PRINCIPLES OF BANKING

AN OVERVIEW OF THE FINANCIAL SERVICES INDUSTRY

Seventh Edition

G. Jay Francis
Susan M. Siegel

AMERICAN
BANKERS
ASSOCIATION ®

This publication is designed to provide accurate and authoritative information in regard to the subject matter covered. It is sold with the understanding that the publisher is not engaged in rendering legal, accounting, or other professional service. If legal advice or other expert assistance is required, the services of a competent professional person should be sought.

From a Declaration of Principles jointly adopted by a Committee of the American Bar Association and a Committee of Publishers and Associations

---

The American Bankers Association is committed to providing innovative, high-quality products and services that are responsive to its members' critical needs.

To comment about this product, or to learn more about the American Bankers Association and the many products and services it offers, please call **1-800-BANKERS** or visit us at our website: **www.aba.com.**

© 2001 by the American Bankers Association
Seventh Edition

Cartoons on the following pages are reprinted with permission:
    Pages 35, 53, 79, 97, 121, and 145 are Frank and Ernest © 1988, 1994, 1995, 1996, and 1997
        by Thaves.
    Page 207 © 1996 Theodore Goff.
    Pages 183 and 227 © 1998 and 1997 Randy Glasbergen.
    Pages 1, 13, 165, and 247 © 1998 American Bankers Association by Sharon C. Lamberton.

Catalog Number: 058600

ISBN: 0-89982-107-3

Printed in the United States of America
10 9 8 7 6 5 4 3 2 1

CONTENTS

EXHIBIT LIST

ABOUT THE AUTHORS

G. Jay Francis has been a banker for 20 years, rising through the ranks from teller, to branch manager, to assistant vice president in branch administration, to residential mortgage lender and finally to his current position as assistant vice president/information security officer at Univest Corporation of Pennsylvania. He has taught Principles of Banking in every conceivable format, most recently designing activities for the new online Principles of Banking initiative. His banking knowledge, coupled with his degree in education, has helped him bring creativity and insight both to the classroom and to the Internet. Through this text and his teaching efforts, Jay's sincere hope is to help those who are new to banking to gain understanding and appreciation of the financial services industry.

Susan M. Siegel is an education and training consultant to the financial services industry. She has been writing seminars, instructor's manuals, and correspondence courses for ABA for 25 years and has contributed her expertise in instructional design to many ABA textbooks. Most recently, Susan has been working on the electronic versions of ABA courses for Internet delivery. She worked closely with Jay on this edition of *Principles of Banking* to reflect his thoughts in a style that can be clearly read and understood by newcomers to the world of banking.

ACKNOWLEDGMENTS

The American Bankers Association and the authors thank the task force members who reviewed and commented on the manuscript of this textbook. They provided invaluable guidance on both substance and depth of content. Several people also contributed the "Did You Know" and "Customer Tips" exhibits and examples, and the website references you see throughout the text. Special appreciation is extended to:

Orrin M. Anderson
Vice President and Branch Manager
Western Mall Branch
The First National Bank in Sioux Falls
Sioux Falls, South Dakota

Ron Asher
Vice President
U.S. Bank
Boise, Idaho

Amaury Betancourt
Loan Review Examiner
Risk Management Division
Hamilton Bank, N.A.
Miami, Florida

W. Bryan Blount
Vice President
Commercial Banking
SunTrust Bank
West Palm Beach, Florida

Linda M. Brooks
Assistant Vice President and
Customer Service Supervisor
Rayne State Bank & Trust Co.
Rayne, Louisiana

Yvette Brooks
Manager
Office of Training and Development
Louisiana State University
Baton Rouge, Louisiana

David Cherrington
Assistant Vice President
Operations
Bank of Lancaster County
East Petersburg, Pennsylvania

Sherry P. Criswell
Senior Vice President
Human Resources and Operations
First National Bank of De Witt
De Witt, Arkansas

Kevin M. Donohue
Registered Representative
Fin-Plan Investments, Inc.
Souderton, Pennsylvania

Nessa Feddis
Senior Federal Counsel
American Bankers Association
Washington, D.C.

William Hood
Compliance Generalist
American Bankers Association
Washington D.C.

B. Mott Jones
Vice President, Retired
First Tennessee Bank
Memphis, Tennessee

PREFACE

This seventh edition of *Principles of Banking* is a revision of the textbook by Francis, Hecht, and Siegel, published in 1998. This version, like all its predecessors, was developed to introduce students who are new to banking to the evolution of banking, basic banking principles, and current changes in the financial services industry. It takes a practical approach and presents a conceptual overview of the fundamentals of banking along with contemporary issues and developments critical to an understanding of banking today. While new technology, regulation, and attitudes have always had an impact on banking, never has this been more the case than in the past few years. This revision addresses these changes, most notably in the areas of customer service, emerging technology, and expanded banking powers and markets.

Changes in This Edition

The authors of the *Principles of Banking* textbook continue their straightforward, customer-focused approach to the content in this edition. The degree of detail needed by more experienced bankers to function in specific jobs has been eliminated in favor of presenting the type of broad information appropriate for entry-level bankers to understand the workings of financial institutions as a whole.

The *Principles of Banking* textbook has several elements that make it an effective learning tool.
- The writing style is clear and easily understood by those new to banking.
- Each chapter begins with real-life situations faced by bank customers, to help you understand your role in connecting customers with bank products and services. These situations are referenced throughout the chapter, helping you understand how the concept you are learning applies to real customers.
- "Did You Know" boxes throughout the textbook add an element of fun and interest with little-known facts and banking trivia.

- "Customer Tips" boxes assist you in helping customers with specific problems.
- Each chapter ends with a list of additional resources, including websites.
- This seventh edition begins by defining the bank as a business and describing the role of the bank employee—especially when it comes to customer service. The concept of a bank employee with a customer service focus is a consistent theme throughout the text.
- Chapters 6 and 7 have been redesigned and reorganized. Chapter 6 discusses the flow of a check through the banking system, while chapter 7 defines a bank's "back room" deposit operations. Chapter 7 also closes with a concentrated discussion of loss prevention issues.
- Interspersed throughout the textbook, particularly in chapter 2, is a discussion of the new powers given to banks under the Gramm-Leach-Bliley Act.
- The lending chapters (8 and 9) have been reorganized so that the related areas of funds management and bank investments appear together in chapter 9, leaving chapter 8 to focus on policy, loan underwriting, and loan categories.
- Chapters 12 and 13 have been completely rewritten. Chapter 12 reflects the latest in specialized products and services, including investment brokerage and insurance services. Chapter 13 focuses on Electronic Financial Services, including EFTS and Internet banking products.
- Answers to the end-of-chapter discussion questions are provided at the back of the text.
- Each chapter ends with a comprehensive summary that highlights the major concepts in the chapter. To get the most from reading each chapter, consider reading the summary twice—once before beginning the chapter to put the material in context, and again after finishing the chapter as a review.
- The textbook ends with a glossary of terms that defines the words that appear in bold type throughout the preceding text, as well as other terms commonly used in the banking industry.

Text Organization

The text is presented in 13 chapters. Chapter 1, Banking and You, introduces the bank as a business and stresses the bank employee's customer-focused approach to these functions. Chapter 2, The Evolution of Banking, traces the development of banking from its unregulated beginning to the present day, with an emphasis on the Gramm-Leach-Bliley Act. Chapter 3, The Federal Reserve and its Regulatory Partners, describes the structure and function of the Federal Reserve and introduces other regulatory agencies that affect our organizations.

Chapter 4, The Deposit Function, discusses the deposit function, types and ownership of accounts, and authority to open accounts. Negotiable instruments as they relate to checks are covered in chapter 5, which also includes a discussion of endorsements and holder in due course. Payments are covered in chapters 6 and 7: chapter 6 addresses the collection process through which a check flows from its receipt at a teller's window to its presentation at the paying bank; chapter 7 addresses back-room operations and security issues.

Chapters 8 and 9 explain the lending function. Chapter 8 shifts the focus from deposits and related activities to the lending function—loans and loan underwriting. Chapter 9, Funds

Management and Bank Investments, presents discussions on the management of bank funds, interest rate determination, and bank investments.

Chapter 10, Measuring and Reporting Financial Performance, explains the importance of accurate accounting and describes basic accounting records (including the balance sheet and income statement) and methods, and performance ratios. Chapter 11, Marketing and the Customer Service Function, introduces the marketing concept and gives bankers a greater understanding of their customers' needs, wants, attitudes, and behaviors. Basic components of marketing such as market research and new product development are also covered. Chapter 12 covers specialized products and services such as trust services, cash management, global banking, investment brokerage, and insurance services.

Finally, Chapter 13, Electronic Financial Services, looks at the world of electronic banking. It covers EFTS, Internet banking, and bank cards. The chapter also discusses some of the loss prevention issues that are inherent in the electronic environment.

Objectives of this Course

After successfully completing this course, you will be able to
- discuss the relationships banks have with their customers and their communities and describe the traditional, non-traditional, and electronic services that banks provide
- explain the evolution of commercial banking in the United States and the federal legislation that shaped its development
- describe the creation of the Federal Reserve System and the Fed's role as the agent of monetary policy and as a bank regulator
- discuss various deposit instruments, the many ways customers can make deposits, deposit regulations, and the means tellers have for establishing a customer's identity
- define negotiable instruments as they relate to checks and describe the features that make a check negotiable
- distinguish between paying a check and cashing a check and explain the procedures for paying checks received through the check clearing system, including relevant regulations and consequences of wrongful dishonor
- explain the process a bank must go through to post a check to an account and discuss controls and security measures that protect the bank and tellers from losses due to fraud
- discuss the legal restrictions on bank loans, describe the role of the bank's board of directors in establishing and overseeing lending policy, and identify basic loan categories
- explain the objectives of funds management, including asset/liability management, and the objectives of bank investments
- recognize the importance of accurate accounting data and describe the categories on the balance sheet and income statement
- discuss the components of the marketing concept and how understanding customers and market research lead to the success of marketing efforts

- explain specialized services offered by banks including trusts, safe deposit services, and global banking services, and newly expanded brokerage and insurance services authorized by the Gramm-Leach-Bliley Act
- describe how electronic funds transfer systems and bank cards facilitate purchases, discuss home banking options for consumers and cash management options for businesses, and explain some of the systems developed to provide security and prevent loss

1

BANKING AND YOU

... And since you're going to the store, I'd love some pickles, some pistachio ice cream, and a custodial savings account for little Johnny!

Learning Objectives

After completing this chapter, you will be able to do the following:

* delineate the multiple roles of bank employees, beyond their specific job duties, including serving customers, being responsible, maintaining customer confidence, and acting professionally
* discuss traditional, non-traditional, and electronic services that banks provide and give examples of each
* explain the financial services provided by banks to the customer and discuss how banks contribute to the economy and to the community
* describe a typical bank organization, including a financial holding company structure
* explain the motivation behind banking industry mergers and acquisitions and the move toward alliances with other companies
* define the bolded terms that appear in the text

Introduction

Each chapter of *Principles of Banking* begins with a series of situations bank customers encounter that can be addressed by the products, services, or operations discussed in the chapter. The purpose of these situations is to remind you that the bank does not just accept deposits and make loans; it serves actual customers with a variety of needs. While a customer with a headache can walk into any drug store and pick up pain medication without the assistance of the pharmacist, this is not the case with banking services. Bank customers rely on bank employees for the products and services they need. Customers rely on the knowledge and professionalism of tellers, customer service representatives, loan representatives, and others to help assess and meet these needs.

So, while the chapters discuss products, services, regulations, and procedures, remember that none of them would exist without the primary link between the customer and the solution—you! Although *Principles of Banking* is not a textbook about customer service, the situations serve as a constant reminder that customer service cannot be separated from banking. The answer to a customer's problem might be overdraft protection or a certificate of deposit, but the customer cannot get that answer without your help. It is important that today's banker have a working knowledge of all areas of the bank so he or she can give the right answer to the customer.

The first two situations below focus on you, the bank employee, and the unique career opportunities banking provides. In situation 3, the customers need the assistance of a banker to address a problem. The chapter presents solutions to these and other problems customers encounter.

Situation 1

Donna dropped out of high school and worked at a variety of minimum-wage jobs for a few years. As a result of a job placement program, Donna began working at a bank. While employed, she managed to receive her GED (a high school equivalency degree). Donna has recently been promoted to department supervisor—a career with a future. Donna is now a confident, self-assured individual.

Situation 2

Jane started at the bank years ago as secretary to the president. She retires this year as a senior vice president in charge of Human Resources. In the interim, she received a bachelor's degree from the local college, paid for by the bank's educational reimbursement program. She has traveled to human resources conferences in major cities throughout the United States, thus staying current professionally.

Situation 3

You are a customer service representative in your branch. Customers Matthew and Verna Abraha, who came to work in the United States several years ago from the Caribbean, have always wanted a home of their own. They have found the house they want, but they now need a mortgage to buy it. Another customer, Lynn DePalma has her own successful interior decorating business. She has never worked for a company that offered a pension plan. She would like to set aside a portion of her income for retirement security but is unsure what plans are available for a person in her situation. These customers come to you for help. What options can you offer?

Financial needs and services are as varied as the customers who come to a bank, thrift institution, credit union, or other financial institution. This chapter gives an overview of the types of services provided by banks. It presents a typical bank organization and describes the multiple roles of bank employees. It also introduces the bank's role in electronic financial services, setting the stage for subsequent chapters.

The Role of the Bank Employee

Employees of financial institutions are responsible for performing their jobs in an outstanding manner, thinking independently, using good judgment, completing assignments promptly, asking questions, and making constructive suggestions. One of the most important aspects of a position in a bank will always be working with customers in a friendly yet professional manner.

Bank Employees Serve Customers

"Customers" are not only depositors and borrowers. They are also bank employees who depend on one another to fulfill their job responsibilities. Customer-focused banking means providing customers with good personal service, confidently and professionally. To do this, employees must know their jobs well. A helpful and pleasant attitude combined with job knowledge leaves a positive impression with customers and fellow employees.

Bank Employees are Responsible

Bank employees are responsible for their actions in many areas in addition to their specific job duties. They are responsible for upholding the policies and procedures of the organization. They are responsible to those they report to and for those reporting to them. Most importantly, they are responsible to the customers and to the stockholders.

Bank Employees Maintain Customer Confidence

The financial services industry is based on customers' confidence in its institutions and employees. Because banks handle and safeguard the funds and assets of others, the highest standards of business ethics must be maintained. The law requires that even minor deviations from established bank policies be reported to regulatory authorities. These policies are usually stated in the bank's code of ethics.

Code of Ethics

A **code of ethics** is a set of guidelines adopted by top management and the board of directors to direct employee actions that might reflect on the institution. The code is useful in answering employee questions concerning policy on receiving gifts from customers, serving on public boards, taking outside jobs,

---

Did You Know?

A satisfied customer will tell 3 to 5 people about the bank, while a dissatisfied customer will tell 15 to 20 people about a bad experience with a bank, restaurant, or any other business.

(Smith Marketing Research, Lexington, Kentucky, *Bankers News*)

and other matters. Employees are normally required to read the code and certify periodically that they are in compliance. Most codes include the following points, among others:

- Banking business is confidential. All confidential matters must be respected and must not be discussed with or divulged to anyone except those who are authorized to receive the information.

- Dishonesty and fraudulent activity of any kind will not be tolerated.

- An employee's behavior must always reflect positively on the integrity of the institution.

- Employees may not accept money or gifts that are given for the purpose of influencing them in the performance of their duties.

- All employees are expected to practice wise personal financial management. To hold the respect and confidence of the public, employees must be beyond reproach in this regard. If employees cannot take care of their own money, customers cannot be expected to trust the bank to take care of their funds and assets.

Conflicts of Interest

Bank employees should never place themselves in situations that could be viewed as conflicts of interest. A **conflict of interest** occurs when two interests are at cross-purposes with each other. The conflict becomes a **breach of conduct** when personal gain or self-interest takes precedence over the employee's job duties. The appearance of a conflict can be just as damaging as an actual conflict. It is important to remember that the existence of a conflict is not necessarily wrong. What is wrong and most damaging is concealing the conflict or dealing with it improperly.

Bank Employees Are Professionals

Bank employees deal with customers as well as other employees on a regular basis. Their professional attitude and appearance set the tone for the entire bank. In general, professionals are:

- organized, keeping their work areas neat, answering messages and following up customer inquiries promptly, and getting to work on time

- positive, recognizing the importance of serving customers, maintaining a positive attitude, being honorable and sincere, and acting confidently and decisively

- well presented, dressing appropriately, maintaining eye contact, treating customers with courtesy, respect, and empathy, and maintaining a business-like (rather than casual) posture

- confident, handling problems, keeping promises, being a good listener, and knowing the bank's products and services

Bank Employees Have Career Opportunities

As the world of banking changes, so do the career opportunities available in commercial banks. There will always be a need for the most visible positions—customer service representatives, tellers, and other front-office staff and supervisors. There are also many opportunities in traditional banking careers such as accounting, auditing, compliance, human resources, and corporate support services. As financial product and service offerings expand, so do career opportunities. The bank employees in situations 1 and 2 took advantage of career opportunities in their institutions. Following are just some of the areas where bankers are enjoying career growth.

Sales

Information about the new products and services has to somehow reach the customer. Banks now actively promote the benefits of these products and services. Of course, it is every banker's job to sell appropriate products and services, but some bank employees are dedicated to this task full time. In larger institutions, the sales teams specialize according to product. Retail banking, business banking, insurance sales, investment products, and trust services are all examples of sales avenues open to today's bankers.

Operations

Operational support departments offer individuals the opportunity to work behind the scenes. These departments provide support, for example, to the customer contact staff by servicing deposits and loans, and processing insurance claims. Operations personnel are among the first to incorporate new technology and electronic software to more efficiently accomplish their increasingly challenging tasks.

E-Business or E-Commerce

E-business or **e-commerce** is a major growth area for banks, as it is for most businesses. From web design and hosting to business-to-business

endeavors to providing Internet service, this field will continue to show explosive growth.

Technology

Probably no two people think of the same thing when they hear the word technology, and for good reason. Technology's reach is vast, as are its career opportunities. Examples of technology careers include:

- programming, design, and maintenance of the bank's mainframe computer
- PC support through hardware servicing, software support centers, LANs (local area networks) and WANs (wide area networks)
- PC banking, including website design, service integration, sales to customers, phone support, and training

Banks, like other businesses, are always looking for trained personnel to fill positions. However, banks already have a long history of training existing employees in new areas. This tradition has not changed. In addition to in-bank, job-specific training, many banks offer reimbursement for education and training as part of their benefits packages. Employees can often get American Institute of Banking (AIB) certification or diplomas, college degrees, specialty certifications and designations, and other education and training opportunities for free or at a reduced cost—just for working at a financial institution. The bank employees in situations 1 and 2 received education, training, and career opportunities through their banks.

Services Banks Provide

Traditional Financial Services

In its simplest terms, traditional banking involves taking money from those who have it (depositors) and giving it to those who need it (borrowers). The money banks make to operate is the difference between the interest they pay for deposits and generate from loans.

Why do depositors choose to save their money in a bank rather than in a coffee can buried out back? Banks provide a secure way of safeguarding depositor savings. Banks also pay depositors for the use of their money, in the form of interest on their savings. Business customers benefit from deposit accounts by having a safe, easy way to clear checks and pay bills.

What benefit do loan customers get? Loan customers can significantly increase their buying power and improve their quality of life by using loans to fund large purchases. Many consumers would be unable to buy a house, a car, or a college education for their children without the assistance of loans. Business customers use loans to expand their markets, purchase new equipment, and modernize their facilities. Like millions of others, the Abrahas in situation 3 might benefit from a traditional bank product—the mortgage loan. Lynn DePalma, the business owner, can save for retirement using a specialized retirement account. She might also use loans for her business.

Banks complement basic deposit and loan services with related products and services that have historically allowed them to grow and be profitable, and to serve their communities. These other traditional services include trust, payment, and safekeeping services.

Non-traditional Financial Services

Until the 1970s, banks stuck with their core product lines both because regulation prevented expansion into non-traditional areas and because business continued to be good. As competition from other financial services providers began to affect profitability, banks began looking for ways to expand their product lines. At first, banks offered new products that circumvented the regulations (chapter 2) and, over time, benefited from the deregulation of the industry. Because of legislation passed in 1999, (chapter 2) banks, insurance companies, and brokerage firms can now enter each other's traditional domain. Banks can offer these non-traditional products and compete on an equal basis.

The bank of the not-too-distant future will be a supermarket for financial services. It will offer convenient locations and a wide range of financial products. The line between banks, insurance companies, and brokerage firms will blur. Customers will be able to go to the bank for car insurance, homeowner's insurance, title insurance, and annuities. These same customers will also be able to purchase stocks and bonds from the bank. They will encounter bank experts and specialists in all of these areas.

Electronic Financial Services

Technology has been a major growth area for all sectors of the economy, including financial services. Technology has brought customers a convenience not thought possible just a decade ago. It is now possible to order groceries, buy a car, and do all your Christmas shopping without even stepping away from your computer. In a recent study conducted by the ABA, customers ranked convenience as the most important reason for maintaining a primary relationship with a bank. Since about 40 percent of U.S. households have computers, it makes sense for banks to offer their customers the convenience of online or electronic banking services. Currently, customers can check account balances, pay bills, and even apply for loans online. Because of recent congressional action recognizing the validity of electronic signatures, options for customers will expand to include online loan closings and other contractual arrangements.

Several banks have been established as **Internet banks**. Internet banks do not have traditional "bricks and mortar" branches. They exist in cyberspace over the Internet. Internet banks generally offer higher interest rates on deposits and lower interest rates on loans. Customers do all of their banking from their home or business PC. This topic will be covered more fully in Chapter 13.

Marketing and Cross-selling Services to Customers

Between traditional and non-traditional services, and all the possibilities technology offers, banks are creating hundreds if not thousands of new products and services. One of the biggest challenges for banks is communicating the existence and benefits of these new offerings to customers, old and new. Many customers are not aware of products and services that will simplify or enhance their financial lives. Many will still go to an insurance company for their insurance needs, a brokerage for investments, and the bank for everything else, even though they may be able to do all of this at the bank. Many are not taking advantage of the convenience of using their computers to manage their finances.

Banks that are succeeding in the new financial marketplace are finding ways to get customers thinking about using the bank for all their financial needs. One strategy already in use that also has great future potential is

cross-selling. Cross-selling involves offering products that relate to a product a customer uses or wants. For example, if a customer wants a mortgage, the banker can cross-sell other products that would be of use, such as:

- a safe deposit box to store the important mortgage papers
- a checking account with automatic payment to ensure that the mortgage payment is made on time
- a home owner's policy through the insurance subsidiary
- a personal line of credit to help with the incidentals of new home ownership

The Bank in Your Community

Banks provide a safe and convenient place for customers to take care of their financial needs. However, banks mean much more to customers, the community, and the economy. When banks do their jobs well they build strong communities, help families grow, educate children, help develop businesses, and generally improve society and the quality of life.

Banks Provide Financial Services

Banks are a fundamental part of the economy. As described earlier, they provide a broad range of traditional, non-traditional, and electronic services to an equally broad range of

Did You Know?

Banks provide more loans to farmers and ranchers than anyone else. Nearly 40 cents of every dollar borrowed by farmers and ranchers comes from banks.
(American Bankers Association)

customers, including individuals, businesses, and government. Banks are increasingly interested in providing a full range of financial services for their customers.

Banks Provide Customer Service

In situation 3, two different bank customers needed more than a "product" off the banking shelf! They needed the knowledge and understanding of a bank employee who could assess their problems and suggest appropriate solutions. In the same day, the customer service representative might suggest mortgage loan assistance programs for the couple from the Caribbean, an Individual Retirement Account (IRA) for the small business owner, and a host of services to other customers. In addition, the bank professional's knowledge of the bank's products and understanding of the broader needs of the customer are put to good use suggesting related services to make these customers' lives easier.

Banks Contribute to the Economy

Through the payments system, banks facilitate the flow of money throughout the United States and around the world. Without this system, the global economy would collapse. Through the lending process, banks create money. These loans allow communities to grow and prosper.

Banks are also businesses and are concerned about profits, efficiency, and effectiveness. A financially healthy bank is important to its stockholders, its community, and the financial services industry as a whole.

Banks also have the ability to create money through the loan process. As banks make more

and more loans, they directly support the success of communities.

Banks Contribute to the Community

How many volunteer organizations in your area does your bank support with donations? How many employees donate their time to organizations like Habitat for Humanity, the United Way, the American Heart Association, and the Boy Scouts and Girl Scouts? How many events or Little League and soccer teams does your bank sponsor? How many educational and cultural events, like Books for Tots, Career Days, school partnerships, and concerts does your bank sponsor?

These questions should give you some idea of the many ways bankers contribute to their communities. In addition to providing the capital that helps businesses, jobs, and communities grow, bank employees are visibly active in all aspects of community life.

The Bank as a Business Organization

Typical Bank Organization

The typical bank has a **corporate structure**: it is a legally chartered business venture, operated for profit with stockholders, directors, and officers, just like any corporation. Its charter is granted either by the state in which it is organized or by the federal government through the Office of the Comptroller of the Currency. The bank's stockholders elect its directors, who are the active, governing body of the corporation. Directors are responsible for the bank's operations, regulatory compliance, and performance; they can be held legally liable for their actions. Directors appoint the bank's officers.

The board of directors usually functions through various committees, such as auditing, trust, and credit.

The bank's chairman of the board often is the chief executive officer, who is responsible for the basic policies that guide the institution. The bank's president is typically the chief administrative officer, who is responsible for implementing policies and supervising operations. Depending on the size and scope of the institution, various organizational levels may be created so that specific individuals are responsible for functional areas. Exhibit 1.1 shows a typical commercial bank organization.

While names may vary, a typical bank has the following departments:

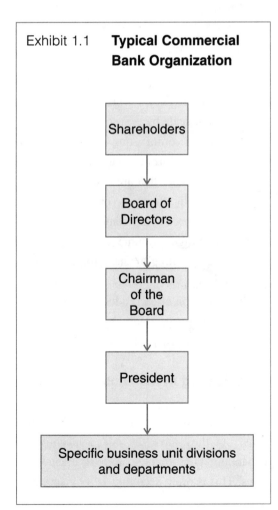

Exhibit 1.1 **Typical Commercial Bank Organization**

Shareholders

Board of Directors

Chairman of the Board

President

Specific business unit divisions and departments

• The Commercial/Business Banking department delivers loan, deposit, and payment services to businesses.
• The Consumer Banking department delivers loan, deposit, and payment services to individuals.
• Human Resources finds, trains, develops, and compensates staff for the bank.
• The Marketing department studies who the customers are, what they want, and how to deliver and promote products and services.
• The Data Processing/Operations department provides high-quality information to the bank and customers.
• Funds Management balances the bank's need for liquidity, safety, and income.
• Finance and Accounting provides information on how efficiently and profitably the bank is run.
• The Audit/Loan Review function makes sure the bank is safe from risks such as internal and external fraud and poor-quality loans.
• The International department services the bank's international consumer and business needs.

Financial Holding Companies

Some banks are organized as **financial holding companies** (FHCs). The FHC owns the stock of the bank or banks and is under the jurisdiction of the Federal Reserve. Some FHCs will enter into banking-related activities such as brokerage or insurance services. A financial holding company can own banks in more than one state, thus facilitating interstate banking. It can own one bank or many banks. Exhibit 1.2 shows a typical organizational chart for a financial holding company.

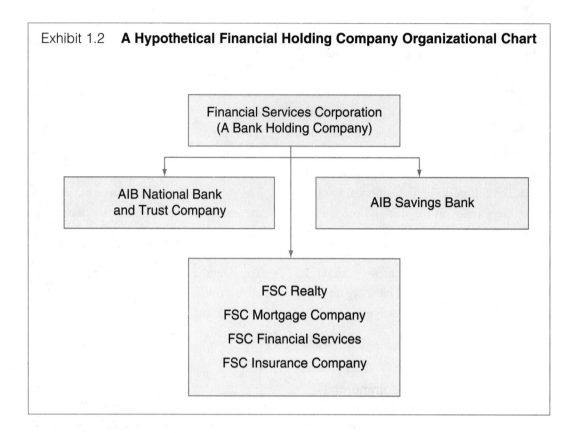

Exhibit 1.2 **A Hypothetical Financial Holding Company Organizational Chart**

Financial Services Corporation
(A Bank Holding Company)

AIB National Bank
and Trust Company

AIB Savings Bank

FSC Realty

FSC Mortgage Company

FSC Financial Services

FSC Insurance Company

Consolidation of the Banking Companies

Mergers and Acquisitions

In the late 1980s, there were about 12,500 commercial banks in the United States. By the year 2000, this number had dwindled to about 8,700. This decline in numbers is not the result of bank failures—banks have been very strong through the recent decade of economic boom. It is not because bankers have lost interest in banking— the number of new, start-up banks has been at an overall high the last few years. The number of banks is declining because of **mergers** and **acquisitions**. Many banks are combining forces (merging) or purchasing other institutions (acquiring) to form larger banking companies.

Through mergers and acquisitions, banks are eliminating duplicate efforts and becoming more profitable. They are taking advantage of economies of scale by:

- reducing or eliminating support departments that perform the same tasks
- closing branches that are in close proximity and combining them into one
- using data processing centers that can support the larger volume of the combined banks, eliminating the need for two distinct systems

Consolidation often produces lower operating costs, expanded earnings potential, and greater profitability for the combined banks.

Participating in the Global Economy

Large banks combine for all of the above reasons, but they have the added incentive of expanding their markets into strategic locations. This is often accomplished by acquiring other banking companies. International banks are also combining to offer expanded banking services on a global scale.

Business Alliances in Banking Companies

Banks have traditionally been known for their independence, wanting independent systems to support their independent operations. Current business practices, however, are reversing that trend. It is now common for an independent bank to seek outside vendors or the services of other banks (such as data processing centers) for technology or other services. Often, these vendors have other bank clients using the same, or similar products. For example, a bank may purchase a maintenance software system that is similar to one purchased by other banks of similar size. The vendor, not the bank, is responsible for upgrading the software to make it consistent with the latest regulatory changes or latest technology. Whereas in the past the bank may have developed and customized its own software system, doing so today may no longer make economic sense. The benefits of partnering with other companies that are responsible for upgrading the computer systems may far outweigh any negatives from the loss of independence.

Currently, banks are in the process of forming many types of alliances. They combine to offer joint lending programs, splitting the responsibilities (management, administration, financing, and so forth) according to their capabilities. They seek outside companies to service, repair, maintain, and upgrade their bank's computer hardware and networking software, ensuring access to the latest technology without bearing the costs of employees and support.

While banks may be giving up some of the independence and ability to customize they

enjoyed in the past, these new alliances provide significant cost savings and a high level of service.

Summary

Bank employees are responsible for more than their specific job duties. They serve their customers in many capacities while being accountable to other employees and upholding the policies and procedures of the bank. They maintain customer confidence by conducting themselves ethically and avoiding conflicts of interest. Finally, bank employees are professional in attitude, appearance, and work habits.

Traditional banking services include deposits, loans, and payments. Banks are expanding their offerings to include non-traditional products such as insurance and brokerage services. They also take full advantage of the opportunities available through electronic financial services.

As with any business, a bank's profitability depends on its ability to meet its customers' needs. In banking, these needs are primarily for deposit, payment, and credit services. Bank employees know their bank's products as well as their customers' needs and attempt to match the two whenever possible. Banks contribute to their communities through loans and involvement in community activities, and to the economy by facilitating the flow of money.

A typical bank organization's corporate structure begins with shareholders. Responsibility for governing the bank corporation rests with the board of directors that appoints and oversees the bank president and appoints the bank's officers. Banks usually operate through a committee structure. In a bank holding company, shares of one or more banks are owned by the holding company.

Mergers and acquisitions in the past decade have substantially reduced the number of banks. The resulting institutions are more efficient and profitable. Combined banks compete more effectively, both nationally and globally. Banks are also seeing the advantages of forming alliances with other banks and vendors for specialized services.

Review and Discussion Questions

1. If all bankers are supposed to be "selling" the products and services of the bank, why is sales a major career avenue for bankers?

2. What are non-traditional bank services and why do banks want to provide these?

3. How do banks contribute to their communities?

4. What is the difference between a typical commercial bank and a financial holding company structure?

5. Why are banks willing to give up some of their independence and use outside vendors or other banks for services?

Additional Resources

Banking and Finance Terminology. Washington, D.C.: American Bankers Association, 1999.

Dealing Effectively with Co-Workers. Washington, D.C.: American Bankers Association, 1999.

Ethical Issues for Bankers. Washington, D.C.: American Bankers Association, 1999.

Referring Mutual Funds and Securities Customers. Washington, D.C.: American Bankers Association, 1999.

Referring Trust Customers. Washington, D.C.: American Bankers Association, 1999.

Revitalizing Customer Service. Washington, D.C.: American Bankers Association, 1999.

Web Resources

Your bank's website
ABA Banking Journal www.banking.com/aba
American Bankers Association www.aba.com
Federal Reserve Bank of New York
    www.newyorkfed.org

2

THE EVOLUTION OF BANKING

Interstate Banking Circa 1890

Learning Objectives

After completing this chapter, you will be able to do the following:

- discuss the early banking system and its influence on the current banking system
- list and explain the major provisions of the National Bank Act
- describe how the Federal Reserve Act of 1913 addressed major problems remaining in the system after passage of the National Bank Act
- describe the impact the Great Depression had on banks, and the resulting legislation
- discuss legislation enacted since the 1980s, including the Gramm-Leach-Bliley Act of 1999, that demonstrates a philosophy of less regulation, and describe some of the new products that have resulted
- discuss the new rules to strengthen bank lending, including the Financial Institutions Reform, Recovery, and Enforcement Act and the Federal Deposit Insurance Corporation Improvement Act, and list and explain the key provisions of the 1999 Gramm-Leach-Bliley Act
- `define the bolded terms that appear in the text

Introduction

Picture yourself conducting business in the 1700s and 1800s. The financial system then was not nearly as reliable as it is today.

Situation 1

In 1780, a textile merchant in Philadelphia purchased dyes from a dye merchant in Philadelphia. He gave the dye merchant a promissory note, drawn on a community bank, for the purchase amount. A Philadelphia tailor purchased textiles from the textile merchant, also paying with a promissory note drawn on the community bank. However, the tailor also wanted fabric made with a cotton he had heard about that was grown in Virginia. How could the textile merchant purchase this Virginia cotton?

Situation 2

Nathaniel is a New Hampshire furniture builder. It is 1887, and he has just finished and delivered handmade dining room and bedroom sets to a successful Texas cattle rancher. The cattle rancher paid Nathaniel with a check drawn on a Texas bank. By taking the check to his local bank, the furniture maker hopes for payment in three to four weeks. How does his bank obtain payment for the Texas check?

Now see the difference a century makes! The next situation takes place in 2002.

Situation 3

Justin opened checking and savings accounts when he graduated from college a couple of years ago. Recently, he inherited money from his great-grandmother. Since he is very satis-fied with the service he receives at his bank, he decides to deposit the money into his savings account until he can decide what to do with it. His banker suggests that he talk to a financial counselor, who offers him a mutual fund. Justin inquires about the stock market and is surprised when the financial counselor can help with that, too. He is surprised even more when he asks to withdraw some of the money to pay his car insurance bill and is referred to the bank's insurance agency for a quote. Justin leaves thinking how convenient it is to get all of his financial needs taken care of in one place—and with people he knows and trusts! How can one bank provide such a range of services?

The first two scenarios were not uncommon 100 to 200 years ago. We take for granted how the current banking system facilitates trade and other transactions. Situation 3, which depicts today's banking environment, provides a sharp contrast to the early banking years.

The previous chapter discussed current bank functions, corporate structure, and community goodwill. However, banks did not always command such a solid leadership position in their communities. This chapter traces the evolution of the banking system in the United States from its chaotic, unstructured, and unregulated early days to the present, where almost every aspect of banking is regulated.

The Early Banking System and Its Weaknesses

The early settlers came to America from countries where government involvement and control in private business were very strong. In fact, many countries had central banks either owned or strongly controlled by the government. Fearing a repetition of the negative consequences of government control in their home countries, the early settlers created a banking "system" with a large number of unrelated and unregulated banks. There was no common currency and no system to clear notes. As a result, the current U.S. banking system still consists of a large number of privately owned banks.

Having local banks that were not governed by a central authority created problems. When the colonies became independent of Great Britain, they traded predominantly among themselves. Boston merchants traded with Boston merchants, Philadelphians with Philadelphians, and Virginians with Virginians. The colonists knew each other, they knew the other merchants, and they knew the bank in their community. However, in situation 1, the cotton farmer in Virginia and the textile merchant in Philadelphia did not know each other. Trade was further inhibited because neither merchant had faith in the other's bank. This spurred many difficulties with the new country's trade growth between settlements or

colonies. Economically, the United States could not prosper.

In addition to hampering trade, the fragmented early banking system created problems for currency. Because there were no restrictions on ownership and the requirements for capital were very low, anyone could own a bank. Capital is the excess of assets over liabilities. In banking, capital defines the strength of the bank to withstand economic downturns. The owner of a bar and grill could also own a bank and change the name of the establishment to Country Bar, Grill, and Bank. Every bank issued its own notes. **Notes**, or banknotes, are promises by a bank to pay the amount of money designated on the face of the note (chapter 5) when presented to the bank. The problem with the early banknotes was that one never knew if the note would be paid when it was presented to the bank. The bank might refuse or be unable to pay the note, or the bank might no longer exist. Because there were no standards for the issuance of notes, any bank could issue them in any form (exhibit 2.1). This lack of control led to counterfeiting and the printing of notes on nonexistent

| Exhibit 2.1 | **Banknote Issued by the Bank of Morgan, Georgia, 1857** |

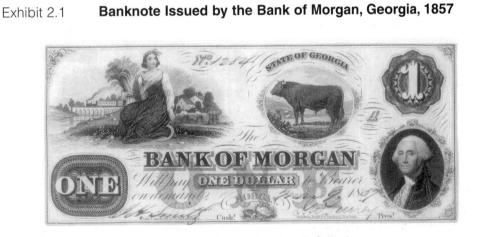

Source: The Smithsonian Institution, National Numismatic Collection

banks. Another problem with the unrestricted issuance of banknotes for currency was that the money supply could vary drastically. With every bank issuing its own notes, the money supply could rapidly grow without control and fuel inflation. **Inflation**—too many dollars chasing too few goods—became a real problem during the early period of banking.

Attempts to Form a Central Bank

When confidence in the banking system had fallen to its lowest point, Congress was persuaded to strengthen the faith of the public and improve the monetary system. Alexander Hamilton, Secretary of the U.S. Treasury, proposed the formation of a new bank that would have the direct involvement and backing of the federal government. His plan was approved by Congress, and the First Bank of the United States opened in Philadelphia in 1791—only fifteen years after the signing of the Declaration of Independence.

By all counts, the First Bank of the United States was a success. Faith and confidence in the banking system were restored, and the actions of the bank benefited the public. However, banks whose notes were redeemed for coin and currency by the new bank strongly opposed it. So did others. The opposition was so strong that Congress refused to renew the charter, and the First Bank of the United States closed in 1811.

Without a central bank, many of the same problems recurred, including poorly run, undercapitalized local banks, limited access to credit, and lack of faith in the system of currency. Once again, confidence in the banking system was extremely low. Congress responded to the demands of the public for a sound banking system, and the Second Bank of the

United States was formed in 1816. It functioned very similarly to the First Bank with the added benefit of acting as a depository for the federal government. The Second Bank met the same fate as the First Bank, and for basically the same reasons. When the bank's 20-year charter expired, Congress once again bowed to political pressure and refused to renew the charter. Andrew Jackson, who was elected president in 1828, strongly opposed all forms of centralized government, including centralization of the banking system.

The period from 1836 to 1863 has been described as the darkest in U.S. banking history. The need for a sound and trustworthy banking system had never been greater, yet there was no response on the part of the government to address this need. The geographic expansion, population growth, and economic prosperity of the years preceding the Civil War had created an ideal climate for the growth of commercial banking, but many of the banks that had opened were poorly capitalized and lacked prudent management. It became apparent that the original concept of the colonists, allowing virtually any individual or group to establish a bank and operate it without supervision or regulation, was not valid or acceptable.

Did You Know?

The period in the mid 1800s, between the failure to recharter the Second Bank of the United States and the passing of the National Banking Act of 1863, became known as the period of wildcat banking. Banks located their office for currency redemption in remote areas where only wildcats lived. People would fear for their lives in approaching these banks to redeem their paper money for gold or silver.

Of the 2,500 state banks that were formed between 1826 and 1860, more than 1,000 closed within ten years of opening; by 1862 more than $100 million had been lost through bank failures.[1] Forged, depreciated, and counterfeit bank notes were so prevalent that various publications of the time list as many as 5,500 types of worthless paper. Public resentment of banks became so strong that by 1852, nine states had enacted laws prohibiting banking.[2]

How could the country grow and prosper without a stable, sound banking system?

National Bank Act

The U.S. banking system and the economy were in serious trouble in 1862. The country was engaged in civil war, government expenditures exceeded revenues, and the inflation rate hit 13 percent.[3] President Lincoln needed a new source of revenue and assigned the task of finding it to the secretary of the treasury, Salmon P. Chase. Secretary Chase was also given the monumental task of overhauling and reforming the banking system. Chase set to work and in 1863 persuaded Congress to pass the National Currency Act, later renamed the National Bank Act. Exactly what the banking system needed, it has survived the passage of time and created the foundation for today's banking system.

The act contained four major provisions aimed directly at solving the most pressing problems of the time (exhibit 2.2). It (1) created national banks, (2) created the Office of the Comptroller of the Currency (OCC), (3) introduced the national banknote, and (4) established a system of required reserves.

National Banks

Because one of the banking system's major problems was instability, the national bank was created to instill public confidence in banks. Like state banks, national banks were privately owned but were **chartered**—authorized to conduct banking business—by the federal government. The charter requirements were very strict, requiring that the bank be

---

Exhibit 2.2   **The National Bank Act of 1863**

National banks created

- privately owned
- federally chartered
- adequately capitalized
- competently managed

Office of the Comptroller of the Currency created

- charter, examine, and regulate national banks

National banknote introduced

- standard design with the issuing bank's name
- backed by Treasury bonds

Required reserves established

- vault and teller cash
- balances with a national money center bank

adequately capitalized and competently managed. As an added incentive to ensure adequate capital, the stockholders could be held personally liable if the bank failed. The act also established legal lending limits based on a percentage of capital. The lending limits helped reduce the risk to the bank in the event that a borrower could not repay a loan.

The establishment of national banks created a dual banking system that exists to this day. The term **dual banking system** means that the banking system has both state-chartered and nationally chartered banks. All state-chartered banks were given the opportunity to convert to a national bank charter if they could meet the stricter federal requirements. Many banks declined to take advantage of this option, choosing instead to remain state banks with no chartering requirements and fewer regulatory restrictions. State banks could offer the same products and services as national banks without the regulatory burdens imposed on the national banks. Even today there are fewer national banks (about 2,700) than state-chartered banks (about 6,700).

In 1865, in an effort to induce state banks to convert their charters, Congress passed additional legislation imposing a ten percent tax on notes issued by state banks. This additional tax was a burden on state banks, but the increasing

Did You Know?

During the Civil War period, the Bureau of Engraving and Printing was called on to print paper notes in denominations of 5 cents, 1 cent, 25 cents, and 50 cents. The reason for this was that people hoarded coins because of their intrinsic value, which created a drastic shortage of circulating coins.

(Bureau of Engraving and Printing)

acceptance of checks gave them relief. Instead of issuing notes, the state banks could deposit loan proceeds directly to checking accounts. If checking accounts had not been developed, more state banks would have converted to national charters.

To distinguish national banks from state banks, national banks are required to either include the word "national" in their names (for example, Union National Bank and Trust Company) or add the words "National Association" (abbreviated as "N.A.") to the end of their names (for example, Citibank, N.A.).

Office of the Comptroller of the Currency

The Office of the **Comptroller of the Currency** was created by the second provision of the National Bank Act. Its function was and still is to charter, examine, and issue regulations governing national banks. As part of the Treasury Department, the OCC ensures sound banking practices to help reduce the high rate of bank failures and to restore confidence in the banking system. The OCC was required to make periodic reports to Congress on the financial stability of national banks.

National Banknotes

The lack of a national currency and the problems associated with every bank issuing its own unique notes were addressed by the introduction of the national banknote. Only national banks were given the authority to issue national banknotes. With the exception of the issuing bank's name, the notes were a standard design (exhibit 2.3), which helped reduce rampant counterfeiting. National banks issuing notes were required to buy a quantity of

Treasury bonds and pledge them as security against the notes. This requirement served three purposes: first, it raised needed money for the federal government. National banks became almost a guaranteed source of funds for the government. Second, it gave the public confidence in the notes. The public knew that the note represented more than just a piece of paper, because it was backed by Treasury bonds. Third, it kept the amount of each bank's notes proportionate to its capital. This also was an important factor in instilling public confidence in the national banknotes.

Required Reserves

Before the National Bank Act, depositors had completely lost confidence in the banking system and were reluctant to put money in any bank. Their fears were well founded, because there were no assurances that banks would be able to meet depositors' demands for withdrawals: banks were not required to keep cash or balances available to meet withdrawal demands. The National Bank Act addressed this problem as well, by establishing a system

of **reserve requirements** (chapter 3). Every national bank was required to keep reserves against its deposits and notes as additional protection for depositors. Reserves could consist of vault cash or a balance maintained with a national bank in a designated money center city. A money center is a city with an active money market and financial community, such as New York, Chicago, or San Francisco. Since New York City had become the nation's financial center, reserve balances were often kept with major New York banks, which paid interest on the balances. The concept behind the reserve requirements was that the bank would have available in a money center bank either cash or demand deposit balances to meet depositor withdrawal demands.

The Federal Reserve Act of 1913

Weaknesses after the National Bank Act

While the National Bank Act went a long way toward restoring confidence in the banking

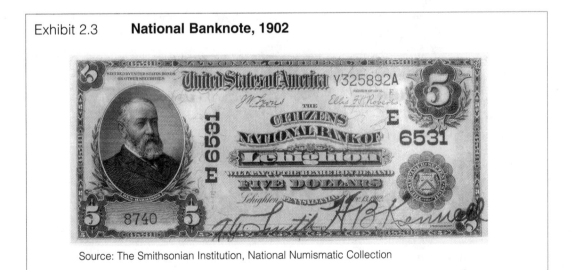

Exhibit 2.3   **National Banknote, 1902**

Source: The Smithsonian Institution, National Numismatic Collection

system, it still fell short of solving all the attendant problems. Three remaining weaknesses were:

- no check collection system
- inflexible currency
- pyramiding reserves

No Check Collection System

The inadequacy of the check collection system meant there was a staggering amount of **float** (items outstanding and in the process of collection), in addition to a great deal of fraud. A check drawn on a bank in the western states could take weeks to be paid by that bank when deposited with a bank in the east. The Texan's check would be deposited in a New Hampshire bank account, and the New Hampshire bank would send the check directly to the Texas bank. Not only would the furniture maker in New Hampshire in 1887 (situation 2) have to wait weeks for his payment from Texas, but there was always the chance that the check would be returned.

Transportation and communications were also so slow in the nineteenth century that they further aggravated the problem of float. Most banks began using a larger bank that offered check clearing services to clear their items. The problem with this process was that the check had to flow through a number of banks before it reached its final destination.

This system created an excellent environment for check fraud (chapter 6). Checks drawn on accounts with insufficient funds or on a closed or nonexistent account could be used to make purchases, and the merchant would not know until considerably later whether the check was good.

Inflexible Currency

The money supply was directly tied to the level of government bonds and therefore unable to expand as needed in the economy as a whole. A national bank could issue notes only if it could purchase the bonds to pledge as security for the note. As the need for an expanding money supply grew along with the economy, the actual amount of notes did not keep pace. The amount of currency in circulation was based on the Treasury bonds held by the issuing bank. As the economy grew, tax revenues increased, and these Treasury bonds were repaid. The amount of currency in circulation shrank, causing severe problems for the expanding economy of the early 1900s.

Pyramiding Reserves

The reserve requirement of the National Bank Act gave stability to the banking system, but it also created problems for some banks. Smaller, rural banks used the larger, stronger, city banks as depositories for their reserves. City banks, in turn, placed their reserves with even larger, stronger banks. The result was a concentration of **pyramided reserves** in the New York City banks—a financial pyramid with New York City at the apex. To pay interest on these reserve accounts, the New York banks used the deposited funds to make short-term loans, usually to brokerage firms— firms that arrange contracts for the purchase and sale of stocks and bonds.

When banks outside New York City needed large amounts of currency to meet their financial obligations, they were forced to withdraw portions of their reserves. This drain on the New York banks compelled them to raise immediate funds by calling in loans they had made to the brokerage firms. The pyramiding of reserves led to money panics when banks lower in the funds pyramid needed money for growth in their community, and the banks that held their money could not return it on time.

How the Federal Reserve Act Addressed these Problems

Fifty years later, these problems were addressed by the Federal Reserve Act of 1913.

With the help of the banking community, economists, and the regulatory authorities, Congress passed the Federal Reserve Act of 1913, creating the Federal Reserve System (the Fed) (chapter 3). The major thrusts of the Federal Reserve Act (exhibit 2.4) were to address the weaknesses remaining after the National Bank Act, stabilize the banking system, and develop an agency to be responsible for the nation's money supply.

National Check Clearing System

Two of the three problems remaining after the National Bank Act were solved by the creation of Federal Reserve districts. The country was divided into 12 Federal Reserve districts, each with a Federal Reserve bank. Member banks located within a Federal Reserve district could send checks to the Federal Reserve bank in their district. This system gave member banks a method of clearing checks by using the services of its local Federal Reserve bank. Non-member banks contracted with member banks to process or clear out-of-town checks through the Federal Reserve. The Federal Reserve bank would present the checks to paying banks either directly or indirectly—that is, through another Federal Reserve bank. A number of Federal Reserve banks have branches that perform many of the same functions as the Federal Reserve banks themselves. This is covered in greater detail in chapter 3.

Decentralized Reserves

The 12 Federal Reserve districts also solved the problem of pyramided reserves. The act gave the Federal Reserve the authority to set reserve requirements and to change those requirements as needed. Member banks were allowed to keep their reserves in the Federal Reserve bank or branch located in their district. This procedure allowed the reserves to be spread across the country rather than centralized in any particular part of the country, as they had been under the National Bank Act.

Exhibit 2.4   **Federal Reserve Act of 1913**

National check clearing system
- 12 Federal Reserve districts
- reduced float
- faster check collection

Decentralized reserves
- bank reserves within the Federal Reserve district
- local control over bank reserve requirements

Federal Reserve notes
- notes not backed by government securities
- basic form of U.S. currency today

Federal Reserve Notes

The problem of the inflexible currency also was solved by the Federal Reserve Act, which allowed the Federal Reserve to issue Federal Reserve notes. Because the notes did not have to be backed by government securities, the limiting characteristics of the national bank-notes were eliminated. An example of a Federal Reserve note may be found in any-one's wallet; it is the basic form of U.S. currency today.

The Great Depression

The 1920s are often referred to as the Roaring Twenties. The economy turned upward at the end of World War I in 1918 and continued growing throughout most of the 1920s. Consumers, bankers, and investment professionals were convinced that the stock market would continue to rise. No one wanted to be left out. People without enough money to play the stock market simply borrowed from banks, paying for a percentage of the stock with their own money and financing the rest—a practice called buying on margin. In turn, investors were allowed to borrow money using stock as collateral, because everybody believed the stock market boom would continue. On October 28, 1929, many people's lives changed dramatically. The stock market that could not fail did exactly that. The day of the market crash, paper values decreased by $14 billion. It was the beginning of the longest depression the world had ever seen. For more than ten years, the country struggled toward an elusive recovery. Unemployment reached 25 percent, and desperation was high. World War II finally gave the United States the economic boost it needed to pull out of the Great Depression as demand for equipment and supplies increased business activity.

Impact of the Crash on Banks

The crash and the events that followed had a significant impact on the banking system (exhibit 2.5). Many customers defaulted on their loans. The stock certificates they had put up for collateral were worthless or had declined so far in value that the debt could not be satisfied. As the economy worsened, businesses in growing numbers went into bankruptcy, fired their workers, and found themselves unable to repay their bank loans. Bank loan losses soared. By the end of 1930 more than 1,300 commercial banks had closed their doors, and by 1933 7,000 more had failed. Customers lost about $7 billion in deposits as a result of these bank failures. Many were unable to withdraw funds to meet everyday living expenses simply because there was no cash to distribute.

By March 1933, 22 states had declared banking holidays—temporary bank closures—

Exhibit 2.5 **Effects of the Great Depression**

- $14 billion of paper security value losses
- 10 years of elusive recovery
- 25 percent unemployment
- 8,300 bank failures
- $7 billion in lost customer deposits

---

and President Roosevelt was finally forced to declare a seven-day, nationwide banking holiday. Only the banks that were considered strong enough to survive were allowed to reopen.

Factors Contributing to the Crash

Once again, the public had lost confidence in the banking system. Many people had lost their jobs and their life savings, and something had to be done. What had gone wrong? Answers to that question vary. Some critics think that because proper controls were not in place, the crash could not have been prevented. Others believe that while the controls were basically inadequate, the Federal Reserve had the power or could have obtained the power from Congress to do something, but instead did nothing.

History can be a good teacher, and after the crash, the lessons of the past showed how government intervention could restore public confidence. Congress again was called on to invoke banking reform. In analyzing the causes of the stock market crash and the extensive bank failures, it identified four contributing factors:

1. *Interest on demand deposits*. Banks were allowed to pay interest on demand deposits (chapter 4). In an effort to attract deposits and fund the demand for loans, banks increased the amounts they paid in interest. This tremendous interest expense lowered bank earnings, and the banks in turn eased credit policies so that more loans could be made to offset interest expenses.

2. *Securities (stock) underwriting*. Banks were also allowed to underwrite securities issues. In other words, they were allowed to buy entire issues of new stock and place the

issues on the market. A bank would guarantee the sale of the securities and collect a fee for handling the issue. Banks would also lend money to borrowers for purchases of stock underwritten by the bank. In theory, the bank could make money on both the loan interest and the sale of the securities.

3. *Lack of margin requirements*. Some banks exercised caution and required margins as high as 45 to 50 percent, but more controls were needed. Requiring stock purchasers to put up more cash would have reduced the number of stocks purchased, and banks would not have exposed themselves to so much risk.

4. *Lack of depositor protection*. When large numbers of banks failed, depositors lost their deposits and had no recourse against the banks.

Resulting Legislation

On the basis of beliefs about these contributing factors, Congress moved ahead with legislation to reform the banking system.

Glass-Steagall Act

Taking into consideration all the contributing factors, Congress passed the Banking Act, more commonly referred to as the **Glass-Steagall Act**, in 1933. The act made broad changes to the banking system, with the following major provisions; it:

- prohibited banks from paying interest on demand deposits
- raised minimum capital requirements of national banks
- prohibited member banks (banks that were members of the Federal Reserve System) from underwriting securities issues and otherwise prohibited member banks from

affiliating with organizations dealing in securities

- allowed the Federal Reserve Board to forbid any member bank to use Reserve credit for speculative purposes
- created the Federal Deposit Insurance Corporation (FDIC) to protect depositors at FDIC-insured banks

Securities Exchange Act of 1934

In 1934 Congress passed the **Securities Exchange Act**, which gave the Federal Reserve the authority to set margin requirements. All loans made by banks that were collateralized by securities were subject to the margin requirements. In the interest of protecting the public, the act was amended in 1964 to require all publicly held banks to make certain financial disclosures. Additional amendments affecting banks were made in 1975.

Banking Act of 1935

The Glass-Steagall Act and the Securities Exchange Act once again strengthened the banking system and restored public confidence. To further strengthen the system, Congress extended the regulatory powers of the Federal Reserve by passing the Banking Act of 1935, also referred to as the **Federal Deposit Insurance Act** of 1935, and amended the Glass-Steagall Act. The Banking Act of 1935 authorized the FDIC to:

- set standards for operations at FDIC member banks
- examine those banks to ensure compliance with the standards
- take action to reduce the potential of troubled banks failing
- pay depositors if an insured bank failed

National banks, already required to be Fed members, now had to belong to the FDIC; other commercial banks might join if they wished. Mutual savings banks, which had already been given the right to become members of the Federal Reserve System by the Glass-Steagall Act, were also permitted to join the FDIC. Savings and loan associations were insured by the Federal Savings and Loan Insurance Corporation until it was abolished in 1989 by the Financial Institutions Reform, Recovery, and Enforcement Act of 1989, which is discussed later in this chapter.

A Change in Philosophy

The last two decades have shown a decided shift in philosophy regarding bank regulation. Congress has recognized the need for banks to be able to compete in an ever-changing marketplace. In the 1980s, regulation relaxed to the point where banks began to offer new products to challenge non-bank competitors. Subsequent problems with bank and savings and loan lending portfolios led to more regulation to strengthen bank lending. Most recently, however, banks finally were given the ability to compete on an equal basis with other financial services providers.

Under its regulatory authority, the Fed enacted Regulation Q, which put limits on the amount of interest that could be paid on savings and time deposits. In an attempt to offer a product for which banks could offer competitive interest rates, New York banks introduced the large-denomination ($100,000 or more) certificate of deposit (CD) in 1961. Because of the size and terms of these CDs, they were exempt from the restrictions of Federal Reserve Regulation Q. Success in attracting funds to this new vehicle, however, was not sufficient to compensate for the limits imposed by Regulation Q on other types of deposits—mostly for customers who could not purchase a $100,000 CD.

In 1971 brokerage firms introduced the money market mutual fund, a new type of mutual fund designed for customers with less than $100,000 to invest. At the same time that banks, restricted by federal regulation, could pay only 5 or 5.25 percent interest on savings accounts used by these same customers, money market funds were paying 8 percent or more. Interest rates began to rise rapidly in the mid- to late-1970s, and banks started to experience what is referred to as **disintermediation**. This term means that customers withdrew their money from banks and other depository institutions in order to earn higher rates of interest on other types of investments.

As interest rates increased, banks had to pay higher rates to compete, and bank profits were reduced. State-chartered banks that belonged to the Fed began to question whether this membership was worthwhile. Although as members they could take advantage of the Fed's services, they also were unable to earn interest on the reserves required and kept by the Fed. Some national banks whose membership in the Fed was required considered the possibility of changing to state charters so that they could withdraw from the Fed and free up their reserves. In 1978, 99 commercial banks withdrew from membership in the Fed, and the percentage of commercial bank deposits subject to reserve requirements decreased from 80 percent in 1970 to 69 percent in 1979.[4] The Federal Reserve believed that this exodus weakened its ability to control the flow of money and credit, because fewer banks were subject to its reserve requirements.

An Expanding Marketplace

Most, if not all, of the banking legislation enacted between 1933 and 1980 implemented new regulatory controls or strengthened old ones. Even 50 years after the stock market crash and the Great Depression, the memory of the primary causes of those problems lingered in the minds of legislators, regulators, and the general public. This increase in control, however, had a negative impact on banks as customers turned to investments offered by less regulated, non-bank competitors who were offering higher interest rates.

For years, banks competed among themselves with little competition from outside sources for traditional banking functions. The bulk of a bank's deposits was in the form of demand deposits on which the bank paid no interest. This all changed as non-bank institutions that were not subject to the same regulatory controls entered the market. In addition to other commercial banks, banks now faced significant competition from the following:

- **Credit unions** offer limited financial services to members who, by law, must share a common bond, such as being teachers or federal employees. Because they are federally tax exempt, offer a limited range of services, and often have company-provided facilities, credit unions have minimal expenses and can offer credit and other products and services at a reduced cost to their members.

- **Savings and loan associations** (S&Ls) were originally chartered to provide mortgage credit to their customers. They are generally owned by depositors rather than stockholders. For years, commercial banks were not particularly interested in tying up their funds by making mortgage loans, allowing the S&L industry to grow and prosper without competition.

- Most **savings banks** are former savings and loan associations, and they operate and are *member* owned in much the same way. Many mutual savings banks, however, are *stock issuing institutions*, and are insured by the FDIC. Many savings and loans have changed their charters and names to federal savings bank (FSB) primarily to have the word "bank" in their title. Others have dropped the word "savings" altogether to distance themselves from the savings and loans and to be recognized as offering more expanded financial services.

- **Brokerage firms** help customers buy stocks, bonds, and mutual funds. They are not FDIC-insured, but offer similar insurance through the Securities Investor Protection Corporation (SIPC). As will be discussed later in this chapter, new legislation will now allow banks to offer brokerage services to their customers.

New Products to Challenge Non-bank Competitors

Depository Institutions Deregulation and Monetary Control Act of 1980

The tight rein on banking powers remained until 1980, when Congress passed the **Depository Institutions Deregulation and Monetary Control Act**. Addressing the problems described in the previous section, this act was the most important single piece of banking legislation since 1933. It redefined banking powers and allowed banks and savings and loan associations to offer new products that could compete against their non-bank com-

petitors. This act marked the beginning of a series of legislative acts, culminating in the 1999 Gramm-Leach-Bliley Act, which dismantled prior regulation and gave banks the freedom to compete.

The Depository Institutions Deregulation and Monetary Control Act allowed financial institutions to become more competitive through deregulation and the Fed to gain more control of the money supply. The act contained the following major provisions:

- Maximum FDIC coverage was increased to $100,000.

- All institutions offering accounts that permit payment to a third party (such as a checking account) were required to maintain reserves against those deposits.

- Federal Reserve Regulation Q, which established limits on the amount of interest a bank could pay on deposits, was to be gradually phased out. (This phaseout was completed in 1987.)

- All financial institutions were allowed to apply for loans from the Federal Reserve. Previously, only member banks had this borrowing power.

- The Federal Reserve was ordered to charge for all of its services (chapter 3).

- Savings and loan associations and credit unions were allowed to make commercial loans and to offer trust services.

- All financial institutions were allowed to offer negotiable order of withdrawal (NOW) accounts. (A NOW account is an interest-bearing account on which a customer may write checks. It is not a demand deposit account, however, because the bank must reserve the right to require the depositor to give the financial institution seven days' advance notice before withdrawing the funds.)

Garn-St Germain Act

In 1982, Congress passed the **Garn-St Germain Act** to help banks and other depository institutions further compete. The act allowed banks to offer two new types of deposit products, the money market deposit account (MMDA) and the super NOW account. The MMDA was basically a savings account with the following features:

- unlimited interest rate on balances of $2,500 or more
- a maximum 5.25 percent interest rate on balances of less than $2,500
- available to all depositors
- unlimited withdrawals are possible by person or by mail
- a limit of three check transfers per month
- a limit of six preauthorized third-party transfers per month
- federally insured deposits

The super NOW account is a NOW account with no transaction limitations and no interest-rate ceiling, as long as a balance of at least $2,500 is maintained. The accounts may be offered only to customers who qualify for NOW accounts.

These two types of accounts did give banks some competitive relief. The fact that the accounts were federally insured made them more attractive to some customers than the money market mutual funds. Banks continue to offer MMDA, super NOW accounts, and NOW accounts today. Customers are more likely to recognize these by their product names such as "interest checking" (NOW accounts) or "high interest savings accounts" (MMDAs).

Many bankers, however, felt that Congress did not go far enough in its deregulation effort to allow banks to better compete against brokerage firms. The provisions of the Glass-Steagall Act, prohibiting banks from underwriting securities and paying interest on demand deposits, remained intact.

New Rules to Strengthen Bank Lending

As has been evident throughout history, banking legislation is often passed in reaction to a crisis. In the 1980s, the crisis was in bank and S&L loan portfolios.

Deteriorating Loan Portfolios. During the 1980s, commercial banks reported severe problems resulting from deteriorating loan portfolios. Banks that had granted huge loans to less developed countries had to add billions of dollars to their loan loss reserves as full repayment of principal and interest on these loans became unlikely. Other banks with large concentrations of loans to real estate developers and to companies in the oil and gas industries reported increasing losses. Real estate sales in 1988 and 1989 plummeted in many parts of the country, and large amounts of unoccupied office space could be found in major cities where overbuilding, financed largely by the banks, had taken place. These large loan write-offs led to an unprecedented number of bank closings. In 1989, 206 FDIC-insured banks were closed, the highest figure in FDIC history.

By the 1980s, however, the savings and loan associations were in serious trouble as well. The total number of savings banks and S&Ls fell from 5,172 to 2,549 by June 1992[5]. Many of the S&Ls experienced losses; the Federal Savings and Loan Insurance Corporation (FSLIC) reported a net loss of $11.6 billion for 1987,[6] and 510 S&Ls were classified as insolvent, with assets worth less than their liabilities.[7]

Though no factor is the sole cause for the S&L crisis, two contributing factors can be pointed out: narrowing spreads and inexperience with new deposit and loan products.

Narrowing Spreads. In the late 1970s interest rates increased significantly, and the S&Ls paid higher rates for deposits. The problem was that the loans they made were fixed-rate loans; as market rates rapidly increased, the **net interest spread**—the difference between loans and interest income and interest expense (deposits)—was narrowed until all profits were squeezed out and a loss resulted. The rates paid on deposits rose faster than the rates that were charged on the loans (exhibit 2.6).

Inexperience with New Deposit and Loan Products. Another problem was that as a result of the Monetary Control Act of 1980, thrifts found themselves offering deposit and loan products that they had not previously offered. In many cases the deposit products were given away to attract the transaction accounts. Some thrifts offered rates 3 or 4 percent above prevailing market rates to keep or attract deposits. Many S&Ls were making loans in areas in which they had limited experience; their inexperience resulted in large losses.

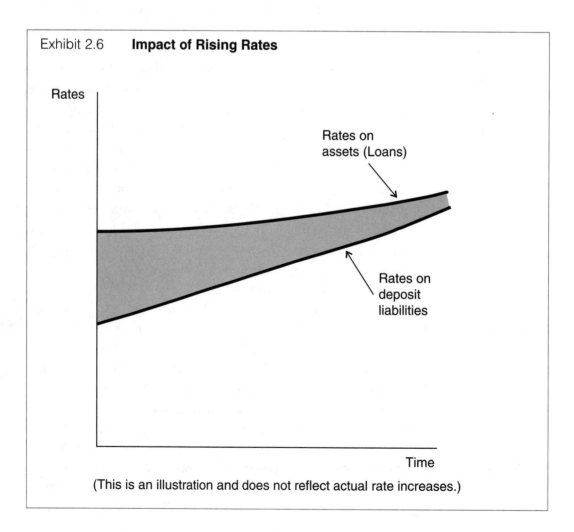

Exhibit 2.6   **Impact of Rising Rates**

Rates

Rates on assets (Loans)

Rates on deposit liabilities

Time

(This is an illustration and does not reflect actual rate increases.)

Financial Institutions Reform, Recovery, and Enforcement Act

The pendulum began swinging back toward regulation and controls (exhibit 2.7) as Congress reacted to the loan crisis by passing the **Financial Institutions Reform, Recovery, and Enforcement Act of 1989 (FIRREA)**. FIRREA completely restructured the S&L insurance and regulatory agencies. The primary purpose of the act was to reform and consolidate the federal deposit insurance system to restore the public's confidence in the S&L industry. The FSLIC and the Federal Home Loan Bank Board (which was the regulatory agency overseeing the S&Ls) were abolished, and their functions were transferred to the FDIC, the Office of Thrift Supervision (OTS)—to oversee and regulate thrifts, the Federal Housing Finance Board, and the Resolution Trust Corporation(RTC)—to deal with insolvent thrifts and sell their assets. New capital requirements were also established, and the act appointed the FDIC as the administrator of two separate insurance funds:

- The Bank Insurance Fund (BIF), which insures the deposits of the BIF member banks
- The Savings Association Insurance Fund (SAIF), which insures the deposits of all SAIF member savings associations

FIRREA provided the RTC with funding, estimated at the time at $166 billion, to close insolvent S&Ls, sell their assets, and pay depos-

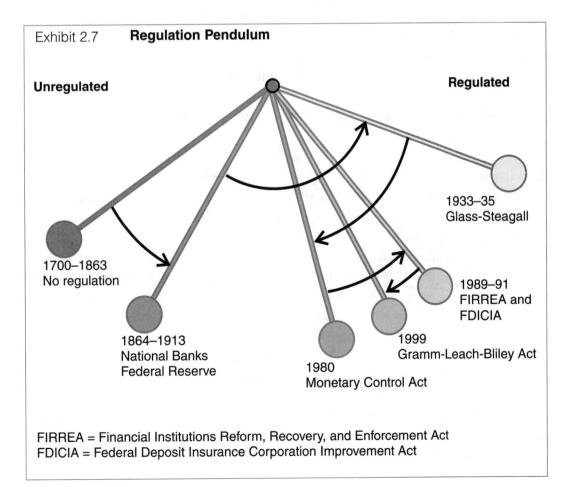

Exhibit 2.7   **Regulation Pendulum**

Unregulated

Regulated

1933–35
Glass-Steagall

1700–1863
No regulation

1989–91
FIRREA and
FDICIA

1864–1913
National Banks
Federal Reserve

1999
Gramm-Leach-Bliley Act

1980
Monetary Control Act

FIRREA = Financial Institutions Reform, Recovery, and Enforcement Act
FDICIA = Federal Deposit Insurance Corporation Improvement Act

itors where necessary. The cost exceeded original projections as the RTC found itself with portfolios of junk bonds to liquidate and billions of dollars in assets to sell, including yachts, hotels, resorts, paintings, and office buildings.

In addition to the liquidation, FIRREA also gave the RTC or the acquirer of a thrift institution the authority to break the original contract between the issuer of a CD and the customer and then quote a lower rate to reduce interest expense.

Federal Deposit Insurance Corporation Improvement Act of 1991

Many bankers thought FIRREA would address the problems plaguing the S&L industry and the troubled commercial banks and that Congress would give the banking industry additional relief through deregulation. Instead, Congress passed the Federal Deposit Insurance Corporation Improvement Act (FDICIA) of 1991.

The FDICIA recapitalized the Bank Insurance Fund by allowing the FDIC to borrow an additional $30 billion from the Treasury. It also substantially revised bank regulation and supervision for both domestic and foreign banks by requiring on-site examinations, annual audit requirements, and revised bank accounting standards.

As a result of the FDICIA, banks are required to meet new safety and soundness standards, including operational and managerial standards, officer and director standards, and compensation standards. Banks perform assessments to determine their credit exposure to correspondent banks. Restrictions were placed on state-chartered banks by prohibiting them from engaging in activities that are prohibited for national banks.

The Truth in Savings Act is part of FDICIA and is implemented by Regulation DD. The purpose of the act is to assist consumers in comparing deposit accounts offered by financial institutions and to provide ongoing information about the accounts. The regulation governs checking, savings, and CD accounts that are held by or offered to individual consumers for non-business purposes. It requires the use of the **annual percentage yield (APY)** when providing interest rate information to customers. APY is a percentage rate that reflects the total amount of interest paid on an account and is based on the interest rate and the frequency of compounding for a 365-day period. Regulation DD is covered in greater detail in chapter 4.

Despite what appeared to be further control of banking, the trend toward overall deregulation continued.

New Opportunities to Compete

Gramm-Leach-Bliley Act of 1999

Hailed as the "most significant overhaul of the financial services industry laws since the Great Depression," the Gramm-Leach-Bliley Act (also known as the Financial Modernization Bill) repeals key provisions of the Glass-Steagall Act and provides the financial services industry with the tools it needs to compete in today's economy. Banks, security firms, and insurance companies can now enter each other's businesses and affiliate with each other. Because Justin in situation 3 happens to need financial services in 2002, he will be one of the first to benefit from the convenience of getting all his financial needs met at one bank. A few years earlier, this would not have been possible.

Gramm-Leach-Bliley is far-reaching legislation, much of which is beyond the scope of this text. In addition, because it is new legislation, it remains to be seen how regulatory authorities will interpret the provisions and direct how banks and other financial institutions will act within its scope. Of relevance to this text are three primary aspects of the law:

- the creation of two new entities
- protection of financial privacy
- disclosure requirements for ATMs

Financial Holding Companies and Financial Subsidiaries. The act authorizes the establishment of two new kinds of entities through which banks can engage in a range of new services.

1. A Financial Holding Company (FHC) is a new kind of bank holding company that expands activities currently permitted by bank holding company affiliates to include insurance and brokerage services. Previously, bank holding companies could only engage in activities closely related to banking.

2. A **Financial Subsidiary (FS)** differs from an FHC in that it may not engage in non-financial activities such as insurance or brokerage. As a subsidiary of the bank, however, it can engage in the sale of any financial product without geographic limits. This will have implications for nationwide banking.

Financial Privacy. The increase in options banks can now offer their customers brings with it an inevitable increase in the exchange of consumer financial information. Gramm-Leach-Bliley includes provisions to protect financial privacy and ensure customers that information will not be exchanged to third parties without their permission. The act accomplishes this by:

1. giving customers the right to instruct their bank not to provide information on their behalf to non-affiliated third parties

2. preventing the financial institution from providing account information to unaffiliated third party marketers or telemarketers

3. requiring financial institutions to establish a privacy policy and to make this policy available to customers annually

4. requiring the financial institution to be sure that it protects the security and confidentiality of its customers' information

ATM Disclosures. The Gramm-Leach-Bliley Act requires banks to disclose surcharges for ATMs. These disclosures must be placed on the ATM machines and must appear on the screens themselves. Customers may choose to not pay the fee and cancel the transaction.

Summary

The banking system in the United States has been developing for more than 200 years. Major developments in the banking system have resulted from reactions to crisis. The industry has gone from a completely decentralized and unregulated system to one of the most monitored segments of the economy.

The early American banking system was unstructured and unregulated; it could not support the needs of a growing industrial nation. Congress passed the National Bank Act in 1863 to begin stabilizing the faltering banking system. The National Bank Act created national banks, the Office of the Comptroller of the Currency, national banknotes, and a system of reserves. The National Bank Act did solve many of the problems plaguing the banking system, but other problems remained. The national banknote was an inflexible form of currency, and the money supply could grow only in proportion to the amount of government securities issued. There was no check

Exhibit 2.8	**Chronology of Banking Legislation and Events**
1791–1811	First Bank of the United States
1811–1816	Bank failures increase
1816–1836	Second Bank of the United States
1836–1863	Chaos in the banking system
1863–1864	National Bank Act
1913	Federal Reserve Act
1929	Stock market crash; start of the Great Depression
1933	Glass-Steagall Act
1934	Securities Exchange Act; start of the FDIC
1935	Banking Act or Federal Deposit Insurance Act
1970–1980	"Disintermediation" in the banking system
1980	Depository Institutions Deregulation and Monetary Control Act
1982	Garn-St Germain Act
1989	Financial Institutions Reform, Recovery, and Enforcement Act (FIRREA)
1991	Federal Deposit Insurance Corporation Improvement Act (FDICIA)
1999	Gramm-Leach-Bliley Act

collection system, and the reserves were concentrated in money center banks.

The Federal Reserve Act of 1913 was passed to address the weaknesses left by the National Bank Act. The Federal Reserve Act established the Federal Reserve System and solved the problem of the pyramiding of reserves and the lack of a check collection system by creating 12 Federal Reserve districts. Reserves could be maintained in the Federal Reserve banks, and the 12 Reserve districts were used to establish a nationwide check collection system. The inflexible currency problem was solved by the creation of the Federal Reserve note, which constitutes our basic currency today.

The economy's rapid expansion after World War I led to some careless banking practices that resulted in massive bank failures. The stock market crash of 1929 led to many bank failures, which in turn deepened the Great Depression. Until the Depression, banks were allowed to underwrite securities issues and to pay interest on demand deposits. In 1933 Congress passed the Glass-Steagall Act, which placed significant controls on banks. The act

prohibited payment of interest on demand deposits, prohibited banks from underwriting stocks or investing in common stock, authorized the Fed to control bank loans for securities, and created the FDIC.

In 1980, Congress passed the Depository Institutions Deregulation and Monetary Control Act. The act allowed banks to compete more evenly with non-bank competitors by lifting some restrictions on banking activities. The Garn-St Germain Act was passed in 1982 to allow banks to better compete with mutual funds.

During the 1980s, narrowing interest spreads and inexperience with new deposit and loan products, in addition to other factors, caused unprecedented losses to savings and loan associations. Commercial banks also experienced high loan losses during that time but were not as seriously affected. In 1989 Congress stepped in to avert significant individual losses by passing FIRREA. This act created the Office of Thrift Supervision and the RTC, authorized billions of dollars to clean up distressed loans, and addressed a number of other issues.

In 1991 Congress decided that more fine-tuning was required, and FDICIA was passed. FDICIA provided for additional funds for failed banks and S&Ls. Regulation DD, which implements the Truth in Savings Act, is part of FDICIA and requires that information be provided to customers, allowing them to compare deposit accounts.

The 1999 Gramm-Leach-Bliley Act has forever changed the face of banking by finally allowing banks to compete in the full financial marketplace. While expanding the powers of banks to offer insurance and brokerage services, the act also protects a consumer's right to financial privacy.

Review and Discussion Questions

1. Describe the banking period prior to the passage of the National Bank Act.

2. What is meant by the term "dual banking system"? Does the dual banking system exist today?

3. How did the Federal Reserve Act solve the problems of pyramided reserves and check collection?

4. What impact did the Great Depression have on the banking system?

5. What does disintermediation mean?

6. How does the Gramm-Leach-Bliley Act protect a consumer's right to financial privacy?

Notes

1. As chronicled by Bartlett Naylor in "Bankers Spilled Blood in Nation's Early Years," *American Banker* (January 1987): 24.

2. See Elvira and Vladimir Clain-Stefanelli's *Chartered For Progress: Two Centuries of American Banking* (Washington, D.C.: Acropolis, 1975), 68-69.

3. See Naylor, p. 24.

4. See Peter D. Schellie's *Manager's Guide to the 1980 Monetary Control Act* (Washington, D.C.: American Bankers Association, 1981): 23.

5. Phil Roosevelt, "Top Thrifts Boost Their Share of the Industry's Deposits," *American Banker* (May 1989): 1.

6. See Jim McTague, "FSLIC's 1987 Deficit Put At $11.6 Billion By Regulators," *American Banker* (April 1988): 1.

7. From Nathaniel C. Nash's "Record Loss for Savings Industry." *New York Times*, 25 March 1988, Sec. D, p. 1.

Additional Resources

ABA Banking Journal. American Bankers Association, monthly magazine.

Bankers News. American Bankers Association, bi-weekly newspaper.

Money and Banking. Washington, D.C.: American Bankers Association, 1998.

Web Resources

American Bankers Association www.aba.com

Board of Governors, Federal Reserve
www.federalreserve.gov

Federal Deposit Insurance Corporation
www.fdic.gov

Office of the Comptroller of the Currency
www.occ.treas.gov

3

THE FEDERAL RESERVE AND ITS REGULATORY PARTNERS

Learning Objectives

After completing this chapter, you will be able to do the following:

* describe why the Federal Reserve System (the Fed) was created and list its primary purposes
* describe the structure of the Federal Reserve, including the 12 districts, the Board of Governors, and the Reserve banks and branches
* list and describe the services offered by the Fed
* explain how the Fed and other agencies use their powers to enforce regulations and supervise and examine banks
* explain inflation and describe the role of banks in creating money
* describe how the Fed uses reserve requirements, discount operations, and open market operations to implement monetary policy
* define the bolded terms that appear in the text

Introduction

Federal Reserve actions have an impact on your job and your customer's financial lives, as shown in the following situations.

Situation 1

It's June and time for graduation. A customer comes to your window asking for 20 crisp, new $50 bills to give as graduation presents. You do not have any to give to the customer but offer to order them for delivery next week. The customer agrees and is curious about where the bills will come from. How do you respond?

Situation 2

One day, Federal Reserve Chairman Alan Greenspan mentioned that he thought inflation might be heating up a little. Immediately, this comment was a lead story on the news. Within one hour of Greenspan's words being reported, the stock market had dropped. What do you say to a customer who asks about this?

Situation 3

The Kowalskis are buying a home and have applied for a mortgage loan. In the six weeks that pass between the loan application and closing, mortgage loan rates change three times. Each time, the Kowalskis call you to inquire about the change in rate. They do not understand how something so remote could affect the interest rate on their loan. How do you explain market reactions to Federal Reserve actions?

The Federal Reserve, our country's central bank, has a significant effect on our individual lives as well as on the national and international banking system. In the process of carrying out monetary policy, the Federal Reserve influences employment, interest rates, the availability of credit, and even our standard of living. A remark by the chairman of the Board of Governors of the Federal Reserve can cause public reaction and affect the stock market worldwide.

For obvious reasons, this type of power and influence should not be subject to politics. Thus the Federal Reserve has been allowed to operate autonomously, because any hint of political pressure on the Fed could inhibit its effectiveness.

Although highly independent, the Federal Reserve interacts with policy-making entities of the federal government. The chairman of the Board of Governors reports regularly to Congress and meets frequently with the president and the government's chief financial officers and economic advisers.

In recent years, the Fed has taken on an increasingly larger role in the international economy. The Federal Reserve Board monitors movements in foreign exchange rates along with other economic developments. It participates, together with the U.S. government and many of its agencies, in international financial policy and various international forums. The Fed is in constant contact with other nations' central banks and its monetary actions influence the price of U.S. goods on world markets.

This chapter discusses the creation of the Federal Reserve System and its organizational structure. The tools of monetary policy and how the Fed uses them, Federal Reserve regulations, and the services offered by the Fed are covered in detail. The chapter also addresses other government agencies that have an impact on the banking system.

Creation and Duties of the Federal Reserve System

As described in the previous chapter, Congress recognized that the National Bank Act did not solve all of the problems in the banking system. It passed the Federal Reserve Act in 1913 to address the unresolved issues.

Creation of the Federal Reserve System

Control of the Federal Reserve System was a perplexing issue. There was tremendous opposition to private ownership of the central bank, fearing that a self-interested private sector could not act effectively as a regulator of the banking system. On the other hand, sentiments were equally strong against giving control to the government. Government control not only would put the Fed under constant political pressure from special-interest groups, but also would place it at the mercy of public opinion—neither of which would always be in the best interests of the country.

Solving the economy's serious problems called for action. There were three major defi-ciencies remaining after the passage of the National Bank Act: lack of a check collection system, an inflexible currency, and pyramiding of reserves. Congress was under pressure to solve these problems and create an autonomous system for controlling the money supply and administering credit. It responded by passing the Federal Reserve Act of 1913, which created the Federal Reserve System (our central bank) to regulate money and the availability of credit. The act provided that the entire system would be privately owned by its member banks.

Duties of the Federal Reserve

The Federal Reserve was given many responsibilities designed to correct the flawed check collection system, the inflexible currency, and the pyramided reserves. Exhibit 3.1 lists the duties of the Federal Reserve System.

Structure of the Federal Reserve System

The Federal Reserve System consists of 12 Federal Reserve districts. Exhibit 3.2 shows

---

Exhibit 3.1 **Duties of the Federal Reserve System**

The Federal Reserve's duties fall into the following four general areas:

* Conducting the nation's monetary policy by influencing the money and credit conditions in the economy in pursuit of full employment and stable prices

* Supervising and regulating banking institutions to ensure the safety and soundness of the nation's banking and financial system and to protect the credit rights of consumers

* Maintaining the stability of the financial system and containing systematic risk that may arise in financial markets

* Providing certain financial services to the U.S. government, the public, financial institutions, and foreign official institutions, including playing a major role in operating the nation's payment system

Source: Board of Governors of the Federal Reserve System.

---

the 12 districts and the cities where each Federal Reserve bank and each Federal Reserve branch is located. Each Federal Reserve district contains a Federal Reserve bank with a board of directors. Each Federal Reserve bank is owned by the member banks in the district. The member banks hold stock in the reserve bank. Although the Federal Reserve System is privately owned, the stockholders (the member banks) do not have total control of the system in the same way stockholders normally control a company; the member banks exercise control through election of six of the nine directors of the local Federal Reserve banks. The other three are appointed by the Board of Governors of the Federal Reserve System. The activities of the Federal Reserve banks and the overall activities of the Fed are governed by the Fed's Board of Governors (similar to a company's board of directors).

Board of Governors of the Federal Reserve System

The **Board of Governors** consists of seven members appointed by the president of the United States and confirmed by the Senate. The governors are appointed for terms of 14 years. These terms are arranged so that one expires every two years in order to insulate the governors from political pressure. As a means of ensuring fair representation, no two members of the board may come from the same Federal Reserve district. The U.S. president appoints one of the governors as chairman and another as vice chairman for four-year terms.

Exhibit 3.3 lists the major responsibilities of the Board of Governors of the Federal Reserve.

Federal Reserve Banks

Each Federal Reserve district has a Federal Reserve bank, and most Reserve banks have branches. The structure of the 12 district banks allows them to serve the needs of the local members and to ensure that there is local representation at the national level. In this way, unique local needs are acknowledged and incorporated into a larger national scope. The local Federal Reserve banks will also provide information on the regional economy. The banks issue economic surveys, statistical reports, and tables of financial data that help define the condition of the local economy. Much of this information is available to the general public. Each Reserve bank is governed by a nine-member board of directors. While each Reserve bank is a separate corporation, the public nature of the organization is indicated by the way the directors are selected. (Six are elected by the member banks, and three are appointed by the Board of Governors.) To ensure that segments of the economy other than the financial segment are given equal representation, only three of the six directors elected by the member banks may be bankers. The other three are chosen from other fields. This structure was necessary to satisfy the objections of those who supported private ownership but were concerned about the possibility of too much banking influence. The boards of directors are responsible for the efficient operation of the Reserve banks. Exhibit 3.4 lists the primary functions of the Federal Reserve district banks.

Federal Reserve Services

One of the original purposes of the Federal Reserve System was to provide basic banking

Exhibit 3.2 **Federal Reserve Districts and Branch Cities**

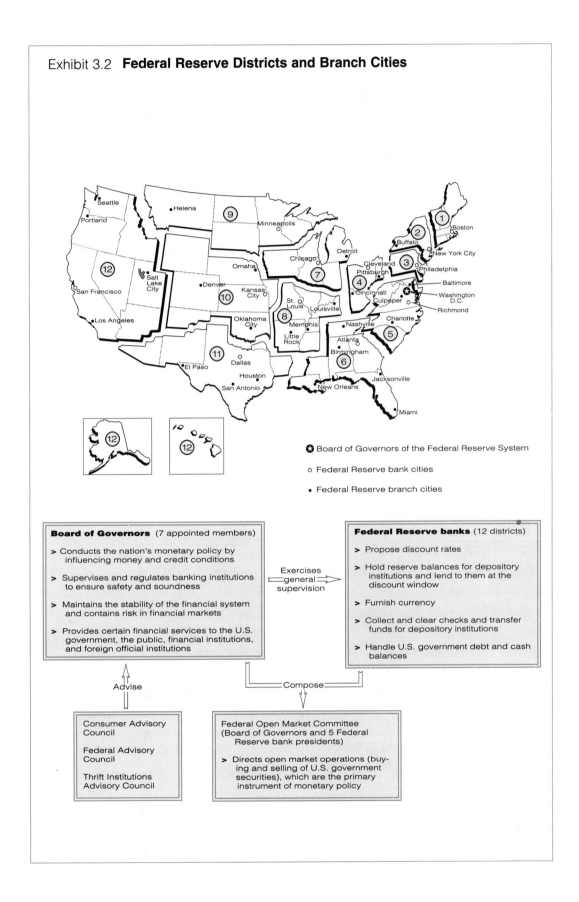

⊛ Board of Governors of the Federal Reserve System

o Federal Reserve bank cities

• Federal Reserve branch cities

Board of Governors (7 appointed members)

> Conducts the nation's monetary policy by influencing money and credit conditions

> Supervises and regulates banking institutions to ensure safety and soundness

> Maintains the stability of the financial system and contains risk in financial markets

> Provides certain financial services to the U.S. government, the public, financial institutions, and foreign official institutions

Exercises general supervision

Federal Reserve banks (12 districts)

> Propose discount rates

> Hold reserve balances for depository institutions and lend to them at the discount window

> Furnish currency

> Collect and clear checks and transfer funds for depository institutions

> Handle U.S. government debt and cash balances

Advise

Compose

Consumer Advisory Council

Federal Advisory Council

Thrift Institutions Advisory Council

Federal Open Market Committee (Board of Governors and 5 Federal Reserve bank presidents)

> Directs open market operations (buying and selling of U.S. government securities), which are the primary instrument of monetary policy

services to member banks. From its inception until 1980, the Fed provided almost all its services free of charge (lending money was the exception) but only to its member banks. In 1980, Congress, through the Monetary Control Act of 1980, mandated that the Fed charge for its services, including float. Fed services that carry a fee are

- coin and currency
- check processing
- Fedwire
- automated clearing house
- settlement
- securities safekeeping

The act further provided that the fees be priced explicitly, that they cover all direct and indirect expenses incurred by the Fed, and that the Fed offer non-member banks all the services it offers member institutions for the same fees.

> **Exhibit 3.4** **Functions of the Federal Reserve District Banks**
>
> - Propose discount rates
> - Hold reserve balances for depository institutions
> - Lend at the discount rate to member banks
> - Furnish currency and coin
> - Collect and clear checks
> - Transfer funds for depository institutions
> - Handle U.S. government debit and credit balances

Coin and Currency

The Fed supplies banks with coin and currency to meet customers' withdrawal demand. Because many retail businesses, as well as individuals, rely on their banks to provide coin and currency, banks have to keep a sufficient supply of coin and currency on hand. Most banks store this money in their vaults or safes. Vault cash, along with correspondent bank balances and teller cash, is a form of reserves that banks use to meet their reserve requirement. The Fed also accepts shipments of coin and currency from banks and ensures that mutilated currency is destroyed. The banker's response to the customer in situation 1 would be that new $50 bills are ordered from their branch of the district's Federal Reserve Bank.

Check Processing

The Fed offers **check clearing services, collection services,** and **return items services** to banks. The rules governing these services are established under Regulation J and Regulation CC. Approximately 40 percent of the nation's interbank checks are currently processed by the Fed, and an even larger percentage of return items are processed by the Fed. The Fed also offers other check-related services referred to as payer bank services (chapter 13) that assist banks in offering services such as controlled disbursement accounts to corporate customers. A controlled disbursement account (chapter 13) is a demand deposit account on which the corporate customer writes checks and the bank advises the customer of the dollar amount of the checks that will be posted to the customer's account that night. The customer then wires money into this account to cover the checks being paid. This service allows customers to manage their funds instead of leaving them in a checking account that does not pay interest.

Fedwire

Fedwire services are also provided by the Fed to many U.S. banks. Fedwire services are governed by Regulation J and are also subject to Article 4A of the Uniform Commercial Code. Banks that do not maintain an account with the Fed typically use the services of a correspondent bank that does maintain a Fed account. A customer who wants to transfer funds from his or her account to a beneficiary with an account at another bank issues a funds transfer at his or her bank. The bank initiates a funds transfer instruction to the Fed through the use of the Fed's Fedwire system. The Fed then initiates a funds transfer instruction to the beneficiary's bank or to another Federal Reserve bank. In the end, the funds are paid to the intended beneficiary. Large corporate customers and other financial institutions are the largest users of this service. Most wire transfers are initiated through the Fed, but banks may also issue wires through the **Clearing House Interbank Payments System (CHIPS)**, operated by the New York Clearing House.

Automated Clearing House

Some banks use the services of private sector processors, but the Federal Reserve is the primary provider of automated clearing house (ACH) services. ACH transactions (chapter 13) are paperless electronic debit and credit transactions. Just like checks, ACH transactions are presented to the paying bank or the receiving bank. The Fed maintains the software to sort the transactions and present them to the paying or receiving bank.

Settlement

In addition to actually performing the services described above, the Fed also offers settlement services. When a bank sends checks to the paying bank or sends a Fedwire, payment is made by one bank to the other. The Fed provides this **settlement** service, or payment, through Federal Reserve accounts. The Fed charges and credits these accounts at different times. For example, if a bank transfers funds to another bank, the Fed charges the sending bank's account and credits the receiving bank's account simultaneously. Check transactions are settled at different times, based on when the Fed receives payment for the checks it presents to the paying bank. The Fed monitors these transactions and discourages banks from creating intra-day overdrafts, referred to as daylight overdrafts. These overdrafts occur when items posted to a bank reserve account bring the account into a negative balance.

U.S. Government Services

Fed services are extremely important not only to banks but also to the U.S. government: the Fed serves as its bank. An individual who receives an income tax refund or other disbursement of funds from the government is actually receiving a check drawn on the Fed. If the disbursement of government funds is made through an electronic transfer of funds, as in the case of Social Security payments, the appropriate government account with the Fed is reduced. The inflow of all funds to the federal government also goes through the Fed. As the fiscal agent for the U.S. Treasury, the Fed is responsible for issuing and redeeming all federal government obligations.

Enforcement, Supervision, and Examination

Among the Fed's many roles is the enforcement of banking law through implementing regulations and the supervision and examination of banks to ensure their safety and soundness.

Regulations to Implement Laws

The Federal Reserve Act gave the Board of Governors of the Federal Reserve the authority to issue rules, regulations, and guidelines that apply to both national banks and state member banks. The various regulations provide the Fed with the means to carry out congressional policies and to control the flow of money and credit.

When Congress passes banking-related regulatory legislation, it directs the Fed to formulate regulatory requirements to implement the provisions of the act or law. An example is Regulation E, titled Electronic Funds Transfer, that was issued to implement the provisions of the Electronic Funds Transfer Act of 1978. Typically, the Fed publishes a proposed regulation for comment, allowing all interested parties the opportunity to react to it. If the Fed is convinced that the comments are valid, it typically modifies the regulation, unless doing so is prohibited by the act the regulation is meant to implement. In addition to issuing regulations, the Fed also issues comments to the regulations. The official comments on a regulation are interpretations issued by the staff of the Board. Good-faith compliance with the official staff commentary generally affords the bank protection from violating the regulation.

As of March 2000, 31 Federal Reserve regulations had been implemented. Each regulation is assigned a letter of the alphabet. Having used letters A to Z, the regulations started over at AA, and now extend through EE. A summary of the Federal Reserve regulations is presented in the appendix of this book.

Regulations address relationships between the Fed and member banks for such items as loans to depository institutions, reserve requirements, member stock in the Fed, and check collections. The regulations also address loans by members to directors and executive officers, assessment of risk, and interlocking relationships with securities dealers. Consumer protection and disclosure regulations apply to areas such as truth in lending, truth in savings, expedited funds availability, and electronic funds transfers.

Certain Federal Reserve regulations also apply to entities other than member banks. Examples of regulations that go beyond member banks are those governing corporations engaged in foreign banking, margin requirements, consumer protection, and non-bank activities of foreign banks that have branches in the United States. The Fed also has regulatory authority over the activities of bank holding companies.

Supervisory Agencies

The Fed is one of four agencies with the authority to supervise banking activities. The other agencies are the Office of the Comptroller of the Currency, the Federal Deposit Insurance Corporation, and each state's banking authorities.

Office of the Comptroller of the Currency

The Office of the Comptroller of the Currency has jurisdiction over all national banks and is responsible for chartering, examining, and supervising them. All applications for national bank charters, all requests by any national bank for opening new domestic or foreign branches or for offering new services, and all mergers or acquisitions involving national banks must have OCC approval. This agency's many functions are carried out

through regional administrative offices throughout the country.

Federal Deposit Insurance Corporation

The Federal Deposit Insurance Corporation (FDIC) is responsible for supervising and examining all federally insured commercial banks and savings banks (through the Bank Insurance Fund) and savings and loan associations (through the Savings Association Insurance Fund). It sets enforceable standards for its members, can examine any FDIC-insured financial institution at any time, and may act to prevent the failure of an insured bank by bringing about a merger with or acquisition by a stronger insured institution. It may also take other positive action to prevent an insured institution from failing—for example, by buying the troubled bank's assets or providing an infusion of capital funds.

State Banking Departments

Each state has its own banking department responsible for chartering, supervising, and examining the state-chartered non-member banks within the boundaries of the state. Banks' applications for state charters are submitted to the banking departments of the individual states and must pass qualifying tests. If the proposed new bank desires membership in the Federal Reserve System or the FDIC, its application must be reviewed and approved by those agencies.

Other Enforcement Agencies

Other government agencies have an impact on banks. For example, the FBI is charged with investigating bank robberies, employee theft, embezzlement, and criminal acts. The Secret Service investigates counterfeit currency. The IRS enforces tax law on banks and uses the banking system to freeze bank accounts for tax evaders. The IRS also reviews currency transaction reports for money laundering activity. The influence of government agencies will increase as banks and bank holding companies expand services as allowed under the 1999 Gramm-Leach-Bliley Act. Because of that, banks and bank holding companies will come under increased scrutiny by the Securities and Exchange Commission and the individual state departments of insurance.

Agency Examinations

Examinations by the Fed and the other agencies are intended to ensure that banks are operating prudently, obeying all regulations and laws; and accurately reporting their financial condition. Examinations also provide comfort and confidence to depositors.

Periodic bank examinations have become an accepted part of our banking system. Every commercial bank receives at least one such examination each year. More frequent examinations are conducted if they seem warranted by conditions in a particular bank. All national banks must be members of the Federal Reserve System, and all Fed member banks must be insured by the FDIC. Therefore, national banks are subject to examination by the OCC, the Fed, and the FDIC. It is impossible, however, for each regulatory agency to examine every bank under its jurisdiction.

To avoid duplication and waste, federal regulatory agencies have agreed on an examination format. The primary examining responsibility is assigned to one agency, which then transmits the results of its findings to all other interested agencies and to the bank's board of directors (exhibit 3.5).

This system does not inhibit any agency from conducting its own, separate examination of a particular bank when justified by conditions. For example, if the OCC identified a problem at a national bank, the Fed and the

Exhibit 3.5 Bank Regulatory Authorities

Type of Bank	Regulatory Authority	Annual Examination Conducted by
National bank	Comptroller of the Currency Federal Reserve FDIC	Comptroller of the Currency
State member bank	Federal Reserve FDIC State banking department	Federal Reserve*
State non-member insured bank	FDIC State banking department	FDIC
State non-member noninsured bank	State banking department	State banking department

* Examinations of state-chartered member banks are often conducted jointly by Federal Reserve and state banking department examiners.

FDIC could, on the basis of the OCC's report, immediately examine that bank if they felt doing so was appropriate.

Monetary and Credit Policy and the Tools of Control

The National Bank Act did not address the issue of the nation's money supply. (The basic money supply, termed M1, includes the coin and currency in circulation, demand deposits, and traveler's checks.) As the agent of monetary policy, the Federal Reserve was given this responsibility. Prior to the establishment of the Federal Reserve, the money supply was not controlled or managed, and the results were devastating to the economy. No mechanism existed to provide the money and the credit needed to support an expanding economy, yet for economic growth to occur, business needed a source of credit and banks needed money to lend.

There was also no mechanism to control **inflation**, which occurs when too many dollars are chasing too few goods. A non-monetary example is used here to explain the concept of inflation. The case of Beanie Babies, while not inflation in the true sense, shows how prices can rise (inflate) under certain circumstances.

Beanie Baby toys were a purchasing phenomenon in the 1990s. If every parent who wanted one of the rarer, and therefore harder-to-find Beanie Babies, had had the purchase price to spend, and if there had been enough toys for everyone, the price would have remained constant. As it happened, the supply of some Beanie Babies was limited and the demand was high. Parents were willing to spend double or triple the purchase price to secure one of these toys, which artificially pushed up, or inflated, the price.

Similarly, the Federal Reserve has the responsibility to ensure that the money supply does not outpace the needs of the economy. Too many dollars for too few goods could result in a rise in the price of those goods, or inflation.

The Fed influences the entire economic environment by taking specific actions to influence the flow of money and credit. However, the Fed always takes into consideration **fiscal policy**—the activities of Congress and the president in the areas of taxation and government spending. Fiscal policy determines how much revenue the government expects to collect and how much it will spend. **Monetary policy** works to control the flow of money and credit without political concerns. The impact of monetary policy also can be realized faster than changes in fiscal policy, as shown by the immediate reaction to Alan Greenspan's comment in situation 2, because the Fed can act quickly to implement changes. Changes in fiscal policy require an act of Congress.

Role of Banks in Creating Money

The Fed establishes ranges for the growth rate of the money supply on the basis of a number of economic factors. The Fed then uses its tools for monetary control to keep the money supply within those ranges. Banks play an important role in the growth of the money supply because of their ability to create demand deposits.

Banks create money for demand deposits through a combination of the deposit and the loan functions. When banks make loans, they also increase the volume of demand deposits. Here is an example of how demand deposits are increased: ABC Bank has $10,000 in cash assets—part of the stockholders' original investment—and $0 in demand deposits. A consumer borrows the $10,000 in cash from ABC to buy a car and pays the $10,000 cash to the car dealership. The dealership deposits the $10,000 to its checking account, also at ABC. Now ABC Bank's demand deposits are increased by $10,000, and its money supply is also increased. After the transaction, the bank has $10,000 in loans, $10,000 in cash (the dealer's deposit) and $10,000 in demand deposits; the stockholders' investment does not change. Exhibit 3.6 uses a T-account to show how this transaction would be shown in the bank's books (bank accounting is discussed in chapter 10).

If the bank has a reserve requirement of 10 percent, the bank must keep 10 percent of its demand deposits in cash or balances at the Federal Reserve. In this example the bank must keep $1,000 as reserves (10 percent of $10,000), so it has only $9,000 available to lend to other customers ($10,000 minus

$1,000). If the bank lends out its available $9,000, that $9,000 will be deposited in the same or another bank in a demand deposit account. The result of this transaction is that demand deposits are created and increased by $9,000, as is the money supply. The fact that the deposits may not be made to the same bank is irrelevant. The point is that money loaned by banks ends up in demand deposits that can be loaned out again after reserves are kept, causing a recycling of funds.

Tools of Monetary and Credit Policy

The Federal Reserve exercises its monetary and credit policy through three tools: (1) reserve requirements, (2) discount operations, and (3) open market operations. These instruments of monetary policy can be used by the Fed to increase or decrease the growth rate of the money supply by encouraging or discouraging borrowing.

Exhibit 3.6 **How Banks Create Money**

BANK BALANCE SHEET BEFORE LOAN

Assets		Liabilities	
Cash	$10,000	Deposits	$ 0
		Stockholder equity	$10,000
Total Assets	$10,000	Total liabilities & stockholder equity	$10,000

BANK BALANCE SHEET AFTER LOAN

Cash	$10,000	Deposits	$10,000
Loans	$10,000		
		Stockholder equity	$10,000
Total Assets	$20,000	Total liabilities & stockholder equity	$20,000

Reserve Requirements

The Federal Reserve requires banks to set aside a portion of their deposits in a non-interest-bearing reserve account at the Federal Reserve as a means of safeguarding customer deposits. The Fed uses changes in the reserve requirement to decrease or increase the amount of money a bank has available to lend. If the Fed decides to stimulate the economy by increasing the money supply, it decreases the reserve requirement. Conversely, a decrease in the reserve requirement increases the amount of money banks have available to lend.

For example, a decrease in the reserve requirement from 15 percent to 10 percent would make 5 percent more funds available for lending purposes. If the reserve requirement were 15 percent, a bank would be required to hold $1,500 in reserve on demand deposits of $10,000 (15 percent of $10,000), thereby limiting to $8,500 the amount available for loans. If the reserve requirement were reduced to 10 percent, that same $10,000 would make $9,000 available for loans. In this example, reducing the reserve requirement from 15 percent to 10 percent increases the money supply by an additional $500.

Conversely, if the Fed were concerned about inflation and wanted to decrease the money supply, it could increase the reserve requirement. If the reserve requirement were increased from 15 percent to 20 percent, the amount of the $10,000 in demand deposits available for loans would be reduced from $8,500 to $8,000 and growth in the money supply would be reduced by $500.

Until the Monetary Control Act of 1980, only Fed member banks were affected by the Fed's reserve requirements (see the Federal Reserve Services section in this chapter). **Non-member banks** maintained their reserves with other financial institutions according to the laws of their individual states. Since implementation of the Monetary Control Act, all banks that have transaction accounts (specifically, accounts that make payments to third parties) must keep reserves at the Fed.

Please note that we are using a $10,000 figure here for the sake of illustration. In the real economy, the change would be measured in billions of dollars!

A decrease in the reserve requirement also ought to improve banks' profitability. Banks are not paid interest on reserves, but a bank can lend or invest the additional funds made available by the reduction in the reserve requirement. Banks, however, manage their loans and investments to ensure that these additional funds are put to work.

Banks whose reserves at the Fed are temporarily larger than required may lend these excess reserves, called **Fed funds**, to another bank whose reserves are temporarily short. Since these transactions take place by adjusting the reserves of the two institutions on the Fed's account books, no money actually changes hands. The funds typically are sold to the other institution overnight. The institution selling the Fed funds charges the other institution interest for the use of the funds. The rate charged, called the **Fed funds rate**, is set by the banks rather than the Fed. Although the Federal Reserve does not set the Fed funds rate, it establishes the rate's range and influences it by increasing or decreasing the amount of reserves available. If the rate rises too rapidly and remains high because the demand for funds exceeds the supply, the Fed makes additional funds available to meet the demand and thereby reduces the rate.

Like any other commodity, money is subject to the law of supply and demand. The interest rate is the price of money, and if the demand for money is high and the supply is low, the price (interest rate) rises.

Discount Operations

The Fed influences loan demand and the easing or tightening of credit through the discount rate. The discount rate is the rate charged by the Fed on loans it makes to financial institutions. Unlike the Fed funds rate, the **discount rate** is set by each of the 12 Federal Reserve banks. Each Reserve bank can change the rate whenever appropriate, subject to review by the Board of Governors. In general, the discount rate is uniform throughout the Federal Reserve System. As a result of the Monetary Control Act, all financial institutions offering transaction accounts have the privilege of applying to the Fed for short-term credit.

The Fed uses the discount rate to encourage or discourage borrowing, depending on the impact it is trying to make on the money supply. If the Fed wants to increase the money supply, it reduces the discount rate to encourage borrowing. During an economic recovery, the Fed wants to expand business growth and activity (exhibit 3.7). By reducing the discount rate, the Fed is attempting to make credit available, to encourage borrowing for business expansion, and to increase the money supply. The Kowalskis in situation 3 saw the interest rate on their mortgage loan change several times while they waited for approval. If the rate had gone too high, they might not have purchased the house and the Fed's attempt to discourage borrowing would have been successful. Banks create money through the deposit and credit functions. As businesses and consumers borrow money, those dollars end up in demand deposit accounts, thereby increasing the money supply. On the other

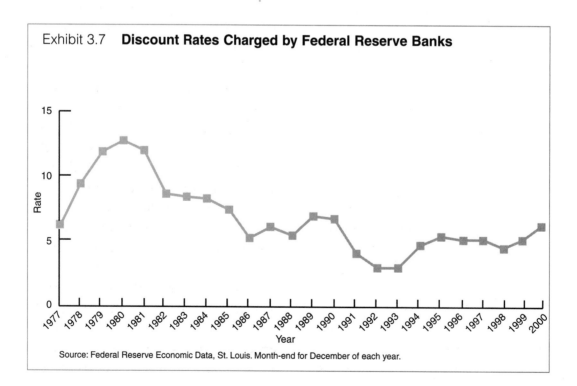

Exhibit 3.7 **Discount Rates Charged by Federal Reserve Banks**

Source: Federal Reserve Economic Data, St. Louis. Month-end for December of each year.

hand, if the Fed wants to discourage borrowing to reduce the growth of the money supply, it increases the discount rate. The increase in the discount rate often signals an increase in the cost of funds for banks, which in turn increases the rates banks charge to customers. The increase in rates discourages borrowing and results in a decrease in the growth of the money supply.

Open Market Operations

By far the most powerful tool available to the Fed in its role as the agent of monetary policy is the **open market operations** of the **Federal Open Market Committee (FOMC)**. The FOMC consists of the seven members of the Board of Governors plus the president of the New York Federal Reserve Bank and four other Reserve bank presidents. They meet every six weeks to project levels of economic activity—three-to-six months in the future. Their actions to increase or decrease the growth rate of the money supply is based on these projections.

The FOMC is responsible for system-wide administration of monetary policy. One of the basic functions of the FOMC is to determine the amount of government obligations (bills, notes, and bonds) to be sold and redeemed each week. After each meeting of the FOMC, where short-term and long-term monetary needs are determined, a directive is issued to the New York Fed, which has been designated as the agent to buy and sell government obligations for the accounts of all Federal Reserve district banks.

The purchase or sale of government securities by the Fed immediately increases or decreases the money supply and affects the availability of short-term credit. If the FOMC

decides to make more credit available by increasing the money supply, it issues a directive to the New York Fed to purchase government securities from banks and the public. When the securities are sold by banks, businesses, or consumers, the Fed credits the reserve accounts of banks. Banks in turn credit the demand deposit accounts of the sellers, thereby increasing demand deposits.

For example, the Fed purchases $5 billion in government securities, and pays for the securities by crediting the banks' reserve accounts. If the banks owned the securities, they will use the money to make loans, and the proceeds will be deposited to demand deposit accounts. If the securities were owned by other investors (individual or business), the banks will directly credit the sellers' checking accounts. Either way, the proceeds issued by the Fed for the securities end up in demand deposits and thereby increase the money supply by $5 billion.

On the other hand, if the FOMC decides to tighten credit by reducing the growth rate of the money supply, it issues a directive to the New York Fed to sell government securities held by the Fed. When the securities are purchased by banks and the general public, the Fed charges banks' reserve accounts for the amount of the securities. The banks then charge their customers' demand deposit accounts, thereby reducing the money supply.

As this example shows, the operations of the FOMC can have an immediate impact on the money supply and the availability of credit, whereas the changes in reserve requirements and the discount rate usually have a delayed impact. However, because of media coverage and comments by financial experts, a change in the reserve requirement or the discount rate can have an instant impact on the

Exhibit 3.8 **Fed Tools and Their Effects**

Reserve Requirements	Increase	Slow, lagging effects on banks and the economy. It decreases the money supply and availability of loanable funds if inflation needs to be checked.
	Decrease	It stimulates the economy by increasing the supply of loanable finds.
Discount Operations	Increase Discount Rate	Moderately fast effect on banks and economy. It discourages borrowing and the money supply shrinks when inflation is becoming a problem.
	Decrease Rate	Has opposite effect during economic recovery when the Fed wants to expand business activity.
Open Market Operations	Purchase Securities	Immediate, powerful effect on banks and economy. Increases money supply in paying for purchases by crediting the reserve accounts of banks.
	Sales	Tightens credit by reducing money supply in times of rising inflation.

Source: Amaury Betancourt, Loan Review Examiner, Hamilton Bank, N.A.

economy—specifically, on the stock market—because the change signals the Fed's direction. An increase in the discount rate signals a tightening of the money supply and an increase in interest rates, which could have an immediate effect on the stock market. Exhibit 3.8 summarizes the effect of the basic Federal Reserve monetary and credit tools on the economy.

Summary

The Federal Reserve plays a major role in both the national and international economies. The Federal Reserve System was created by the Federal Reserve Act of 1913 to eliminate many of the problems not solved by the National Bank Act. Through the establishment of the 12 Federal Reserve districts, a nationwide check collection system was created, and the problem of pyramided reserves was resolved. In its role as the agent of monetary policy, the Fed was made responsible for managing the money supply.

The Fed provides many services to member banks, including supplying coin and currency, check processing, Fedwire, automated clearing house, settlement, and securities safe-keeping.

The Fed operates as both a competitor and a regulator by offering services in competition with correspondent banks. The Fed issues regulations to perform its duties as the agent of monetary policy and to implement the provisions of various laws created by Congress; it is also the primary federal supervisor of state-chartered member banks. The Fed helps the government maintain a sound banking system and assists in reinforcing public confidence.

The Fed controls the ability of banks to create money through three primary tools of monetary control: (1) changes in the reserve requirement, (2) discount operations, and (3) open market operations. Banks create money through the deposit and credit functions, and the Fed uses reserve requirements and the discount rate to encourage or discourage the use of credit. The Fed's most powerful tool is the operations of the Federal Open Market Committee, which the Fed uses to influence the money supply through the purchase and sale of government securities.

Review and Discussion Questions

1. List the four basic duties of the Federal Reserve.

2. How is the Federal Reserve structured?

3. What services are offered to banks by the Federal Reserve?

4. How is the Fed used to implement regulatory legislation?

5. Describe how banks create money.

6. Briefly describe the tools of monetary control, and explain how the Fed uses them.

Additional Resources

Law and Banking: Applications. Washington, D.C.: American Bankers Association, 2000.

Money and Banking. Washington, D.C.: American Bankers Association, 1998.

Reference Guide to Regulatory Compliance. Washington, D.C.: American Bankers Association, 2000.

The Federal Reserve System: Purposes and Functions, Washington, D.C.: Board of Governors of the Federal Reserve System, 1994.

Web Resources

American Bankers Association www.aba.com

Code of Federal Regulations
www.access.gpo.gov/nara/cfr/

Federal Deposit Insurance Corporation
www.fdic.gov

Federal Reserve Bank
www.federalreserve.gov

House Committee on Banking and Financial Services www.house.gov/banking/

National Credit Union Association
www.ncua.gov

Office of the Comptroller of the Currency
www.occ.treas.gov

4

THE DEPOSIT FUNCTION

Learning Objectives

After completing this chapter, you will be able to do the following:

* define the deposit function and distinguish among the various types of deposit accounts
* describe various types of individual and business account owners, noting considerations for banks in dealing with each type of account
* explain the difference between identity, authority, and capacity when opening an account and list acceptable forms of identification
* differentiate among coin and currency, cash items, and noncash items
* describe several ways customers can make deposits
* give an overview of the requirements of four deposit regulations, including Regulations DD, CC, E, and D, and the coverage of FDIC
* define the bolded terms that appear in the text

Introduction

The following situations demonstrate different customer needs for opening, managing, and depositing to accounts. While customer-focused banking usually means helping customers find the right solutions to their problems, this has to be balanced with protecting the bank against loss.

Situation 1

A retired couple comes to you with the following problem: they are planning to travel extensively in their new RV. They have arranged to have their pension checks automatically deposited into their checking account and want to give their daughter the ability to pay bills and otherwise manage the account while they are away. However, they also want access to cash from the account while they travel across the country. What arrangements can you suggest to cover these needs?

Situation 2

A man asks you to help him open a joint account for himself and his wife, who is not present. He wants to open the account by depositing checks from an out-of-state company. He is very polite and friendly and is hoping to withdraw several thousand dollars right away to help him get settled. What steps can you take to help him and to protect your bank?

Situation 3

You are the new accounts representative at your bank. A potential customer approaches you with a check for $250,000 payable to a corporation. He claims that he is the president of the corporation, but he has no documentation to substantiate his claim. He says he will obtain the proper documentation at an upcoming meeting of the board of directors, but he must open the account today. He adds that if he is unable to open the account immediately at this bank, he will take his business elsewhere. Opening the account could result in a substantial customer and a long-lasting, mutually beneficial relationship, or it could result in a $250,000 loss to the bank. What course of action should you take regarding his request?

Situation 4

A customer of yours owns a retail store and cannot make deposits during the day when the bank is open. The store owner calls you and says he wants to deposit $2,000 into a general account. He has $800 in coin and currency, $900 in checks drawn on this bank, and $300 in checks drawn on other banks. The owner does not want to leave the money in the store overnight, but will get to the bank too late to make a deposit at the teller window. What cash management service will you recommend to your customer?

Each of the above situations provides challenges for a bank in accepting deposits, providing deposit services, and limiting fraud. This chapter discusses the deposit function, the documentation required to open an account, and the risks faced by banks in offering accounts and accepting deposits.

Deposit Function

The **deposit function** is the traditional banking function of accepting funds for credit to checking, savings, and other types of deposit accounts. If there were no deposits, there would be no need for the other two principal banking functions—payments and lending. Banks would have no need to pay instruments drawn on deposits and, because most funding for loans and investments is generated by deposits, banks would have no funds to lend. The deposit function also provides customers a safe place to keep their coin and currency.

Through the deposit function, customers can simply deposit checks or other items in their accounts and receive credit. Hundreds of billions of dollars are deposited in and withdrawn from commercial banks each year. The bulk of a bank's daily deposit activity consists of checks rather than coin and currency. Since checks are so widely used, the total dollar value of all the checks deposited each day is far greater than the daily deposits of coin and currency. As technology develops and becomes more accepted, more money will flow in and out of accounts electronically through such means as direct deposit, automated clearing houses (ACHs), wire transfers, and Internet operations.

Deposit Safety and Customer Convenience

Depositors believe that the bank is responsible for safeguarding their deposits at all times while making them available for withdrawal at some future date. If a bank robbery or other loss of funds takes place, the depositor is protected against loss. Banks, always conscious of this need for safety, protect and use depositors' funds prudently for loans and investments. A bank should always be able to honor a legitimate request for payment from an account.

Convenience is also extremely important to bank customers. Banks go where their cus-

tomers are—in grocery stores, for example. Banks make their offices and facilities readily available while simplifying banking transactions. Extra banking hours, drive-in windows or teller stations, and automated teller machines (ATMs) have also become commonplace. Banks are also becoming active players in the electronic realm with such services as online banking, electronic bill payment, and web-based loan application and approval. Bank cardholders can now access their accounts for cash withdrawals worldwide through linked ATM networks. ATM machines not only meet customer needs and provide greater convenience, but also reduce a bank's transaction costs and allow banks to offer around-the-clock banking services

Many banks now offer the convenience of PC banking. Customers can issue bill payment instructions and conduct other banking business over the Internet.

Demand Deposits vs. Savings and Time Deposits

Deposits at banks may be placed in a checking or savings account, or used to establish some form of time deposit. The depositor's intention is different in each case. Checking account deposits (demand deposits) are made because the customer intends to withdraw the funds in the very near future to pay bills and meet expenses. Basic checking accounts do not earn interest. However, banks offer other types of accounts that allow customers to earn interest on funds they plan to withdraw in the very near future. In today's economy, customers tend to leave minimum amounts in non-interest-bearing accounts, while placing most of their funds in accounts that will generate interest. Savings and time deposit accounts earn interest and are generally used to deposit funds not immediately needed by the customer.

Demand Deposits

The largest single element in the nation's money supply are the **demand deposit** balances, against which checks are issued. Demand deposits are so named because the total amount on deposit, or any part of it, is payable "on demand" and can be converted into coin and currency after the deposited funds are collected and available. If you have an available balance of $100 in your checking account, you can write a check for that amount and present it to a teller for immediate payment of $100 in cash.

Traditionally, checking accounts existed only at commercial banks. Today, thrift institutions compete aggressively for these accounts, and members of credit unions can participate in a similar arrangement using share drafts (which are like checks) as payment vehicles.

Federal laws also allow banks to offer automatic transfer services (ATS). With ATS, a customer can write checks that exceed existing balances and the bank, by prior arrangement, will automatically move funds from the customer's savings account to the checking account to cover the checks.

Savings and Time Deposits

Savings accounts differ from demand deposits in that banks can require a seven-day notice of withdrawal from savings accounts. Therefore, while in practice few banks actually require such notice, these accounts cannot be considered demand deposit accounts. Savings accounts do have one thing in common with demand deposit accounts—they have no maturity date. Deposits and withdrawals can be made at any time over a period of days, weeks, or years. By contrast, time deposit accounts have specific maturity dates, at least seven days from the date of deposit. Whenever a time deposit is withdrawn before maturity, there usually is a penalty for early (premature) withdrawal. Banks pay interest on both savings and time deposit accounts.

In addition to certificates of deposit (CDs), other time deposits include Christmas, Hanukkah, and Vacation Club accounts. Deposits are generally made weekly to these accounts in small amounts to help customers accumulate funds for these annual events.

The ratio of demand deposits to savings and time deposits is important for two reasons. One, the bank pays interest on savings and time deposits as well as on some demand deposits, and the turnover rate for demand deposits is extremely high. Two, every deposit accepted from a customer is a liability—not an asset— for the bank that accepts it. It is an obligation that must be repaid at some future date. Deposits represent the largest percentage of liabilities on almost all bank balance sheets. At the same time, as the bank's raw material, these deposits are the primary and most important source of funds to be put to profitable use as loans and investments. Because time deposits with stated maturities remain with the bank for longer periods of time than demand deposits do, these funds are generally used for longer-term bank loans and investments. High-turnover demand deposit funds are put to short-term use.

Type and Ownership of Accounts

The type of account opened by a customer, whether individual, joint, partnership, corporate, or other, determines the ownership of the account, what identification is required, and what documentation is necessary to establish the capacity and the authority of the person opening the account. The type of account also determines the rights, obligations, and liabilities of the parties to the account. The implications of ownership are discussed in the following sections. Exhibit 4.1 shows the types of consumer and business account owners to be discussed.

Consumer Owners

Individual Accounts

An individual account is an account opened for and owned by an individual. The individual is the sole owner of the account, and no other person has any rights concerning it. When the account owner dies, the account normally becomes part of his or her estate.

When opening individual accounts, banks are mostly concerned with establishing the account owner's identity. Banks have policies and procedures that dictate the forms of identification required to open an individual account and the types of documentation or references needed.

At a minimum, banks require at least one form of primary identification, typically something with a photograph such as a driver's license or passport, and a piece of secondary identification like an automobile registration or social security card. (Appropriate types of identification will be covered more fully later in this chapter.) In addition, banks require other banking references and will usually check the databases available from credit reporting services.

Individuals are properly identified to ensure that they are the persons they represent themselves to be. Proper identification substantially reduces the risk that the person opening the account will use the account for fraudulent purposes.

Sometimes a customer might want to give someone else the authority to sign checks or make other decisions for his or her account. This can be accomplished through a power of attorney. A **power of attorney** (exhibit 4.2) is a legal document that authorizes a person (the attorney-in-fact) to act on behalf of another person (the principal).

Powers of attorney vary depending on the wishes of the account owner. He or she can grant a general power of attorney, which gives the attorney-in-fact unlimited authority over the account, or a special power of attorney

---

Exhibit 4.1 **Type and Ownership of Accounts**

Consumer	Business
–Individual	–Sole Proprietorship
–Joint	–Partnership
–Fiduciary	–Corporate
	–Public Funds
	–Unincorporated Organizations

Exhibit 4.2 **Power of Attorney Form**

	DEMAND ACCOUNT
	SAVINGS ACCOUNT

ACCEPTED BY	OFFICE

Know all Men by these Presents

That _____

do make, constitute and appoint _____

_____ true and lawful attorney for _____ and in _____

name:

1. To withdraw all or any part of the balance in _____

account number _____ in

THE INSTITUTE NATIONAL BANK

by drawing checks, if a demand account; or, by giving the required prior notice and by executing the proper withdrawal order or receipt if a savings account.

2. To endorse notes, checks, drafts or bills of exchange which may require _____ endorsement for deposit as cash in, or for collection by said bank.

3. To do all lawful acts requisite for effecting any of the above premises; hereby ratifying and confirming all that the said attorney shall do therein by virtue of these presents.

This power of attorney shall continue in force until due notice of the revocation thereof shall be given in writing.

In witness whereof _____ have hereunto set _____ hand and seal this _____ day of _____,
two thousand and _____

SIGNED, SEALED AND DELIVERED
IN THE PRESENCE OF }

_____

which limits the authority to a specific duty or function and to a limited period of time. Powers of attorney cease at the death of the person who grants the power of attorney. For example, a customer may place a power of attorney on a checking account but not on a savings account or certificate of deposit, denying access to these other accounts. The retired couple in situation 1 wants their daughter to be able to pay their bills while they are away. The daughter can be given power of attorney over the couple's checking account only, and the power of attorney could be revoked when the couple returns from their trip.

Just as they do with identification, banks have policies and procedures to follow when accepting a power of attorney. It is important to follow these procedures, which ensure that, among other things, the power of attorney was authorized by the principal.

Joint Accounts

A joint account is an account opened in the names of and owned by two or more depositors. Joint accounts can be held either in joint tenancy with full right of survivorship or as tenants in common (exhibit 4.3).

A typical joint tenancy account with full right of survivorship has the word "or" separating the names of the account owners (Bill Wiltshire *or* Peggy Wiltshire). In an account like this, either one of the account holders may make deposits, write checks, make withdrawals, transfer funds, access the account electronically, stop payment on checks, close the account, or otherwise treat the account as his or her own. Only one signature is required.

When one of the account holders dies, the funds in the account typically pass to the surviving account holder(s) in accordance with state law and without need to establish an estate.

Joint tenants in common accounts usually have the word "and" separating the names of the holders (Mike Harris *and* Jackie Harris). These account holders must act together. For example, both Mike's and Jackie's signatures would be required to make a deposit or withdrawal from the account. Roommates might find a tenants in common account to be the most convenient way to share expenses. Since all of their signatures are required on checks drawn on the household account, none of the roommates can use the funds without the others' knowledge. Joint tenants-in-common accounts need greater monitoring, requiring the bank to verify that all account holders sign checks or withdrawal slips. If the bank pays checks with only one signature when it has agreed to require the signatures of all the account holders, the bank could be liable to the account holders who did not sign the checks or withdrawals.

Establishing identification is just as important in opening joint accounts as it is in opening individual accounts. Bank procedures vary. Some require that all the joint account holders be present to sign the signature card, while others might allow a signature card to be mailed from one or more of the joint account holders.

In most circumstances, the account agreement holds each account holder responsible for the transactions on a joint account, including overdrafts.

Fiduciary Accounts

The term fiduciary means one who acts for the benefit of another. A **fiduciary** account is an account opened by a representative for the benefit of another. Some examples of fiduciary accounts are guardianships, conservatorships, trust accounts, and estate accounts. In all

---

Exhibit 4.3 **Joint Accounts**

| Right of survivorship | "or" | husband and wife act independently |
| Tenants in common | "and" | roommates act together |

cases, each account has a representative (such as a guardian) and a beneficiary (such as a minor child) or person for whose benefit the account is held. The accounts take many different forms and require several different types of documentation, depending on the type of account opened.

An example of a simple fiduciary account is an account opened "in trust for" a minor child. In this example, a mother and father open a fiduciary account for their newborn child. This simple account usually involves only a basic document and may not involve large balances. When opening the account, the bank will obtain identification from the representative (the parents), just as if opening an account for an individual.

An account established for the executor or administrator of a substantial estate is far more complicated, requires extensive documentation, and may carry large balances until the estate is finally settled. Before opening an estate account, the executor or the administrator provides the bank with court-issued documents establishing the estate of the deceased and appointing the administrator or executor of the estate.

Guardianship accounts can also be complicated, and they require substantial documentation. The laws governing **guardianships** may vary from state to state, but in general a guardianship account may be opened only with court documentation. In many cases, withdrawals may be made only by a court order. Policing these accounts usually requires special handling by experienced banking officers.

Many states have adopted the Uniform Fiduciaries Act, which contains provisions that apply to fiduciary accounts and provides guidelines for banks on the type and extent of documentation that banks should obtain. The act also outlines the steps in maintaining and policing fiduciary accounts.

Business Owners

Sole Proprietorship Accounts

A sole proprietorship is a business owned by an individual called a proprietor. The business may be in the name of the proprietor or in a trade name ("trading as" or "t/a"), or the phrase "doing business as (dba)" may be used. Examples are Winston's, or Winston's Coffee House, or James Winston doing business as Winston's Coffee House. In each example, Winston is the owner of the business, and he alone has the right to open an account or authorize someone to open an account for him. When a proprietorship is operated under the individual's own name, a bank requires identification, references, and signature cards to open the account, much as it does in the case of an individual. However, when any name other than the individual's is used, the connection between the owner and the fictitious trade name should also be established legally. The proprietor provides the bank with the legal registration form required by the state. This might be a business certificate, a fictitious name registration, or a certificate of registration of trade name.

A sole proprietor has the right to open an account, make deposits, stop payment, and conduct his or her account in any manner he or she wishes. Checks payable to the proprietor or to the proprietorship may be deposited to the sole proprietorship account. The proprietor can authorize another individual as a signer on the account, but this person would not have the same rights to the account as the owner.

Partnership Accounts

When two or more individuals enter into a business together, they may form a partnership. The business may operate under the names of the individual partners (for example, Harris, Wink, and Harris), or it may use a trade name. Partnerships are widely used in real estate ownership and in many law firms, accounting firms, and brokerage houses. Most states have adopted laws pertaining to the conduct of this type of business and the rights and obligations of each partner. These laws directly relate to the bank's handling of the account.

A legal document called a *partnership agreement* is usually drawn up at the time the partnership is established. The agreement states the contributions each partner has made to the business, the nature of the business, and the proportions in which each partner will share in profits or losses. Any one member of the partnership may be empowered to act for all the others, so that his or her actions are legally binding on all the other partners.

In opening an account for a partnership, a bank obtains signatures from all the partners who will be authorized to issue checks, apply for loans for the partnership, and otherwise deal with the bank. This form is normally called a partnership resolution. The bank also obtains a copy of the partnership agreement, either on the bank's own standard form or on another legally acceptable form. If the partnership operates under a trade name, the bank also keeps a copy of the business certificate on file—the same as was required of the sole proprietor discussed earlier.

Partnership law generally states that the death of any one partner automatically terminates the partnership; however, provisions are made for the surviving partners to reorganize the partnership. When a partner dies or new partners are added to the firm, the bank obtains new documents that reflect the changes.

Corporate Accounts

A corporation is a legal entity or an artificial person created by state or national law. A corporation has the right and capacity to enter into contracts. A corporate account is opened in the name of the corporation, and the corporation is the owner of the account. Anytime a bank interacts with the corporation—lending money, for example—it interacts with the corporation, not its stockholders, directors, or officers.

A corporation can be identified by its legal name, which includes "Inc.," "Corporation," "Incorporated," or "Limited." For example, if Winston incorporated his coffee house, he would have to change the name from Winston's Coffee House to, say, Winston's Coffee House, Inc.

Corporations are the same as individuals and partnerships in that the corporation is a legal entity, but the similarity ends there. The corporation cannot act on its own; it must act through representatives. The stockholders, who own the corporation, elect the board of directors, who are the governing body of the corporation and are responsible for conducting its business. Only the directors can establish the legal right to open and operate a bank account.

To verify the authority to open an account, the bank reviews the corporate resolution (exhibit 4.4)—a document prepared by the board of directors when it resolves to open an account. When the account is opened, a certified copy of the resolution is filed with the bank. In addition to other information, the corporate resolution authorizes certain officers to

Exhibit 4.4 **Corporate Resolution Form**

	ACCOUNT NUMBER
CORPORATE RESOLUTION	OFFICE
	ACCEPTED BY
	DATE

_____
(account title)

"RESOLVED, that an account in the name of this Corporation be established or maintained with the INSTITUTE NATIONAL BANK and that all checks, drafts, notes, or other orders for the payment of money drawn on or payable against said account shall be signed by any _____ (indicate number) person or persons from time to time holding the following offices of this Corporation.

_____   _____   _____

_____   _____   _____

Indicate title only; not individual's name.

FURTHER RESOLVED, that said INSTITUTE NATIONAL BANK is hereby authorized and directed to pay all checks, drafts, notes and orders so signed whether payable to bearer, or to the order of any person, firm or corporation, or to the order of any person signing the same.

The undersigned Secretary of _____ _____ (name of corporation) hereby certifies that the above is a true and correct copy of a resolution regularly adopted by the Board of Directors of the Corporation at a duly called meeting of the Board held on _____ (date), at which a quorum was present and voting throughout; and that said resolution is presently in full force and effect.

I further certify that the persons named below are those duly elected or appointed to the Corporate Office or capacity set forth opposite their respective names.

NAME	TITLE

In Witness Whereof, I have hereunto set my hand and affixed hereto the Corporate Seal of this Corporation."

Corporate Seal

_____
Secretary

Dated:

sign checks or otherwise issue instructions to the bank concerning the account. The resolution may also authorize the corporation to borrow money from the bank or, more likely, a separate resolution will cover the corporation's borrowing needs.

The question of authority is important in a bank's relationship with a corporation. Only individuals authorized by the directors can do business with the bank on behalf of the corporation. Therefore, when the corporate resolution mentions official titles (such as vice president or treasurer), the bank keeps on file the names and signatures of the persons who hold those titles and who are authorized to transact business on the corporation's behalf. This file is updated constantly with new signature cards as new people are given authority or authority is lost through death, retirement, or other means. While banks are careful to identify those authorized to transact business, the corporation may bear some liability for unauthorized transactions if it is shown that the corporation's negligence contributed to the loss.

In addition to knowing who can transact business for the corporation, banks keep records on the limits to the authority of each signer. The president, for example, may have unlimited authority, while the vice president of finance can sign checks up to only $100,000. It is also possible that several people will need to combine their signatures to be acceptable under the resolution, as shown below.

Individually		Combined (any two)
VP	$5,000	$25,000
Comptroller	$5,000	
Secretary	$5,000	

Unlike an individual or a partnership account, neither a corporate account nor the operation of a business is affected by the death of a stockholder.

Public Funds Accounts

Thousands of governments receive and disburse funds on behalf of the communities and citizens they serve. In most instances, the funds involved are collected and used for the public's benefit; the general term public funds account is used to describe all relationships opened for any department, agency, authority, or other component of any federal, state, or local government or political subdivision.

The unit of government officially appoints the banks with which it wishes to open accounts. State and local laws usually prescribe the procedures that establish public funds accounts at banks.

Documentation of public funds accounts usually consists of signature cards listing the authorized signers and some form of official letter or notice appointing the bank as a depository. The letter or notice is typically issued by the head of the unit of government.

In general, all such accounts are secured by segregated, specific assets in the bank's possession; that is, the bank sets aside U.S. government obligations or other assets of unquestioned value as collateral to protect the deposited funds. This collateral provides an additional guarantee that public funds will never be lost. If a bank does not possess or cannot obtain enough government securities or other satisfactory assets to be pledged for this purpose, it must decline a new public funds account.

Unincorporated Organizations

Banks are asked to open deposit accounts for all sorts of unincorporated organizations such as churches, bowling leagues, soccer teams, class reunions, and disaster relief funds. While these are not "businesses" in the traditional sense, many banks tend to treat them as business accounts. Accounts established for social or fraternal groups, not-for-profit and unincorporated associations and societies, and other informal types of entities can create interesting situations for banks.

Important issues with unincorporated organizations are (1) establishing the authority to open the account and (2) authorizing the person or persons who will sign checks. Unlike a corporation that has a board of directors, an unincorporated organization may not have an established governing body. Because such organizations usually are not listed in state or local government records, the bank relies largely on its knowledge of the parties it will be dealing with when it establishes such accounts. Signature cards always are required. Each situation dictates what additional letters, forms, agreements, or special documents should be obtained. The bank's attorneys are often consulted when dealing with these types of organizations.

After the account is opened, unincorporated organizations frequently send letters changing the authorized signers. The organization occasionally documents the meeting where the new officers were elected and provides the bank with the minutes of the meeting.

Authority to Open Accounts

A customer must open an account before the bank can accept items for deposit. The account-opening process entails much more than filling out forms at the new accounts desk. In opening the account, the bank

- establishes the identity of the person opening the account
- determines that the person has the legal capacity to open the account
- ensures that the person is authorized to open the account

By opening an account, a bank enters into a contractual relationship that gives the cus-tomer the ability to extend credit to himself or herself, provides the customer with the vehicle to convert checks and other instruments into cash, and creates a number of other situations that could result in a loss to the bank. The same principle that applies to making a loan applies to opening an account: Know as much as you can about your customer!

Establishing Identity

The bank establishes the identity of the person opening the account in order to protect the bank from loss. But how can a bank determine that the individual who wishes to open an account is the person he or she claims to be and is someone with whom the bank would want to do business? Unfortunately, there is no foolproof way. Forgers can counterfeit driver's licenses, auto registrations, credit cards, and other forms of identification. A passport is often regarded as ideal identification, yet few people have them, and most people who do have one rarely carry it with them. Bank staff members, then, must evaluate the identification that is offered according to bank policy and procedures, and employ an element of judgment.

New Accounts representatives are the bank's first line of defense against all types of new account fraud. Bankers who open accounts walk a fine line between keeping undesirable customers from opening accounts and not discouraging potentially valued customers. Bank policies and procedures vary, but generally, bankers:

- Require at least one form of primary identification (driver's license, passport, U.S. Armed Forces ID, state- or bank-issued ID, or a work ID with a photo) and at least one form of secondary identification (automobile registration, birth certificate, union card, local credit card, voter registration card, government ID, Social Security card, and so forth).

- Check to see if the customer's home or place of work is close to the bank. If not, inquire as to why the customer wants to open an account at that bank.
- Check that the customer's employment information is valid after the account is opened by calling the customer at the workplace to thank him or her for opening an account.
- Consider the source of funds used to open an account. Be wary of large cash deposits and large checks from out of state.
- Consider using prior bank references or credit bureau reports.
- Search databases for undesirable customers—those who have had problems at other banks, including insufficient funds, fraud, bankruptcy, or other judgments

In addition to establishing the identity of the customer, IRS regulations in most instances, require that banks verify a customer's Taxpayer Identification Number (TIN) through **TIN Certification**. TIN Certification is the process of confirming that a customer's tax identification number is correct, and that he or she is not subject to back-up withholding (requiring the bank to withhold and pay to the IRS 31 percent of interest, dividends, and other payments) or exempt from withholding. For TIN Certification, the customer completes IRS Form W-9 (see exhibit 4.5). For tax reporting purposes, the W-9 is one of most important documents for a financial institution to receive and retain. Banks generally require these for all entities that are required to file a return.

An incident that actually occurred at a bank illustrates how difficult it may be to discover fraud. A customer opened an account in the name of a pest exterminator company. Because he had convincing identification—even a business card with a picture of a bug on it—the new accounts clerk did not question whether the man was actually the person he represented himself to be. After opening the account with cash, this con artist made legitimate deposits to his account with cash and checks for about three weeks. During that time he also cashed checks at various branches around town and got to know a number of tellers by name. After three weeks, he put his scheme into action. He deposited to the account a number of checks drawn on closed accounts around the country, and before the bank received notification of return, he withdrew the funds from the account. He absconded with the money and was never seen again.

Remember the man in Situation 2 who wanted to open a joint account for himself and his wife? The out-of-state checks and the absence of his wife should be red flags to any new accounts representative. Bank policy most likely dictates that, in this case, starter checks would be denied until the initial deposit has cleared, thereby preventing loss.

The bank must establish the identity of the person opening the account, even if the person opens an account with cash. There are strict reporting requirements to help detect potential money **laundering** (the practice of moving large amounts of cash received from cash-based illegal business—like selling drugs—through many accounts or banks to hide the source of the money). Forged checks, identity theft, kiting (chapter 7), stolen checks, and other instances of fraud are all compelling reasons to establish the customer's identity. In many situations, the bank is liable for losses due to new accounts fraud.

Exhibit 4.5 **IRS Form W-9**

Form **W-9** (Rev. December 2000) Department of the Treasury Internal Revenue Service	**Request for Taxpayer Identification Number and Certification**	Give form to the requester. Do not send to the IRS.

Please print or type

Name (See **Specific Instructions** on page 2.)
Susan E. Smith

Business name, if different from above. (See **Specific Instructions** on page 2.)

Check appropriate box: ☒ Individual/Sole proprietor ☐ Corporation ☐ Partnership ☐ Other -

Address (number, street, and apt. or suite no.)
456 Cherry Street

City, state, and ZIP code
Portsmouth, RI   02871

Requester's name and address (optional)

Part I   **Taxpayer Identification Number (TIN)**

Enter your TIN in the appropriate box. For individuals, this is your social security number (SSN). **However, for a resident alien, sole proprietor, or disregarded entity, see the Part I instructions on page 2.** For other entities, it is your employer identification number (EIN). If you do not have a number, see **How to get a TIN** on page 2.

Note: *If the account is in more than one name, see the chart on page 2 for guidelines on whose number to enter.*

Social security number
| 1 | 2 | 3 | 4 | 5 | 6 | 7 | 8 | 9 |

or

Employer identification number

List account number(s) here (optional)

42-1234567

Part II   **For U.S. Payees Exempt From Backup Withholding** (See the instructions on page 2.)

Part III   **Certification**

Under penalties of perjury, I certify that:

1. The number shown on this form is my correct taxpayer identification number (or I am waiting for a number to be issued to me), **and**

2. I am not subject to backup withholding because: **(a)** I am exempt from backup withholding, or **(b)** I have not been notified by the Internal Revenue Service (IRS) that I am subject to backup withholding as a result of a failure to report all interest or dividends, or **(c)** the IRS has notified me that I am no longer subject to backup withholding, **and**

3. I am a U.S. person (including a U.S. resident alien).

Certification instructions. You must cross out item **2** above if you have been notified by the IRS that you are currently subject to backup withholding because you have failed to report all interest and dividends on your tax return. For real estate transactions, item **2** does not apply. For mortgage interest paid, acquisition or abandonment of secured property, cancellation of debt, contributions to an individual retirement arrangement (IRA), and generally, payments other than interest and dividends, you are not required to sign the Certification, but you must provide your correct TIN. (See the instructions on page 2.)

Sign Here	Signature of U.S. person		Date

Purpose of Form

A person who is required to file an information return with the IRS must get your correct taxpayer identification number (TIN) to report, for example, income paid to you, real estate transactions, mortgage interest you paid, acquisition or abandonment of secured property, cancellation of debt, or contributions you made to an IRA.

Use Form W-9 only if you are a U.S. person (including a resident alien), to give your correct TIN to the person requesting it (the requester) and, when applicable, to:

1. Certify the TIN you are giving is correct (or you are waiting for a number to be issued),

2. Certify you are not subject to backup withholding, or

3. Claim exemption from backup withholding if you are a U.S. exempt payee.

If you are a foreign person, use the appropriate Form W-8. See Pub. 515, Withholding of Tax on Nonresident Aliens and Foreign Corporations.

Note: *If a requester gives you a form other than Form W-9 to request your TIN, you must use the requester's form if it is substantially similar to this Form W-9.*

What is backup withholding? Persons making certain payments to you must withhold and pay to the IRS 31% of such payments under certain conditions. This is called "backup withholding." Payments that may be subject to backup withholding include interest, dividends, broker and barter exchange transactions, rents, royalties, nonemployee pay, and certain payments from fishing boat operators. Real estate transactions are not subject to backup withholding.

If you give the requester your correct TIN, make the proper certifications, and report all your taxable interest and dividends on your tax return, payments you receive will not be subject to backup withholding. **Payments you receive will be subject to backup withholding if:**

1. You do not furnish your TIN to the requester, or

2. You do not certify your TIN when required (see the Part III instructions on page 2 for details), or

3. The IRS tells the requester that you furnished an incorrect TIN, or

4. The IRS tells you that you are subject to backup withholding because you did not report all your interest and dividends on your tax return (for reportable interest and dividends only), or

5. You do not certify to the requester that you are not subject to backup withholding under 4 above (for reportable interest and dividend accounts opened after 1983 only).

Certain payees and payments are exempt from backup withholding. See the Part II instructions and the separate **Instructions for the Requester of Form W-9.**

Penalties

Failure to furnish TIN. If you fail to furnish your correct TIN to a requester, you are subject to a penalty of $50 for each such failure unless your failure is due to reasonable cause and not to willful neglect.

Civil penalty for false information with respect to withholding. If you make a false statement with no reasonable basis that results in no backup withholding, you are subject to a $500 penalty.

Criminal penalty for falsifying information. Willfully falsifying certifications or affirmations may subject you to criminal penalties including fines and/or imprisonment.

Misuse of TINs. If the requester discloses or uses TINs in violation of Federal law, the requester may be subject to civil and criminal penalties.

Cat. No. 10231X

Form **W-9** (Rev. 12-2000)

Despite their desire to attract new business, banks must be selective in opening accounts. The bank has no obligation to open an account if the potential customer fails to meet the requirements established by the bank.

Recently, there has been growing concern over a new type of fraud referred to as identity theft (see chapter 7). Criminals obtain one or more pieces of identification and social security numbers from their victims, either through mail theft or other means. The pictures and signatures on these pieces of identification can be altered using graphic software, and used to open fraudulent accounts in the victim's name.

Capacity

Before opening an account, the bank determines that the person opening the account has the legal capacity to do so. Having legal capacity means that the person or organization is recognized under the law as being a legal entity with the right to open an account. Most people have the capacity to open accounts, but a person who is considered a minor or incompetent normally does not have the legal capacity to do so. Banks also encourage organizations to open accounts, and these organizations also are required to provide some proof that the corporation, partnership, or other organization exists.

Minors can, in fact, have checking accounts as long as the accounts are co-owned or otherwise guaranteed by a responsible party. To accommodate requests for such accounts, banks will often ask a parent to sign as a responsible party.

Authority

The person opening the account is asked to prove that he or she has the authority to open and use the account. An individual opening an account in his or her name need only produce proper identification. On the other hand, an individual opening an account on behalf of another person will be asked to produce proof that he or she has the authority to act on behalf of that other person. For example, a man representing himself as an executor of an estate is asked to produce the court-approved documentation appointing him as the executor. A person opening an account in the name of a corporation or a partnership will want to bring the proper documents issued by the board of directors or the partnership authorizing that person to open the account. The "corporate president" in situation 3 wanted to deposit a check made out to a corporation but had no identification giving him authority to do so. If the bank presented with this dilemma had an established documentation policy, this account would not have been opened. As tempting as the large deposit is, the customer should have been advised to return with the proper documentation from his board of directors. If the proper documentation is not produced, the bank may find out too late that the person opening the account lacked authority to do so. A person acting without proper authority could illegally deposit company checks into this account and withdraw the money, thereby stealing from the company and opening the bank to possible litigation.

Types of Deposit Items

Customers often want to deposit coin and currency, checks, drafts, traveler's checks, money orders, bonds, bond coupons, intrabank transfers, foreign currency, foreign checks, checks drawn on other banks, negotiable notes, drafts with documents attached, and all sorts of other items into their accounts. Except for coin and currency, the bank is responsible for collecting funds on these items and converting them into an available account balance for the customer's use. The bank acts as the customer's agent and collects the funds through a number of different methods, depending on the type of item deposited.

Coin and Currency

Coin and currency obviously do not require collecting. The customer deposits the money into his or her account, and the bank typically makes the funds available on the day following the day of the deposit. Although the bank does not have to present coin and currency to a payer to collect the items, expenses are still incurred. Teller salaries for handling and processing coin and currency and the cost of shipping excess cash to the Federal Reserve (including transportation, fraud prevention, and security) make up the bulk of the bank's cost. Many banks do not charge individuals or small businesses for processing cash deposits; however, large commercial customers such as grocery stores and other retail establishments may be charged a fee for handling coin and currency deposits.

Cash Items

Many people mistakenly believe that the term "cash item" means coin and currency, but a cash item is an item that flows through the collection process without need of special handling. Banks are willing to give cash items, such as checks, immediate but provisional credit. Immediate credit means the bank immediately posts the amount of the deposit to the customer's account. Provisional credit

means this credit may be reversed if the item that was deposited is returned unpaid by the paying bank.

After the teller takes the cash items for deposit, the items and the deposits are processed in large numbers in the bank's operations department (chapter 6). The items are sent by various means to the paying bank and payment is made. The bank can use automated equipment or imaging to process these items at a relatively low cost per item. The primary characteristics of cash items are that they can be handled in bulk and that the amounts of the items are reflected in the book and collected balances.

Checks are cash items. They are a set of instructions, issued by account holders, ordering the bank to pay the amount to the payee who presents the checks. They are relatively inexpensive for the bank to collect because they do not require special handling through the collection process. For example, payment is not dependent on any event. Unless there is something wrong with the check, the paying bank pays it when presented.

When a cash item is deposited into an account, the ledger or book balance reflects the amount of the deposited check. While different terms may be used at different banks, generally the book balance, or ledger balance, is the balance in an account after all the deposits or credits have been added and all the checks and other debits have been subtracted. However, just because the book balance reflects the amount of the check, it does not necessarily mean that the money is actually in the account. In order for the money to be credited to the account, the amount must be "collected" from the paying bank. The difference between the book balance (the amount noted in the account) and the collected balance (the cash balance in an account that can be used if not subject to any holds) is called float.

Book Balance – Collected Balance = Float

If the check being deposited is drawn on the bank in which it is deposited (an on-us check), no float is generated because the check can be collected immediately. The book balance and the collected balance are the same. Likewise, a deposit containing coin and currency does not contain float, again because coin and currency do not need to be "collected." This also results in the same book and collected balances. Any cash item that is sent to another bank or payer/drawee does generate float. The length of time a check is in float depends on when the Federal Reserve or other clearing agent makes the funds available to the presenting bank.

As the bank receives payment for checks drawn on other banks, the collected balance is adjusted to reflect the availability of those funds (exhibit 4.6). For example, a customer deposits a $1,000 check drawn on another bank into a checking account. If the balance in the account was $100 before the deposit was made, the book balance is $1,100 afterward, and the collected balance is $100. If the cus-

tomer withdraws funds from the account before the funds are collected, the balance in the account is reduced by the amount of the check, and the collected balance may be a negative balance. If a check in the amount of $400 is presented and paid on the account in this example, the book balance is $700 ($1,100 – $400), and the collected balance is –$300 ($100 – $400).

Another term used in banking that may have different meanings at different banks is **available balance**. The available balance is the collected balance minus any holds plus any memo-posted credits. A **hold** is a restriction on the payment of all or part of the balance in an account. Examples of holds are teller holds, account attachments, garnishments, and court-ordered holds. A memo-posted credit is an indication on an account that a credit will be posted to the account during the next posting period. A direct deposit is an example of a credit that would be memo-posted.

Here is an example of available balance: a customer deposits a $1,000 on-us check in a checking account. The book and collected balances are $1,000. A teller places a hold on the account for a check the teller has paid in the amount of $600. After the hold is placed, the

---

Exhibit 4.6 **Book and Collected Balance**

Beginning balance	$ 100
Check deposited drawn on another bank	1,000
Book or ledger balance	1,100
Float	(1,000)
Collected balance	$ 100

If a check is then paid for $400, the balance would change as shown below:

Book balance	Collected balance
$1,100	$ 100
– 400	– 400
$ 700	$ – 300

book and collected balances remain at $1,000. On the other hand, the available balance is $400 ($1,000 balance – $600 hold).

This example assumes that the bank does not actually deduct the amount of the check from the balance at the time it is presented. Exhibit 4.7 demonstrates how the deposit made by the retail store owner in situation 4 would affect the available balance in his account. In addition to the deposit, the store owner issued one check to an employee for $275 to cover expenses for an upcoming trade show. The business's operating account has also been credited with a $425 electronic deposit from a customer who banks by personal computer.

Unless the processing system used by the bank is an online, real-time system—that is, transactions are posted as they are received—posting (chapter 6) occurs sometime in the late evening or early morning. The book and collected balances are updated after the posting. The available balance is updated not only after the post, but also each time a hold is placed or some other transaction is memo posted.

Non-cash Items

Non-cash items are items that require special handling and cannot be processed in bulk. For example, a draft that cannot be paid unless an auto title is attached is a non-cash item. Another example of a non-cash item is a foreign check that must be converted to U.S. dollars. Upon receipt of these non-cash items, the teller either enters the items for collection or sends them to a special department for processing.

Since the non-cash items are not sent to the bank's operations department with cash items, the deposits are not posted to the customer's account. Therefore, they are not given immediate provisional credit. When a teller receives a deposit containing non-cash items, the teller issues a collection receipt to the customer. The customer's account is given delayed credit for the deposit, so the amount of the deposit is not reflected in the customer's balance. The customer is given credit for the deposit when the bank is paid for the non-cash item. This means that a non-cash item, unlike a cash item, does

---

Exhibit 4.7 **Available Balance**

Existing account balance	$	500
Deposit		
• coin and currency		800
• checks drawn on our bank		900
• check drawn on other banks		300
Book or ledger balance	$	2,500
Float		(300)*
Collected balance	$	2,200
Check paid against operating account		(275)
Electronic deposit from another account		425
Available balance	$	2,350

* Checks drawn on another bank are not available for immediate credit. Therefore, the amount is temporarily float.

not create float. Exhibit 4.8 lists other differences between cash items and non-cash items.

How Customer Deposits Are Made

Customers make deposits in a number of different ways. Some customers feel better making their deposit in person, at a bank branch teller's window. That way, they know when the bank received the deposit and they obtain a receipt to prove it. Banks have gone to great expense to make tellers available to these customers by building branches in convenient locations and by installing drive-in windows. Other customers are less concerned about making deposits in person and will take advantage of other convenient services.

While tellers are involved in most deposit transactions, they do not always come into direct contact with the customer. For example, a **night depository** is a locked, secured safe into which the customer may place deposits. These deposits are processed at the beginning of the next business day. The bank typically gives the customer a key to the night depository for the purpose of making deposits after the bank is closed. This service is used mostly by small businesses with late hours. Some of these small businesses deposit coin and currency in the night depository to avoid leaving cash unsecured in their place of business. Night depository service would be an appropriate solution for the retail store owner in situation 4 at the beginning of the chapter. The store owner had a large deposit of cash and checks that he did not want to leave in his store overnight.

Many customers take advantage of **direct deposit**, which allows governments, employ-

---

Exhibit 4.8 **Characteristics of Deposited Items**

Cash Items

- Give customer immediate, provisional account credit
- Create float (time lag between account crediting and collection)
- May be payable on demand
- Must not have documents attached
- Must not carry special instructions or require special handling
- Inexpensive; processed in bulk
- Payable in U.S. funds

Non-cash Items

- Give customer delayed (deferred) credit
- Do not create float (account not credited until collection is completed)
- May or may not be payable on demand
- May have documents attached
- Require special individualized handling; may carry specific instructions
- More expensive to handle
- May or may not be payable in U.S. funds

Examples

- Checks

Examples

- Promissory notes
- Drafts with attached documents
- Coupons
- Checks drawn on banks outside of the United States

ers, and companies to make the deposit for them. Direct deposits are processed through the Automated Clearing House (ACH) (chapter 13), which is an organization run by the Federal Reserve to process paperless transactions. Instead of issuing checks, the government, employer, or company delivers a computer tape or a diskette, or transfers the information electronically to the bank. When the information is received, the bank makes credit entries to the customer's account. Through ACH, customers are assured of secure and immediately available account deposits.

The ACH is also used by commercial customers to transfer funds between accounts in the same bank and between accounts maintained at other banks. Commercial customers can even transfer funds from numerous other banks into one central account.

As another deposit option, customers can request that the bank transfer funds from one account to another. Many banks offer telephone, personal computer or Internet transfer services, whereby the customer can transfer funds between accounts at the same bank from the comfort of a home or office. Consumers are protected in their electronic transfer transactions by Federal Reserve Regulation E, which is discussed later in this chapter.

Customers may also make deposits at automated teller machines(ATMs). ATMs provide a safe, convenient way to make deposits and offer a number of other services, such as cash dispensing, balance inquiries, and transfers between accounts. Customers can even purchase postage stamps and movie tickets at some ATMs. In some areas of the country, banks accept non-customer deposits at ATM machines. Many local ATM networks have joined national networks, allowing customers

to have access to their accounts virtually anywhere in the country, and often anywhere in the world. This will be a big help to the retired couple mentioned in situation 1 who can use their ATM card as they travel.

Another deposit option is to wire funds from the customer's bank to another bank. Some banks allow customers to initiate wire transfers by telephone or PC while others require customers to issue wire transfer orders in person.

Typically, banks issue wire transfers through the Federal Reserve's Fedwire service (chapter 3). The customer issues an instruction called a payment order to the bank, describing who is to receive the wire (the beneficiary), the amount of the wire, the date the funds are to be transferred, and any other instructions. The bank charges the customer's account and issues a payment order to the Fed, which transfers the funds in accordance with the bank's instruction. Most banks charge a fee on both the sending and receiving ends for performing wire transfer services.

Deposit Regulations

The federal government has enacted many laws over the years, designed to protect consumers in their banking relationships. To enforce these laws, they have given responsibility to various oversight agencies, like the Federal Reserve, to implement enforcement regulations. Several of these relate specifically to the deposit function. Four are highlighted in this section, including Federal Reserve Regulation CC, which implements the Funds Availability Act; Regulation DD, which implements the Truth in Savings Act; and Regulation E, which implements the Electronic Funds Transfer Act, and Regulation D known as Reserve Requirements for Depository Institutions. The insurance protection under FDIC is also discussed here.

Regulation CC

Federal regulations require banks to provide certain disclosures to customers before accounts are opened. For example, Federal Reserve Regulation CC requires banks to disclose availability of funds before a transaction account, such as a checking account, is opened. A depository bank (where funds are initially deposited) may make funds available to the customer in accordance with a schedule provided in the regulation, or the bank can make the deposits available in a shorter period of time. The availability of the deposited items is based on the location of the bank on which the check is drawn. A check drawn on a bank in the same check-processing region as the depositary bank is called a **local check**; a check drawn on a bank not located in the same check-processing region is called a **non-local check** (chapter 6). A depositary bank generally must make funds from local checks available to the customer no later than the second banking day after the day of deposit; non-local checks, no later than the fifth day. The depositary bank may extend these times for certain deposits. To do so, it *must* place a hold on the deposit, as required by regulation.

The bank may make the deposit items available to the customer sooner than required, e.g., on the day following the day of deposit. If the bank makes the funds available on the next business day, it may reserve the right to invoke a "case-by-case" exception. A case-by-case exception may be invoked for any reason and allows the bank to hold funds up to the time

Did You Know?

The American Bankers Association estimates that the average bank must comply with nearly 6,000 pages of regulations, statutory language, policy statements, regulatory commentary, and legal analysis.

permitted by the general Regulation CC funds availability schedule.

In addition, banks may hold funds beyond the general funds availability schedule under certain "safeguard" exceptions, including, for example, funds in excess of $5,000 and funds from checks the bank has reasonable cause to believe are uncollectible. If one of these exception holds is placed, the bank can hold funds from a non-local item up to 11 business days and for a local check up to 7 business days. If a bank invokes an exception, it must notify the customer in writing (see exhibits 4.9 and 4.10). Banks must alert customers to their funds availability policies. Usually, this policy is posted near the teller windows.

Regulation DD

The Truth in Savings Act was enacted in December 1991 as part of the Federal Deposit Insurance Corporation Improvement Act. The Federal Reserve Board issued Regulation DD to carry out the provisions of the Truth in Savings Act on September 14, 1992. The purpose of the act is to assist consumers in comparing deposit accounts offered by financial institutions and to provide ongoing information about the accounts. The regulation governs almost all checking, savings, and time deposit accounts that are held by or offered to individual consumers for non-business purposes.

Exhibit 4.9 Sample Notice of Hold

Notice of Hold

Account Number: _____ Date of Deposit: _____

Amount of Deposit: _____

We are delaying the availability of $(*amount being held*) from the deposit. These funds will be available on the (*number*) business day after the day of your deposit.

We are taking this action because:
- ☐ A check you deposited was previously returned unpaid.
- ☐ You have overdrawn your account repeatedly in the last six months.
- ☐ The checks you deposited on this day exceed $5,000.
- ☐ An emergency, such as failure of communications or computer equipment, has occurred.
- ☐ We believe a check you deposited will not be paid for the following reasons:

_____

_____

_____

[If you did not receive this notice at the time you made the deposit and the check you deposited is paid, we will refund to you any fees for overdrafts or returned checks that result solely from the additional delay that we are imposing. To obtain a refund of such fees (*description of procedure for obtaining refund*).]

Payment and Calculation of Interest

Financial institutions must calculate interest on the full principal balance in the account each day by using methods specified in the regulation. The same method must also be used for determining the minimum balance required to earn interest.

Disclosures

Financial institutions must provide customers with a disclosure about an account before the account is opened. The disclosure must be in writing and in a form the consumer may keep. The disclosure must reveal the

- interest rate
- annual percentage yield

- frequency of interest compounding
- minimum balance requirements
- fees
- transaction limits
- additional information found in the account agreement

When providing interest rate information to customers, bank employees must quote the **annual percentage yield (APY)**, a yield or total return that reflects the total amount of interest paid on an account; it is based on the interest rate and the frequency of compounding for a 365-day period.

Other Provisions

Financial institutions must notify customers if changes in terms, such as a reduction in APY,

Exhibit 4.10   **Reasonable Cause Notice of Hold**

Notice of Hold

Account Number: _____   Date of Deposit: _____

Amount of Deposit: _____

We are delaying the availability of the funds you deposited by
the following check: _____
(description of check, such as amount and drawer)

These funds will be available on the (*number*) business day after the day of your deposit.
The reason for the delay is explained below:

☐ We received notice that the check is being returned unpaid.
☐ We have confidential information that indicates that the check may not be paid.
☐ The check is drawn on an account with repeated overdrafts.
☐ We are unable to verify the endorsement of a joint payee.
☐ Some information on the check is not consistent with other information on the check.
☐ There are erasures or other apparent alterations on the check.
☐ The routing number of the paying bank is not a current routing number.
☐ The check is postdated or has a stale date.
☐ Information from the paying bank indicates that the check may not be paid.
☐ We have been notified that the check has been lost or damaged in collection.

Other: _____

_____

_____

[If you did not receive this notice at the time you made the deposit and the check you deposited
is paid, we will refund to you any fees for overdrafts or returned checks that result solely from the
additional delay that we are imposing. To obtain a refund of such fees (*description of procedure
for obtaining refund*).]

will affect them adversely. The notice must be given to customers 30 calendar days in advance of the effective date. Notice is not required when interest rates on variable-rate accounts decrease, when third-party check printing fees increase, or for time deposit accounts that mature in less than one month. Financial institutions are also required to provide customers with maturity notices on certain CDs.

If a financial institution mails a periodic statement, the statement must include the following disclosures:

- APY earned
- amount of interest earned
- fees imposed
- length of the statement period

The regulation also contains specific requirements when financial institutions advertise deposit accounts. An advertisement may not describe an account as "free" or "no cost" if any maintenance or activity fee may be imposed on the account, and advertised interest rates must be stated as an annual percentage yield.

Regulation E

Regulation E governs **electronic funds transfer systems (EFTS),** which move funds to and from consumer accounts without paper checks. Regulation E was adopted to implement the provisions of the 1978 Electronic Funds Transfer Act. The act stipulates the obligations of both consumers and bankers who make electronic funds transfers. Covered transactions include ATM transactions, point of sale debit transactions, and most consumer-initiated telephone transfers. Regulation E:

* generally limits a consumer's liability to $50 for unauthorized use of an EFT service
* requires banks to provide consumers with periodic statements describing electronic funds transfers
* requires the bank to provide procedures for resolving errors and to periodically disclose the procedures to consumers
* requires banks to ensure that a receipt is made available to a consumer at the time an electronic funds transfer is made at an electronic terminal, such as an ATM

Regulation D

Rules governing interest bearing accounts are found in Regulation D. The rules that are part of Regulation D came about with the passage of the Depository Institutions Deregulation Act of 1980. This act eliminated all federal interest rate ceilings on deposit accounts (chapter 2).

Reg D includes definitions of deposit accounts such as demand, savings, and time deposits, as well as more specialty types of accounts such as transaction accounts, NOW accounts, and money market deposit accounts. Definitions of these accounts can be found earlier in this chapter.

The regulation also addresses rules regarding reserve requirements on those deposit accounts (chapter 3).

FDIC Insurance Protection

As we know from chapter 2, the FDIC was created in 1933 to restore public confidence in the nation's banking system. The FDIC insures deposits at the nation's more than 10,000 banks and savings associations. The purpose of the FDIC with regard to deposit accounts is to insure depositors against losses up to $100,000. These losses would occur to account holders as a result of their bank's failure and the FDIC choosing to close the bank rather than merge it into a stronger bank.

The FDIC enacted new rules in 1999 that allow joint account holders to be insured individually rather than per account. Under the old rules, a husband, wife, and child who jointly owned a $300,000 account would have been insured for only a total of $100,000. Under the new rules, each owner is entitled to $100,000 of protection. Since there are three owners in this case, the entire $300,000 account would be insured.

The new rules also expand the insurance beneficiaries on payable-on-death accounts. In addition to spouses, children, grandchildren, parents, and siblings can be eligible for insured benefits.

The FDIC publishes a brochure called "Your Insured Deposit" which outlines all the coverage requirements.

Summary

The deposit function of banks plays an important role in the economy. Banks provide both a safe place for depositors to keep their coin and currency and an economical method for payees of checks and other items to obtain payment for those items. Bank customers deposit all types of items requiring collection, including cash items and non-cash items. If banks did not perform this collection service, customers themselves would have to present these items to the payers.

Banks offer a number of safe and convenient methods for customers to make deposits: (1) in person in facilities provided by the bank, (2) in night depositories and ATMs 24-hours a day, and (3) electronically via the ACH and other methods. Customers can also transfer funds through a number of other convenient methods.

Banks exercise caution in opening accounts and ensure that the depositor provides the bank with proper identification. The customer may act in a number of capacities, and the bank requires proper documentation to establish the authority of the customer to act on behalf of the entity.

Federal Reserve regulations apply to a number of products and services offered by banks. For example, Regulations CC and DD require banks to make certain disclosures about the availability of funds and the terms and conditions of deposit accounts before the accounts are opened. The intended purpose of these regulations is to require financial institutions to provide information about deposit accounts so that potential customers can make informed decisions about opening accounts. Regulation E protects customers who make electronic transactions and Regulation D provides definitions of deposit accounts and other specific account types.

New rules for FDIC insurance have expanded coverage for joint owners.

Review and Discussion Questions

1. Why is the deposit function so important to depositors?

2. Why is it important to properly identify a person opening an account?

3. When opening accounts, why is it important for banks to establish the authority of the customer to use the account? What three steps does the bank take to accomplish this when opening an account?

4. Distinguish between a cash item and a non-cash item.

5. List several ways customers can make deposits.

6. What is the purpose of Regulation DD, and how has its enactment benefited bank customers?

Additional Resources

ABA Bank Compliance Magazine. Washington, D.C.: American Bankers Association, bi-monthly magazine.

Cross-Selling Deposit Products. Washington, D.C.: American Bankers Association, 1999.

Deposit Account Fraud Survey Report. Washington, D.C.: American Bankers Association, 2000.

Deposit Products and Services for Small Businesses. Washington, D.C.: American Bankers Association, 1999.

FDIC Public Information Center, 801 17th Street, NW, Room 100, Washington, D.C. 20434, (800) 276-6003.

Law and Banking: Applications. Washington, D.C.: American Bankers Association, 2000.

Law and Banking: Principles. Washington, D.C.: American Bankers Association, 2000.

Managing Your Checking Account. (Pamphlet) Washington, D.C.: American Bankers Association.

Retail Banking Survey Report. Washington, D.C.: American Bankers Association, 2001.

Web Resources

American Bankers Association
www.aba.com
FDIC Your Insured Deposit
www.fdic.gov/deposit/deposits/
insured/index.html
Federal Deposit Insurance Corporation
www.fdic.gov
Federal Reserve Bank www.federalreserve.gov
Internal Revenue Service www.irs.ustreas.gov

5

CHECKS AS NEGOTIABLE INSTRUMENTS

Learning Objectives

After completing this chapter, you will be able to do the following:

- describe what makes a check negotiable
- distinguish among the various parties to negotiable instruments and explain their liabilities
- distinguish among the various types of specialized checks
- describe how negotiable instruments are transferred
- distinguish among the various types of endorsements
- explain the concept of holder in due course and explain how this designation facilitates collection
- define the bolded terms that appear in text

Introduction

Knowing what makes a check a negotiable instrument and how a negotiable instrument works helps you protect your customers and the bank. The following situations show how important the concept of negotiability is to your relationship with your customers.

Situation 1

An insurance company issues a claim check jointly to Wayne Simms and Alice Simms in the amount of $50,000. Wayne forges Alice's endorsement on the check and deposits it to their joint checking account. One year later, Wayne and Alice are divorced, and Alice realizes she never endorsed the insurance check. She contacts the depositary bank, declares that her name was forged on the check, and demands payment from the bank. What is the bank's liability in this situation?

Situation 2

Franco and Lena are settling on a house tomorrow. The settlement company will not accept a regular check for the closing, for fear that it will be dishonored. Franco and Lena do not want to bring a large amount of cash to the settlement but they do not know what other options they have. What would you suggest to solve their dilemma?

Situation 3

Joel endorses his paycheck by signing his name on the back. Someone steals the check and cashes it at your teller window. Joel contacts your bank and demands that the bank pay him the amount of the check. What is the bank's liability in this case?

What are the rights and obligations of the individuals and banks in the above situations? Who absorbs the losses a bank experiences? (More often than not, it's the bank, whether or not it is legally obligated!) How can banks protect themselves from the risks associated with dishonored checks? This chapter discusses the rights, liabilities, and obligations of those who use negotiable instruments, the banks on which they are drawn (payee banks), and the banks that cash the items or take them for deposit (payor banks).

Negotiable Instrument Defined

When people write checks, they fill in the required information—the date, the payee (entity to whom the check is payable), and the amount (in numbers and words)—and sign their names. To most people, that check is payment for goods, services, or other obligations, and will end up as cash in someone's pocket or a credit to someone's account. Conversely, when people receive checks from others, they expect those checks to be exchanged for cash at the teller window or credited to their bank accounts. Most people never think about the collection process, let alone the complicated web of rights and obligations that accompany the check and that allow all of us to take its use for granted.

However, that check and other similar instruments (drafts, notes, and certificates of deposit) have a legal classification, accompanied by guidelines affecting everything from the wording on the instrument to the responsibilities of each party if the check is dishonored to the protections afforded those who take the risk of clearing the instrument. These items are called **negotiable instruments.**

In the United States, negotiable instruments are governed by Articles 3 and 4 of the **Uniform Commercial Code** (UCC), which is a set of model laws that facilitate the handling of banking and business transactions. Each state decides individually whether to adopt these laws.

The first thing to know about a negotiable instrument is how it is defined by the UCC. An item must meet very strict criteria to be considered negotiable. According to Section 3-104 of the UCC a negotiable instrument is "an unconditional promise or order to pay a fixed sum of money, with or without interest or other charges described in the promise or order." The UCC further specifies that the promise or order must be in writing and signed by the person issuing the instrument, and must also

- state that the instrument is payable to order or to bearer at the time it is issued or at the time it is transferred to another person
- be payable on demand or a specific future date
- contain a specific amount of money to be paid
- be issued without any conditions to payment

Exhibit 5.1 **Negotiable Instruments**

Negotiable instruments are

- Payable to order or bearer
- Payable without conditions
- Payable for a specific (fixed) amount of money
- Payable on demand or a specific future date
- Always in writing and signed by the issuer
- An order or promise to pay

A check is a **demand draft** drawn on a bank. A **draft** is a form of negotiable instrument. Therefore, a check is a negotiable instrument.
Check = demand draft
Demand draft = negotiable instrument
Check = negotiable instrument

In short, the instrument must be payable on demand (when presented by the holder) or at a definite time ("pay five days from the issue date"), the amount of payment must be specific and fixed ("pay $50"), and there can be no conditions to payment (such as "pay this amount if the contractor finishes the work"). Exhibit 5.1 lists the main components of a negotiable instrument. Each is explained in greater detail below. The explanations will focus on checks as negotiable instruments. This book does not permit a discussion of the other types of negotiable instruments.

Payable to Order or to Bearer

We see the words "pay to the order of" followed by a blank line on our checks again and again. We write in the name of the telephone company or the Cub Scout troop without even noticing the printed phrase. These words, however, mean something to the bank. Without this order ("pay to the order of"), the check is not negotiable. This requirement is important because it prevents someone from using an item that was never intended to be negotiable (like those genuine-looking "checks" that arrive in the mail saying "You may have already won $10,000,000!"). Checks are the only exception to this requirement because checks are intended to be negotiable instruments. Preprinted checks may have the words "pay to" instead of "pay to the order of." These checks are still considered to be negotiable instruments.

An instrument is payable to bearer if the words "bearer" or "cash" appear on the instrument, or if it otherwise indicates that the person in possession of the instrument is entitled to payment. A check that is made payable to an identifiable person and endorsed by that person becomes a bearer instrument.

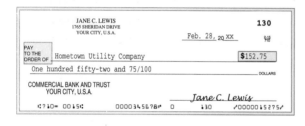

Unconditional Order or Promise

As stated above, checks contain a written order to the bank to pay the amount of the check to the person specified. This promise or order cannot be dependent on any conditions—it must be unconditional. For example, a check may not contain the statement "If he paints the house, pay to the order of Leonard." If an instrument does contain a condition to payment, it is not a negotiable instrument.

Fixed Amount of Money

The promise or order to pay explained above must be for a fixed amount of money. The

amount can be in U.S. dollars or in a foreign currency and must be clearly specified on the face of the instrument, in monetary terms. It may not be stated in terms of something of value that could be converted to money, such as the amount of one ounce of gold, even though the value of one ounce of gold can be easily determined.

Payable on Demand or at a Definite Time

Because it is important to the discussion of the time component of negotiability, the concept of **presentment** will be introduced here. Presentment (chapter 6) is defined in Article 3 of the UCC as "demand for payment made by the person entitled to payment." Basically, the check or draft must be physically presented to the bank to be paid. For example, if Cindy calls the bank to verify a check given to her by Jeff, Cindy has not made presentment. On the other hand, if Cindy takes the item to a teller and asks for cash, presentment has been made. In recent years the concept of electronic presentment (chapter 13) has been introduced and accepted.

To be negotiable, an instrument must be payable at a known time—either now (payable on demand) or at a specific date in the future. An instrument that is payable on demand, like a check, can be presented for payment whenever the person who possesses the instrument desires. Conversely, it is not payable on demand at the will of the issuer. For example, if Mr. Jones issues a check to Ms. Young and states that he will pay the check sometime after he returns from vacation the instrument is not payable on demand and therefore is not a negotiable instrument.

Some negotiable instruments other than checks can also be paid at a definite time in the future. For example, an instrument might state that it is payable ten days after the date of issue.

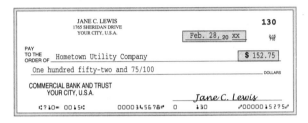

Written and Signed

The next condition for a negotiable instrument is that it must be in writing and signed by the drawer. A verbal agreement to pay $500 to a merchant for a washing machine does not constitute payment for that machine with a negotiable instrument. A written check from the buyer, however, would be negotiable if it is properly signed.

A negotiable instrument signed by a signature machine or stamped with an individual's signature is considered valid, as are "identifying marks" like Xs. Banks may have policies regarding these special types of signatures. In many cases banks will work with customers to

arrange these special solutions ahead of time, often calling on the services of a notary.

Parties to Negotiable Instruments and Their Liabilities

The parties to a negotiable instrument are called by different names depending on the type of instrument. Their liabilities also differ. One party that is common to all types of negotiable instruments is the **endorser**. An endorser is any person who makes an endorsement—the signature or mark made to negotiate the instrument.

Parties to Drafts

A check drawn on a bank is the most common example of a draft. Parties to a check are:

- the **drawer**—the person or party who writes the check
- the **drawee**—the bank that holds the checking account
- the **payee**—the person or party to whom the check is written (exhibit 5.2).

Banks also regularly see insurance drafts, which are used by insurance companies to pay claims. While often negotiated regularly as checks, insurance drafts are *not* checks. A check would be payable on demand. Creating drafts to pay claims allows insurance companies time to examine the drafts before they are paid. A check is payable on demand and cannot be examined by the drawer unless special arrangements are made with the bank.

Liability of the Parties

All parties to negotiable instruments are liable, or legally accountable, for various

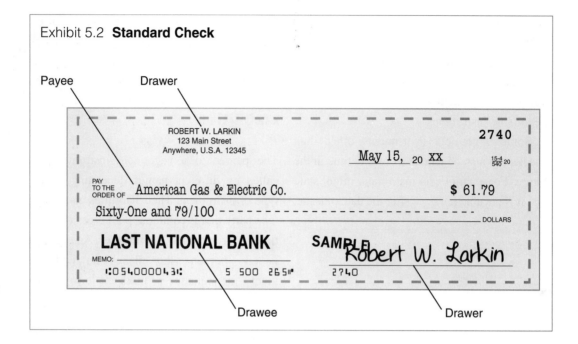

Exhibit 5.2 **Standard Check**

Payee   Drawer

ROBERT W. LARKIN
123 Main Street
Anywhere, U.S.A. 12345

2740

May 15, 20 XX   15-4/540 20

PAY TO THE ORDER OF _American Gas & Electric Co._ $ 61.79

Sixty-One and 79/100 - DOLLARS

LAST NATIONAL BANK

SAMPLE   _Robert W. Larkin_

MEMO:

⑆054000043⑆ 5 500 265⑈ 2740

Drawee   Drawer

aspects of the transaction. The liability of the parties depends on the capacity in which they sign. (A person is liable on an instrument only if he or she signs it.) Following is a discussion of the liabilities of the parties to a check. The liability of parties to other types of negotiable instruments is not covered in this text.

Liability of the Drawer

The drawer (person writing the check) is liable for paying the instrument even if it is dishonored by the drawee (the bank). **Dishonor** means that the drawee has refused to pay the instrument when presented. The most common reason for dishonor is insufficient funds. A draft or check must be presented to the drawee bank before the drawer is required to pay it. For example, if Jeff issues a check to Cindy, she cannot file suit against Jeff to collect the amount of the check until she has presented the check to the drawee bank and the check has been dishonored.

Liability of a Drawee

A drawee bank has an obligation to all drawers to pay checks that are properly payable (chapter 6) and therefore must accept all such instruments for payment when presented.

Liability of an Endorser

The person or party who endorses and transfers an instrument that is presented for payment and dishonored must take the instrument back and pay the amount. However, the instrument must be returned, and notice of dishonor must be given, in a timely manner in order for the endorser to be liable. Continuing the above example, Cindy deposits the check issued to her by Jeff into her account. The bank dishonors the check for insufficient funds. Since Cindy has presented the check for payment (by depositing it into her account) and it has been dishonored, the endorser (Jeff) must take the dishonored check back and pay Cindy the amount. Just because the bank will not pay the check does not mean that Jeff doesn't have to!

Another liability taken on by an endorser who transfers an instrument is a warrant that there are none of the following problems with the instrument:

- It is not stolen.
- It has not been altered.
- It does not contain any forgeries.
- No other person has a claim to it.
- The endorser does not have any knowledge that the drawer or acceptor is unable to pay the item when it is presented.

For example, someone forges Bill's name on a check and transfers the check to Betty. Betty, who does not know that Bill's endorsement is forged, endorses the check and deposits it in her account with the First Deposit Bank. Later the check is returned to the First Deposit Bank because of the forged endorsement. Betty has to take the check back from the bank because it contained a forged endorsement, even though she was not aware of it. This warranty liability exists even if timely notice of dishonor is not given.

Betty also would have to take the check back in the following examples:

- if the amount of the check had been changed without the drawer's authority
- if Betty had known that the drawer of the check was insolvent and could not pay the check
- if Betty had known that the signature of the drawer was forged

Types of Checks

There are many everyday situations when a standard check is not accepted as payment. An individual closing title on a new home, or buying an expensive automobile or item of jewel-ry, for example, may be required to supply an instrument that gives the payee greater assurance of actual payment. Too many things can happen from the time a check is issued until it is paid by the drawee bank—the account on which the check is drawn may not have sufficient funds to pay the check, the check may contain a forgery, or the drawer may decide to stop payment on the check. Consequently, some payees may require that the person making payment do so with some type of check that is issued by a bank or that is more likely to be paid than a personal check. Following are examples of checks that provide a greater guarantee of payment. Please note that not all banks and businesses around the country use all of these items. Banks in some parts of the country, for example, do not use certified checks but issue cashier's or treasurer's checks instead.

Cashier's Check or Treasurer's Check

A cashier's check (exhibit 5.3) is issued by a national bank and drawn on that bank; the bank is both the drawer and the drawee. A treasurer's check is issued by a state bank and drawn on that bank. Banks often use cashier's or treasurer's checks to pay their own obligations or to pay out loan proceeds. These checks may also be sold to customers who require an official instrument of the bank, and they are often used by customers as a less expensive alternative to certified checks (see next section, Official's Check or Teller's Check).

The bank issuing a cashier's check is obligated to pay the check even if the purchaser wants to stop payment. For example, a customer purchases a cashier's check to pay for a new computer. When the computer does not work, the customer contacts the bank to stop

Exhibit 5.3 **Cashier's Check**

| **Back Beach First National Bank** | 63-000 / 000 |

88597

BACK BEACH, U.S.A. ___May 2___ 20 __XX__

PAY
TO THE
ORDER OF ___ABC Developers, Inc.___ $ ___178.00___

THE SUM 178 DOLS 00 CTS _____ DOLLARS

Cashier's Check

REMITTER ___Kit Walker___

Margaret A. King
AUTHORIZED SIGNATURE

⑆088597⑆ ⑇0000⑈0000⑇ ⑆000 0004⑈

payment on the check. However, despite the customer having a good reason to stop the payment, the bank has no right to refuse to pay the check. Article 3 of the UCC provides that the bank is obligated to pay these items. But what if the check is lost or stolen? Article 3 does allow the issuing bank to issue a stop payment (chapter 6) on a cashier's or treasurer's check, but only after the purchaser or the payee has given the bank a declaration of loss. The declaration of loss is a statement signed by the purchaser or the payee that the check has been lost or stolen and has not been negotiated. The stop payment becomes effective 90 days after the issuance of the check. If the check is presented for payment, however, and paid during the 90-day period, the issuing bank is discharged from its obligation on the check and on the stop payment. Banks often require purchasers of cashier's checks to post a bond for twice the amount of the check.

Official's Check or Teller's Check

An official's or teller's check is similar to a cashier's check, except that it is issued by one bank and drawn on another bank or payer. The obligation of the issuing bank for these checks is the same as described above for cashier's checks. That is, the bank is obligated to pay the check even if the purchaser does not want it paid.

Issuing official's or teller's checks instead of cashier's checks has several advantages for issuing banks. First, checks are supplied by the payer bank, so there is no cost to the issuing bank. The payer bank also maintains the blank check stock, reconciles the official check account, stores the paid checks, and provides customer service to both the issuing bank and to the issuing bank's customers. Banks can also gain increased float time on these checks because they will clear on a bank out of the area. The balances in the account are directly swept into interest-earning accounts until the balance is called for to pay incoming checks. Banks make interest income from official's and teller's checks. Interest income is more limited with cashier's or treasurer's checks.

Certified Check

A certified check (exhibit 5.4) is a check for which funds have been set aside by the bank on which it is drawn. A customer who wants a check certified presents his or her check to the bank. The bank immediately debits the funds from the customer's account and puts them in a special "certified checks outstanding" account. When a bank certifies a check, the original order to pay is transformed into the bank's promise to pay. Certified checks are legal liabilities of banks. They are useful in many instances, such as that described in situation 2. Franco and Lena can use a certified check for the closing costs for their house, and it will be accepted by the settlement company.

To complete the certification process, the bank places an official bank stamp and signature on the check. The certified check is then marked, and the magnetic ink character recognition (MICR) line is covered with the certified check account number or is mutilated so that it will not be charged to the drawer's account. As part of the certification stamp, the drawee may also use some form of perforation to prevent any tampering with the amount.

Negotiation and Transfer

Bill writes a check payable to Betty. Betty endorses the check and presents it to the bank for payment. Technically, what has happened in this seemingly simple transaction is that Bill negotiated the check by transferring it to Betty. Betty became a holder of the check since she was in possession of it and it was payable to her by name. Betty, in turn, negotiated the check by transferring it, and the status of holder, to the bank. In short, negotiation transfers possession of a negotiable instrument to a holder.

If Bill had written the check "to cash" and given it to Betty, she would still qualify as a holder. However, if Bill had written the check to himself and given it to Betty without endorsing it, Betty would not be a holder. Bill's endorsement is required for Betty to become a holder. If the person to whom an instrument is transferred does not become a holder, negotiation has not taken place.

Instruments Payable to an Identifiable Person

Negotiation of an instrument payable to an identifiable person requires the endorsement of the identifiable person and delivery, or transfer, of the instrument. An identifiable person is an actual person or a legal entity such as

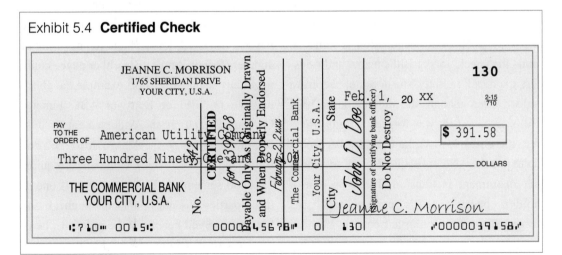

Exhibit 5.4 **Certified Check**

a corporation. If the payee is not an identifiable person or entity, the check is payable to bearer. For example, a check payable to Bill is payable to an identifiable person. On the other hand, checks payable to "cash" or "bearer" are not payable to an identifiable person. Negotiation on checks of this nature takes place by delivery alone.

Endorsements

Negotiation of an instrument payable to an identifiable person requires the endorsement of that person. If the endorsement of the payee is forged, then negotiation does not occur, and the rightful owner can make a claim against the person in possession of the instrument. For example, a check payable to Bill requires Bill's endorsement for negotiation. If someone finds the check, forges Bill's name, and transfers the check to Betty, she does not become a holder, even though she did not know that Bill's endorsement was forged. If Betty transfers the check to Earl, he does not become a holder, either. No subsequent party to whom the instrument is transferred can become a holder, because Bill's endorsement was forged. This is an important concept because holders are given certain protections (dis-

cussed later in this chapter) that non-holders do not receive.

If the bank takes the check with the forged endorsement, the bank is subject to a claim directly from Bill or a claim from the paying bank for breach of the transfer warranty. The bank, as an endorser, warrants that the check does not contain a forged endorsement and that no person has a claim to the instrument. Remember that Bill has not benefited from the amount of the check. In this example, Bill's endorsement is forged and he has a claim to the check. The bank would most likely absorb the loss. This is the reason many banks and other businesses are reluctant to take third-party checks. Situation 1, in which Alice Simms's husband forged her signature on an insurance check, is not uncommon. Most likely, the bank will have some liability for the amount of the check to Alice Simms. However, the account was joint and Alice had access to or benefit from the forgery, so she may have some liability, too. Often, the courts must decide the percentage of liability in such cases.

Checks Payable as "And" or "Or"

A check or draft payable to joint payees (Bill and Betty) requires the endorsement of all the payees. If the check is payable to one payee or another (Bill or Betty), then either payee could negotiate the check. For example, a check payable to "Bill or Betty or ABC Finance Company" requires the endorsement of only one of the payees. A check payable to "Bill and Betty and ABC Finance Company" requires the endorsement of all three payees. If one of these parties has not endorsed the check and has not received benefit of the proceeds, he or she may have a claim against the others.

Instruments Payable to Bearer

Negotiation of an instrument payable to bearer requires only delivery of the instrument; it does not require an endorsement. Any person in possession of an instrument payable to bearer is the holder of the instrument. Negotiation takes place regardless of whether the transfer was voluntary or involuntary. A check payable to cash is payable to bearer, and any person in possession of the check is the holder regardless of how he or she obtained it. For example, Ralph writes a check to Elena, and Elena endorses the check and gives it to Cindy. Cindy becomes the holder of the check, and no further endorsement is necessary to negotiate the check. After Elena endorses the check, any person who has possession of the check is the holder.

If Cindy takes the check to a teller to obtain cash, most banks would require Cindy to endorse the check in order to identify the person to whom the cash was given and because the endorser is obligated (see previous Liability of an Endorser section) to take the item back upon dishonor and timely notice of dishonor.

Endorsements

Endorsements can be made in a number of ways, depending on what the payee intends to do with the item. The item can be transferred to another person, converted to cash, deposited to an account, or used for a number of other purposes. The principal types of endorsements (exhibit 5.5) are: blank, special, and restrictive.

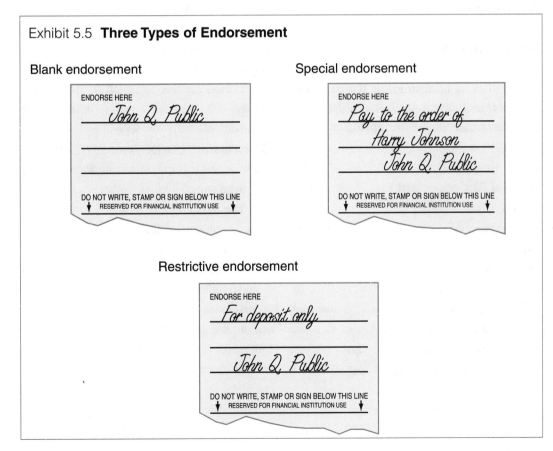

Exhibit 5.5 **Three Types of Endorsement**

Blank endorsement

Special endorsement

Restrictive endorsement

Blank Endorsement

A **blank endorsement** (or an endorsement in blank) consists simply of the signature of the payee and is the most common form of endorsement. The endorsement is placed on the back of the check, near the top. The endorsement area is now identified as the "top" portion of a check. Regulation CC designates the top one-fourth of the check for endorsements, and most check printing companies will provide the space. An instrument endorsed in blank becomes a bearer instrument and may be negotiated without any other endorsement. An instrument endorsed in blank may be used for any purpose. For example, Bill owes Earl $500, and Betty issues a check to Bill in that amount. Bill can simply endorse the check in blank and give it to Earl as payment for the debt.

In situation 3, Joel endorsed his paycheck in blank and then it was stolen. It has now become a bearer instrument that can be cashed by anyone who finds it. While the bank may not be legally liable to Joel for the check amount, it may choose to reimburse him to retain his goodwill.

Special Endorsement

Rather than endorse the check in blank, Bill could endorse the check to Earl. The endorsement might state, "Pay to the order of Earl,"

and then Bill would sign under that statement. This is called a **special endorsement**. With an endorsement such as this, only Earl could negotiate the check.

A special endorsement may also be used if the payee of a check is sending it to another person through the mail. For example, Bill's mother lives in a home owned by Bill. The home sustains fire damage, and the insurance company issues a check to Bill. Bill can put a special endorsement on the check to make it payable to the order of his mother and then mail it to her knowing that further negotiation of the check would require her endorsement.

Restrictive Endorsement

The payee or other holder of an instrument can restrict the purpose for which an instrument may be used. In a **restrictive endorsement**, the payee or other holder of the instrument, in addition to signing his or her name, identifies the purpose of the transfer and restricts the use to which the instrument can be put. The most common restrictive endorsement, used for depositing an item to an account, is "For Deposit Only." Endorsed this way, the instrument can be used only for deposit to an account; any other use is prohibited. The item cannot be cashed, used to purchase a cashier's check, or deposited to an account other than that of the person endorsing the check.

Any endorsement, including a restrictive endorsement, can be canceled by the person making the endorsement. For example, if Bill endorses a check for deposit only, he can cancel that endorsement by deleting it or scratching through it and endorsing it in another manner. The deletion, however, should bear Bill's initials. This type of cancellation is not desirable, but it is allowed. Cancellation of the endorsement by any person other than the payee or holder, however, is not valid.

Bank-provided Endorsement

Under the current version of Article 4 of the UCC, the bank automatically becomes a holder of an unendorsed instrument when it is accepted for deposit to the payee's account or other holder, or is cashed for the payee or holder. The bank no longer needs to stamp an item with "For deposit to." The bank becomes the holder of the instrument for all purposes, including becoming a holder in due course (discussed later in the chapter). Before Article 4 was revised, the depositary bank did not become a holder of the instrument until the endorsement was supplied.

A bank can still supply a missing endorsement. If a customer failed to endorse an item, and the item itself did not require the personal endorsement of the payee, the bank could provide an endorsement that stated, "For deposit to the account of the within named payee." This endorsement is usually stamped on the item at the time it is deposited. The bank typically supplies the endorsement when items are received for deposit through the night depository, the mail, or the automated teller machine.

These provisions concerning the endorsement are helpful to depositary and payer banks. The depositary bank can accept deposits without having to inspect each check for an endorsement before accepting it for deposit. However, the bank must still ensure that the proceeds reach the right party. The paying bank also receives benefit in that it may pay the item without having to examine the endorsements.

Regulation CC Endorsement Requirements

Federal Reserve Regulation CC states endorsement requirements regarding the placement of an endorsement on a check (see exhibit 5.5). The depositary bank is responsible for ensuring that its endorsement meets the requirements of the regulation and is placed in the proper location. The depositary bank also must ensure that the customer does not interfere with the area of the check designated for the depositary bank's endorsement. However, the depositary bank must still accept the item back even if a check is delayed in being returned because of the placement of the endorsement or because the endorsement of the depositary bank was obstructed by the depositing customer making the deposit.

Holder in Due Course

Individuals, businesses, and banks are willing to accept negotiable instruments, especially checks, as a method of payment because most are collected. Negotiable instruments are processed freely through the clearing system and given value (cash or credit) because they have protections. Accepting a negotiable instrument without being liable for any claims and defenses against it is known as being a **holder in due course**—an important concept in the banking business.

To attain the status of holder in due course:
1. The person must be a holder of a negotiable instrument (see the Negotiation and Transfer section).
2. The holder must take the instrument
   - for value
   - in good faith

- without notice that the instrument is overdue or has been dishonored
- without knowledge that the instrument contains an unauthorized signature or has been altered
- without knowledge of any claim to the instrument or any defenses against payment of the instrument

If these requirements are not met, the holder is not holder in due course. The holder takes the instrument subject to all claims and defenses against payment of the instrument. Details and examples of each requirement follow.

Value

The instrument is accepted for value, either cash or a performance of a promise. For most instruments, value is determined by cash or check. An example of non-cash value would be Rudy agreeing to paint Bob's house and actually doing so. Rudy has given non-cash value.

Good Faith

The instrument must be taken in good faith. This means that the holder must be honest in accepting the negotiable instrument and must practice reasonable commercial standards. If the holder knows an instrument is stolen, then he or she is not acting in good faith and is not a holder in due course. For example, if a check cashing company cashes for Bob a check payable to Rudy without asking for identification, then it did not practice reasonable commercial standards and is not a holder in due course.

Overdue and Dishonored Instrument

The holder of the instrument takes the instrument without notice that it is overdue or dis-

honored. A check is considered overdue 90 days after being issued. After the 90 days, the check is overdue and the holder who takes it cannot become a holder in due course. The holder can transfer the check for payment, but the legal protections are not there. Another situation is the dishonored instrument. For example, the bank will not cash a check for Betty because the account is overdrawn. The bank stamps the check insufficient funds and gives it back to her. The check is dishonored. Betty then persuades Earl to cash the check. Earl is not a holder in due course, because the check had been dishonored previously.

Unauthorized Signature or Alteration

The instrument must not contain an obvious alteration (such as erasure or strikeover), a forged signature, or any other sign that it was altered or completed after it was issued. If a check payable to Bill appears to have been changed from Phil to Bill, the holder is not a holder in due course.

Claim or Defense

In the same example, the holder has knowledge of a check with an obvious alteration (originally payable to Phil), and knows that someone else may have a claim to the instrument or a defense against its payment. By holding this check, the holder has knowledge of a claim and a defense against payment, therefore the holder is not a holder in due course. For example, Roger hires Joel to paint his house and issues a check to Joel in advance. Joel agrees not to cash the check until the job is done. Knowing the facts, Laura cashes the check for Joel, and Joel never paints the house. Because Laura had notice that Roger has a defense against paying the check, she is not a holder in due course.

Facilitating Collection

In a typical example, Dave writes a check to pay his utility bill (see exhibit 5.6, below). The check is deposited by the utility company into its bank account (the bank is known as the depositary bank). The depositary bank sends the check through the collection process, through the Federal Reserve, back to Dave's bank for payment. Neither the depositary bank nor the Federal Reserve knows Dave. Why are they so willing to accept responsibility for collecting this check? The answer is the protec-

tions provided by being a holder in due course. Dave's check is a negotiable instrument. It has value, it was accepted in good faith, and neither the depositary bank nor the Federal Reserve had notice that the check was overdue, dishonored, or contained an unauthorized

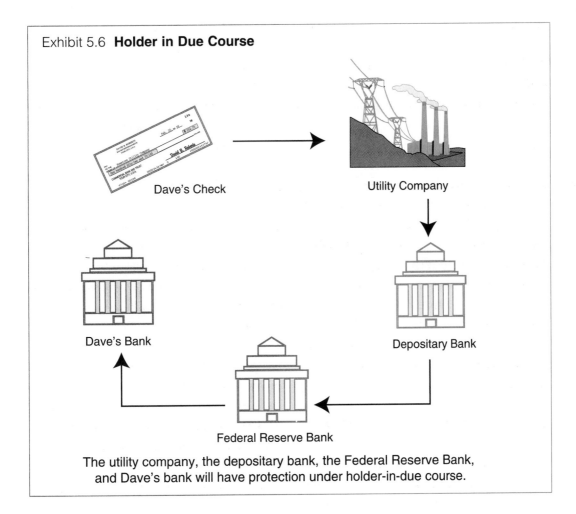

Exhibit 5.6 **Holder in Due Course**

Dave's Check

Utility Company

Dave's Bank

Depositary Bank

Federal Reserve Bank

The utility company, the depositary bank, the Federal Reserve Bank, and Dave's bank will have protection under holder-in-due course.

signature or claim. Therefore, the depositary bank and the Federal Reserve both agree to act as transfer agents for the check's collection back to Dave's bank.

Holder in due course gives the depositary bank and the Federal Reserve recourse for collecting checks if they are returned unpaid. Without holder in due course, neither would be willing to accept checks for clearing. Imagine how the utility company and the millions of others who send checks through the clearing system would receive payment. They would have to go directly to the issuing bank—a slow, cumbersome, and expensive process.

Summary

Negotiable instruments have existed for a long time, and they serve an important function. Because they are used as a form of payment and flow across state lines, they are governed by a uniform set of laws known as the Uniform Commercial Code (UCC). The UCC governs all aspects of negotiable instruments, including the requirement that an instrument meet certain specifications before it can be considered a negotiable instrument. If the instrument does not meet those requirements, it is not a negotiable instrument. Negotiable instruments have multiple parties whose rights, liabilities, and obligations are defined in the UCC and are dependent on the capacity in which they sign the instrument.

Because of the nature of negotiable instruments, they must flow freely within our economy from person to person. This transfer of possession and title of negotiable instruments is accomplished through negotiation. The requirements of negotiation depend on whether the instrument is payable to an identifiable person or to bearer. If the instrument is

payable to an identifiable person or persons, negotiation requires the endorsement of all the payees and delivery of the instrument. If the instrument is payable to bearer, negotiation occurs simply through delivery of the instrument. The instrument may be endorsed in a number of ways, depending on the intended use of the instrument. It may be endorsed in blank and transferred freely, or it may contain an endorsement that designates the specific purpose for which the instrument may be used.

To encourage the acceptance of negotiable instruments as a form of payment and to promote negotiation, the UCC provides a preferred status called holder in due course. A holder in due course takes an instrument free of all claims and all defenses on the part of any person. If the holder meets all the requirements of a holder in due course, he or she is assured of obtaining payment on the instrument. Payment will be made to the holder in due course even if another person has a claim to the instrument or the drawer or payer has a defense against payment.

Review and Discussion Questions

1. Define the term "negotiable instrument."
2. List the parties to a check.
3. Distinguish among a cashier's or treasurer's check, a teller's or official's check, and a certified check.
4. Distinguish between a check payable to bearer and a check payable to an identifiable person.
5. Explain the difference between a "blank endorsement" and a "special endorsement" and discuss when each is used.
6. Discuss how holder in due course affects the banking system.

Additional Resources

Banking and Finance Terminology. Washington, D.C.: American Bankers Association, 1999.

Law and Banking: Applications. Washington, D.C., American Bankers Association, 2000.

Law and Banking: Principles. Washington, D.C., American Bankers Association, 2000.

Web Resources

Cornell University Legal Information Institute
www.law.cornell.edu/topics/negotiable.html

6

CHECKS AND THE PAYMENT FUNCTION

Checking Accounts

I DON'T WANT TO PUT A STOP PAYMENT ON MY CHECK, JUST A YIELD RIGHT OF WAY UNTIL I CAN MAKE A DEPOSIT.

THAVES

Learning Objectives

After completing this chapter, you will be able to do the following:

- distinguish between paying a check and cashing a check, explaining the teller's role in this process
- explain the conditions under which a check is and is not properly payable
- explain how items are prepared for processing through the encoding and proof functions
- describe the item capture and sorting process, including an explanation of check routing symbols and ABA Institution Identifiers
- list and discuss the various check clearing alternatives
- define the bolded terms that appear in the text

Introduction

Nowhere is the knowledge and skill of the teller more critical than in the payments function, which often starts at the teller window, where tellers are the first line of customer relations. As the following situations demonstrate, the teller has many roles—each one important in protecting the bank and the customer from financial loss.

Situation 1

A man who does not have an account with the bank gives you his paycheck, which is drawn on another bank, and requests cash. The man maintains that he works for a local business that has prearranged check-cashing privileges with the bank; however, the man has forgotten to bring his employee identification card. He produces other identification. You have to decide whether to cash this check. What tools do you have to help you decide?

Situation 2

Jim issues a check to pay for a new chain saw. Later that afternoon, the chain saw stops working. He comes to your teller station furious about the chain saw and wants you to stop payment on the check immediately. Can you help him?

Situation 3

A customer presents an on-us check for payment at your teller window. The new year 2000 has just begun and you are aware that many customers are still writing "1999" on their checks by mistake. This check, however, is dated April 25, 1998. What would you say to your customer about this check?

The above situations illustrate the breadth of the teller's role and demonstrate that the job entails far more than the accuracy, friendliness, and good customer service that customers have come to expect. Tellers start a process that eventually involves not only several other bank departments, but also other financial institutions and clearing facilities throughout the country and around the world. This chapter explores the payment function, from paying and cashing checks at the teller window to preparing them for processing to following them as they work their way through the clearing system.

When customers deposit checks to their checking accounts, they are not concerned with how the checks are forwarded to the paying bank and collected. They just want to know how soon they can use their money. To remain competitive, banks make customer money available as quickly as possible. Technology and automation have allowed banks to process checks much faster and less expensively than they could just a few years ago. Before automation, the check collection process was very slow and expensive, and customers had to wait a long time for funds to be made available to them. Today, with check processing equipment capable of processing checks at speeds of up to 2,500 items per minute, the check collection process takes much less time. Banks are using various means to speed up the collection process so that funds are made available to customers as quickly as possible at the lowest cost. With the advent of electronic check presentment and image technology, the trend will continue.

The Teller's Role

The general public is unaware that there is a difference between **paying** and **cashing** a check. Most people think that when they convert a check into cash by presenting it over the counter to a teller, the check is being cashed. Although seemingly a technicality, the difference is significant. All bank employees, especially tellers, should know and understand the different meaning of the two terms.

A bank has an obligation to its own customers to pay a check that is properly payable. A teller pays a check when he or she gives cash to the person presenting a check drawn on that bank (an on-us check). Conversely, the teller is cashing a check when he or she gives cash to the person presenting a check drawn on another bank. A bank has no obligation to cash a check.

Paying Checks

When someone issues a check, that person intends the check to be paid by the drawee unless he or she stops payment on it. When an on-us check is presented to the bank at the teller window, it can be deposited in an account or presented for immediate payment over the counter. An on-us check can also come to the bank through the Federal Reserve, a correspondent bank, or by directly presenting it from another local institution. When an on-us check is presented for payment over the counter to a teller, the teller is making final payment on the check. Final payment means the bank is accountable for the amount of the item. When a bank makes final payment, the bank cannot later decide to dishonor and return the check.

> Paying a check: giving cash for an on-us check
>
> Cashing a check: giving cash for a check drawn on another bank

The following is an example of the impact of final payment. Dan issues a check drawn on First Deposit Bank to Jean. Jean goes to a branch of the First Deposit Bank, endorses the check in blank (chapter 5), and presents it to a teller. The teller gives Jean cash for the check. At that point, the check is finally paid; the First Deposit Bank cannot return the check even if the balance in Dan's account is insufficient to pay the check. Upon final payment, Dan's obligation to pay the check and Jean's obligation to take the check back are discharged. (Dan, however, is liable should an overdraft be created by paying the check.)

Because making final payment on an on-us check presents a risk for the bank, it is important that the teller examine the check and the account on which the check is drawn to ensure that the person presenting the item is properly identified. There are both visual and nonvisual tests a teller can perform when inspecting a check (exhibit 6.1). Nonvisual tests include determining whether:

- the check is drawn on an open account
- the account has sufficient and available funds
- a stop payment has been issued on the check
- any type of hold has been placed on the account

Visual tests include:

- verifying that the check is not altered
- properly identifying the person presenting the check
- verifying that the check is dated properly
- ensuring that the check is properly endorsed and that the check does not contain a restrictive endorsement
- verifying the signature on the check by comparing the check to the signature card on file

Exhibit 6.1 **Visual and Nonvisual Tests for Inspecting a Check**

Nonvisual Elements

o		Has a stop payment order been placed on the check?
o		Has a hold been placed on the account?
o		Is there sufficient balance to cover the check?
o		Is the account balance available to the drawer?

Visual Elements

o		Is the item an actual check drawn on the bank?
o		Is the signature genuine and authorized?
o	□	Has the check been altered?
o	□	Is the check properly dated?
o	□	Is the check properly endorsed?

o = paying a check   □ = cashing a check

Even if no additional endorsement is needed to negotiate a check, such as a check payable to cash that is already endorsed in blank (chapter 5), many banks require the person presenting the check to endorse it so that the person to whom the cash was paid can be identified.

Online systems now allow tellers to view an image of the bank's record of the customer's signature so that it can be compared to the actual signature on the check. This helps to reduce instances of forged signatures for the bank. To ensure that the funds are available when the posting process is completed later that day, many banks also place a teller's hold on the funds when the check is paid. Some financial institutions—primarily savings and loan associations, savings banks, and credit unions—actually post the check to the account through the online system.

On-us checks are drawn from accounts that are in the bank's computer files. Therefore, the teller has all the information necessary to pay a check at his or her fingertips, just as if the item had been presented directly to the bank's deposit operations department. The teller can do nonvisual tests (exhibit 6.1) to determine if the account has insufficient funds or has been closed, if a stop payment has been placed on the check, or if any other reason exists for refusing to pay (dishonoring) the check. The bank can pay a check only if it is properly payable. By paying a check that is not properly payable, the bank could be liable to the customer for the amount of the item. For example, Anne presents an on-us check from Bob at the teller window. Since the teller knows Anne is a regular customer, he does not check Bob's account information. The teller pays the check and only later discovers that there were insufficient funds in Bob's account.

In this situation, the bank could ask Anne (the payee) to make good on the check but would have little ability to collect. Since Bob's account is overdrawn, the bank may still collect from him. On the other hand, if the bank dishonors a check that is properly payable (chapter 7), the bank could be liable to the drawer for wrongful dishonor. For example, a teller returns an on-us check that is presented for payment. The teller indicates that a hold had been placed on the account, when in fact, none had. As a result, the account holder has to pay a fee to the party who did not receive payment. The bank may be liable for this fee because of the wrongful dishonor.

If the teller refuses to pay the check, the person presenting the check is entitled to a reason for the refusal. In some instances, the teller may be asked to write the reason (e.g., insufficient funds, account closed, payment stopped) on the check so the person presenting the check can show that his or her attempt to present it failed, and for what reason.

Cashing Checks

On any business day, large volumes of payroll, dividend, tax refund, public assistance, and personal checks drawn on other banks may be presented to tellers to be cashed. Tellers assume a far greater risk in giving cash in exchange for these items than in paying checks. When cashing a check, the teller has no way to determine the sufficiency of funds, whether the account is open or closed, whether a stop payment has been placed on the check, whether the drawer's signature is genuine and authorized, or any of the other reasons why the drawee might dishonor the check. As highlighted in exhibit 6.1, tellers can only verify whether the check has been altered and if it is properly dated and endorsed. They cannot perform any of the nonvisual tests or verify the signature of the maker.

Although banks are not obligated to cash checks, they do so for at least two reasons. First, the person presenting the check usually has an account with the bank and may wish to cash the check instead of depositing it to the account. Second, the bank may have other

Did You Know?

The number of checks written in 2000 is estimated to be 68 billion.

(American Bankers Association)

relations with the maker of the check, such as loans or other banking services, and the bank may wish to cash the checks as a courtesy to the customer. For example, XYZ Corporation carries its main corporate account at Bank A but also maintains a payroll account with Bank B. The corporation asks Bank A to cash payroll checks presented to it with proper employee identification and signs an agreement protecting Bank A against any losses. The corporation's employees are told that they can cash their payroll checks at Bank A. Bank A is providing a service for the employees of the corporation in hopes of maintaining their relationship with the corporation and maintaining or developing a relationship with the employee.

If the bank cashes a check and the check is not paid by the drawee, the endorser remains liable on the check, and the bank may collect the amount of the check from the person who cashed the check or any other previous endorser. The bank may also look to the maker of the check for payment. In situation 1, the teller must balance the bank's relationship with the local business, the bank's policies on proper identification, and the customer's satisfaction.

Most banks establish check-cashing policies and procedures that determine the authority of a teller to cash checks. In general, this authority reflects the teller's experience and possibly his or her past performance. Dollar limits can be established for new tellers and subsequently increased as they gain more experience. Inevitably, however, situations arise in which a person presenting a check to be cashed must be referred to a supervisor or a more senior banking officer. (Situation 1, in which a man without the proper identification tries to cash a paycheck drawn on another bank, may be such a case.) If the referring is done tactfully so the individual understands the reasons for it, no ill will is created.

Properly Payable Items

A bank may pay a check on a customer's account only if the check is properly payable. "Properly payable" is not specifically defined in the UCC, but it basically means the check does not have any forged or unauthorized signatures, alterations, stop payment order, or other reason why the depositor would object to the bank's paying the check.

Signatures

A valid signature is necessary for a check to be properly payable. A check is not properly payable if it contains a forgery or an unauthorized signature. However, the customer may be responsible for some types of unauthorized signatures, particularly if the customer uses a stamp or a computer-generated signature. If the customer does not have procedures in place to prevent someone from using the stamp or computer file, this failure would be considered negligence on the part of the customer. The bank would not have to refund the amount of the checks.

Under Articles 3 and 4 of the UCC, an employer's forged signature could be considered valid (that is, the employer would be held liable) if the check were signed by an employee and the employee had responsibilities related to issuing checks. For example, Ellen works for a doctor, and her duties include writing checks for the doctor's signature, mailing the checks, and reconciling the bank statement. Ellen forges the name of the doctor on several checks payable to herself. Under Articles 3 and 4, the signature could be considered a valid signature of the doctor; in other words, the doctor would be liable for the checks. Articles 3 and 4 also apply to forgery of the doctor's endorsement.

The customer also has an obligation to examine his or her bank statement and report any unauthorized signature to the bank within a reasonable time (see Chapter 7).

Endorsements

A check with a forged or missing endorsement is not properly payable; the customer is entitled to a refund from the bank unless the customer was negligent in issuing the check and the customer's negligence substantially contributed to the forgery. For example, an insurance company insures two people named Jim Long. The company issues a check payable to Jim Long and sends it to the wrong Jim Long, who endorses the check for payment. The insurance company's negligence contributed to the forged endorsement. The endorsement is considered valid, and the insurance company cannot object to the bank's paying the check.

Joint Payees

A check payable to joint payees that does not contain all the payees' endorsements is not properly payable, and the drawer has a right to object to its being paid. As with other checks, certain defenses are available to the bank. For example, a check payable to Ellen Smith and Bob Smith must be endorsed by both to be properly payable. If Ellen endorses the check and it is paid by First Deposit Bank, Bob Smith can object because he is entitled to the proceeds and he has not received any benefit from the check.

Alterations

An altered check is one in which a material change has been made, such as a change in the payee or the amount. (Making notation on the check or changing information on the line designated "memo" is not an alteration of the check.) An altered check is not properly payable; however, the check is properly payable for the original amount. For example, a check in the amount of $100 that is altered to $1,000 is not properly payable for $1,000, but it is properly payable for $100.

Stop Payments

The UCC gives a customer the right to stop payment on a check. Therefore, a check on which payment has been stopped is not properly payable. The order may be given orally or in writing. An oral **stop payment** is valid for 14 days, and a written stop payment is valid for six months. The customer must renew the stop payment at the expiration of the six-month period to keep the stop payment in effect. In situation 2, Jim wants to stop payment on his new chain saw until it works properly. He can issue an oral stop payment on the check that will be in effect for 14 days. If the problem is resolved in that time, the check will again become payable. If not, Jim will have to extend the stop payment with a written request to the bank.

Accurate Description

The customer is obligated to provide the bank with information that accurately describes the check to be stopped. For example, if the customer describes check 221 in the amount of $14.65 payable to Janet but actually meant check 212 in the amount of $16.24 the bank would be justified in paying the check. Complications arise when the customer comes close to stating the correct amount but does not state it exactly. In anticipation of this, most banks' computer software looks for check amounts a certain percentage above and below the amount the customer provides. A range of about 10 percent to 15 percent is normal. For example, if a customer estimates the check amount to be $100, the computer would flag checks between $90 and $110 for manual inspection. Most banks require the specific check number and will cue their systems to flag that check. Sometimes, when a customer really is not sure but can provide some information, the bank will manually watch the account at a greater cost to the customer.

Sufficient Time

The stop payment order must be given in such a manner as to allow the bank sufficient time to stop payment on the check. The definition of a reasonable amount of time depends on a number of factors, including the manner in which the stop payment order is given and the capabilities of the bank. Stopping payment often becomes a race against the clock. The payee may be in the branch at 9:00 a.m. cashing the check, and the drawer may be at another branch or on the phone issuing a stop payment. In this situation, the bank would not have sufficient time to stop the check. But if the customer calls the bank at 9:00 a.m. to issue the stop payment and the payee presents the check to a branch one hour later, the notice is probably sufficient if the bank has an online system to alert all its branches to the stop payment. On the other hand, if the bank does not have an online system and stop payments have to be entered in a log at a central location, the bank needs more time to make the stop payment order effective.

Although the customer has the right to stop payment on a check, many banks charge a stop payment fee for processing stop payments. Banks incur expense performing this service and use the fee to help offset those costs.

Postdated Checks

In the past, a check was not properly payable before the date on the check. If the bank paid a check before the date on the check, the bank could be liable to the customer for any damages caused by payment of the check. If payment of the check caused other checks to be returned, the bank could be liable to the customer for wrongful dishonor.

Current regulations recognize that banks do not and cannot examine every item presented for payment. The bank is liable to the customer for paying the check prior to the date on the check only if the customer notifies the bank that he or she issued the postdated check. Procedures for issuing a postdated check notification are similar to those for issuing a stop payment order: reasonable notice must be given to the bank for the order to become effective, and the customer must accurately describe the item. The notice is valid for 14 days if given orally and six months if given or confirmed in writing.

Stale-dated Checks

Much confusion surrounds the definition of a **stale-dated check** and whether a bank should pay a stale-dated check. Article 4 of the UCC authorizes the bank to pay the check as long as it exercises good faith: For example, a bank pays a check it thinks the maker wants paid, such as a dividend check. If the bank does not notice that the check is older than six months and has no reason to know that the customer did not want the check paid, the bank is justified in paying the check. On the other hand, if a teller notices that the check is almost two years old (like the check in situation 3), good faith probably requires the teller to inquire whether the customer wants the check paid.

The following situation is fairly common: The customer issues a stop payment on a check. Six months later the stop payment order expires, the customer does not renew it, and the check is presented for payment some time later. The bank is still within its rights to pay the check. When the stale date section and the stop payment section of Article 4 are considered together, the conclusion is that (1) a bank may pay a check that is older than six months old and (2) a written stop payment is valid for six months. If the customer does not want the check paid after six months, he or she must renew the stop payment. In the absence of a renewal, the bank may pay the check. Note that U.S. government checks are considered stale after one year.

Death or Incompetence of a Customer

The death or incompetence of a maker does not affect the bank's right to pay a check, unless the bank has knowledge of the facts. Even with knowledge of the maker's death, the bank may pay checks up to ten days after the death of the maker unless an interested party stops payment on the checks. The UCC does not define "an interested party."

In the case of incompetence, the person must be judged incompetent by a court. Without the proper court judgment, a family member cannot demand that the bank not pay checks of an incompetent customer. Once the account holder has been judged incompetent, the bank cannot pay checks after the date of the judgment. In most cases the account is closed by the guardian or whomever the court appoints to handle the affairs of the account holder, thereby avoiding potential losses to the bank.

Wrongful Dishonor

The bank is required to honor a check that is properly payable. If the bank fails to do so, the bank could be liable to the customer for wrongful dishonor of the check. A bank will be liable to its customers for wrongful dishonor if it:

- fails to pay an item drawn on sufficient collected funds
- pays a check subject to a stop payment order and then dishonors other checks that would have been paid if the stop payment order had been followed
- holds the wrong account pursuant to the service of an attachment order or IRS levy and then dishonors checks presented for payment
- mistakenly applies funds against an obligation not owed by the depositor, leading to the dishonor of checks
- closes its depositor's account without giving reasonable notice of the closure and dishonors checks that were outstanding before the account was closed

Under the revised Article 4, the bank is not liable for wrongful dishonor when it dishonors a check that would overdraw the account, unless the bank has an agreement to pay checks in the overdraft. In determining the sufficiency of funds, the bank has to check the balance only one time after presentment of the item, and the bank may select the time it checks the balance.

If the bank has wrongfully dishonored a check, the bank is liable for the amount of actual damages caused by the wrongful dishonor.

Encoding and Proof

Once an item is accepted for cash, payment, or deposit, it is processed for collection. Deposit slips, the items deposited, cashed and paid checks, loan payments, and other transaction items received by the teller are sent, in most cases, to a central location for processing. The transactions on customers' accounts are processed, and the checks drawn on other banks are sent for collection. The checks paid by the teller and other items received by the teller are posted (paid) to the accounts of the depositors (chapter 7) unless the bank posts the transactions on-line at the teller's window. Before automation, this posting process was done manually by making entries in a ledger. Since the process is now automated, the items are prepared for automated processing before they leave the teller's window.

Exhibit 6.2 shows how items presented from various points (branches, other departments, customers, other banks) are processed, from presentment to the depositary through presentment to the paying bank. Each step is discussed in this section.

Item Preparation

When items are received in the item preparation area, they are prepared for **proofing** and

Exhibit 6.2 **Presenting Items for Payment and Posting**

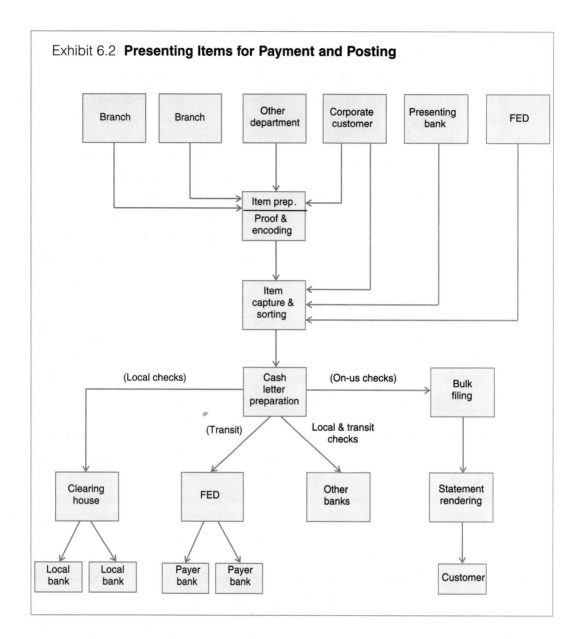

encoding. The exact manner in which the work is prepared depends on each bank. While there is no right or wrong way to prepare the work, some common standards are followed. Staples, paper clips, and rubber bands are removed. All items are set to face forward and right side up. Only the items that are to be captured are sent through the proof and encoding function. Cash, interoffice mail, and other items are separated. If the customer deposits cash, the teller substitutes the cash with a document usually called a cash-in ticket. The cash stays in the teller's drawer, and the cash-in ticket is put with the deposit ticket. If the customer receives cash back from a deposit, the teller uses a document typically referred to as a cash-out ticket to balance the deposit.

Some banks process checks first; others process deposits first. Again, there is no right or wrong way; the bank's capture system determines whether the debits or the credits are processed first. However, depending on the bank's chosen order, the preparation area ensures that the correct group of items—debits or credits—goes first. Otherwise, errors could occur and slow down the capture process. It is important for the work to be prepared before being sent for encoding since, once the automated process has started, any manual intervention slows it down.

Encoding Function

Encoding, commonly known as **magnetic ink character recognition (MICR),** made possible the automation that has revolutionized check processing in banks. Many functions that previously had to be performed visually and manually are now computerized. MICR made it possible for checks and other encoded documents to be read directly by high-speed reader/sorters.

The MICR line on a check is read by magnetic ink character recognition equipment to capture data such as the amount, account numbers, and check numbers. (Each numeral from 0 through 9 has been designed to contain a unique quantity of magnetized ink particles so that the machines that read the numerals cannot mistake one for another.) This information is stored for posting the transactions later.

The American Bankers Association (ABA), which participated in developing the encoding system, specified the placement of MICR information on all checks and required that all checks be within a specified size range (exhibit 6.3). A specific place is designated on the check for the **ABA Institution Identifier** (formerly the ABA transit number), the account number, the check number, the amount, and some other special designations. As the MICR

program gained acceptance throughout the banking system, the Federal Reserve issued a regulation stating that unencoded checks would not be treated as cash items. (Using the MICR system, banks also began supplying customers with deposit slips on which the account numbers were preencoded.) With these preencoded items, the chance for errors decreases significantly.

Every financial institution today uses its own system of assigning account numbers to customers. The system may indicate the type of account (business, personal, correspondent bank, or other) and the unit (department or branch) within the bank that handles the account. New checks issued to depositors contain the bank's identifying number (see the Item Capture section) and the customer's account number. They usually contain a sequential check number that is used by the bank in preparing statements, stopping payment on checks, and providing automated telephone inquiry services.

Whenever a customer asks the bank to provide a blank, unencoded check called a counter check, all the MICR information is encoded subsequently so that the item can be processed through automated equipment. Many banks have eliminated counter checks to reduce the risk of fraud.

Although the customer's account number, the check number, and the bank's identifying number are typically preprinted on the check, this information is encoded by the bank on some checks, deposits, and other items. Since

Exhibit 6.3 Placement of MICR Data on Checks

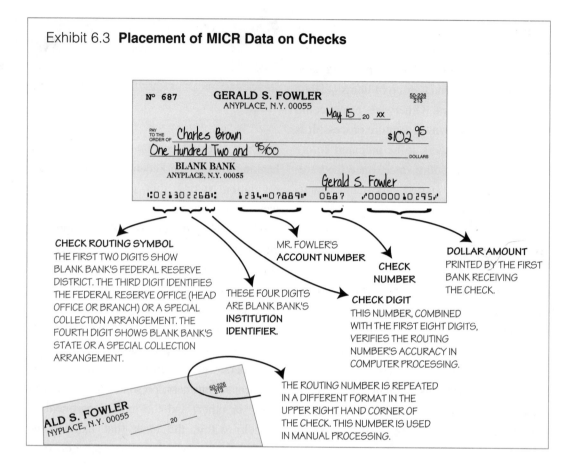

CHECK ROUTING SYMBOL
THE FIRST TWO DIGITS SHOW BLANK BANK'S FEDERAL RESERVE DISTRICT. THE THIRD DIGIT IDENTIFIES THE FEDERAL RESERVE OFFICE (HEAD OFFICE OR BRANCH) OR A SPECIAL COLLECTION ARRANGEMENT. THE FOURTH DIGIT SHOWS BLANK BANK'S STATE OR A SPECIAL COLLECTION ARRANGEMENT.

THESE FOUR DIGITS ARE BLANK BANK'S INSTITUTION IDENTIFIER.

MR. FOWLER'S ACCOUNT NUMBER

CHECK NUMBER

CHECK DIGIT
THIS NUMBER, COMBINED WITH THE FIRST EIGHT DIGITS, VERIFIES THE ROUTING NUMBER'S ACCURACY IN COMPUTER PROCESSING.

DOLLAR AMOUNT
PRINTED BY THE FIRST BANK RECEIVING THE CHECK.

THE ROUTING NUMBER IS REPEATED IN A DIFFERENT FORMAT IN THE UPPER RIGHT HAND CORNER OF THE CHECK. THIS NUMBER IS USED IN MANUAL PROCESSING.

---

the amount of the item cannot be preencoded except by a large corporate customer or a correspondent bank, the bank usually encodes the amount. The encoding machine not only encodes the amount of the check, but it also proves the deposits at the same time.

Proof Function

Tellers do not prove (balance) deposits when they are made by customers unless the bank uses an online posting system. The deposit is proved to ensure that the amount placed on the deposit ticket matches the amount of the items included in the deposit. The customer may have made a mathematical error, included an extra item, or listed an item that is not included with the deposit. The deposit is proved at

this point—the last time the deposit is balanced individually. After this proof function, the system is balanced on the basis of total debits and credits and not on the basis of individual transactions.

If the deposit does not balance, the proof operator either balances it or passes it on to another area in the proof department to perform this function. If an item is missing, the deposit usually is made for the entire amount as listed by the customer, and a debit adjustment is made to the account. If the deposit includes an unlisted item, the account is given a credit adjustment for the amount of the extra item. If the customer made an error in addition or subtraction, a debit or credit adjustment corrects the error.

Some commercial or governmental customers provide the bank with special instructions for correcting errors. They may ask that copies of the transactions be made and sent to the local office and that a copy go to the main office. Or they may instruct that correcting entries be made to an account other than the deposit account, or handled in another manner.

The items from the proof department are typically batched in groups of 250 to 300 items, or whatever number of items the bank considers manageable. If the work is out of balance or a bundle of work is dropped, the error can be found and corrected much more easily if all the work has been batched together.

Item Capture and Sorting

After items have been proofed and encoded, they are ready for true automated processing— that is, item capture and sorting. Every paper transaction, regardless of whether it is a deposit or a loan transaction, goes through the item capture process. Item capture is the process of gathering information about the items, such as the dollar amount of the items, whether the items are debits or credits, the accounts to which the transactions are to be posted, the types of applications (loans or deposits), the check numbers, the amount of float assigned to a deposit, and the number of items included in a deposit.

Once items are captured, they go through sorting for further processing or for presentation to the payer. On-us checks are sorted by statement cycles or account number; deposit slips, savings withdrawals, and club coupons are sorted; other internal documents are separated and sent to various places within the bank; and local and transit checks are presented to the drawee for payment.

Item Capture

Banks perform item capture in a number of ways, using various processing systems and pieces of equipment. Some smaller banks conduct the capture function on a multipocket proof machine that performs the proof and encoding function, the capture function, and the sorting function. Larger banks typically use single-pocket proof machines for proof and encoding, and perform the capture on high-speed document processors (referred to as reader/sorters) that process 2,500 items or more per minute.

As the items pass the reader head on the document processors, the machine reads the MICR line and "captures" the information on the item. If the bank runs credits first, the system knows that the debit items that are to follow are assigned to the credit. If the credit is a deposit to an account, the system captures the account number to which the deposit is to be made and the amount of the credit. The system also analyzes the debits being deposited and assigns the proper amount of float, if any, to the deposit on the basis of the checks. The float assignment is based on the bank ABA Institution Identifier on which the check is drawn.

A check drawn on another local bank is referred to as a **local clearing item**, and a check that is not a local item is referred to as a **transit item**. Typically, the bank captures only the amount and the routing ABA Institution Identifier of local clearing and transit items. The entire MICR line of an on-us item is captured. The system captures the account number, the amount of the check, and the sequential check number. This information is stored for processing later, when the debits and credits are posted to the accounts.

The system identifies the bank on which a check is drawn by the ABA Institution Identifier on the check. Before 1910, many larger banks in money market centers, serving networks of correspondent banks, had developed their own system to identify the drawees to whom they sent checks most frequently. Early in the twentieth century, however, the growth of the banking system and the increase in check volume created a need for a uniform, nationwide program of bank identification to expedite the process of sorting checks according to drawees.

The American Bankers Association resolved the check sorting problem by developing and implementing a national numerical system, identifying every commercial bank in the United States. In 1911 the ABA published the first Key to Routing Numbers Book (Key Book), a reference book listing the **national numerical system** number (also called the **ABA Institution Identifier**) assigned to every bank. It is the most frequently used reference work for identifying a bank or determining its geographic location. The Key Book is updated each year as new banks are formed and others go out of existence. It is available in electronic format. Now that thrift institutions commonly offer checking accounts and credit unions allow their customers to issue share drafts (the equivalent of checks), the Key Book also lists the ABA Institution Identifiers assigned to them.

> ABA Institution Identifier: a national numerical system, identifying every commercial bank in the United States
>
> Check routing symbol: identifies the Federal Reserve district facility to which the check can be sent for clearing

ABA Institution Identifier

The ABA plan specified that the ABA Institution Identifier for each institution would be shown in the upper right-hand corner of all checks drawn on it. This number always consists of two parts separated by a hyphen. The prefix numbers (preceding the hyphen) identify where the drawee is located—1 through 49 identify major cities, 50 through 99 identify states, and 101 identifies territories and dependencies (exhibit 6.4). The suffix (following the hyphen) identifies the individual financial institution in the city, state, or territory.

If a check has been mutilated in processing and the drawee's name is no longer legible, the Key Book immediately identifies the drawee through the ABA Institution Identifier. A check drawn on a small, rural bank can be identified as easily as a check drawn on a large bank in one of the nation's money market centers.

Check Routing Symbol

Until 1945 the ABA Institution Identifier was the only means of identifying banks, aside from their printed names on each check. However, as check usage continued to grow, it became apparent that an additional aid in sorting was needed. With the help of the Federal Reserve Committee on Check Collections, the American Bankers Association introduced the **check routing symbol (or Federal Reserve routing symbol)**. This symbol does not identify a particular bank; rather, it identifies the Federal Reserve district facility to which the check can be sent for clearing. It is used to determine the availability given by the Fed if the check was sent to it according to a specific timetable.

The ABA plan combined the ABA Institution Identifier and the check routing symbol in frac-

Exhibit 6.4 **Guide to ABA Institution Identifiers**

Prefix numbers
For guidance in use of the system, the following geographical division has been made:
Numbers 1 to 49 inclusive are city prefixes

1	New York, N.Y.	14	New Orleans, La.	26	Memphis, Tenn.	38	Savannah, Ga.
2	Chicago, Ill.	15	Washington, D.C.	27	Omaha, Neb.	39	Oklahoma City, Okla.
3	Philadelphia, Pa.	16	Los Angeles, Calif.	28	Spokane, Wash.	40	Wichita, Kan.
4	St. Louis, Mo.	17	Minneapolis, Minn.	29	Albany, N.Y.	41	Sioux City, Iowa
5	Boston, Mass.	18	Kansas City, Mo.	30	San Antonio, Tex.	42	Pueblo, Colo.
6	Cleveland, Ohio	19	Seattle, Wash.	31	Salt Lake City, Utah	43	Lincoln, Neb.
7	Baltimore, Md.	20	Indianapolis, Ind.	32	Dallas, Tex.	44	Topeka, Kan.
8	Pittsburgh, Pa.	21	Louisville, Ky.	33	Des Moines, Iowa	45	Dubuque, Iowa
9	Detroit, Mich.	22	St. Paul, Minn.	34	Tacoma, Wash.	46	Galveston, Tex.
10	Buffalo, N.Y.	23	Denver, Colo.	35	Houston, Tex.	47	Cedar Rapids, Iowa
11	San Francisco, Calif.	24	Portland, Ore.	36	St. Joseph, Mo.	48	Waco, Tex.
12	Milwaukee, Wis.	25	Columbus, Ohio	37	Ft. Worth, Tex.	49	Muskogee, Okla.
13	Cincinnati, Ohio						

Numbers 50 to 99 inclusive are state prefixes organized by region

	Prefix number(s)
Eastern States	50 to 58
Hawaii	59
Southeastern States	60 to 69
Central States	70 to 79
Southwestern States	80 to 88
Alaska	89
Western States	90 to 99

Eastern		**Southeastern**		**Central**		**Southwestern**		**Western**	
50	New York	60	Pennsylvania	70	Illinois	80	Missouri	90	California
51	Connecticut	61	Alabama	71	Indiana	81	Arkansas	91	Arizona
52	Maine	62	Delaware	72	Iowa	82	Colorado	92	Idaho
53	Massachusetts	63	Florida	73	Kentucky	83	Kansas	93	Montana
54	New Hampshire	64	Georgia	74	Michigan	84	Louisiana	94	Nevada
55	New Jersey	65	Maryland	75	Minnesota	85	Mississippi	95	New Mexico
56	Ohio	66	N. Carolina	76	Nebraska	86	Oklahoma	96	Oregon
57	Rhode Island	67	S. Carolina	77	North Dakota	87	Tennessee	97	Utah
58	Vermont	68	Virginia	78	South Dakota	88	Texas	98	Washington
		69	West Virginia	79	Wisconsin			99	Wyoming
59	Hawaii					89	Alaska		

Number 101 is the territory and dependency prefix

Within prefix number 101 the following suffix numbers are reserved for territories and dependencies

Puerto Rico	200 to 299
Mariana Islands, Midway Islands, Marshall Islands, and Wake Island	300 to 399
American Samoa	400 to 499
Guam	500 to 599
Virgin Islands	600 to 699
Caroline Islands	700 to 799
Canal Zone	800

tional form in the upper right-hand corner of each check. The check routing symbol is the lower portion (denominator) of the fraction; the upper portion (numerator) is the ABA Institution Identifier. The routing symbol consists of four digits that designate the Federal Reserve district and the Federal Reserve bank or branch that serves the drawee (exhibit 6.5)

The first two digits of the routing symbol identify the drawee's district, and the third digit represents the office of the Federal Reserve Bank that services that bank. The fourth digit formerly designated availability but no longer does so. The 06 in the routing number 0650 designates a check drawn on a bank in the 6th Federal Reserve district (Atlanta); the 5 indicates branch number 5 (New Orleans); and the 0 completes the four digit requirement.

Routing Symbol and ABA Institution Identifier in the MICR Line

The ABA Institution Identifier is included in the MICR line to enable the capture equipment to identify the bank on which the check is drawn. An additional digit has been added to the ABA Institution Identifier as a self-check digit that verifies the correct encoding of the information. The self-check digit is determined with a mathematical formula that uses the routing and ABA Institution Identifiers. For example, a check drawn on Union National Bank and Trust Company of Souderton, Pennsylvania, contains the routing transfer number 0319-1343-8. The digits 0319 identify the Federal Reserve district and branch, 1343 designates Union National Bank, and 8 is the self-check digit. If an error were made in encoding any one of the eight digits of the ABA Institution Identifier, the self-check digit would not be 8 and the error could be flagged.

The ABA Institution Identifier is also used to identify on-us checks. Many banks use the same area in the MICR line (called a field) where the ABA Institution Identifier is placed to identify internal documents such as savings documents, loan documents, and general ledger tickets.

Other Capture Functions

In addition to capturing the data, the document processor also sorts, films, endorses, applies a

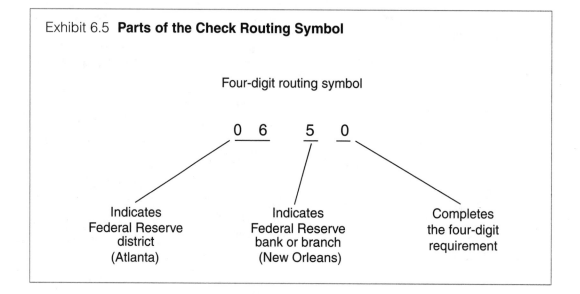

Exhibit 6.5 **Parts of the Check Routing Symbol**

Four-digit routing symbol

0 6   5   0

Indicates Federal Reserve district (Atlanta)

Indicates Federal Reserve bank or branch (New Orleans)

Completes the four-digit requirement

sequence number, and may even scan the items for imaging. Most document processors contain cameras that film the items during the capture process. This film becomes part of the bank's permanent records and is used for research and for producing copies of items when requested by customers, administrative summonses, and court subpoenas. As the items are being filmed, the document processor sprays a sequence number on the check. The same number is put on the film and is passed to the posting system. By referring to reports, and the bank statement, the bank can obtain the sequence number to locate the item on film. Without this number, the task of locating the item would be extremely difficult, if not impossible.

Sorting

In performing the sorting process, the bank is concerned about meeting certain deadlines and tries to keep the number of passes to a minimum. The initial pass (or run) of the items through the document sorter is referred to as the prime pass; the bank attempts to make a final disposition of the items on the prime pass. Sometimes, the bank may have to make additional passes to sort the items.

The document sorter has bins, or pockets, to which the items are sorted. Each pocket is numbered and is assigned to a certain type of item; the pocket also may be assigned by bank or location to which the checks will be sent for collection (the end point). For example, pocket 1 may be designated for on-us checks; pocket 2 may be for checks to be presented to the local clearing house; pockets 3, 4, and 5 may be for checks the bank will present directly; pockets 6 and 7 may be for transit checks to be presented to the Fed or correspondent banks; and so on.

The bank performs balancing procedures during the entire capture and sorting process. After all the items have been sorted, the bank makes a final disposition of them. The on-us items are kept by the bank and put aside for further processing. The local clearing and transit checks are prepared to be sent to their final destination. Each transit pocket or end point is totaled, and a cash letter is prepared. A cash letter—a listing of all of the checks being sent to an end point—acts as a deposit ticket. The checks and the cash letters are bundled together and are prepared for transportation to the designated end point. A batch header is also prepared to act as an offset entry to the checks. It is usually a credit, since the debits (checks) must equal the credits.

Float, the dollar value of checks in process for collection, is assigned to deposits during the capture and sorting process in a relatively complex process involving a number of steps. The bank knows in advance how long it will take to collect items, because the clearing agent—the Fed or correspondent bank offering check collection services—to which the checks will be sent for collection provides the bank with an availability schedule. An **availability schedule** is a listing of bank ABA Institution Identifiers, each of which (or group of which) is assigned a certain number of days' availability. From this availability schedule, the bank knows when the funds will be made available to the bank. The bank then creates its own availability schedule and assigns float to the deposit on the basis of that availability schedule. As the items are being captured and sorted, the system reads the ABA Institution Identifier on the check, sorts the check to the assigned pocket on the sorter, and assigns the float. For example, the customer deposits a check drawn on Depositors National

Bank, and the customer's bank has assigned two days' float to this item. During the sorting process, the sorter reads Depositors' ABA Institution Identifier, and on the basis of this number, the check processing system assigns two days' float to the deposit.

The document processor cannot read all items during the prime pass. Sometimes the information is not encoded in MICR, the check is mutilated, there is an error in the information or a defect in the magnetic ink, or a number is misread, to name a few reasons. Items that cannot be read are called rejects; they must be repaired and reentered in the system, often by placing the defective item inside a document carrier—an envelope with a transparent front that is encoded and processed.

Clearing Alternatives

Banks may choose from a number of methods, known as **clearing alternatives**, for presenting checks to drawees. The bank can clear the checks by sending them directly to the drawee, using a clearing house, or using the services of the Fed or a correspondent bank. Most banks find it necessary to use a combination of all these methods.

Banks consider a number of factors in determining the best clearing alternatives. The four major factors banks consider all relate to speed and cost. They are

- availability
- deadlines
- price
- transportation

Certain other factors may be considered, such as correspondent relationships and other services offered by the clearing agent, but these four are the major factors and are examined together. If availability were the only consider-

ation, for example, the bank would make direct presentment of all items, because the quickest way to obtain available funds for an item is to present the item directly to the drawee. If a bank in Florida had an item for $12.50 drawn on a bank in California, it could present the check directly to the drawee to obtain the funds immediately; but the transportation cost to present the item directly to the bank in California would far outweigh any potential benefit of receiving immediate funds. On the other hand, if the check were for $12.5 million, making a direct presentment of the item might be sensible.

To determine the clearing alternative and select a clearing agent, the bank analyzes all the items to be collected. The analysis includes determining the total dollar volume and number of items drawn on a particular bank and on banks in a particular Federal Reserve district or city.

Local Items

Selecting the clearing alternative is less complicated for items drawn on local banks and other financial institutions than for transit or non-local checks, because there are fewer choices. The checks can be presented directly to the local banks, to a correspondent bank, or to a clearing house.

Direct Presentment

Local checks can be easily presented directly to local banks by bank messenger or local courier. As always, speed and cost are considered together to determine whether this method of presentment is desirable in a particular case. One of the major considerations in local presentment is sorting capacity. The bank may not have the capacity to sort the items to prepare the individual cash letters, and the benefit derived from the local presentment may not offset the cost of increasing the bank's sorting capabilities.

Many banks that enter into local clearing arrangements do not charge a fee for items presented to one another; rather, they agree to swap items free of charge. The method of settlement for the local items could be by check, credit, or debit due to and due from bank accounts; by Fedwire; or by credit to a Fed or correspondent bank account.

Presentment through Correspondents

Correspondent banks offer a wide variety of services, of which check collection is the most traditional. A bank that maintains a correspondent account with a larger bank often relies on it to present and collect checks. Thrift institutions similarly use their commercial bank correspondents for this purpose.

In processing and collecting checks, correspondent banks simply accept the day's deposited items and treat them as they do all other deposits; that is, they credit the sending bank's account, sort the items, and present them to drawees. Exhibit 6.6 shows a basic check collection system.

Non-local or Transit Checks

Transit checks can be presented directly to the drawee, to a correspondent bank, to the Federal Reserve, or through a private check collection service. To justify this **direct sending** to a drawee and to offset the transportation cost, the bank must have substantial dollar volume of checks. One method of reducing the transportation expense, however, is for several banks in one location to combine

their cash letter sends and share in the transportation cost. Even when transportation cost is shared, it is often difficult to justify direct sends. Therefore, the bank must consider other options. The most prevalent methods for clearing transit items are through the Federal Reserve, through a correspondent bank, or through a combination of the two. A bank may decide to use the Fed's service for some end points and a correspondent for others.

Presentment through Correspondents

Presentment of transit items through a correspondent bank is similar to presentment of local items; however, a correspondent offering transit clearing typically offers more sophisticated service for transit items. Many times the services offered by a correspondent are similar to services offered through the Fed (see the next section, Presentment through the Federal Reserve). Correspondents sometimes offer better availability than the Fed or lower pricing for specific end points.

Payment for cash letter services can be made by a direct payment to the correspondent, or the fee may be offset by balances. The fee may be the same regardless of the method of payment, or the price may vary by method of payment depending on whether the correspondent is encouraging balances. When the fee is offset by balances, the correspondent bank can use these balances to make investments or loans. In addition to a per-item fee, some correspondents charge a cash letter fee for each cash letter presented.

The method of settlement varies from bank to bank; however, the most prevalent method is through due-to and due-from accounts. Payment could be made through the methods previously discussed.

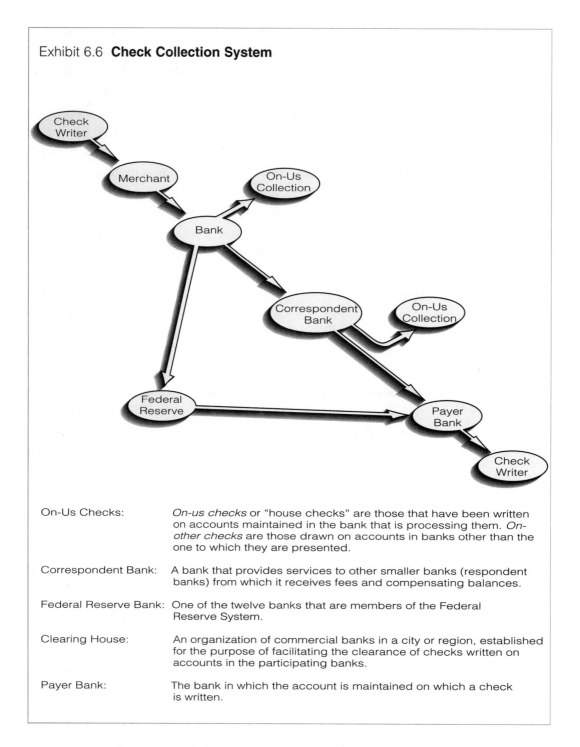

Exhibit 6.6 **Check Collection System**

On-Us Checks:	*On-us checks* or "house checks" are those that have been written on accounts maintained in the bank that is processing them. *On-other checks* are those drawn on accounts in banks other than the one to which they are presented.
Correspondent Bank:	A bank that provides services to other smaller banks (respondent banks) from which it receives fees and compensating balances.
Federal Reserve Bank:	One of the twelve banks that are members of the Federal Reserve System.
Clearing House:	An organization of commercial banks in a city or region, established for the purpose of facilitating the clearance of checks written on accounts in the participating banks.
Payer Bank:	The bank in which the account is maintained on which a check is written.

Presentment through the Federal Reserve

The Federal Reserve Act established the first nationwide system for collecting non-local checks. Each of the 12 Fed district banks serves as a center for check collection in its area so that non-local checks flow quickly and efficiently among the districts. Each Federal Reserve bank has branches within its district.

Some districts also have regional check processing centers (RCPCs) because of the geographic size of the district. Fed banks pay one another for the dollar amount of each day's processing through the Interdistrict Settlement Fund. This fund is maintained at the Federal Reserve headquarters in Washington, D.C., where the daily records of all processing are maintained.

A bank with a relatively small volume of non-local checks might present all of them through the Fed. To do so, the bank would forward unsorted work destined for any or all of the 12 districts to its local Fed branch. This program is referred to as the "mixed deposit program." Larger banks that have more volume and use the Fed's services typically sort local city items into cash letters and other Fed city items into one commingled cash letter.

Electronic Check Presentment

The Federal Reserve offers a service to banks whereby the Fed captures the MICR line of checks drawn on a bank and transmits the information to the paying bank. The paying bank then uses that file to post the checks to customers' accounts. At present, this process, called **electronic check presentment (ECP)**, is used mostly by smaller banks with low volumes. The disadvantage of using ECP is that these banks rely completely on the accuracy of the Fed; most do not have systems to check the electronic file against the actual checks. The Fed films the items, however, and supplies the bank with a copy on request.

ECP also is conducted on a local and national basis between banks. Some local banks have begun swapping electronic files, with the paper to follow, for local clearing items. On a national basis, a number of banks send electronic check files to one another, subject to certain rules and regulations. The electronic file is sent to the drawee and followed by the actual check; presentment is not considered made until the actual check is presented to the bank. Most of the banks involved in both local and nationwide ECP programs have installed or are installing sophisticated ECP systems to create, transmit, and post the electronic files. These systems create documentation to track transactions, match the electronic transaction to the actual check, and perform a number of other functions. One system even creates electronic return notifications to speed up the return notification process and reduce the risk of loss.

While the above system is in place for several banks throughout the country, the Fed continues to test new systems. One such ECP system captures and stores an electronic image of the check. Drawees can access a secured Federal Reserve website through the Internet to see images of the stored checks. Once they have these images, banks can decide whether to pay and post the check to the maker's account. This process facilitates payment decisions since checks are available as soon as they are received by the Federal Reserve through the depository bank. Ultimately, this could reduce float time by one day. Another example is a pilot project in Montana, in which banks use electronic pictures of checks so they do not have to physically move the checks from one location to another.

Summary

Banks receive checks over the counter to be paid or cashed, and they also receive checks in deposits and in payments made to the bank.

Some of these items are drawn on the bank, and some are presented to other paying banks. When a teller pays out cash on a check drawn on that bank, the teller is paying the check. Once the check is finally paid, the liability of all of the parties to the check is discharged; that is, the bank cannot return the check to any of the endorsers on the check after it is paid. For this reason, the teller must ensure that the check is properly payable and that the account on which the check is drawn has sufficient funds to pay the check. When a teller pays out cash on a check drawn on another bank, the teller is cashing the check. The risk in cashing a check is that the teller cannot determine whether the check is backed by sufficient funds, is drawn on an open account, has a valid signature, or is subject to a stop payment order, in which case the check may be dishonored by the paying bank.

The bank presents to the paying banks checks it cashes and receives. The checks are sent from the branch or other source of receipt to the proof and encoding area, where the checks are prepared for automated processing. The transactions are balanced, and the amount and other information are encoded in MICR on the checks, deposits, and other items. After the items are encoded they are sent to the item capture area, where the data on the MICR line are captured and used for posting the transactions. The checks that will be sent to other banks for payment are bundled into cash letters and presented to the paying banks. These checks are presented either directly to the paying banks or indirectly through a correspondent bank or the Federal Reserve.

In determining its clearing alternatives, the bank weighs availability, deadlines, price, and transportation. These factors are considered together to obtain the optimum clearing strategy.

Many banks are taking advantage of new technology and are presenting checks electronically to the paying bank. After the checks are presented, the paying bank settles with the presenting bank. Settlement may be made in a number of ways, including debit and credit to accounts, check, wire, or settlement through Federal Reserve or correspondent bank accounts.

Review and Discussion Questions

1. Describe the difference between paying a check and cashing a check.

2. What tests must a check pass to be properly payable?

3. What functions are typically performed in the item preparation, encoding, and proof functions and what are their purposes?

4. Describe the item capture and sorting process, including the information that is typically captured.

5. What is electronic check presentment?

Additional Resources

ABA Key to Routing Numbers (electronic or print versions). Thomson Financial Publishing.

Fedpoints 8 (Float) and *31 (ACHs)*. New York: Federal Reserve Bank of New York.

"If You Pay by Check," Electronic Check Council, NACHA.

"If Your Check Bounces," Electronic Check Council, NACHA.

Law and Banking: Applications. Washington, D.C., American Bankers Association, 2000.

Law and Banking: Principles. Washington, D.C., American Bankers Association, 2000.

Web Resources

Check Resources from the Federal Reserve
  Bank of New York
    www.ny.frb.org/bankinfo/
Consumer's Guide to Direct Deposit
    www.stls.frb.org/banking/epaymnts
Electronic Direct Payment
    www.ny.frb.org/bankinfo/payments/
    master2.htm#ecash
National Automated Clearing House Associ-
    ation www.nacha.org

7

DEPOSIT OPERATIONS AND LOSS PREVENTION ISSUES

Learning Objectives

After completing this chapter, you will be able to do the following:

- explain the process a bank must go through to post a check to an account, including examining rejects and preparing reports
- distinguish between in-filing and bulk filing
- explain various ways that banks prepare statements and return checks to customers, and define the customer's duty to examine these statements
- explain the return item process and the impact of Regulation CC
- discuss controls and security measures that protect the bank and tellers from losses due to fraud
- describe fraud schemes perpetrated on customers, such as identity theft and bank examiner schemes
- define the bolded terms that appear the text

Introduction

Checks move through the banking system as the amounts are added to one account and subtracted from another. Checks in the payment process are a target for thieves, as are the tellers and other frontline personnel as well.

The following situations demonstrate some facets of the payment process and one of the hazards that tellers face.

Situation 1

A grandmother mails a birthday check to her granddaughter 300 miles away. Since she has sufficient funds in her account, the grandmother assumes that her granddaughter will be able to cash this check and further assumes that the amount will be subtracted from her own account. What happens to the check as it moves through the system that gives the grandmother such confidence?

Situation 2

Donna receives a statement from her bank every month. She throws it in the desk drawer without looking at it. What risks is she taking? How could this affect her checking account? What would you advise Donna to do?

Situation 3

Toward the end of the day, an agitated customer approaches the teller window and hands the teller a note. The note advises the teller that this is a robbery and that the robber has a gun. The teller remains calm and agrees to comply with the demands in the note. While opening her cash drawer, the teller secretly sets off a silent alarm, all the while studying the face of the robber. How has the teller's training prepared her for acting appropriately in this situation?

Situation 4

A teller closes out his cash drawer at the end of the day. Because it was payday at three local companies, it has been particularly busy. He has had to go to the vault four times for additional currency and has processed many split deposits, where customers deposit part of their paychecks and receive money for the rest. On the first attempt, his drawer does not balance. Knowing that a courier will be there in 15 minutes to take his items for processing, he begins again, trying to detect his error. What controls does the bank have in place to help tellers reduce the chance for error?

Every one of the 100 million checks that flow through the check collection system daily must be processed (in some cases, still manually processed) and each special circumstance handled individually. Without the technological advances that have automated most of the processing of today's massive volumes of checks, the task would be almost impossible. It appears that the checkless society will not come about in the near future, because customers like checks and are not willing to give them up completely. Therefore the banking industry must continue to look for better, faster, and cheaper ways to handle checks.

The current method of processing checks, transferring the transactions around the country and returning the checks to the customer, is undergoing a tremendous change from paper-based to electronic processing. Many banks are experimenting with electronic processing in combination with paper, and many more will follow their lead in the years to come. For now, however, most U.S. checks are processed through the existing paper-based systems. This chapter discusses those systems in relation to paying checks received from the check clearing system. The chapter also discusses the security challenges banks face in keeping their customers, employers, and funds safe from criminals.

Receipt by the Paying Bank

Checks are received by a paying bank in a number of ways. Chapter 6 addressed checks received over the counter (at the teller window). This chapter addresses receipt of items directly from other banks, through the local clearing house, and from the Fed (in-clearing). Regardless of how checks are received, the bank must follow basically the same procedures.

In-clearing Capture

When a bank or the Fed presents cash letters (chapter 6) to the paying bank, the paying bank must prepare the items for capture, capture the data on the checks, and settle for the items. In-clearing capture procedures are similar to over-the-counter capture procedures with one main difference. Since the items presented by the Fed and other banks are all checks drawn on the paying bank, the entire MICR line must be captured on these items. If any of the MICR characters cannot be read by the document sorter, the items are rejected and the error must be corrected to ensure that the data are entered properly in the posting system. The items do not have to go through the encoding function, because encoding was done by the depositary bank

where the items were originally deposited or cashed.

In addition to capturing the data on the checks, the bank films the items and assigns sequence numbers, which are also put on the film and passed to the posting system. This sequence number is used by the bank to locate items on the film.

The Fed presents items to the paying bank, or has them available for pickup by the paying bank, throughout the day until 2:00 p.m. (the deadline established in the Uniform Commercial Code). Correspondent and other banks make direct presentment at some time in the morning. Some banks have accelerated this process; instead of presenting the items in the morning, they make a late evening exchange.

Posting

Posting is the process of adding deposits to an account balance and subtracting checks and other withdrawals from that balance. The grandmother in situation 1 has no doubt that the check she sent as a present will result in cash for her granddaughter and a debit from her own account. But a great deal of activity is necessary for that to happen. Data from the capture runs (including items presented over the counter and from in-clearings) are stored throughout the day. At the end of the day, when the bank has completed all of its capture runs, the transactions are posted to the accounts. Deposits and other credits are usually posted first, and then the debits are posted. The entire MICR line is read on on-us checks, and all of this information—the account number, the amount, the check number, and the sequence number—is passed to the posting system. The account number is used to post the check to the proper account, and the amount must be present for the account to be charged. The check number is also used in posting, to identify which checks have been paid on the account. Most banks provide this information on the customer's bank statement, indicating the date the check was paid, the amount, the check number, and the routing-transit number to help identify the transaction should it need to be traced.

Before checks are posted to the account, a number of other functions are performed internally by the bank's system, which must determine if the account has sufficient funds to pay the check. If it does not, the system may either reject or pay the check. Some banks post all checks, causing an **overdraft,** and later reverse those checks the bank decides not to pay; other banks reject all checks and reenter the ones they wish to pay; still others assign overdraft limits to the account, post the check if it is within the limit, and reject the check if it exceeds the limit. The system also may check the collected balance and the available balance. Some banks pay checks on the basis of the collected balance in the account, not on the basis of the ledger balance.

The bank also determines whether the customer has issued a stop payment on a check and whether a hold has been placed on the account. Most systems identify checks on which payment has been stopped by the check's amount and account number. If the check being presented has a stop payment order, the system rejects it. If a hold has been placed on the account for some reason, all the checks are rejected until reviewed by the bank.

After the items that will not be posted have been identified, the posting process can be completed, and the balance in the accounts can be updated. The order in which banks post the debits to accounts varies. Some banks may choose to post small debits first; some to post large debits first; and others to post debits randomly as they are presented. Banks also may post debits based on the risk a bank takes. For instance, a bank might post over-the-counter items first so that checks cashed by tellers will be paid before checks coming from outside the bank. Electronic items are usually posted before checks coming from outside the bank. The bank then sorts the items by category. First, the items that will not be posted are separated from those that will be. Items that will not be posted are sent to a department (often called the exception processing department) for further processing. Items that will be posted must be sorted by statement cycle or fine-sorted by account number. If the bank bulk-files checks (see the Document Examination and Filing section), the checks are sorted by statement cycle. If items are not bulk-filed, they are fine-sorted by account number.

Posting Rejects

Posting rejects, or nonprocessed items, are items that have been rejected during processing because of insufficient funds, stop payments, or holds. These items require special handling. They must be reviewed by the bank, which has to decide which checks it will pay and which checks it will return.

Insufficient Funds

The decision to pay or return checks has been automated by many banks. Some banks do, however, still make this decision manually. With an automated system, each bank officer is assigned certain accounts. If an account balance is not sufficient to pay a check, the customer's entire account relationship assigned to that officer is pulled up on a screen or computer terminal. This gives the bank officer an overview of the entire relationship and helps the officer decide which items to pay and which items to return. In a manual system the insufficient funds checks are listed in a journal, and a bank employee manually reviews the list and makes the decision.

Regardless of how the decision is made, the checks that will be paid are posted to the account, and the checks to be returned (see the Return Items sections) are processed and sent back to the previous endorser.

Stop Payment Checks

Checks that are rejected because of a stop payment are examined to determine whether the check matches the stop payment order description. This examination process varies from bank to bank. When a stop payment is placed, the customer usually provides the bank with a complete description of the check, including amount, number, date, and payee. When examining the check, the bank compares the information contained in the stop payment notice to the information on the check. If the rejected check is the stop payment check, it is sent to the return item section for return to the previous endorser.

Holds

Banks place holds on customers' accounts for a number of reasons. The bank may suspect the customer of check kiting (described later in the chapter) and may want to examine the checks being presented; the bank may want to examine the signature on every check that is presented on a particular account; or the bank

may have received a court order freezing the funds in the account. Whatever the reason, the checks drawn on the account on which the hold is placed must be initially rejected, then examined, and then either paid or returned.

If the bank places a hold on an account with the intention of not honoring checks drawn on specific deposits, the bank must meet the requirements of Regulation CC. While banks may place a case-by-case hold on deposited local checks for two days, and non-local checks for five days, many have an availability policy that allows customers to have next-day availability with a case-by-case hold (chapter 4). With such a policy, banks must notify the depositors when the funds are going to be held longer. Regulation CC allows a bank to extend a hold on an account for certain reasons called exceptions (7 days for local checks and 11 days for non-local checks). If the bank invokes one of the exception holds as provided by Regulation CC, the bank must notify the depositor in writing. The notice must include the amount of the deposit held, the customer's account number, the date when the funds will be made available, and certain other information (refer to exhibit 4.9).

A bank may invoke an exception for the following reasons:

- The deposited check was previously returned.
- The customer has repeatedly overdrawn the account within the previous six months.
- The checks deposited for the day exceed $5,000.
- An emergency has occurred, such as computer or communications failure.
- The bank has reason to doubt that the item being deposited by the customer will be paid by the paying bank.

Depending on the type of item being deposited, the bank can extend the availability of the item for one to six days. If the bank invokes the hold because it doubts the collectibility of the item, the bank may choose to use a "reasonable cause" hold notice (refer to exhibit 4.10).

Reports

The more extensive and sophisticated the bank's computer system, the greater its ability to supply customized reports useful for many purposes. Many systems have online capabilities to provide information to tellers and other departments. In addition to online inquiries, banks also produce a number of daily paper and microfiche reports. The most commonly produced reports for deposit accounts are the following:

- trial balance, showing all debits and credits posted on the previous business day and the closing account balance for each depositor
- lists of all drawings against insufficient or uncollected funds
- reports on all opened and closed accounts that have shown large increases or decreases in balances
- stop payment and hold reports
- reports of posting rejects
- lists of dormant accounts

These reports and listings are used by all areas of the bank for various reasons. The trial balance report, for example, may be used to determine the balance on an account or to determine whether an item has been paid. The dormant account report is used to identify accounts that have been classified as dormant (inactive) but have had some type of transaction posted to the account; in such a case the bank may want to examine the transaction to ensure that it was proper.

Document Examination and Filing

Before the posting process was automated, banks manually posted checks to accounts. Checks did not bear account numbers; the bank clerk had to locate the account by the customer's name and compare the signature on the check against the signature on file. Clerks also examined checks for other points of negotiability and to ensure that they were properly payable. Checks were examined for postdates, stale dates, alterations, endorsements, and any other defects that would affect payment.

As the volume of check transactions grew, posting checks to accounts by customer name became too difficult, and banks began assigning account numbers to customers to speed up the posting process. The process was still manual, but now the customers' ledgers were filed in account number sequence. As long as volumes were manageable, banks continued to examine each check and to verify signatures. As the posting process was automated, banks continued the tradition of examining each check, even though the actual debiting of the account was done by computer. Customers' signature cards were put in files in account number sequence, and each check was examined for proper signature, date, and other details. This method of filing is referred to as in-filing. As check volumes continued to grow, in-filing checks and examining signatures became too difficult. With advances in technology, the concept of bulk filing was introduced. **Bulk filing** is a method of filing checks in bundles that are sorted by statement cycle. Only selected checks are examined under the bulk filing method.

Laws governing payment of checks were based on the manual system of paying and filing checks. When all banks in-filed checks and examined each check, this became the reasonable commercial standard in the industry. Article 4 of the UCC, governing the relationship between the bank and its customer, required a bank to exercise "ordinary care"; that is, the bank had to exercise the industry's reasonable commercial standards. If a dispute arose between the customer and a bank over a forged signature, the bank had to prove that it had exercised ordinary care. Even with the introduction of bulk filing, although banks stopped examining every signature, the courts continued to apply the stricter standard of examination.

Today most U.S. banks bulk-file checks, and many establish a dollar limit for the examination of signatures; that is, only checks above a certain dollar amount are examined. The limit for examination varies from $2,500 to $100,000, depending on the bank. Some banks also randomly check signatures, regardless of the amount. Reviewing the signature on every check would be very costly for banks. Since such a small percentage of checks going through the system are actually "bad," banks have determined that it is less costly to write off these losses than to try to prevent them through signature verification. Each bank decides the level of loss it is willing to take and establishes its check examination policies based on that risk. The current version of Article 3 of the UCC defines "ordinary care" in a way that should benefit banks. It gives them the flexibility to apply standards of business common in their area and does not require them to examine checks unless the individual bank policy specifically directs them to.

This definition shifts the law away from signature verification, as long as the actions of the bank are reasonable in comparison with its own procedures and the procedures of other banks.

The way a bank sorts checks depends on whether the bank in-files or bulk-files checks. Some banks bulk-file individual accounts and in-file commercial accounts because commercial account holders will often request that checks be returned to them.

In-filing

In-filing is a method of filing checks in account number order. Checks must be sorted in account number sequence daily, then filed manually in account number sequence. The process is labor-intensive, and the costs of in-filing are substantial.

Each account is assigned a statement cycle indicating when the statement will be prepared and mailed to the customer. At statement-rendering time, the checks must be pulled from the files, counted, and verified against the statements to ensure the customer receives all the checks due, and that there are no extras. Then the checks are inserted with the statements and mailed to the account holder.

Bulk Filing

Bulk filing takes advantage of technology and substantially reduces a bank's processing cost. In a bulk file environment, the checks are sorted daily in bundles by statement cycle and filed. If the bank examines the signatures, dates, or other details of any of the checks, they are sorted separately into account number sequence. Some banks have automated the signature verification function and use either film-based or image-based signature verification. Even with these systems, an employee is required to compare the signature on the check to the signature on the signature card.

At statement-rendering time, the checks are sorted into account number sequence, and dividers are inserted to separate the accounts. The checks are then taken to the statement preparation area, where the statements are processed manually or are rendered on automated statement-rendering equipment. Exhibit 7.1 demonstrates this process.

Statements

Each checking account is assigned a statement cycle when the account is opened, designating the date on which a statement is automatically produced by the bank's computer system. The cycles, mostly for personal accounts, are established by the bank so that statements are evenly distributed throughout the month to prevent peaks and valleys in the bank's workload. Commercial accounts are usually cycled on the last day of the month unless the customer has requested a different cycle. Some commercial customers request statements weekly or even daily, though the majority of these customers will use an electronic means. Savings statements normally are rendered quarterly unless the account has electronic funds transfers (EFTs), in which case Regulation E requires that the statements be rendered monthly.

Return of Checks

Banks render statements in a number of ways. Some customers receive checks. Some do not, in a process called truncation or check safekeeping (see the Check Truncation and Check Safekeeping section). Most banks do not return deposit tickets or savings withdrawal slips with the bank statement.

The typical statement-rendering process at most banks works as follows: the statements are printed in account number sequence, and the checks are sorted into account number sequence. In an automated process, a bar code is printed on the statement, indicating the number of debit items that accompany the bank statement. Then the checks are counted by the equipment, and if the number matches the number on the bank statement, the machine seals the envelope and puts postage on it. The statements are then ready to go to the post office. To take advantage of the presort discount, some banks use equipment to presort the statements by zip code before mailing. Other banks hire a third party to perform this function.

In a manual operation, the checks are counted by hand or with the aid of a document counter. The number of items is then compared with the number on the statement, and the statements are placed in an envelope and mailed. This process is very labor-intensive.

Check Truncation and Check Safekeeping

Check truncation, or check safekeeping, means the bank keeps the checks and stores them for the customer. The bank prints the date the check was paid, the amount of the check, and the check number on the bank statement. Customers who do not get their checks returned may use and retain duplicate checks. The customer can get a copy of the check from the bank upon request. Some banks charge a reduced service fee for this type of account, because postage and handling costs are lower for the bank.

Exhibit 7.1 **Bulk Filing Statements**

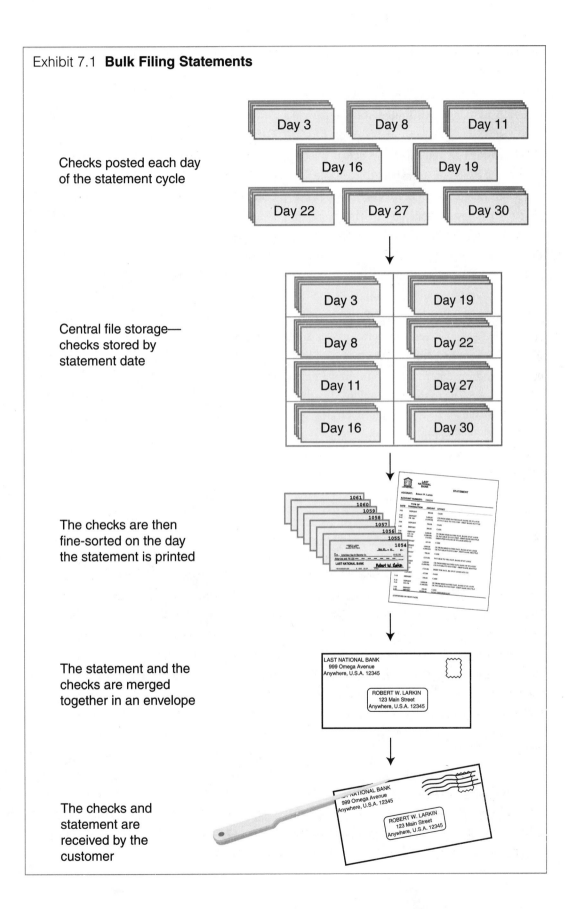

Checks posted each day of the statement cycle

Central file storage— checks stored by statement date

The checks are then fine-sorted on the day the statement is printed

The statement and the checks are merged together in an envelope

The checks and statement are received by the customer

Image Statements

Image statements are receiving considerable attention by banks. An **image statement** is a statement that contains an image of each paid check. Instead of returning the actual check, the bank uses an image scanner to scan checks, and small images of 15 or 18 checks are printed on regular statement paper. This paper is much easier to store than the actual checks. Image statements may reduce some postage and handling expense, but the initial investment in the image scanning equipment and the image software is substantial. Banks experience other savings in reduced sorter passes and faster statement preparation. As the cost of this equipment drops, more banks will offer image statement services to their customers.

Some banks are using the Internet for image technology. By clicking on a check's description line, customers can see an image of the check.

Combined Statements

In addition to checking account statements and savings account statements, some banks offer combined statements. A combined statement combines the information from a number of accounts into a single statement. Depending on the software capabilities of the bank, the statement may contain checking, savings, bank card, time deposits, and loan information. A combined statement may reduce postage expense for the bank and be more convenient for the customer.

Combined statements are for bank products and services only. Regulations prohibit these statements from containing information about investment accounts, annuities, money market mutual funds, and other non-traditional accounts. Account information on these other products is provided in separate statements to the customer.

Customer's Duty to Examine Statements

Customers have a duty to examine bank statements and related items with "reasonable promptness." Since the UCC does not define what constitutes "reasonable promptness," many banks are specifying a time frame (such as 30 days) in the account agreement. If a customer does not examine his or her statement within this time and only later finds a forged check in the statement, the customer may lose the ability to fully recover the funds. The revised Article 4 of the UCC lets the courts allocate responsibility for the loss on the basis of the negligence of the parties; that is, if both the bank and the customer are negligent, they share the loss.

For example, a doctor's secretary begins forging checks on the doctor's account in January and continues doing so until she is caught in October of the same year. The bank statement is rendered on the last day of each month, and the secretary was responsible for balancing the statement. If the doctor had examined his January 31 statement, discovered the forgeries, and reported them to the bank before March 2, the bank would have been liable for the loss. Instead, he is liable for all the loss from February 15 until the day in October when he discovered and reported the forgeries.

Remember Donna in situation 2 who does not check her statements when they arrive? Donna risks being unable to fully recover a loss to her account by not checking her statement within 30 days.

Dishonored Items

Very few checks that are issued are returned without being paid. However, banks spend a disproportionate amount of money on the return item process. Even with today's automation and technology, return items require much manual handling on the part of both the paying and the depositary banks. Many items are dishonored for reasons already discussed, such as stop payment orders, insufficient funds, and so forth. Others may be suspected of being fraudulent, as will be discussed later in this chapter.

There are two categories of **return items**: outgoing return items and incoming return items. Outgoing return items are checks, drafts, and other instruments returned by the paying bank. Incoming return items are checks, drafts, and other instruments that are received by the depositary bank to be charged back to depositors' accounts.

Outgoing Return Items

After the decision is made during the posting process to pay or return checks, checks to be returned must be prepared for their return trip to the depositary bank—the bank where the check was originally deposited. Congress, through the **Expedited Funds Availability Act (EFAA)**, mandated the Fed to reduce the return time in order to notify the customer about the return as quickly as possible. Regulation CC, which implements the EFAA, sets a timetable within which items must be returned. The regulation allows the bank to return an item directly to the depositary bank, or to the Fed or other central facility that acts as a **returning bank**.

The paying bank must also return the check by its midnight deadline. The midnight dead-line is defined in the UCC as midnight of the banking day following the banking day of receipt of the item. A paying bank must return a check in an "expeditious manner." A check is returned expeditiously if it meets one of two tests established by Regulation CC: the two-day, four-day test and the forward collection test. The two-day, four-day test establishes certain time frames in which checks must be returned—two days for a local check and four days for a non-local check. The forward collection test establishes the return time on the basis of how a similarly situated bank would handle the check for forward collection.

In preparation for return, the paying bank must indicate on the face of the check that the check is returned and the reason for return. Most banks stamp the reason for return on the front of the check, such as "insufficient funds" or "payment stopped." The paying bank must prepare a return cash letter and return the items. Return items are settled in the same manner as forward collection items.

Large-dollar Notification

Regulation CC requires the paying bank to notify the depositary bank of the return of all items in the amount of $2,500 or more by 4:00 p.m. local time on the second day following presentment of the item to the paying bank. For example, a paying bank that receives a check on Monday must give notice of dishonor to the depositary bank by 4:00 p.m. on Wednesday. The notice must contain the following:

- name and routing number of the paying bank
- name of the payee(s)
- amount
- date of the endorsement of the depositary bank

- account number of the customer(s) of the depositary bank
- branch name or number of the depositary bank from its endorsement
- trace number associated with the endorsement of the depositary bank
- reason for nonpayment

The bank is required to supply only information that can be obtained from the check. The notice may be given by any reasonable manner, including return of the item, written notice including a copy of the check, telephone, Fedwire, or telex. Return of the item meets the notification requirement if the check is received by the depositary bank by the notification deadline.

The depositary bank is required to send notice of return to its depositor by midnight of the banking day following the day of receipt of the notice.

Incoming Return Items

The depositary bank receives incoming return items from the Federal Reserve, from returning banks, from paying banks, and from its own deposit operations department. Regardless of the method of receipt, the bank must settle for the returns on the banking day of receipt. Upon receipt, the bank identifies the account to which the check was deposited or the other source of receipt. If the process is manual, the bank must examine the instrument and refer to tapes, reports, and film. If the process is automated, the bank can locate the account to which the item was deposited through the online system. Some banks are automated to the point that the return cash letter can be captured on the bank's high-speed sorting equipment. The capture system reads the MICR line and refers to a file called an "all

items file" that lists all the items handled by the bank on a specific day. From the all items file the system can determine the account to which the item was deposited.

After the bank has located the proper account or other source (the check may have been a loan payment or a teller-cashed item, for example), the item must be charged back to the account or the proper department. The way this is done varies from bank to bank, depending on whether the system is manual or automated. The item must then be sent back to the depositor along with a copy of the charge-back.

Some commercial customers give the bank special instructions to follow when items are returned. These instructions may include directions not to charge the items back to the account but instead to hold the returns at a branch, or to charge the checks to another account, or to send copies of the returns to the home office. Whatever the instructions, the bank must follow them if it agrees to perform the special instructions. Many banks charge a fee for return items and for special instructions.

Fraud Schemes and Security Issues

The very nature of banking provides swindlers, thieves, and confidence men and women with opportunities to apply their illegal practices. Criminals who seek to defraud banks often are highly skilled in developing new methods to deceive banks or to frustrate a bank's security measures. Of course, banks must contend with the threat of bank robbery. This most dangerous situation puts bank customers and personnel at risk, making the loss of funds far less important. But thieves do not always wear masks and carry guns. Greater losses to banks occur through various forms of check fraud. This type of crime can be perpetrated against tellers and customers.

Bank Robbery

When the famous bank robber Willie Sutton was asked why he so often chose banks as his target, he replied, "Because that's where the money is." In the annual crime statistics published by the Federal Bureau of Investigation, one of the most alarming figures is the annual increase in bank holdups. Despite all that banks have done to make robberies difficult to commit and unprofitable to the perpetrators, their frequency continues to grow. Bank robbery is automatically a federal offense.

Every banking facility potentially tempts the would-be robber. This temptation is compounded when the bank has not taken the proper measures to keep tellers' supplies of cash to a workable minimum or when proper security measures are lacking. Law enforcement authorities have repeatedly said that some banks virtually invite holdups by ignoring the essentials of internal security.

Even when banks rigorously control cash supplies, holdup attempts still occur with alarming regularity. Days when banks are known to have larger amounts of cash on hand—during the Christmas shopping season or on active payroll days, for example—are often targeted by robbers.

Although banks do have a basic responsibility to protect depositors' funds, tellers should not contemplate individual acts of heroism. Lives are often at stake during bank holdups because robbers can be irrational, desperate, and unpredictable. Tellers who try to use force or put up any show of resistance dur-

ing a holdup attempt risk not only their own personal safety, but the safety of others who happen to be on the premises at the time.

Most banks are legally required to equip their premises with cameras and holdup alarms. In addition, many have installed bulletproof plastic shields in front of each teller's station. Some banks limit access to the lobby, requiring customers to show identification before they are allowed in the bank. Nevertheless, no type of security system can be more effective than the actions the teller, as the first line of defense, takes during a holdup. Teller training programs normally emphasize that physical resistance is unwise and that tellers should take positive action. Tellers, however, can help the authorities apprehend criminals by following certain basic procedures.

For example, tellers should make every effort to remain calm during a holdup attempt and to take note of the bandit's physical characteristics. Exhibit 7.2 provides a sample physical description form that is helpful in this respect.

Tellers can activate silent alarms by using a foot pedal or device in the cash drawer. Decoy or marked money can be handed over in the hope that it can be traced to the perpetrator. Some banks even prepare special bundles of money that contain an exploding device filled with a conspicuous dye. Anything given to the teller, such as a holdup note, should be kept so that fingerprints or other identifying evidence can be checked.

Exhibit 7.2 Physical Description Form

COLOR ___Caucasian___ SEX ___Male___ NATIONALITY ___European–North___ AGE __25–30__ HEIGHT __6'__ WEIGHT __170__

BUILD ___Husky – well-built___ COMPLEXION ___Light___ HAIR ___Blonde–wavy___ EYES ___Green–large___
     (THIN, STOCKY, ETC.)   (LIGHT, DARK, RUDDY, ETC.)   (COLOR, WAVY, STRAIGHT, LONG, SHORT, HOW COMBED, ETC.)   (COLOR, SMALL, LARGE, ETC.)

NOSE ___Medium___ EARS ___Medium___ GLASSES ___None___ MUSTACHE OR BEARD ___Small mustache___
     (LARGE, SMALL, BROAD, PUG, ETC.)   (PROMINENT, SMALL, ETC.)   (DESCRIBE FRAMES)   (COLOR, SHAPE, ETC.)

MASK OR FALSE FACE ___None___ SCARS OR MARKS ___Small mole on left cheek___
     (TYPE, COLOR, ETC.)   (TATTOOS, BIRTHMARKS, FACIAL BLEMISHES, ETC.)

DISTINGUISHING CHARACTERISTICS ___Confident mannerisms; well-dressed; professional___
     (HOW WOULD YOU PICK THIS PERSON OUT OF A CROWD?)

CLOTHING

HAT ___None___

OVERCOAT ___None___

RAINCOAT ___None___

JACKET ___Blue blazer___

SUIT ___None___

TROUSERS ___Black___

SHIRT ___Light blue___

TIE ___None – open collar___

SHOES ___Black___

OTHER CLOTHING ___None___

MISCELLANEOUS

WEAPON EXHIBITED ___Saturday Night Special___
     (REVOLVER, AUTOMATIC, KNIFE, ETC.)
___chrome color___

SPEECH ___Educated; clear – very precise___
___in directions___

ANY NAMES USED ___None___

MANNERISMS ___Left handed; chewing on___
     (RIGHT OR LEFT HANDED, UNUSUAL WALK OR CARRIAGE,
___toothpick___
     NERVOUS HABIT, ETC.)

PROMPTLY FILL OUT THIS FORM AS ACCURATELY AND AS COMPLETELY AS POSSIBLE AND GIVE IT TO BRANCH MANAGER.

Because every holdup is a traumatic experience for the bank personnel involved, thorough training in the recommended procedures to be followed is absolutely necessary. The importance of remaining calm cannot be overemphasized. Instances in which a teller's simple, calm approach completely frustrated a holdup attempt are numerous.

In one incident, a person who had staged a holdup earlier in the day returned to the same teller in the same bank for a second attempt. Law enforcement officials happened to be questioning the teller when the robber made his second appearance. She was able, calmly and quietly, to point him out, and he was captured at once. The teller in situation 3 is behaving prop-erly during the robbery by remaining calm, complying with the robber's demands, and following bank procedures regarding setting off the alarm when it is safe to do so. She will likely reduce the risk that anyone will be harmed, and will be very helpful to the subsequent investigation.

Exhibit 7.3 is a list of procedures to follow during and after a robbery, from the Mace Anti Crime Bureau.*

Teller Fraud Issues

Besides being the mostly likely target of bank robbers, tellers are also targets for fraud.

---

*Permission to use portions of "Robbery—Know What to Do," ©1997 Mace Anti Crime Bureau, granted by MACB, division of Mace Security International, Inc.

Exhibit 7.3   Know Exactly What to Do in a Robbery

1. Keep cool. Obviously, this is easier said than done. Three factors may help.
    a.   Knowing what to do eliminates the need for making decisions in a crisis environment.
    b.   Most robbers are as nervous as their victim. They want to leave as quickly as possible.
    c.   Most robberies take less than 90 seconds. Keep your cool for two minutes or less and the danger will usually pass.
2. Handle the note carefully. A note may have fingerprints and is primary evidence in a court trial. A robber will usually forget the note if it is placed out of sight. Of course, notes are not always used, but they are becoming more common.
3. Obey instructions. Employees should be assured that this is bank policy and that following a few simple procedures during a robbery is all that is expected of them.
4. Activate silent alarm. Money clips permit tellers to activate a silent alarm without arousing a robber's suspicions. Any unnatural movement, such as reaching under the counter for a pull switch, may invite retaliation and should not be attempted while the robber is present.
5. Get a good look at the robber. Tellers should be especially attentive to identification details. See the Physical Description Form (exhibit 7.2) for items and characteristics that should be noticed if possible.
6. Activate another alarm. After the robber has gone, it's a good idea to pull another alarm just to make sure the police are notified. Seldom-used electrical devices don't always work.
7. Notify supervisor. There have been cases when tellers have simply stood at their stations in shock after experiencing a robbery. During that time witnesses may have left and other customers may have smeared fingerprints or destroyed other evidence.
8. Protect fingerprints. Bank robbers generally do not wear gloves and smooth countertops are ideal for taking fingerprints.
9. Write down description. Although holdup cameras may have photographed the robbery, it will take several hours to develop the film. An immediate description is important. Use the Physical Description Form in exhibit 7.2. Because memory fades rapidly, this should be done as soon after the robbery as possible.

The teller window is one of the first ports of entry for the payments function. As such, tellers have the responsibility to the customer and the bank of recognizing and preventing fraud whenever possible. To aid tellers, banks have numerous controls to limit customer and employee fraud.

Balance and Controls

A teller's principal function is to collect and pay out coin and currency. During these transactions, many opportunities for error occur. Banks use a series of controls to limit loss due to error as well as to theft. Tellers are required to keep strict account of all the cash in their cash drawers. They have a fixed amount of cash at the beginning of the day. This amount varies by bank, depending on security policies and anticipated cash needs, and by teller, depending on level of experience. If a teller needs more cash during the day, he or she may get this from a working supply in the bank vault.

Periodically throughout the day, and certainly at its end, the tellers' work must be balanced. Many tellers want to hold on to all this work until they are absolutely certain they balance. Unfortunately, this is not always possible. Courier pickups are scheduled by the item processing area to ensure the most efficient use of equipment and personnel, and to eliminate or reduce float.

Requiring tellers to balance regularly is part of a system of controls banks implement to reduce the incidence of errors and theft. At the end of the day, vault cash is balanced separately and in combination with the teller's cash. Situation 4, involving the teller whose drawer does not balance at day's end, is a common occurrence for tellers; balancing is made easier by these bank controls.

Common Schemes

Split Deposit Fraud: A **split deposit** is a transaction in which the bank customer wishes to have part of a check credited to an account and the remainder paid out in cash. It is one of the most common types of transactions but one that is frequently used to illegally obtain funds.

Charge-back Check Fraud: In charge-back check fraud (sometimes called returned deposited item fraud), a customer deposits worthless checks drawn on an account at another institution and withdraws the funds before the checks are returned unpaid, creating an overdraft. Another variation of this scheme is for the customer to ask the teller to cash a check drawn on an account at another financial institution, using existing funds in his or her own account as back-up to cash the check. However, the customer withdraws the funds from the account before the check is returned unpaid. This causes an overdraft. This type of fraud can occur in legitimate accounts or in accounts opened solely for fraudulent reasons.

Counterfeit Checks: To create **counterfeit checks**, a legitimate check is scanned into a computer. Then, the payee's name, dollar amount, check serial number, and date are changed but the authorized signature remains as it appeared on the original check. The new counterfeit check is then printed and brought to the teller who sees the legitimate signature and cashes the check. Later, after the criminal leaves, the check is discovered to be fraudulent. The availability of low-cost, high-quality computers, scanners, and printers, along with desktop software programs, has made this crime far more common.

Money Laundering: Although this scheme does not involve a financial loss, criminals see banks and other financial institutions as logical targets for moving illegally gained money through the system. A former director with the International Monetary Fund estimates that at least $600 billion a year is laundered worldwide. Once large sums of cash, most commonly from drug dealing and racketeering, are deposited, they become difficult to trace. This is called **money laundering** because the criminals are attempting to make the money "clean." In an effort to stem the flow of illegal cash through the banking system, the **Bank Secrecy Act** was enacted. This act places strict reporting requirements on banks for deposits or withdrawals exceeding $10,000 in coin and currency. Money orders and cashier's checks for $3,000 or more must also be recorded. Exhibit 7.4 is the IRS 4789 Report Form, which banks are required to file for these transactions under the Bank Secrecy Act.

Other Schemes: Some common fraud schemes perpetrated at the teller window include the following:

- The criminal may forge a bank officer's initials on the back of a check to indicate that it has been approved for cashing when it has not been approved. The teller who does not verify this, or the bank that does not use a

Exhibit 7.4 **Currency Transaction Report**

Form **4789** (Rev. June 1998) Department of the Treasury Internal Revenue Service	**Currency Transaction Report** ▶ Use this 1998 revision effective June 1, 1998. ▶ For Paperwork Reduction Act Notice, see page 3. ▶ Please type or print. *(Complete all parts that apply–See instructions)*	OMB No. 1506-0004

1 Check all box(es) that apply:

a ☐ Amends prior report   **b** ☐ Multiple persons **c**   ☐ Multiple transactions

Part I	**Person(s) Involved in Transaction(s)**

Section A–Person(s) on Whose Behalf Transaction(s) Is Conducted

2 Individual's last name or Organization's name ABC Corporation	**3** First name	**4** M.I.

5 Doing business as (DBA)	**6** SSN or EIN 1:3:3:4:5:6:7:8:9

7 Address (number, street, and apt. or suite no.) 32 Maple Street	**8** Date of birth M M D D Y Y Y Y

9 City Portsmouth	**10** State R I	**11** ZIP code 02871	**12** Country (if not U.S.)	**13** Occupation, profession, or business

14 If an individual, describe method used to verify identity:

a ☐ Driver's license/State I.D.   **b** ☐ Passport   **c** ☐ Alien registration   **d** ☐ Other ....

e Issued by: **f** Number:

Section B–Individual(s) Conducting Transaction(s) (if other than above).
If Section B is left blank or incomplete, check the box(es) below to indicate the reason(s):

a ☐ Armored Car Service   **b** ☐ Mail Deposit or Shipment   **c** ☐ Night Deposit or Automated Teller Machine (ATM)

d ☐ Multiple Transactions   **e** ☐ Conducted On Own Behalf

15 Individual's last name Smith	**16** First name Susan	**17** M.I. E

18 Address (number, street, and apt. or suite no.) 456 Cherry Street	**19** SSN 1:2:3 4:5:6 7:8:9

20 City Portsmouth	**21** State R I	**22** ZIP code 02871	**23** Country (if not U.S.)	**24** Date of birth M M D D Y Y Y Y 0:3 2:5 1:9:6:5

25 If an individual, describe method used to verify identity:

a ☒ Driver's license/State I.D.   **b** ☐ Passport   **c** ☐ Alien registration   **d** ☐ Other ....

e Issued by: State of RI   **f** Number: 9876543

Part II	**Amount and Type of Transaction(s). Check all boxes that apply.**

26 Cash In $ $12,000 .00	**27** Cash Out $ _____ .00	**28** Date of Transaction M M D D Y Y Y Y 0:2 0:2 2:0:0:1

29 ☐ Foreign Currency _____ (Country)   **30** ☐ Wire Transfer(s)   **31** ☐ Negotiable Instrument(s) Purchased

32 ☐ Negotiable Instrument(s) Cashed   **33** ☐ Currency Exchange(s)   **34** ☐ Deposit(s)/Withdrawal(s)

35 ☐ Account Number(s) Affected (if any):
98-6784321   **36** ☐ Other (specify)

Part III	**Financial Institution Where Transaction(s) Takes Place**

37 Name of financial institution XYZ State Bank	Enter Federal Regulator or BSA Examiner code number from the instructions here. ▶ [ ]

38 Address (number, street, and apt. or suite no.) 123 East Main Street	**39** SSN or EIN 1:2:3:4:5:6:7:8:9

40 City Portsmouth	**41** State R I	**42** ZIP code 02871	**43** MICR No. 0350-1513-7

Sign Here ▶	**44** Title of approving official Branch Manager	**45** Signature of approving official	**46** Date of signature M M D D Y Y Y Y 0:2 0:1 2:0:0:1
	47 Type or print preparer's name Susan Teller	**48** Type or print name of person to contact Jeffrey Banker	**49** Telephone number (401) 683-4000

Cat. No. 42004W   Form **4789** (Rev. 6-98)

special daily code along with the officer's initials, assumes a real risk.

- An individual who is trying to obtain cash for a fraudulent check may claim that a bank representative who is not on the premises at the time "always approves my checks."
- Another individual may try to engage the teller in a steady stream of conversation in the hope of creating a distraction.
- The criminal may telephone the teller to give false advance instructions on a check that will be presented for cashing or on a payroll that is to be prepared.
- The individual clips the corners off a $20 bill, attaches it to a $5 bill, and passes it off as $20; this is called the "raised bill" scheme.

Schemes Against Customers

Tellers are not the only ones at risk of fraud. Customers may also be unwitting targets. They can be victims of identity theft as well as direct attempts by criminals to trick them into withdrawing their money.

Identity Theft

Identity theft is, unfortunately, a very fast-growing form of fraud, claiming an estimated 500,000 victims a year. **Identity theft** is the method by which criminals gain unauthorized access to personal information and use it to fraudulently establish credit, incur debt, or take over existing accounts of unknowing victims. It involves the theft of a victim's identifying information, such as social security number or birth date, to apply for credit in the victim's name. The thief uses the victim's credit to purchase merchandise and services. Often, the victim is unaware of the problem until thousands of dollars are charged to the account.

Fraudulent charges can be made to existing accounts once the account number and identifying information are obtained. Thieves get this information by stealing mail from the victim, searching for credit card bills or pre-approved applications in the garbage, or gathering information from cards used in routine transactions.

Credit card companies often detect identity theft before the victim does. Their computer software is designed to detect charges that are uncharacteristic for the cardholder—especially large overseas charges, or large charge amounts over a short period of time.

The trauma to victims is not financial since, by law, their credit card fraud liability is limited to $50 (which is often waived by the bank). Victims are, however, devastated by the destruction of their identity and credit history. In one case, a victim estimated that she spent 400 hours trying to clear her name, only to learn that another fraudulent account was opened two months later. Exhibit 7.5 provides tips for individuals to use in safeguarding their financial information.

Did You Know?

More than 1,400 individuals in this country become victims of identity theft every day.
(American Bankers Association)

Fictitious Payee and Padded Payroll

Fictitious payee and padded payroll are two other situations in which forged endorsements are considered valid. In the former situation, the drawer is induced to issue a check to a fictitious payee. For example, a person sends an invoice to ABC Company asking for payment in the name of XYZ Company, which does not exist. If ABC issues a check payable to XYZ, a fictitious payee, the endorsement is considered valid. In the padded payroll situation, a supervisor or other manager either adds fictitious names to the payroll or requests payments for actual employees and intercepts the checks. For example, Jerry, the shop foreman, adds someone named Phil to his company payroll. Phil is not an employee of the company. He may not even exist. Jerry intercepts the payroll checks and forges Phil's name for endorsement. The forged endorsement is considered valid.

Bank Examiner Scheme

Thieves have been known to tell depositors that they are bank examiners trying to apprehend a dishonest teller. Using this ruse, they ask the customer to withdraw a large sum of money and give it to the examiner to deposit. Of course, the envelope returned to the customer contains newspaper and not cash, but by then the thief has gotten away. The best defense against this and other schemes is to advise depositors to report any requests for cash—from those claiming to be examiners or from others—to the bank and the police at once.

Pigeon Drop Scheme

A variation of the bank examiner scheme is the pigeon drop scheme. An unsuspecting customer is approached by someone claiming to have found a large sum of money and wondering what to do about it. A third person joins the discussion and, as they discuss how they will spend the money and appropriate ways to split it, the victim is drawn in more and more. They eventually decide to formalize the arrangement to split the money by going to a lawyer. The thieves convince the victim to show good faith by putting up some of his or her own money before meeting at the lawyer's. The victim's money will ostensibly be returned when the found money is divided. Of course, the thieves run off and do not meet the victim at the prearranged location.

Check Kiting

Check **kiting** is a fraudulent activity designed to obtain cash from checking accounts that do not have sufficient funds to cover the withdrawals. In a typical check-kiting situation, a customer uses two or more bank accounts to draw against nonexistent balances. For example, the customer opens several checking accounts in different banks, often in different areas of the country. These accounts might be opened with a cashier's check or with cash. Checks are then written to transfer funds from one account to another. These transfers from account to account occur so frequently that the actual funds will not exist in a given account when a check is written on that account. At this point, the customer usually leaves town with more money than originally deposited.

Check kiting works because the banking system uses uncollected funds for a period of days until the check clears. Exhibit 7.6 shows that, from an initial deposit of $1,000 (the amount temporarily deposited in bank A), this check

kiter fraudulently took $2,100 (the total of the three checks cashed at banks B, C, and D.)

To monitor for signs of check kiting, most bank computer systems have kiting reporting systems as part of their daily report function. The system looks for "red flags" such as checks written for even dollar amounts, checks over a certain dollar amount, a high level of account activity, and/or a high level of activity on uncollected funds. Some systems look at weekly activity for evidence of the above.

The first bank to detect a check kiting scheme has the best chance to expose the scam and reduce its losses. When this type of fraud is detected, the bank puts an immediate hold on the account and institutes allowable Regulation CC holds on future deposits. The bank ensures that all future checks are paid on collected funds only. Often the bank will close the account.

Bank Programs to Combat Check Fraud

Banks are constantly trying to stay one step ahead of the criminals in combating check fraud. Some estimates show that bank losses due to check fraud are as high as $25 billion. In addition to effective teller and new accounts training, banks are turning to technology to

---

Customer Tips — Check Fraud

- Don't give your checking account number to people you don't know. Regardless of their claims, they have no business getting such information.
- Reveal checking account information only to vendors you know to be reputable.
- Guard your checkbook. Report lost or stolen checks immediately.
- Read your monthly checking statement and check for fraudulent usage.
- Properly store or dispose of canceled checks, and guard new checks.
- Report any inquiries or suspicious behavior to your bank, which will take measures to protect your account and to notify authorities.
- Do not leave your ATM receipt at the ATM machine. Dispose of it safely and securely.

(American Bankers Association)

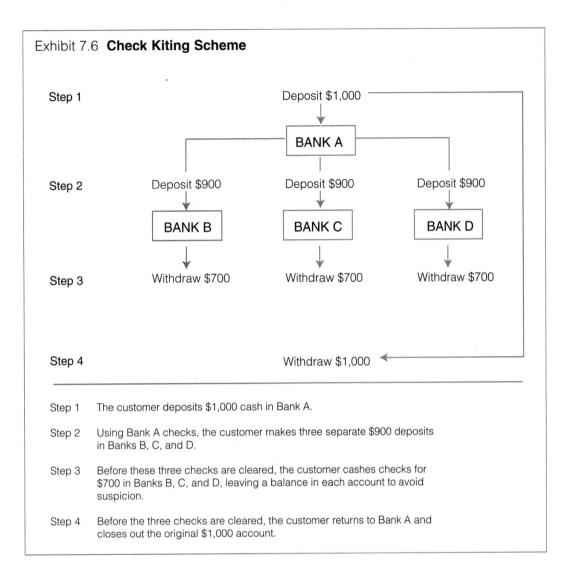

Exhibit 7.6 **Check Kiting Scheme**

Step 1   Deposit $1,000

BANK A

Step 2   Deposit $900   Deposit $900   Deposit $900

BANK B   BANK C   BANK D

Step 3   Withdraw $700   Withdraw $700   Withdraw $700

Step 4   Withdraw $1,000

Step 1   The customer deposits $1,000 cash in Bank A.

Step 2   Using Bank A checks, the customer makes three separate $900 deposits in Banks B, C, and D.

Step 3   Before these three checks are cleared, the customer cashes checks for $700 in Banks B, C, and D, leaving a balance in each account to avoid suspicion.

Step 4   Before the three checks are cleared, the customer returns to Bank A and closes out the original $1,000 account.

help deter fraud. Some of these electronic efforts include:

- electronic storage and verification of customer signatures (see chapter 6)
- thumbprint identification in which a thumbprint reader at the teller window compares the customer's thumbprint with one that has been electronically stored in the bank's records. This technology can also be used for non-customers or employees of local businesses who want to cash their payroll checks drawn on the bank but do not have an account at the bank.

- photo IDs with "invisible" signatures that can be read only by special equipment at the bank. The invisible signature is compared to the endorsement on the check.

As technology improves, it will play a greater and greater role in the war against check fraud.

Summary

Paying banks receive checks from a number of sources. Checks are presented directly from local and other banks, from the local clearing house, and from the Federal Reserve. Regardless of the source, the bank must balance the incoming cash letter and settle for it, capture the information on the checks, and store the information for posting the amounts of the checks to the previous day's balance. In posting checks to a customer's account, the bank must check for sufficient funds and determine whether a hold has been placed on the account or whether payment has been stopped on a specific check.

If the balance in an account is insufficient to pay a check, the bank must decide whether to pay or return the item. If the check is paid, an overdraft is created, which must be covered by the customer. If the check is returned, the bank must prepare the item for the return process. This process requires time, effort, and resources, for which the bank normally charges a fee.

After the posting process is completed, the bank must keep the checks until the statement is rendered. Banks in-file checks, bulk-file checks, or use a combination of the two methods. The bank may verify all the signatures on every check, verify signatures on checks that exceed a certain dollar amount, or verify no signatures.

Banks periodically render bank statements to customers; the customer has an obligation to examine the statement and the items within 30 days after the statement is made available to him or her by the bank. If the customer fails to examine the statement, he or she could be prevented from asserting a claim against the bank for any alterations or unauthorized payments. On the other hand, if the bank is negligent, the bank could absorb the entire loss or share in the loss.

In addition to processing items that are posted to customers' accounts, banks also process return items. Return items are called outgoing returns if they are being returned by the paying bank, and incoming returns if they are being received by the depositary bank. When processing outgoing returns, the paying bank must ensure that the checks are returned within the time established by the UCC and Regulation CC. When processing incoming return items, the bank must identify the customer who deposited the check or otherwise transferred the check to the bank, and charge the amount of the check back to that customer.

Security issues are a major concern for banks. Tellers are the most common victims of bank robbery and various fraud schemes including split deposits, charge-back check fraud, and counterfeit checks. Money laundering is also often attempted at the teller window.

Customers can be the victims of fraud also through identity theft, fictitious payee and padded payroll schemes, and bank examiner and pigeon drop schemes.

Review and Discussion Questions

1. Describe the process of posting.

2. Distinguish between in-filing and bulk-filing.

3. Under the revised provisions of Article 4 of the UCC, what is the customer's duty to examine the bank statement after it is made available to him or her by the bank?

4. Distinguish between outgoing returns and incoming returns.

5. List several points tellers should keep in mind when dealing with a bank robber.

6. Define identity theft and explain why it is such a serious problem for the victim.

Additional Resources

Deposit Account Fraud Survey Report Series. Washington, D.C., American Bankers Association, 2000.

Web Resources

American Bankers Association Consumer Connection: **Identity Theft—Protect Your Financial Identity** www.aba.com

8

THE LENDING FUNCTION

Learning Objectives

After completing this chapter, you will be able to do the following:

* list five reasons why the credit function is important to the bank
* list and discuss the legal requirements for bank loans
* explain the purpose of the lending policy and the board of directors' role in establishing and overseeing this policy
* describe the four stages of the lending process
* distinguish among the four basic categories of loans—real estate, consumer, business, and government loans
* define the bolded terms that appear in the text

Introduction

Each of the following customers has a lending need you can help resolve.

Situation 1

The O'Dells both have stable jobs that provide them with a comfortable income. Three years ago, they finished paying off loans they had taken for their children's education. With the exception of their home mortgage, which they have paid monthly for 20 years, they are debt-free. The O'Dells have applied to your bank for a home-improvement loan. Imagine their surprise when you call to ask them about a negative credit report from a credit bureau. With your assistance, they contact the credit bureau and discover that the college loans they had paid were incorrectly listed as being delinquent. What course of action would you recommend to the O'Dells to correct this error?

Situation 2

Dan Brennan's construction company wants to build a small shopping center in a new suburban community. He needs short-term financing to help construct the center. Since his company will also manage the center when construction is completed, he will need long-term financing as well. How can his bank accommodate his needs?

Situation 3

A large technology company has expressed its intent to build a plant in your community, contingent on receiving financing for the project. This new facility will bring hundreds of much-needed high-tech jobs to your community; however, the multimillion dollar cost of the project exceeds the individual legal lending limits of most area banks, including yours. Does your bank have to pass up this opportunity?

The above situations demonstrate the many lending challenges banks face every day. As the primary source of credit for businesses and consumers, banks have diversified their loan products and enabled their customers to acquire goods and services that stimulate economic growth. To remain financially sound so they can keep providing this stimulus, banks rely on the decisions made by their loan officers and loan committees, who in turn base their decisions on the bank's goals.

This chapter shifts the focus of the text from deposits and related activities to the lending function—loans and the lending process. The deposit function was covered first because, without deposits, there would be no lending function. In the bank, deposits from all accounts are lumped together to provide the funds banks lend. Like a manufacturing company that turns raw materials into a product it can sell in the marketplace, banks use deposits as the raw material for loans. Banks grow as they grow their deposit base and have more funds available to lend. These loans generate income for the bank.

A bank's lending activities are guided by legal requirements and lending policy as well as the bank's specific business goals. The success of any loans—that is, whether they are profitable for the bank—depends on an accurate assessment of their risk and on their being properly priced. Failure to follow these steps exposes the bank to loss. This chapter presents an overview of the lending function and the legal environment in which banks operate, and reviews the stages of the lending process and the various loan categories.

The Lending Function

The lending function is extremely important for many reasons, including the following:

- Of the three cornerstones of banking—the deposit, payment, and lending functions— the lending function represents the most important source of income.
- To qualify as a bank, a bank is legally required to make commercial loans.
- Lending is the most traditional element in the relationship between banks and their customers.
- Under the Community Reinvestment Act, banks are evaluated and given a public rating on their record of helping to meet the credit needs of their communities, including home mortgage and small business and small farm lending.
- The quality of a bank's loans is often key to the institution's survival in today's economy.

Borrowing and lending money have been accepted financial activities since the earliest days of civilization. In the ruins of ancient Babylon, written evidence was found of a loan made to a farmer, who promised to make payment with interest when his crops were harvested and sold. In farm areas of the United States today, equivalent transactions take place: The American farmer who borrows from a bank executes a written promise to repay just as his predecessor in Babylon did thousands of years ago.

The literature and history of the Middle Ages record that goldsmiths, who held their clients' precious metals and other valuables in safekeeping, often made loans against the value of those assets. In the eighteenth centu-ry, the American Revolution was financed in part through loan certificates issued by the two Continental Congresses, and every subsequent war in which the United States has been involved has been financed through heavy borrowing by the federal government.

Today, a great many sources of credit are available. Customers can now apply for credit from a finance company. They also can borrow from an insurance company or from a brokerage firm against the value of their securities. In addition, they can buy merchandise on credit from a retailer, obtain a home mortgage or home equity loan from savings or commercial banks, or borrow from their credit union. As savings depositors, they also may use their account balances as security for loans.

Businesses of every type and size also have many sources of credit open to them in addition to traditional sources of bank credit. Savings banks use their expanded powers under the Depository Institutions Deregulation and Monetary Control Act of 1980 and the Garn-St Germain Depository Institution Act of 1982 to offer commercial loans, as do many commercial financing firms. One business may extend credit to another by selling merchandise in advance of payment. Insurance companies often make large, long-term loans that are used for the construction of shopping centers, office buildings, and factories. Many large corporations, such as General Motors Acceptance Corporation and General Electric Credit, also make large commercial loans.

Instead of borrowing from banks, many large corporations with excellent credit ratings borrow in the money markets by issuing unsecured, short-term promissory notes known as **commercial paper**. Federal, state, and local governments use a wide variety of long- and short-term borrowing techniques to raise funds. Banks themselves often borrow directly from one another or use the facilities of the Federal Reserve to obtain short-term credit.

Despite this diversity of available lenders, banks remain the dominant force in the lending market. More money is borrowed each year from banks than from any other source. Banks are the largest lenders not only because they are required to make commercial loans under the legal definition of a bank, but also because banks often have the most attractive rates available.

Interest on loans constitutes one of banks' largest sources of income. Typically, two-thirds of a bank's yearly earnings results from loan interest—although it's likely the percentage will change when, as a result of the Gramm-Leach-Bliley Act, banks begin generating income from non-traditional sources.

Lending also fulfills each bank's traditional role of service to its customers and communities. The banking industry's full-service philosophy means that banks extend a broad spectrum of credit to every segment of the market. No other lender can match the size or diversity of the credit banks extend.

Bank loans are available to meet the needs of small or large businesses, governments, and consumers. In fact, businesses, governments, and consumers are the three main categories of borrowers. Banks provide about $70 of every $100 borrowed by businesses. Through direct loans to government agencies, and by invest-

ing in the debt obligations that those agencies issue, banks supply about $50 of every $100 borrowed by governments.

The term of a typical bank loan may be as short as 30 days or as long as 30 years. Although some loans are made with collateral, many loans in the United States are made on an unsecured basis, with the bank relying entirely on the borrower's written promise to repay. On any given day, a bank may grant a $2,500 personal loan to an individual, a $750,000 loan to a medium-sized business, and a $50 million loan to a major corporation.

Though many other sources of credit are available, consumers continue to use banks very actively for borrowing purposes. The ability of banks to meet the credit needs of businesses, governments, and consumers is vital to the prosperity of the economy. By granting loans and crediting the proceeds to customers' accounts, banks are directly responsible for creating money, thereby directly affecting the nation's money supply.

Legal Requirements and Lending Policy

Two factors predominate in the oversight of the lending function—legal requirements and bank lending policy. Federal and state lawmakers and bank directors are all concerned with ensuring that the banking system is safe and protects the interests of consumers. Bank directors also have the challenge of making the bank profitable, and they address all of these issues through the lending policy.

Legal Requirements

The impact of bank loans on the nation's economy, the importance of the lending function to a bank's success or failure, and the emphasis on consumer protection in today's society have led to federal and state requirements for bank loans. Bank lending officers are familiar with the following:

- The maximum dollar amount of an unsecured loan to any single borrower is legally limited to a percentage, depending on applicable state or federal laws, of the bank's capital and surplus. **Capital** is the stockholders' investment in the bank; **surplus** is the funds paid for stock in excess of par value plus retained earnings and other gains not distributed. Fifteen percent of a bank's capital and surplus is a common lending limit for unsecured loans. If the loan is fully secured, this limit is usually higher, up to 25 percent to 50 percent of capital plus surplus. This legal requirement helps banks to focus on lending to many customers rather than concentrating too heavily on a single customer; it also encourages their offering loans jointly with other banks.

- The sizes and maturities of real estate loans may be limited by state laws. For national banks, limits on real estate loans are not set by the Office of the Comptroller of the Currency.

- Many state laws set the maximum interest rates that can be charged on various types of credit. Home mortgages, bank card balances, and personal loans are affected by these laws. There are heavy civil and criminal penalties for usury (the legal term for excessive and punitive interest).

- The Community Reinvestment Act (CRA) and each agency's regulations also affect lending. The CRA was passed by Congress in 1977 to prevent redlining and to encourage commercial banks and savings banks to help meet the credit needs of all segments of their communities, including low- and moderate-income neighborhoods. Banks are required to maintain certain loan and deposit information for public review. They are evaluated periodically (by the appropriate regulatory agency) on their performance. Their performance record (CRA rating) is taken into account in considering any application for charters or for approval of bank mergers, acquisitions, and branch openings. The CRA is implemented under Federal Reserve Regulation BB.

- In addition, the following Federal Reserve regulations affect loans made by all banks:

1. Regulation B, which implements provisions of the Equal Credit Opportunity Act (ECOA), prohibits discrimination by a lender on the basis of age, race, color, national origin, sex, marital status, income from public assistance programs, or exercise of rights under the Consumer Protection Act; establishes guidelines for gathering and evaluating credit information; and requires written notification when credit is denied. ECOA applies to all types of credit, including consumer and business credit, although notice requirements are different for large business customers.

2. Regulation Z implements the Truth in Lending Act, a consumer protection law. It applies to credit transactions by banks for personal, household, or family purposes. It prescribes uniform methods for computing the cost of credit, for disclosing credit terms, and for resolving errors on certain types of credit accounts. Consumer loans of $25,000 or less and consumer loans secured by real estate regardless of the amount are covered by Regulation B. Disclosures for these

loans include the cost to the consumer for the credit (the finance charge, the annual percentage rate, and the calculations used to derive these), the credit terms, the consumer's right to rescind in certain types of credit transactions (like home equity loans), and the consumer's fair credit billing rights (for open-ended credit).

Banks are also required to report information about their outstanding loans. To meet these federal requirements, a bank's loan portfolio is divided into detailed categories that give federal authorities a complete picture of lending activity at the branch, regional, and national levels. The detailed categories required for federal reporting are not necessarily consistent with the way banks classify loans for their own internal purposes and are beyond the scope of this text. This chapter instead focuses on the lending products offered by banks and the way they are internally classified.

Lending Policy

A bank is a corporation with a board of directors as its active, governing body. The making of lending policy, or a written statement of the bank's guidelines for making lending decisions, begins at the board level. Directors, usually through membership on a loan committee, are actively involved in the lending function and do the following:

- review the bank's portfolio of outstanding loans to ensure that the bank is meeting the credit needs of its customers and the community in compliance with the Community Reinvestment Act
- assign lending authority in varying amounts to the bank's lending officers so that each

officer knows the maximum amount he or she can approve individually and what combinations of higher authority are needed for larger amounts
- determine what types of loans the bank will consider or refuse to make
- conduct periodic reviews (audits) of the bank's entire loan portfolio to ensure that proper procedures are being followed and that undue risks are not being taken
- tighten overall credit standards when conditions warrant
- implement policies that determine loan collateral, define loan maturities, outline maximum lending to certain business sectors, or set standards for down payments on automobiles or residences
- authorize all loans above a stipulated amount—in other words, loans so large that they exceed the authority of any combination of officers
- establish and monitor legal lending limits as well as minimum loan amounts

All the information staff members require about the organization of the bank's lending function, lending objectives and standards, levels of loan authority, review and charge-off procedures, and loans to the bank's own officers and directors are documented in a comprehensive policy guide and approved by the board of directors. Policy is generally reviewed annually.

The Lending Process

A "borrower" can be a consumer who has obtained a small loan or a nationally known corporation that has borrowed to the bank's legal lending limit. In either case, a standard set of guidelines and principles applies. While banks have different policies and procedures, all follow a general lending process that includes the loan application and interview, investigation, documentation, and management.

All parts of the lending process have a cost to the bank. Loans that are more significant to the bank or that appear riskier may require more in-depth investigation, documentation, or management than a small, less risky loan. Lenders assess each request in terms of its risk, cost, and profitability to the bank, and apply the lending process according to that assessment.

Regardless of the type or size of credit, strict adherence to the lending process helps protect the bank against losses, but cannot completely eliminate losses. No absolute formula or system exists that positively guarantees full and timely repayment of every loan with interest. Borrowers' situations change and this can put the bank at greater risk.

The Application and Interview

The lending process begins with the loan application and the loan interview. The goal of this step is for the loan officer to understand the borrower's needs, gather initial, supporting documentation, and begin to formulate the type of loan that will best meet the borrower's need.

Most banks start the process by using the loan application to gather preliminary information. The loan officer discusses this and other information during the loan interview, which can take place in person, over the phone, over the Internet, or through a third party. The depth of the interview is determined by the level of detail of the loan request. The loan officer, for example, might meet several times with a business owner seeking a complicated commercial loan in order to get a better understanding of the company's financial pic-

ture, while leaving an interview for a car loan to a third party (the car dealer).

Loan officers must be fully aware of bank policy and lending regulations during this phase of the lending process. Consumer protection laws and regulations such as Equal Credit Opportunity Act (Regulation B) and Truth in Lending Act (Regulation Z) are very specific about what constitutes illegal practices in lending. The bank's loan policy also guides the process by establishing criteria for loan size, type, and other terms.

The Investigation

Banks obtain and evaluate all available information when making credit decisions and balance this information against the potential cost of making the loan. There are many sources of information to assist a bank in doing a credit investigation: that is, a formal evaluation of the financial and economic condition of a potential borrower and the borrower's ability to repay the debt. A weak or incomplete credit investigation during the lending process can increase the bank's risk for loan losses.

Individual Loans

Credit investigations for individual or consumer loans usually consist of verifying the applicant's employment, income, credit history, and existing debts. Most lenders subscribe to a basic set of standards when credit is evaluated, especially when analyzing consumer loan requests. These standards are known as the five Cs of credit—character, capacity, collateral, capital, and conditions.

Character: The character of the borrower is the primary consideration. If there is reason to question the borrower's honesty or integrity, the decision to reject the request is immediate; further analysis of the loan is unnecessary. The key question is: Will the borrower repay?

Capacity: The capacity of the borrower to repay is extremely important. Every loan, whether for a nominal amount or millions of dollars, should reflect the bank's judgment that the borrower will have adequate funds for repayment. Assuming the borrower's full intention to repay, the key question is: Can the borrower repay?

Collateral: The next consideration is the **collateral** that may be pledged as part of the proposed loan. Lenders have always sought to protect themselves by obtaining some form of security, usually the pledging of certain assets, that can be used in case of default. Here, the key question or test for all collateral is its marketability in the event it must be sold for repayment of the loan. However, a loan request is not approved on the basis of the value of the collateral. All of the preceding principles must be satisfied before the bank accepts collateral to secure the loan request.

Capital: The borrower's capital position is important. The lender examines other assets that might be used to pay the loan. The key question is: If the income stream were stopped, would the borrower still be able to pay off the loan?

Conditions: The conditions affecting the borrower's ability to repay in the future must receive full consideration. No one remains unchanged from year to year. Jobs change, illness and accidents occur, and family status changes. All these can affect the borrower's ability to repay. Here the key question is: What could go wrong?

Banks subscribe to credit bureaus, which maintain detailed records on consumers' credit history and activities. These bureaus can provide the bank with daily input on new loan applications, repayments, rejected requests for credit, and delinquencies. Information provided by an applicant can be cross-checked with credit bureau reports to determine the accuracy of the application. If a bank declines a consumer loan request on the basis of unfavorable credit information, the bank is required to make that reason known to the applicant as well as to the bureau that furnished the credit report. Because the O'Dells in situation 1 were advised that information in their credit report was holding up their loan approval, they were able to contact the credit bureau and correct an error.

More and more banks are relying on **credit scoring** both to improve the efficiency of the credit investigation and to improve its fairness. A credit score, sometimes called Fair Isaac (FICO) or Empirica credit score, relies on a mathematical formula to determine the likelihood that a borrower will repay a loan, given adverse circumstances. Many factors are considered in this formula, including amount and type of outstanding credit, repayment patterns, and repayment history.

Credit scoring is often used with electronic underwriting. The score is generated electronically, as is a determination of whether the applicant profile falls within the acceptable range established by the bank. This procedure allows the bank to process large numbers of loan applications electronically, referring only those that fall into a pre-defined "gray" area to a loan officer for further evaluation.

Business Loans

Because of the larger loan amounts and increased complexities of commercial loans, the investigative process for businesses is far more detailed, and the sources of information are far more numerous, than for consumer loans.

Loan analysis (credit) department. The starting point is usually the bank's own loan analysis or credit department, where credit files are maintained on each business account and borrower. These files provide a complete history of the bank's relationships with its customers. They contain reports of interviews; copies of correspondence; financial statements supplied by the borrower; internal memos, including previous credit analyses; and data on average balances, previous loans, overdrafts, and loan approval documentation.

Other banks. Credit information can be obtained from banks and other creditors, provided there is a legitimate reason for requesting the information. Banks exchange information with one another on mutual customers, especially when a company is borrowing from more than one bank.

Credit agencies. Credit agencies such as Dun & Bradstreet publish regular business reports, which provide current financial information on a company and include the firm's history, management structure, products, scope of operations, and borrowing history with suppliers.

Suppliers. Because most merchandise is sold with credit terms, it is important that a bank know how a company has paid its suppliers. This information, in addition to being found in credit agency reports, can be obtained through direct contact with the firms that sell to a particular company.

Internet. A growing number of companies have their own websites. These sites often contain information about a company's products, services, history, and other information that may be helpful in the investigation.

Tax information. A bank must determine that all payroll, sales, and income taxes are current and satisfied from prior years. A tax lien imposed for the nonpayment of taxes can place a company in jeopardy and threaten its ability to repay its creditors.

In lending to businesses, banks rely heavily on financial information supplied by the borrower. The information on balance sheets, income statements, supplementary schedules, and projections of future growth and earnings are analyzed to detect trends in the business, compare the borrower with others in the same industry, and help to identify the sources of repayment for current and future borrowings.

In analyzing financial statements, it is necessary to understand the conditions that created increases or decreases in sales or profits. Understanding the management process within a business is also necessary, because financial performance is a result of decisions that are made by a company's managers. Since every business operation assumes risk, the lending bank should be confident that the company's managers are aware of the risks they face and are taking appropriate steps to minimize the potential results of miscalculating a new venture or business opportunity.

Loan Documentation

Loan documentation begins once the decision to make the loan is made. Loan documentation involves obtaining and completing all the necessary forms to secure the lender's interest and comply with federal and state requirements. Failure to properly document the loan could make the loan agreement unenforceable. Proper loan documentation is important because it helps to:

- protect the bank's investment

- ensure that the borrower understands the loan terms
- prevent litigation against the bank
- prevent loan loss for the bank
- prevent compliance violation penalties

Loan documentation is a very detailed process. All documents required by federal and state law must be completed. The loan officer ensures that all sections are completed, the calculations are correct, the collateral description is correct, the signatures and dates have been obtained and witnessed (if necessary), and any alterations have been initialed by all parties.

Lenders also use documentation to meet their obligation to inform borrowers about the major components of the loan. Federal law (most notably Truth-in-Lending regulations) requires that borrowers be informed of such loan details as the repayment program, annual percentage rate, total cost of the loan, consequences of not paying on time, information about collateral, and so forth. Lenders provide disclosure forms and other informative documents during this stage.

The type of documentation required is highly dependent on the type of loan and the location of the bank. Different types of loans require different types of documentation. The quantity and type of documentation will also vary from bank to bank and from state to state.

The loan is considered closed when all the documents are complete, the appropriate forms are signed, the funds disbursed, and the documentation filed.

Collateral

From time to time a bank may use collateral as a means of reducing its risk with a loan customer. Collateral is a specific asset pledged as security for the loan. If the borrower defaults, the bank can sell the collateral. When a bank accepts as collateral government obligations, securities traded on the stock market, savings account balances, or residential or commercial property, it believes that the assigned property can be readily sold if necessary, and that the proceeds of the sale will be sufficient to pay off, or at least reduce, the outstanding loan amount. If the bank takes physical possession of the collateral, it provides for safekeeping and control. The bank registers its security interest in collateral with the appropriate state and local authorities. The lender is said to have a **security interest** when the borrower has entered into an agreement securing the loan with collateral. In the event the borrower is unable to repay the loan, the lender is entitled to obtain possession of the collateral and sell it to repay the loan.

Collateral may strengthen a borrowing situation, but it should never be the sole reason for approving a loan. Borrowers should demonstrate the capacity to repay out of an identifiable source of income, and a bank should not look to the collateral alone as the justification for extending credit. A bank does not succeed by foreclosing, repossessing, or seizing real estate, automobiles, or factories. These steps are taken only when the borrower cannot meet the loan repayment schedule. Furthermore, a bank usually incurs additional costs associated with each foreclosure or repossession. A long time may elapse before the foreclosed, repossessed, or seized property can be sold, and market value of property often deteriorates. During this time, the bank classifies the loan as a non-performing asset. This means the loan is still considered an asset, but it is an asset that does not generate income.

Loan Management

After the loan is properly documented and closed, it moves into the loan management phase. Loan management involves:

- mailing regular statements
- receiving and posting agreed-upon payments
- maintaining current address information
- ensuring that the bank's security interest in the collateral is properly recorded, filed, and returned to the bank
- answering customer inquiries
- reporting the loan to various credit reporting agencies
- maintaining the files and documentation for review and examination by internal and external auditors and by regulatory agencies, and
- closing out the loan when the final payment is received.

The risks a lender assumes do not end when the loan has been approved and placed in the bank's loan portfolio; that is just the beginning. The loan is also monitored throughout its life for signs of trouble. For business loans, the loan officer monitors the company's financial performance. The lending officer usually maintains contact with the company to stay informed of all developments that could affect the repayment of the loan. Individual loans are also monitored for signs that the loan is becoming a problem.

Asset Recovery and Loan Review

In addition to the monitoring by lending officers, banks also need a system of loan review. This process occurs after the loan has been properly documented and closed. Here, a staff of specialists impartially and objectively examine all approved loans for potential problems. Because interest income on loans represents one of the largest sources of bank revenue, and the quality of the loan portfolio is vital for overall asset quality within the bank, loan losses are a source of major concern to shareholders and directors.

Asset recovery departments can help prevent losses by taking timely action for late payments and, in some cases, by restructuring the terms of a loan for the benefit of both bank and borrower. Asset recovery officers watch for any indications of poorly performing loans. They are responsible for examining all loans for which there are late payments, identifying existing or potential problems, and recommending corrective action, including the advisability of an increase in the bank's reserve to cover possible loan losses.

Systematic loan review gives management and directors assurance that lending officers have stayed within their authority, that lending policies and procedures have been followed, that the investigation and analysis process was adequate, and that all necessary documentation on each loan has been obtained and properly filed. If the size of the bank's portfolio warrants, the review may cover both unsecured and secured loans and loans made previously as well as new ones.

The lending process is summarized in exhibit 8.1

Loan Categories

Banks have assumed the role of financial intermediary, accepting deposits and putting them to profitable use. However, as changing market and economic conditions create new customer needs and increase competition in the financial services industry, banks have broad-

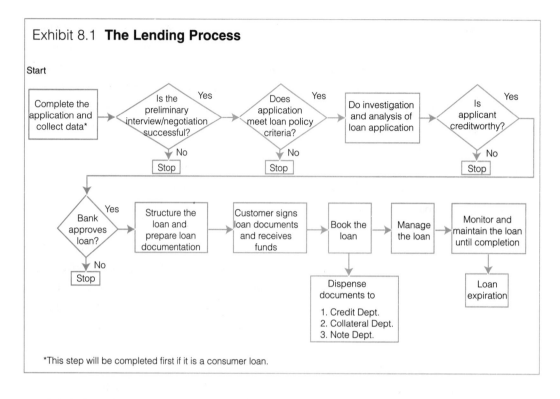

Exhibit 8.1 **The Lending Process**

Start

Complete the application and collect data*

Is the preliminary interview/negotiation successful? — Yes / No → Stop

Does application meet loan policy criteria? — Yes / No → Stop

Do investigation and analysis of loan application

Is applicant creditworthy? — Yes / No → Stop

Bank approves loan? — Yes / No → Stop

Structure the loan and prepare loan documentation

Customer signs loan documents and receives funds

Book the loan

Manage the loan

Monitor and maintain the loan until completion

Dispense documents to
1. Credit Dept.
2. Collateral Dept.
3. Note Dept.

Loan expiration

*This step will be completed first if it is a consumer loan.

ened their loan products and introduced many new types of loans.

As mentioned earlier, banks divide their loans into many detailed categories for purposes of reporting to government agencies and for internal management purposes in monitoring and planning. Many loans fall in more than one category. A large loan to a corporation, shared with other banks, is both a business loan and a loan participation. A home mortgage (or purchase money mortgage) or home equity loan is a real estate credit, yet it is also a loan made to a consumer. Many banks internally classify loans by industry so that they can monitor how much of their portfolio is committed in certain sectors of the economy, such as automobiles, petroleum, tobacco, agriculture, or aerospace. If problems in an industry emerge because of increased competition, an economic slowdown, or other external factors, the bank is aware of the number and size of loans that

may be affected and is in a good position to take necessary action.

For their own purposes, most banks divide their loan operations into categories that reflect their primary customer bases. These categories are

- real estate loans
- consumer loans
- business loans
- government-sponsored loans

Real Estate Loans

Real estate loans can be both consumer- and business-based. It therefore makes sense to put them in a separate category. Banks are involved primarily in two areas of real estate financing: short-term construction loans and longer-term mortgage loans (exhibit 8.2). A real estate developer often requires bank funds to purchase, demolish, and clear existing property and begin erecting a new structure such as a shopping mall, an office park, or a residential development. A bank can accommodate the developer by providing a construction loan.

Construction Loans

Construction loans are relatively short-term loans that are repaid when the builder obtains long-term mortgage financing. The proceeds of the loan are used to buy land, pay architects and contractors for their services, purchase needed materials for building construction, and meet payrolls. Consumers also use construction loans to build their "dream houses." Frequently, a commercial bank provides a construction loan and another lender or combination of lenders extends long-term mortgage credit when the project is completed. However, a commercial bank may fill both of these lending roles if it so desires, as it did for the builder in situation 2. In that case, the bank was able to meet the builder's need for short-term financing with a construction loan for the shopping center. When the center was complete, the bank provided long-term mortgage financing that the builder will repay from renting the retail space.

Mortgage Loans

Real estate credit, or a mortgage loan, is granted knowing payments will be made for many years. The property itself is pledged by the borrower as collateral to secure the loan. For example, banks may extend mortgage loans on office buildings, apartment houses, and shopping centers if there is sufficient evidence that regular income from rents in the project will be more than adequate to meet a schedule of regular payments. These scheduled payments include both interest and principal payments. The loan balance is gradually reduced over a period of time as the payments are made.

In the past, individuals seeking funds to finance home purchases usually obtained mortgages from mortgage companies, savings banks, or other long-term lenders. Savings and

Customer Tips—How to Shop for a Mortgage

Ask Lenders:
* What are the interest rates, fees, and points? (A point is a fee equal to 1 percent of the loan amount, used to lower the interest rate.)
* What types of mortgages do they offer, and what are the terms?
* What is the minimum down-payment required with and without private mortgage insurance?
* Is there a fee to lock in the current interest rate? For how long is the lock-in effective?
* Is there a penalty for prepayment? Are extra payments allowed?
* Is an escrow required for taxes and insurance?
* What are the closing costs?

(American Bankers Association)

loan associations, originally known as building societies, were organized specifically to extend home mortgage credit.

Commercial banks are involved in making residential mortgage loans, also. The introduction of the variable-rate, or adjustable-rate, loan has attracted more diverse lenders to this market. A lender can adjust the interest rate on the mortgage during the term of the loan as rate conditions change and in accordance with the loan contract. Adjustable rates on mortgages work to the advantage of both the bank and the borrower. If interest rates decline, the borrower gets the benefit of the lower rate. If interest rates rise, the bank's risks are reduced because the bank can increase the interest rate.

The practice of selling mortgage loans to investors, such as insurance companies and pension funds, was introduced by commercial banks. Instead of keeping the mortgage loan on its books, the bank sells the loan to an investor. Doing so allows the bank to make money on the sale of the loan and frees those funds so the bank can make additional loans. The bank does not make money from the interest on the loans, but from the fee income and service charges generated from the loan.

Home mortgage loans are based on a number of factors, including the borrower's income and creditworthiness and the appraised value of the home. If the borrower is unable to make the payments, the lender can foreclose on the home and sell it at auction in an effort to recover part or all of the borrower's unpaid balance.

Consumer Loans

As mentioned earlier, in recent years banks have shifted much of their attention to the consumer market, and the needs of this segment have become extremely important in the overall banking picture. **Consumer lending** includes closed-end (installment) loans, bank cards, and other types of open-end (revolving) credit (exhibit 8.3). Revolving or open-end credit is a specified maximum line of credit on which a borrower may draw for a limited period. The balance may fluctuate from zero up to the maximum amount. A home equity line of credit is an open-end credit that is secured by a person's home. Terms allow a lien to be placed on the home and allow for future advances to the consumer up to the amount of the credit line.

Another form of open-end credit is used when a credit card purchase is made. These cards allow a user to travel, entertain, or purchase merchandise on credit and make payment later. With credit cards customers can extend themselves loans. Instead of going through the procedures involved in obtaining a personal closed-end loan, the individual simply uses the bank card to make the purchase. The credit card customer usually receives a monthly statement from the bank containing a description of all the purchases made that month. The customer has the option to pay off the entire balance, make a minimum payment, or pay some amount in

Exhibit 8.3 **Consumer Loans**

* Open-end Credit
  —line of credit
  —home equity line of credit
* Credit Cards
* Installment Loans

between. Banks are required by some states to give the customer a period of time, called a grace period, to pay the balance. If the customer pays the entire outstanding balance shown on the statement before the payment due date, the customer generally is not charged a finance charge. In other words, the customer usually is given an interest-free loan for the grace period.

Credit cards carry a high amount of risk for the bank. Fraudulent charges, stolen cards, and unpaid balances are some examples of these risks. Others will be discussed in chapter 13.

Installment or closed-end loans carry a schedule of fixed monthly payments that can usually be made in a number of ways. For example, the bank may issue the loan customer a coupon book that contains information about the specific payment. The customer sends the coupon along with the payment to the bank, and the bank uses the coupon to give the customer credit for the loan payment on the bank's loan system. Many banks also offer the customer an option whereby the bank automatically charges the customer's checking account for the amount of the loan payment. The loan payment is then shown on the customer's checking account statement.

Consumer loans can be made with or without collateral. For example, if the customer borrows money to buy a car, the bank may ask the customer to secure the loan by pledging the car as collateral. If the customer fails to make

the payments on the car loan, the bank can take the car from the customer and sell it to pay off the car loan. If the customer fails to make the loan payments, the customer is said to be in default, or to have defaulted, on the loan. In making these loans, banks rely on the borrower's ability to repay as outlined in a signed promissory note—a document that contains all the provisions, or terms, of the loan.

Consumer loans have proven attractive to banks for several reasons:

- By making consumer loans, banks are able to compete more effectively with other types of financial institutions and non-bank lenders.
- Interest income makes an important contribution to the annual profits of many banks.
- Consumer loans help banks to become full-service financial services providers.
- Most consumer loans are repaid as agreed.
- Consumer loan customers can often benefit from other bank services.

Business Loans

Loans made to businesses are one of the largest components of a bank's total loan portfolio (exhibit 8.4). A bank today may simultaneously lend $25,000 to a company to finance seasonal purchases of raw materials and lend millions of dollars to an airline to finance the purchase of new aircraft. Some business loans, known as working capital loans, are made for short periods, the most common maturity being 90 days. Short-term loans are often used to provide immediate funds for a business. For example, a toy manufacturer may need short-term financing to buy raw materials so that the finished goods will be available for distribution and sale in time for the peak Christmas season. On the other hand, a corporation that is expanding its factory and buying new equipment needs a capital improvement loan that carries a longer term.

Some businesses use working capital lines of credit to meet seasonal short-term needs. A working capital line of credit is available at any time (much like a consumer line of credit). Banks often require that the loan be fully paid (to zero) at least 30 days of the annual cycle. Rates are typically the prime rate plus a percentage that reflects the risk of the loan. Working capital lines of credit are more convenient than regular short-term bank loans for many businesses.

Did You Know?

An increasing number of banks now use credit scoring in their application review process, particularly for indirect loans.
(American Bankers Association)

Commercial and industrial loans are of many types. In reporting to various regulatory agencies, a bank may classify its loans as secured and unsecured. Loans can also be classified according to purpose and maturity.

Some loans are demand loans; that is, there is no fixed maturity or repayment schedule. The bank can call for repayment at any time, or the borrower can repay whenever convenient. Time loans, on the other hand, have specific maturity dates. From a bank's standpoint, both types have advantages and disadvantages.

Demand loans have allowed banks to make any changes in interest rates that they feel are necessary at any time. Time loans, on the other hand, were traditionally made with fixed interest rates that remained constant throughout the life of the loan. In recent years, banks have shifted this emphasis so that time and demand loans are made on an adjustable-rate basis, which enables the bank to tie loan rates to money market conditions and ease the burden of asset and liability management.

Participations are loans made to a single borrower and shared by two or more banks. In other words, the banks participate with each other in the loan. These shared loans are used for many reasons and are common in commercial and industrial lending. For example, a corporation that requires an extremely large loan may divide it among the various banks with which it maintains accounts. Alternatively, a requested loan may be too large for a single bank to handle legally; that bank therefore offers to share the loan with others. There are legal limits on the amount of money banks can lend to a single borrower, but participations often result from practical rather than legal reasons. One bank may simply wish to diversify its risk because of the size of a requested loan, or to avoid excessive concentration of loans to one industry. In these instances, a bank invites other banks to share the loan. The banks in the community referenced in situation 3 at the beginning of the chapter cannot individually lend the full amount needed to finance the technology company. However, by "participating" with other banks, they will be able to fund the project.

Many banks work directly with automobile and appliance dealers and obtain loan applications from customers who purchase their inventory. These loans are known as **indirect** or third party loans. These dealers can be an important source of new consumer business for the bank.

The bank enters into a floor plan financing agreement by extending credit directly to a dealer, allowing the dealer to maintain an adequate inventory of consumer products for display and sale. In other words, the bank lends the money to the dealer and the bank takes the inventory (appliances, furniture, cars, trucks, boats, and so on) as collateral.

Another product often associated with business loans is the letter of credit. Used mostly for international transactions, a letter of credit is an instrument issued by the bank that substitutes the credit of the bank for the credit of the buyer of goods. Letters of credit are discussed further in chapter 12.

Bank loans are made on the basis of the information available regarding the borrower. "Know your customer" is a banking axiom. Especially in the case of unsecured loans, the bank is expressing full confidence in the borrower's honesty, willingness, and ability to repay. As additional protection on loans to corporations, banks often require the personal guarantees of the **principals**, the primary owners or controllers in the business. If the borrowing company defaults on the loan, the personal guarantors can be called on to make payments. Personal guarantees are often needed in secured loans to small and medium-sized businesses as an additional safety factor.

Government Loans

State and local governments borrow from banks just as consumers and businesses do. Their need to purchase road equipment or police cars or to meet other working capital needs cannot always be financed directly from tax revenues. Consequently the government will seek approval from its board or elected oversight body to take on a bank loan for a specific purpose. Governments will often finance on terms similar to those in business loans. Banks may provide a short-term loan on a tax anticipation basis (using the government's anticipated tax revenues to pay off the debt). Boards and authorities of state and local governments may also borrow from banks (exhibit 8.5).

A second area of government lending is government-sponsored or government-supported programs. Student loans and mortgage loans are primary examples of this type. Governments often support specific groups or institute congressional mandates through loan programs for affordable housing or access to higher education. They have several options for sponsoring or supporting loan programs, which include

- subsidizing loans by guaranteeing them, as do the Veterans' Administration (VA) or Federal Housing Administration (FHA)
- purchasing back delinquent loans such as student loan programs
- acting as a conduit to stimulate the market as do the Federal National Mortgage Association (Fannie Mae) or the Federal Home Loan Mortgage Corporation (Freddie Mac)

Since the end of World War II, the number of home mortgage loans has consistently grown, partly because of assistance provided by such federal agencies as the VA and the FHA. These agencies provide guarantees to lenders if the borrowers default and help provide funds for mortgage loans for the nation's homebuyers. Because their activities involve hundreds of billions of dollars each year, these agencies directly affect the real estate lending functions of commercial banks and savings banks.

The first of these, the Federal National Mortgage Association (commonly known as FNMA, or Fannie Mae), was created in 1938 to supply funds for reasonably priced mortgages in response to the nationwide housing crisis that had arisen during the Great Depression. In 1970 it became a publicly held company; its stock is traded on the New York Stock Exchange. It is an important component of the so-called **secondary market**; that is, it buys home mortgage loans from commercial banks, savings banks, and other lenders to hold in its own portfolio.

The Government National Mortgage Association (GNMA, or Ginnie Mae) was established by Congress in 1968 to stimulate mortgage credit. As a government corporation within the Department of Housing and Urban Development (HUD), Ginnie Mae provides federally backed guarantees that enable housing lenders to raise cash. Ginnie Mae then issues notes and bonds (which are like IOUs) called securities. The mortgages granted by these lenders serve as collateral for the agency's securities, which are sold to investors. In turn, these mortgage-backed securities are sold to investors by brokerage firms just like other stocks and bonds.

The third agency is the Federal Home Loan Mortgage Corporation (Freddie Mac), authorized by Congress in 1970 and owned by commercial banks and savings banks. By issuing bonds, it raises funds that are used to buy the loans granted by mortgage lenders. Freddie Mac also issues mortgage-backed securities that are sold to investors.

Summary

The lending function represents one of the most important sources of income for the bank. While credit is available from many sources, banks are the primary providers of credit to businesses, governments, and individuals.

Federal and state government have enacted laws affecting lending to protect bank safety and soundness and borrowers of credit. When a bank considers a loan, it is guided by these requirements. On the basis of the cost and the bank's own decisions regarding the types of loans it is willing to make, each bank sets its lending policy and gives its loan officers stated amounts of credit authority within which to work.

The lending process consists of four stages, starting with the application and loan interview. During the credit investigation, information is gathered and analyzed to support the loan decision. Loan documentation occurs after the loan has been approved and involves gathering and completing all the required documents, through

---

Exhibit 8.5 **Government Loans**

* Tax Anticipation Loans
* Student Loans
* Mortgage Loans
  —Veterans' Administration
  —Federal Housing Administration
  —Fannie Mae
  —Freddie Mac
  —Ginnie Mae

---

the loan closing. Once the loan is closed, it enters the loan management phase where payments are received and posted, and the loan is monitored for signs of problems.

Bank loans are generally of four types: real estate loans, consumer loans, business loans, and government loans. Extending credit creates a major source of bank income, but at the same time, every extension of credit also carries with it some degree of risk. No absolute formula has ever been devised to eliminate losses completely. The objective of prudent bank lending is to keep losses to a minimum while working to match the needs of the community. In real estate, consumer, business, and government loans, banks follow systematic procedures to achieve that objective. These procedures help protect depositors' funds.

Review and Discussion Questions

1. List five reasons why the lending function is so important to the bank.

2. Identify three Federal Reserve requirements for bank loans.

3. What roles do bank directors play in the overall lending function?

4. Should loans be granted on the basis of collateral alone? Why or why not?

5. Distinguish between construction loans and mortgage loans.

Additional Resources

Analyzing Financial Statements. Washington, D.C.: American Bankers Association, 1998.

Bank Card Industry Survey Report. Washington, D.C.: American Bankers Association, 2001.

Commercial Lending. Washington, D.C.: American Bankers Association, 1999.

Consumer Credit Delinquency Bulletin. Washington, D.C.: American Bankers Association, 2001.

Consumer Lending. Washington, D.C.: American Bankers Association, 2001.

Farm Credit Survey Report. Washington, D.C.: American Bankers Association, 2001.

Home Equity Lending Survey Report. Washington, D.C.: American Bankers Association, 2001.

Installment Credit Survey Report. Washington, D.C.: American Bankers Association, 2001.

Law and Banking: Applications. Washington, D.C.: American Bankers Association, 2000.

Law and Banking: Principles. Washington, D.C.: American Bankers Association, 2000.

Web Resources

Fannie Mae www.fanniemae.com

FDIC CRA site www.fdic.gov/ regulations/community/index.html

Federal Financial Institutions Examination Council (FFIEC) Community Reinvestment Act resource site www.ffiec.gov/cra/

Federal Reserve Board CRA site www.federalreserve.gov/DCCA/CRA/

Freddie Mac www.freddiemac.com

Ginnie Mae www.ginniemae.gov

OCC CRA site www.occ.treas.gov/crainfo.htm

Office of Thrift Supervision CRA site www.ots.treas.gov/cra.html

Robert Morris Associates www.rmahq.org

United States Department of Agriculture www.usda.gov

9

FUNDS MANAGEMENT AND BANK INVESTMENTS

Jenkins, you do have a way with the customers ~
but at this bank, lending is a serious business...

Learning Objectives

After completing this chapter, you will be able to do the following:

- explain the difference between asset management and liability management
- identify the three objectives of funds management in banking and describe how they interrelate
- describe four factors that are considered when determining the interest rate of a loan and distinguish among the discount, prime, fed funds, and LIBOR rates
- describe two major differences in the objectives of loans and investments
- explain credit risk, market risk, and diversification of investments, and discuss how diversification reduces risk
- identify the four types of investments that make up most of the holdings in bank investment portfolios
- define the bolded terms that appear in the text

Introduction

Banks are charged with ensuring that sufficient funds are available to meet their customers' credit and cash needs, while providing a good return for their shareholders. They do this by effectively managing the banks' loanable funds and prudently investing. This chapter explains basic asset and liability management strategies and the funds management objectives of liquidity, safety, and income. It also describes the types of investments that banks are legally allowed to make.

Credit needs vary tremendously and there are any number of credit products available from the bank. The challenge is matching your customer's need with the appropriate credit product, while effectively managing the bank's funds so that money is available to meet credit needs.

It is a testament to the success of bank funds management that most customers take bank services and the availability of credit for granted. The following situations demonstrate this.

Situation 1

The Paulsons have a friend who is selling a luxury car for $25,000. The car is actually worth $30,000, but the owner must sell within two days and has lowered the price. The owner has given the Paulsons the first option on the car if they can come up with the money in that time; otherwise, another buyer is lined up. The Paulsons do not want to get a car loan. They have more than enough money invested in the stock market. However, when they call their stockbroker to sell $25,000 worth of stock, they are told they will not receive a check for seven days. They offer their friend the $10,000

that they have in their checking account and hope that he can wait one week for the balance. Could you have given them better advice?

Situation 2

Elizabeth Markley applied for a home equity loan to pay for renovations to her home. She anticipates spending about $10,000 over a period of two to three years. She already has a mortgage loan from the bank and maintains a savings account and a checking account with overdraft protection. She also has a safe deposit box. When Elizabeth's loan is approved, she deposits the proceeds into her savings account, intending to use the money as needed during the renovation project. How else could this have been handled?

Situation 3

A young entrepreneur is ready to take advantage of a healthy business environment, a strong economy, and favorable interest rates to start a software development company. He seeks a loan from his bank. Because many people in his community have realized that this is a good time to start a business, the bank has been very busy making loans. By the time the young entrepreneur gets his loan approved, the bank has already exceeded its anticipated loan demand. However, rather than deny the loan for lack of funds, how can the bank help this customer?

Banks invest deposited funds to meet cash needs and to generate income. Like any business, a bank's need for vault and teller cash is seasonal. Investing in instruments with varying maturity dates allows banks to have their cash earn interest when it is not needed and to be available when it is needed. Banks are restricted in their investment activities because they are investing other people's money. While high-risk investments might yield a high return for the bank, they also expose the bank to potential loss. Therefore, government regulations limit the types of investments banks can make to those that are "safe," protecting depositors from loss.

Management of Bank Funds

Managing assets (loans and investments) and liabilities (deposits) is the fundamental challenge of banking. However, it is far more complex than simply making sure that the rate charged for a loan is higher than the rate paid for deposits. Banks have an obligation to make loans that service their community and market (consumer, business, and government), and to meet their cash (liquidity) needs. The lending function, therefore, is as much about investments as it is about loans.

It is a widely held misconception that banks possess huge pools of money belonging only to themselves and that they can lend and invest these funds as they see fit. If this were true, a bank would be risking only its own funds when it makes loans. In fact, the opposite is true. Every bank loan represents an effort to put deposited money to work safely and prudently, at a profit, while at the same time meeting the legitimate credit needs of borrowers.

Each bank develops a strategy to manage bank funds, taking the many variables into account. Most banks have found that the most effective funds management strategy is one that simultaneously manages both assets and liabilities.

Asset and Liability Management

An **asset** is anything of value that is owned by or owed to the bank, while a **liability** is anything that is owed by the bank. Loans (owed to the bank) and investments (owned by the bank) are assets for the bank. In previous years, as demand deposits steadily flowed into the bank on an interest-free basis, the banker's task consisted simply of putting those funds to the most profitable use. For years, management primarily focused on the bank's assets—mostly on loans and other investments. Managers were not particularly concerned about the source of the funds—primarily customers' deposits—that were used to purchase the assets.

While **asset management** is still important, **liability management** now must receive at least equal attention. Changes in banks' deposit base require that each institution make periodic decisions about how much it needs in working funds, where additional funds can be acquired, and how much the bank is willing to pay for them in a competitive marketplace. Deposits are a liability to the bank, because the funds deposited are owed to depositors and the depositors expect the bank to return them. Managing the liability side of banking has become increasingly important, because interest-free deposits no longer can be expected to flow in regularly and automatically. Banks work hard to attract new depositors and to retain those deposits once the account has been opened.

Interest paid to depositors constitutes one of the largest and least controllable expenses for most U.S. banks. Banks buy the funds they need for their continuing operations. The interest they pay to depositors must be offset by interest received on loans. Because most of the deposit base consists of interest-bearing time and savings deposits, the bank must ensure that its earnings from loans exceed its payments on deposits. The spread between the two, known as net interest spread, represents the profit spread on loans. Each institution's net interest spread is critical to its efforts to meet payments, generate profits, and grow.

In bank lending, every effort is made to match maturity of loans with maturity of deposits—the principle of matched funding. For example, increased requests from creditworthy customers for loans may require that the bank increase its efforts to acquire funds in the CD market. The rates a bank pays to obtain those deposits directly affect the rates charged on loans. If customers seek long-term loans for factory expansion or the purchase of modern equipment, the bank makes every effort to fund those loans with longer-term deposits. Because demand deposits, on the other hand, tend to remain with the bank for much shorter periods, they can be used to fund customers' requests for short-term loans or for loans that reprice or adjust as market rates change.

This principle of matched funding applies to every component of the bank's deposits and loans. Realistically, it cannot be implemented in every loan situation; however, it is a basic guideline that is followed whenever possible. An institution cannot remain in business for long if it ignores that guideline and embarks on a program of funding long-term, fixed-rate loans with short-term deposits.

Objectives of Funds Management

Because bank loans are made with funds entrusted by customers, a program must exist for the sound management of those funds. These funds management programs are given a high priority and are often managed by the president or CEO at smaller banks and funds management departments at larger banks. This program addresses three objectives: liquidity, safety, and income. Successful bank management requires the balancing of the three, in the order listed. Any emphasis on one objective at the expense of the other two, or any neglect of one objective inevitably causes difficulties.

Liquidity

Every business, individual, institution, and agency of government faces the continual problem of meeting everyday financial obligations. If this can be done with cash or the equivalent of cash, a liquid financial condition is said to exist. An individual who holds sufficient currency, demand deposits, or other assets that can be quickly converted into cash to cover his or her debts, taxes, and other expenses is considered to have a high degree of liquidity. Similarly, a business that pays its suppliers and other creditors without difficulty is considered to have a high degree of liquidity.

On the other hand, an individual or a business may have assets that cannot be readily converted into cash. For example, the owner of large amounts of undeveloped real estate or of a major office building might have difficulty obtaining cash quickly in exchange for those holdings. In this case, the individual or business is said to be in an illiquid position, or a position of illiquidity. The Paulsons in situation 1 have $10,000 in liquid money—money in their checking account that can be converted immediately to cash to pay for the car they want to buy. The money they have in the stock market is less liquid because it takes longer to convert it into cash. However, an astute banker can suggest other means of securing the cash quickly, such as obtaining a stock-secured loan or a simple auto loan.

Liquidity has special importance for a bank. To operate effectively, a bank cannot find itself in an illiquid position. No depositor leaves funds with a bank without expecting to use the funds or to direct that the funds be paid to others. Demand deposits, for example, can be withdrawn at any time by issuing checks. A savings account customer has access to part or all of his or her balance at any time unless the bank exercises its right to demand advance notice of intent to withdraw. Time deposits mature at specified dates and are paid back with interest.

No bank can remain in business long if it rejects customers' requests for withdrawals or payments on the grounds that it cannot meet them. For a bank, then, **liquidity** chiefly means the ability of the institution to meet demands for payments of funds at any time.

The need for liquidity is tied not only to the deposit function but also to the lending function as well. Every bank has customers who have legitimate needs for credit. They expect their bank to meet that need and to make funds available to them. Liquidity also enables banks to provide for the loan demands of customers, and it fulfills the bank's obligation to support community needs as defined in the Community Reinvestment Act.

Depositors' understanding of liquidity is implicit in their making deposits in the first place. Every deposit demonstrates a customer's confidence that the bank will protect the funds and be able to repay them when called on to do so. Without this confidence, people would not put their money in banks. If funds are not available, all the usual patterns of inflow and outflow of funds change. New deposits no longer flow into a bank that is sus-

pected of being illiquid; at the same time, depositors rush to withdraw funds in an effort to protect themselves. The wave of bank failures during the 1930s was caused at least in part by this type of reaction.

For the American public, federal deposit insurance and the other efforts of the federal government to protect depositors' funds have brought a much-needed degree of public confidence. However, the obligation of banks to be sufficiently liquid to meet estimated outflows of funds and to provide for legitimate credit demands remains unchanged, no matter what forms of government protection exist.

Every bank bases its daily operations on a variation of the law of averages. Theoretically, it is possible that all depositors will want to withdraw funds at the same time, but there is little likelihood that they will. It is far more likely that new deposits will arrive at the bank each day while checks and orders for withdrawals are being honored. (Consider a teller's cash drawer in which cash comes in from one customer and goes out to the next. Rarely does a teller spend the whole day giving out cash without taking any in.) A problem arises only when this law of averages is distorted.

When a manufacturer encounters a sudden, unforeseen demand for its product, it usually can cope with the situation by assuring customers that the assembly lines are doing everything possible to meet the sales orders and by promising delivery of the finished goods as soon as possible. Banks, on the other hand, have no such option. They cannot ask customers to wait patiently until a liquidity problem is solved and necessary funds are obtained. Every demand for payment or withdrawal of funds is honored unless there is a compelling reason to refuse it. For this reason, liquidity in banking is essential, and it is always the most important of the three basic objectives in managing bank funds.

The deposit-loan relationship. The relationship between a bank's liquidity position and its lending function has an additional facet. Typically, bank loans are made to existing customers and the proceeds are credited to existing demand accounts, or the loan proceeds are used to open an account. New loans therefore generate additional deposits (see exhibit 3.6). After the bank makes provision for reserve requirements, the deposits can be put to profitable use in the form of additional loans.

If a bank overemphasized liquidity, keeping large supplies of currency in its vaults as protection against possible increases in customers' demands for withdrawals, it would reduce the percentage of its deposits available for lending. In this way its lending function would be impaired and its loan income would shrink. At the same time, the bank would be neglecting its safety requirements, because keeping excessive quantities of currency on hand makes the bank more vulnerable to theft and losses.

Therefore, while always recognizing the primary importance of liquidity, a bank also focuses on two other obligations in its program for funds management: safety and income.

Meeting liquidity needs. Each bank makes its best effort to predict loan demand in relation to its deposit base. If a combination of seasonal and money market conditions and information obtained from existing or potential borrowers indicates that loan demand will increase, and if maturity dates for time deposits and seasonal factors indicate that deposits will probably decrease, the bank requires additional liquidity. If the demand for credit is extremely high, a so-called "credit crunch" may occur, meaning that banks are finding it difficult to meet the legitimate borrowing needs of their markets.

Liquidity needs at banks are usually met through various types of reserves. Primary reserves consist of cash on hand, demand deposit balances held at correspondent banks, and reserves kept at the Federal Reserve. The bank relies on these funds to support its day-to-day operations. Primary reserves offer more liquidity because they are immediately available; on the other hand, they earn no interest. Secondary reserves consist of the highest-quality investments permitted by law (such as Treasury bills) that can be converted into cash on very short notice. These funds serve as back-up reserves. They provide interest income but slightly less liquidity, because they have to be sold to obtain cash.

Safety

Customer confidence in the safety of banks is essential. By avoiding undue risk, banks meet their responsibility to protect the deposits entrusted to them. Depositors need to know that their funds are being fully protected. Creating a climate of customer confidence in the ability of banks to provide safety for deposits has never been more important.

Although the Federal Deposit Insurance Corporation (FDIC) is a form of protection for depositors at insured banks, the banks also work to increase public confidence by practicing care and prudence in lending. Any report of fraud or mismanagement at financial institutions, particularly when improper extensions of credit are included, weakens public confidence. By increasing loan loss reserves, banks have acted prudently and have helped protect depositors against the loss of their funds.

Again, however, balancing the three objectives of funds management is essential; no single factor can be stressed while the other two are neglected. If a bank tried to provide maximum safety, it would never assume any risk by putting deposits to profitable use; it would make only those loans and investments that had no potential for loss. In being overcautious, such a bank would inevitably neglect the legitimate needs of all its customers and community. In addition, its income would shrink because it would lose loan interest.

Income

The third objective that is part of a bank's program for funds management is income. If liquidity and safety were the only factors a bank had to consider, it could build the largest and strongest vault imaginable, keep as much cash as possible on hand under maximum security, and make only those loans and investments that carried an absolute minimum of risk. An adequate supply of currency would always be available to meet demands for withdrawals and payments of funds, and losses resulting from loans and investments would be very small (if any existed at all). This course of action, however, would neglect the income objective.

Unlike banks in some other countries, U.S. banks are not owned by or directly subsidized by the federal government. They are organized for profit, and profit for their shareholders is of primary importance, coupled to a lesser degree with other obligations to customers and communities. A bank that repeatedly shows annual losses or does not demonstrate adequate growth in its annual income soon loses the confidence of its depositors, its stockholders, and the public.

Income, like liquidity and safety, can never be considered alone. Overemphasizing profits while neglecting liquidity and safety can be disastrous. Throughout U.S. financial history, many banks choosing to maximize short-term income at the expense of liquidity and safety have been forced out of business because of unsafe practices.

Interest on loans represents a large portion of a bank's annual income. Therefore, any bank that makes improved earnings its essential goal expands its loan portfolio to build up its interest income. Such expansion involves aggressive efforts to attract new borrowers. Experience clearly shows that this course of action, which was followed by many banks in the late 1920s and early 1930s, leads to a lowering of normal credit standards. Safety becomes a low priority, and banks approve loans that would not otherwise be made, accepting risks that are far beyond prudent norms.

Interest is money paid for the use of money. A borrower who particularly needs funds will pay a higher interest rate. Similarly, a bank that seeks improved earnings while neglecting safety considerations will charge higher rates to reflect the increased risks it assumes. Despite immediate short-term gains in profits, this policy will prove fatal to the bank in the long run as weak loans prove uncollectible and are charged off.

Banks always attempt to increase income, but they must not ignore liquidity and safety requirements while doing so.

Priorities of Funds Management

A program for managing bank funds creates and sustains a balance among the three objectives—liquidity, safety, and income. Doing so requires establishing a schedule of priorities. Since the most fundamental obligation of a bank is to meet all foreseeable demands for withdrawals of funds, the primary focus is on liquidity. A bank's deposit base is always changing, demand deposits even more than savings and time deposits. A bank must be prepared for shrinkage in its deposit base at any time. Any indication that a bank is having difficulty meeting depositors' demands for withdrawals worsens an already critical situation.

Because banks have an obligation to satisfy the legitimate credit needs of depositors and communities, estimates of liquidity needs must also consider loan demand. By law, and as a practical matter, a bank cannot remain in business if it neglects the lending function. In every discussion of liquidity needs, the fact that every segment of the economy relies on banks as a primary credit source must be considered. When an economic slowdown occurs, corporate earnings decrease. Many companies find it necessary to borrow to finance ongoing operations. When corporations are forced to incur additional debt, additional pressure is created on the banks to accommodate them.

Customers tend to deposit funds with banks that meet their requests for credit. If a bank refuses to make a loan to a customer, the customer is not likely to open or maintain an account with that bank. This fact puts pressure on banks to make loans. Some of the loans made by banks are not paid and are ultimately charged off. On the other hand, stockholders look for growth and profits. The stockholders like to see banks make only loans that are paid back. Banks require the highest degree of management skill to reconcile customers' demand for loans with stockholders' desire for enhancement of their ownership in the bank. Again, the nature of the banking business creates demands on banks that make them essentially different from other types of lenders. If, for example, a small loan company or commercial financing firm rejects a request for credit, it loses only the interest income it might have received. If a bank refuses to lend to a longstanding depositor, however, it faces the loss of a valued account as well as the potential interest income, deposit dollars, and service fee income. Remember how the customer in situation 2 had several existing accounts with the bank and deposited her loan proceeds in one of these accounts? Had the bank denied that loan, the bank would not have received the additional deposit, and might have lost all of the customer's accounts. This customer could have been counseled to get a home equity loan that disburses funds when needed.

Interest Rates

Within legal limits, the interest rates banks charge reflect the fact that money is essentially a supply-and-demand commodity, the price of which fluctuates widely. The rate charged on a specific loan usually represents a combination of factors, including the

- cost of funds to the bank
- availability of funds

- risk factors perceived by the bank
- term (or period of time) of the loan

Cost

The basic source of loanable and investable funds for a bank continues to be customer deposits. Today, deposits carry a significant cost to the bank in the form of interest that is paid to depositors. Banks monitor the cost of funds compared to the interest rate charged on loans.

Availability

The Federal Reserve plays a major role in controlling the nation's supply of money and credit by raising or lowering reserve requirements whenever it feels changes are advisable. In addition, the purchases and/or sales of government obligations, as directed by the Federal Open Market Committee, directly affect the availability of loanable funds within the economy. Open market activities affect the level of reserves in the banking system. By purchasing government obligations, the Federal Reserve adds to reserves and makes funds available for banks to lend or invest (chapter 3). Conversely, sales of government obligations through the FOMC's actions reduce reserves in the banking system and pressure interest rates upward. Therefore, banks will need to adjust their price (the interest rate on loans) to reflect the actions of the Federal Reserve.

Risk

Interest rates may be affected by the bank's perception of **risk** (the possibility of sustaining loss on its loans). Within legal limits, banks set interest rates on loans after evaluating the creditworthiness of a borrower. Banks also evaluate risk on the type of loan being made. Some loans have a higher degree of risk than others. For example, unsecured loans are higher risk than home equity loans; motorcycle loans are higher risk than car loans; and debt consolidation loans are higher risk than home mortgages. Some lenders, such as personal finance companies, charge higher rates than banks because of the higher degree of risk they are willing to assume.

Term

The term for which a loan will be outstanding also affects the interest rate charged. The longer the loan term, the greater the uncertainty of repayment and the opportunity for the borrower's credit standing to deteriorate. Therefore, most banks will charge a higher rate to offset some of this risk. For example, the continuing operations of a manufacturer involve risks in the acquisition of raw materials, the production process, the demand for the finished product, and the collection of receivables from customers. If a loan is made for an extended term, there is a stronger possibility that these risks will adversely affect the borrower's ability to repay as scheduled.

Rates—Discount, Prime, Fed Funds, and LIBOR

Just as banks establish the interest rate to charge for their loans, the Federal Reserve determines the rate to charge banks for the use of its funds. Regulation A of the Federal Reserve allows each of the 12 Federal Reserve banks to extend credit to depository institutions and to charge interest on all such loans at the **discount rate**. The Federal Reserve Act requires each of the 12 district banks to establish its discount rate and report the results to the Federal Reserve Board of Governors in Washington, D.C.

The discount rate applies to short-term credit extended by the Fed. In addition, the Fed has established a higher rate for its loans to depository institutions for periods of more than 30 days. The higher, flexible rate is used when a depository institution is under liquidity pressure and is unable to obtain funds on reasonable terms from other sources.

The **prime rate** is a benchmark, base, or reference that a bank establishes from time to time in calculating an appropriate rate for a loan customer. It is widely quoted as an indicator of overall interest rates. In self-protection, especially on longer term loans, a bank may enter into a written agreement with a commercial borrower that the interest on the loan will be at a certain differential from the prime rate (such as prime plus 1.25 percent) as quoted in nationally recognized publications. In this way the bank gives itself the option of adjusting the interest rate as the cost and availability of funds change.

The **Fed funds** rate is the rate one institution charges another for the overnight use of reserve funds. Banks that, because of the day's activity, are short on their reserve requirements borrow overnight from institutions that have excess reserves. The Fed funds rate is not a customer rate. It is a bank-to-bank rate that is usually higher than the discount rate and lower than the prime rate. The Federal Reserve bank, through its Federal Open Market Operations, "targets" a rate for federal funds. The actual rate for fed funds is determined between banks during the day based on availability of reserves in the marketplace. Exhibit 9.1 shows the relationship among these three rates.

Another rate that is sometimes used in bank lending is the LIBOR rate. LIBOR stands for the London Interbank Offered Rate. It is an international money market interest rate that represents the average rate offered by banks for the interbank placement of Eurodollars. The LIBOR rate is determined by calculating the average rate of trade among those banks. It is often used as a benchmark, similar to the prime rate, against which other loans are priced. Banks will often add percentages from LIBOR to determine the rate for a loan.

Bank Investments

Loans are not the only means of putting the bank's funds to profitable use. Banks also invest available funds so that these funds can earn income when not needed for loans. There are two basic differences between loans and bank investments.

The first difference is that banks must give priority to the credit needs of customers and communities; the fundamental business of banking is the lending of money to businesses, units of government, individuals, and other banks. Banks fulfill their obligations by supplying the funds that customers legitimately wish to borrow. An institution that does not make loans fails to meet the legal definition of a bank. Although certain laws also require banks to make investments, there is no comparable pressure on them to do so. Investments have a lower priority and are made only after the demand for loans has been met. When a bank encounters an increased demand for loans, it may choose to sell some of its investment holdings to obtain additional funds to lend. Therefore, banks may sell securities before their maturity. Funding for the software company in situation 3, for example, may be

Exhibit 9.1 **Interest Rate Comparison**

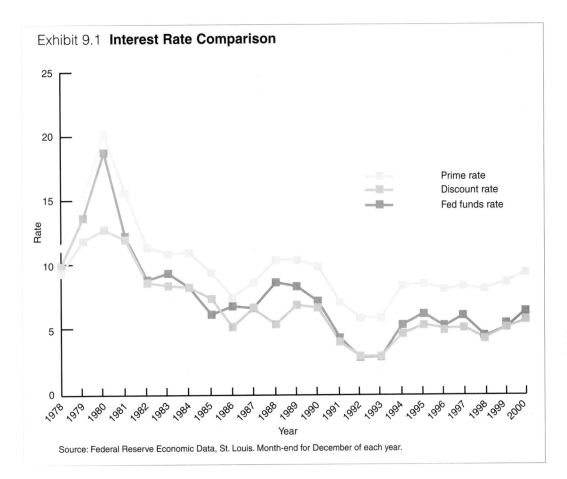

Source: Federal Reserve Economic Data, St. Louis. Month-end for December of each year.

met by attracting additional deposits, or may come from the sale of investment holdings.

The second difference is that the bank negotiates directly on loans and indirectly on investments. In making a loan, a bank negotiates directly with the borrower regarding the amount, purpose, maturity, rate, and other factors. In most cases the bank is dealing with a borrower who is known to it through a deposit relationship. In contrast, when a bank makes an investment it does so indirectly, through a bond dealer or underwriter. The bank relies on investment rating services to determine the quality of the investment and the risk involved. In some cases, local issues of securities may not be rated, and the bank may have to conduct its own inquiries and have its own

investment portfolio officers rate the issues before making an investment. The bank does not negotiate directly with the issuer in most cases; the issuer may not even know who the purchaser is.

Interest on loans and income from investments both contribute to bank earnings, but the purpose of each is different. Banks do not make loans solely to earn income; rather, loans also reflect the bank's obligation to meet the credit needs of its customer base and the community. Investments, on the other hand, are made chiefly for income purposes. The fact that banks do contribute to the general well-being of a community by buying that community's notes or bonds is secondary to the income objective.

Credit Risk vs. Market Risk

Risk enters into every investment activity a bank undertakes. A bank faces two types of risk when putting funds to profitable use: credit risk and market risk.

In loans, the chief concern is **credit risk**—the bank's estimate of the probability that the borrower can and will repay a loan with interest as scheduled. The investments that banks are allowed to make have a lower degree of credit risk than loans. These investments also have a lower rate of return or yield, generating less revenue for the bank. In general, banks are more concerned with a borrower's ability to repay a loan than they are over the ability of the issuer of notes or bonds to meet its obligation to repay. Rather than borrow from a bank, local, state, and federal governments borrow money directly from investors by issuing debt obligations in the form of notes and bonds. Banks act like any other investor and purchase these government obligations directly. In the case of U.S. government obligations there is no question of credit risk, because the federal government guarantees repayment. Similarly, when the full faith and credit of a state, county, or city guarantees an issue of debt securities, they can raise taxes to repay the obligation.

Even these "safe" investments, however, are not without risk. In investments, the chief concern is market risk. **Market risk** is the risk that the market value of a security will decrease because of interest rates and other market conditions. When a holder wishes to sell a security, market conditions and the overall desirability of the security determine market value—the seller cannot control it. The risk is that the market value at the time of sale may be less than the price the holder initially paid for the security.

The price of a bond, for example, may increase or decrease as a result of interest rate fluctuations. Therefore, while U.S. government obligations carry no credit risk, they do entail market risk, because open market yields and interest rates fluctuate with supply and demand. When a bank wishes to sell a government security with a rate lower than the current market rate of interest, it will have to lower the price enough to make its yield comparable to current yields. Depending on the price the bank paid for the security, this selling price could result in a loss to the bank. The price of a security moves inversely (in the opposite direction) to its yield. In periods when interest rates and yields increase, the market price of outstanding bonds decline. When rates and yields fall, the prices of outstanding bonds increase. Under the conditions described above, the sale of the bond generates a loss of principal to the bank. The market price in this case is lower than the bank's original purchase price.

In any given year, a bank may show profits or losses on sales of securities, depending on market conditions during the previous 12 months. In certain cases a bank deliberately sells some of its investments at a loss in order to raise funds to improve its liquidity and uses the proceeds for loans that carry a higher rate of return. Taking such losses can also work to the bank's advantage if the institution has a substantial amount of net taxable income from which the losses can be deducted.

Diversification

For both legal and practical reasons, banks invest their funds in various types of bond issues with varying maturity dates. This method of decreasing risk by investing in assets of different kinds is called diversification.

The legal reasons for diversifying investments in bond issues are twofold:

- First, banks are prohibited from investing directly in any common stock (except in the cases noted below), although their subsidiaries or financial holding companies may do so as a result of Gramm-Leach-Bliley, which limits their investing largely to bonds
- Second, banks are limited in the percentage of their capital and surplus they can invest in the securities of any one issuer, except investments in U.S. government obligations, which is a mandate for diversification.

The first of these restrictions traces back to the thousands of bank failures that occurred during the Great Depression. Before 1933, many banks were active as both underwriters of, and investors in, corporate stock issues. In many cases they were considered to have done this simply in the expectation of making quick profits. They were as optimistic as the general public in believing stock market prices would continue to increase. This activity was not considered a legitimate use of deposited funds. The Glass-Steagall Act of 1933 forced a separation of commercial banking from investment banking, prohibiting banks from underwriting certain types of debt issues and restricting their opportunities for investment.

There are two other cases to note of banks holding investments in common stock: (1) member banks in the Federal Reserve System are legally required to buy and hold stock in their district Federal Reserve bank, and (2) bank holding companies are allowed to buy and hold stock in their various subsidiaries.

Required Investments

In many cases, bank investments are made because of legal requirements. For example, many states require banks to pledge U.S. government obligations to ensure protection for deposits in public funds accounts over and above the coverage provided by the Federal Deposit Insurance Corporation. This means that a depository bank holds and segregates a quantity of federal or state obligations to protect deposits. For similar reasons, the trust powers granted by many individual states to bank trust departments require that federal and state debt issues be set aside to protect the pension, trust, and profit-sharing funds they manage.

Spacing of Maturities

In attempting to achieve the proper combination of liquidity, safety, and income, banks not only diversify their investment portfolios among various issues, but also ensure that their holdings carry a range of maturities. The securities with the shortest maturities provide the bank with a higher degree of liquidity; at the same time, their yields are usually lower than those of the longer-term issues, reflecting the higher risk that long-term debt creates.

Types of Bank Investments

A typical bank's investment portfolio consists almost exclusively of four types of holdings (exhibit 9.2):

- U.S. Treasury/U.S. government obligations
- U.S. government agency obligations
- municipal issues
- miscellaneous investments that meet the highest credit standards, such as bankers' acceptances, certificates of deposit issued by other financial institutions, commercial paper, corporate bonds, and mortgage-backed securities

Exhibit 9.2 **Types of Bank Investments**

U.S. Treasury/U.S. government obligations
* Bills–maturities of less than 1 year
* Notes–maturities greater than 1 year but less than 5 years
* Bonds—maturities greater than 5 years but less than 30 years

U.S. government agencies
* Export-Import Bank
* Federal Home Loan Bank
* Veterans' Administration

Municipal issues
* School district bonds
* State government bonds
* Turnpike commission bonds
* Sewer authority bonds

Miscellaneous investments
* Certificates of deposit issued by other institutions
* Commercial paper
* Corporate bonds
* Banker's acceptances
* Mortgage-backed securities

U.S. Treasury and U.S. Government Obligations

U.S. Treasury bills offer an investing bank a dual advantage. Because Treasury bills are issued with maturities of less than one year, they are immediately marketable, usually with limited risk. They provide liquidity and are part of the bank's secondary reserves. Treasury notes (which carry maturities greater than one year but less than five years) and Treasury bonds (which are issued with maturities greater than five years) are sources of investment income. They are marketable because of their longer maturities, but they carry greater market risk.

U.S. government obligations form the most acceptable type of collateral when a depository institution borrows from the Federal Reserve. The Federal Reserve's loan portfolio can exceed $500 million. This is money owed to the Federal Reserve by depository institutions; in many cases the borrowers pledged government obligations to secure those loans.

U.S. Treasury obligations are backed by the full faith and credit of the federal government.

U.S. Government Agency Obligations

Many banks will also invest in obligations issued by agencies of the federal government (for example, the Export-Import Bank) as well as by agencies that are federally sponsored (such as the Federal Home Loan Banks and the Federal National Mortgage Association). Obligations of all these agencies are to some extent guaranteed by the federal government, yet the interest rates on those obligations are typically higher than the rates on U.S. government obligations of the same maturity. Because of the extra yield, banks frequently invest in agency issues.

Municipal Issues

Municipals is a generic term that describes the bonds issued by any government or government agency, other than federal. A state, city, county, town, school district, or other government unit issues bonds to raise funds that will be used for public purposes. These debt issues supplement the funds the unit of government may receive from taxation.

If the municipal bonds are backed by the full taxing power of the issuer, they are known as full faith and credit obligations. Banks are allowed to act as underwriters for these general obligation bonds; that is, they are permitted to buy them directly from the issuer and distribute them by selling them to investors. Other municipal bonds, known as revenue bonds, are not backed by the taxing power of the issuer but are supported by the direct income expected from a specific project. For example, a state may issue revenue bonds to raise funds to build a new toll road. Each bondholder depends on the profit from the new turnpike's operations to provide a source of repayment. As a result of the Gramm-Leach-Bliley Act, banks are allowed to underwrite revenue bonds as long as the bank is well capitalized.

Unlike U.S. government obligations, which are considered entirely free of credit risk, municipal bonds involve both credit risk and market risk. Their credit risk reflects the fact that no municipal issuer's credit standing can be as high as that of the federal government. For the same reason, their market risk is greater. A bank or other investor wishing to sell municipals may be forced to accept a loss if sold prior to maturity. For example, publicity about the financial problems of a state or city may make municipal issues unattractive to investors, and a change in the credit rating given to a particular municipal bond by one of the major rating agencies immediately increases market risk.

Given the credit and market risk that municipals carry, a good question is, Why do banks consider them to be worthwhile investments? There are two basic reasons.

First, income from municipals is completely exempt from federal income taxes and may also be exempt from state and local taxes. For example, a bank or other investor in Chicago who purchases bonds issued by a unit of Illinois government enjoys exemption from all taxes on the income. On the other hand, if a Virginia bank or investor bought bonds issued by a unit of Illinois government, the exemption from federal tax on the income would still apply, but the income could be subject to Virginia state and local taxes, depending on state laws. The higher the tax bracket of the bank or other investor, the greater the advantage of deriving tax-free income from municipals.

The second reason banks invest in municipal bonds involves the commitment banks make to their communities. Banks recognize that their own well-being, growth, and profitability are closely tied to the economic conditions in their own communities. If a city or town is unable to raise the funds it needs, and its economy and services deteriorate, the banks suffer as well. Every bank investment in municipal issues represents a vote of confidence in the ability of the community to maintain a healthy economy and eventually repay its debts. By investing in municipal bonds, banks act as responsible corporate citizens who give to their local communities as well as receive income from them.

Miscellaneous Investments

Investments such as banker's acceptances, negotiable certificates of deposit, commercial paper, and corporate bonds meet the highest credit standards and are acceptable bank investments.

Banker's Acceptances

Banker's acceptances are drafts or bills of exchange that banks have "accepted" as their own liabilities by pledging their credit on behalf of their customers' credit. For example, a buyer of goods arranges a line of credit with the bank to be used to purchase goods. When the buyer sends the bank a draft ordering the bank to make payment, the bank acknowledges its obligation to pay the draft by marking it "accepted." However, since the draft usually does not come due for several weeks or months (usually when the goods are delivered), it can be sold. When it matures, the new owner presents the draft to the buyer for payment. If for some reason the buyer does not make good on the draft, the accepting bank provides the funds, since that bank has already "accepted" its obligation.

Banks are major investors in banker's acceptances, since these instruments provide liquidity and earnings for the bank's portfolios.

Negotiable Certificates of Deposit

Banks issue negotiable certificates of deposit that one depositor can sell to another investor prior to the CD's maturity. Negotiable CDs have a minimum denomination of $100,000. In the case of smaller banks, the interest rates are negotiated between the banker and depositor; in the case of issues by large banks, rates are usually established daily by bank management. Some banks with excess reserves buy CDs to hold as a highly liquid earning asset. To be attractive to investors, negotiable CDs have an interest rate that is somewhat higher than comparable maturities on the Treasury bill and commercial paper.

Commercial Paper

Short-term unsecured obligations of large and financially sound corporations are known as commercial paper. Firms that issue commercial paper to raise funds have excellent credit ratings, because investors receive no collateral and depend on the firm's reputation for the safety of funds invested. Commercial paper is often used as an alternative source of short-term funds instead of borrowing directly from a bank.

Corporate Bonds

Corporations may raise funds needed to finance expansion by selling **corporate bonds**. These bonds are long-term debts owed to investors. Corporate bonds may be either unsecured or secured by some type of collateral. Some banks may invest in high-quality corporate debt, but few do (and those invest only in relatively small amounts) because the after-tax return on other investments is usually better and because banks are concerned with marketability. Banks prefer to finance business firms directly through loans, rather than indirectly through purchases of credit instruments in the market.

Summary

Banks manage their funds to meet the credit needs of their customers and to generate a profit for their shareholders. They commonly employ an asset and liability management strategy to meet this goal.

The nature of the deposit base in banks has changed dramatically over the years. Interest-earning deposits now constitute the largest portion of that base. Because all deposits are direct liabilities of banks, the overall program of funds management addresses two questions: (1) How much in additional deposits does the institution wish to obtain? and (2) What costs will those new deposits create? By analyzing the types and maturities of deposits it is attracting, and the interest expenses these deposits create, a bank can match its loan and investment policies to its deposit structure. It thereby manages liabilities as well as assets, while assuring itself of an appropriate net interest margin.

If a business, a unit of government, or an individual can readily meet existing debt payments and handle current expenses with cash or the equivalent of cash, a liquid position exists. Liquidity, the first objective of funds management, is important for banks, because they must be able to meet customers' demands for withdrawals of funds and for credit; if they cannot do so, they soon cease to exist. Through a combination of primary and secondary reserves, banks meet their liquidity needs and provide for anticipated withdrawals and payments of funds and for probable loan demand.

Safety, the second objective of funds management, calls for banks to avoid undue risk in their use of customers' money. Prudence in making loans and investments is necessary and is a critical factor in building public confidence.

Income is the third objective of funds management. If a bank overemphasizes income at the expense of the other two objectives, it inevitably lowers its credit standards and builds a portfolio of weak loans that can lead to its downfall.

Bank investments contribute to the overall lending function by putting deposited funds to work, but investments occupy a lower priority than loans in the managing of bank funds. As a group, commercial banks are the largest holders of U.S. government obligations. They have also made substantial investments in the debt issues of state and local units of government, authorities, and agencies. These municipal issues offer tax advantages to an investing bank and also help to provide the flow of funds needed by local governments to provide community services.

When a bank makes investments, it considers both the credit risk and the market risk of a particular obligation; however, no credit risk exists with U.S. government obligations. In many cases bank investments are made because they are used as collateral against public funds accounts, as required by state laws.

With the approval of federal regulators in recent years, many banks have begun to engage in a wider range of securities-related activities.

Review and Discussion Questions

1. Why has liability management become so important in banking?

2. What would be the consequences if a bank chose to overemphasize liquidity while neglecting other factors in funds management?

What would be the consequences of overemphasizing safety at the expense of liquidity and income?

3. Distinguish between the discount rate and the prime rate.

4. How can bank investments contribute to liquidity?

5. Distinguish between credit risk and market risk.

6. List the four types of holdings that typically make up a bank's investment portfolio.

Additional Resources

Commercial Lending and Wholesale Operations Survey Report. Washington, D.C.: American Bankers Association, 2001.

Investment Basics and Beyond. Washington, D.C.: American Bankers Association, 1998.

Portfolio Managers Survey Report. Washington, D.C.: American Bankers Association, 2000.

Web Resources

ABA Securities Association
  www.aba.com/ABASA/default.htm
Federal Reserve Board of Governors
  www.federalreserve.gov/
US Treasury www.treas.gov

10

MEASURING AND REPORTING FINANCIAL PERFORMANCE

**"We're looking for people who can help
make this company profitable again.
I'll read your resume for $200."**

Learning Objectives

After completing this chapter, you will be able to do the following:

- describe the bank's need to maintain accurate accounting data and explain its importance to regulatory authorities, shareholders and investors, bank directors, management, employees, and customers
- compare and contrast cash and accrual accounting methods and describe various recordkeeping methods and reports
- describe the income statement and balance sheet and list several categories of key bank assets and liabilities
- explain how key performance ratios (return on assets, return on equity, capital ratio, net interest spread, and earnings per share) are determined and discuss what each says about a bank's performance
- discuss the impact of financial condition and performance data on shareholders, investors, regulators, other financial institutions, customers, and employees
- describe the financial planning and budgeting process
- define the bolded terms that appear in the text

Introduction

Just as you must be accurate in every aspect of your job, your bank must be accurate in presenting the bank's financial position.

Situation 1

The Jayson Investment Group manages the pension fund for ACME Corp, a large manufacturing business with more than 3,000 employees. Mr. Jayson is considering investing in several bank stocks. He has read annual reports and other financial data from your bank and has set up a meeting with your bank's senior management and auditors to discuss projections for the future. If Mr. Jayson is satisfied with the bank's prospects for the future, he will invest a large sum of money for the ACME Corp. pension fund. What might help him to decide?

Situation 2

Don is taking two years off after high school to make money for college by painting houses. He is hired by a homeowner and finishes the job by December 2000. The homeowner pays him in February 2001. When Don files his 2000 taxes, he claims the expenses but will not report the income until 2001. Down the street, a house is being painted by Rainbow Painting, Inc., a large company with branches throughout the state. Rainbow Painting finishes at the same time as Don (December 2000) and is paid at the same time (February 2001). However, the accountant at Rainbow Painting will report both the income and the expense in the 2000 tax year. How can both situations be legal?

Situation 3

Pat and Larry Ortiz are moving to the Southwest from the Northeast when they retire in a few months. Careful planning and saving over the years have resulted in a substantial retirement investment portfolio that they want to transfer to a financial institution near their new home. In the early 1970s, they had their life savings in a financial institution that failed. Although they did not lose any money, they did not have access to their funds for some time and were scared about the potential loss. Since then, they have become very knowledgeable about financial matters. When they move, they want to make sure the financial institution they select to handle their accounts is well managed and solid. What might help to convince them of this?

The above situations are some examples of how businesses and individuals rely on accurate accounting and financial data to make important decisions. In addition, federal and state regulatory authorities, bank shareholders and investors, other financial institutions, and bank management and employees make use of this data on a regular basis. This chapter describes the reasons why banks keep current and accurate accounting records and the various forms in which the data are presented. It reviews the primary ratios used to measure bank performance, and also discusses planning and budgeting to meet the bank's financial and performance goals. The chapter explains why all employees of the bank—even those whose primary functions are not accounting or auditing —need to have a cursory understanding of bank financial statements and attendant reports.

Importance of Accurate Accounting

Every business, regardless of size and type, must keep current, accurate accounting records to reflect its financial condition and performance, in standard accounting form. Accounting helps a business record its financial data; it is, in fact, the "language of business." Without accurate records a business has no idea whether or not it is making money. The fact that the business is generating revenues, paying bills, paying employees, and paying taxes does not necessarily mean it is making money. The only way that the business can determine profitability is to maintain and analyze accounting records. Businesses also use this financial information for external purposes, such as calculating taxes, borrowing money from financial institutions, and, in the case of publicly held companies, preparing annual reports for stockholders. To reflect its financial position, every publicly held company is required to establish a system of internal controls that includes accurate accounting procedures.

Banks are like any other business. They need to plan accurately, and an essential tool of planning is careful accounting records and budgets. Banks maintain accounting systems to reflect their financial condition and performance. To satisfy regulators, stockholders, and customers, banks must be able to provide data on their condition and profitability, and data must present a true picture of the bank's operations. Errors in accounting data cause closer scrutiny by the Federal Reserve and other regulators.

Because of the nature of the banking business, banks maintain sophisticated systems for posting transactions initiated by both customers and other banks. The information developed through a bank's accounting system is vital to the many individuals and government agencies concerned about the financial strength and profitability of the bank. Among them are

- federal and state regulatory authorities
- bank shareholders or investors
- bank directors, management, and employees
- customers

Federal and State Regulatory Authorities

In every bank examination by federal and state authorities, the examiners verify the accuracy of the institution's financial reports to determine its true financial condition and performance. The Comptroller of the Currency, the Federal Reserve, the Federal Deposit Insurance Corporation, and the state banking departments all require that banks under their jurisdiction file periodic call reports. Call reports contain not only financial data but also a certification by management that the figures are accurate and up-to-date. These reports are filed by national banks, member banks of the Federal Reserve, and non-member state-chartered banks. Often, those reports verify the strength of the bank or identify a troubled institution. These agencies have a particular interest in the strength of financial institutions, so that depositors' funds are protected.

Shareholders or Investors

Bank shareholders are clearly entitled to information. The value of their investment is directly related to the financial data that show where and how the bank acquired funds, how the funds were put to work, and what the results were.

Other investors are also interested in information such as how similar banks have performed and how sound the bank's capital position is. They want to judge the growth potential of the institution (particularly the growth of the stock) and the likelihood of getting a good return on their investment. The pension investor in situation 1 has an even greater obligation to analyze accounting information about the bank since he is responsible for investing other people's retirement money. The importance of producing accurate information reaches far beyond the walls of the bank.

Customers

Many customers carefully scrutinize published data showing the bank's financial condition and its profitability. Depositors have a natural and ongoing interest in the strength of the bank. More sophisticated businesses will analyze several banks to ensure that their businesses will have a strong financial partner. Large businesses do not want to change banks regularly—they want to make the right choice from the start. Large depositors (over $100,000) and smaller depositors alike want to know their money is in good hands. A bank that pays attention to its own profitability has more credibility with depositors. Customers choose a bank for more than its prices or innovative products.

Bank Directors, Management, and Employees

For internal management purposes, each bank provides daily updates on all of its asset, liability, income, expense, and capital accounts.

For directors, senior officers, and other staff members, bank accounting identifies the branches, departments, and services that directly generate profits or losses.

Banks operate today in an increasingly aggressive, competitive environment. To meet the challenge, they place far more emphasis on planning than ever before. Bank directors and senior managers set the institution's mission and objectives and develop policies and strategies that produce the best use of bank resources. Planning leads to managerial decisions and ties together all the component parts of the bank. The annual budgeting process and the effort to forecast future conditions and events are important elements in this overall planning process.

Through information provided by the bank's accounting systems, management can decide what needs to be done in the areas of asset and liability planning, what funding will be needed, its cost, and the uses to which acquired funds will be put. Managers rely on a thorough review of the bank's financial data when deciding whether to eliminate unprofitable branches or subsidiaries, correct deficiencies, or reduce expenses in one place and commit additional resources to another. The data also are used by the board of directors and senior officers in developing goals and policies. Of course, all such financial information is kept confidential. These policies, in turn, establish the daily practices that staff members follow in contributing to growth and profitability. In this way, accounting forms the basis for the entire planning process.

Basic Accounting Methods

To manage its funds for all concerned parties, a bank keeps records of all transactions. These records are used by a bank to post and balance daily transactions, research information for customer inquiries, resolve errors, report financial data, and meet regulatory requirements. As transactions are processed, they are entered into journals and ledgers as part of the bank's posting and bookkeeping functions. Banks use double-entry bookkeeping when posting transactions as a method of control and to produce required records.

Double-entry Bookkeeping

The fundamental technique used in bank accounting, known as **double-entry bookkeeping**, requires that each transaction affect two accounts and be recorded in a balanced set of entries. Every debit must have an equal offsetting credit, and total debits must equal total credits.

Posting a **debit** means making an accounting entry that increases an asset or expense account and decreases the liability, income, or capital account. Posting a **credit** means making an accounting entry that accomplishes the reverse; credits increase liability, income, or capital account, and decrease an asset or expense account.

For example, a customer deposits $100 in currency in a checking account. The transaction is recorded by (1) a debit, which increases the cash account, and (2) a credit, which increases the demand deposit account. The cash account is an asset of the bank because it represents something of value that the bank owns or that is owed to it; the demand deposit account is a liability because it represents money owed to a customer. Exhibit 10.1 demonstrates this concept.

Cash and Accrual Accounting Methods

Basic accounting principles recognize that individuals and businesses need different methods of recording income and expenses. To meet this need, there are two basic accounting methods: cash and accrual.

Exhibit 10.1 **Double-entry Bookkeeping**

Asset accounts		=	Liability accounts		+	Capital accounts	
Debit for increases	Credit for decreases		Debit for decreases	Credit for increases		Debit for decreases	Credit for increases

Income accounts		–	Expense accounts		=	Net profit
Debit for decreases	Credit for increases		Debit for increases	Credit for decreases		

Asset of cash	=	Liability of demand deposits	+	Capital
+ 100	=	+ 100	+	–0–

Individuals and small businesses typically use the **cash accounting** method. Under this system, entries to the individual or business records are made only when cash is actually received as income or paid out as an expense. Don in situation 2 uses the cash accounting method. He does not recognize (claim for tax or bookkeeping purposes, etc.) the income from painting the house until he receives the payment in February 2001, even though he actually completed painting the house in December. On the expense side, however, he has to recognize the expenses he incurred in painting the house (such as new paintbrushes, paint, and payroll) as those expenses were paid in 2000.

Banks, like many other businesses, use the accrual method of accounting to recognize income and expenses. Under the **accrual accounting** method, income and expenses are recognized as the income is generated and as the expenses occur even though the income is not actually received or the expenses are not actually paid. Rainbow Painting, Inc., in situation 2 uses the accrual accounting method, recognizing the income from painting the house in December even though payment was not actually received until the following February. Likewise, expenses are recognized at the point they are incurred and not when they are actually paid. If Rainbow had incurred expenses in December 2000 but did not actually pay its suppliers until the following February, under the accrual method of accounting the company would have to recognize the expense in December.

Banks use the accrual method of accounting to accurately reflect the payment of interest on liabilities (expense) and the receipt of interest on loans (income). For example, interest must be paid to holders of certificates of deposit at maturity and to savings account customers at the end of each quarter. Under cash accounting, no entries are made on the bank's books until the actual payout to customers takes place, even though the interest expense was actually incurred at an earlier date. Under the accrual method of accounting, the bank accrues interest payments daily that it must make to the customers and recognize as an expense. For the same reason, when a customer borrows $25,000 from the bank and agrees to pay it 90 days later, cash accounting does not recognize that the bank earns interest each day throughout the three-month loan. Under the accrual accounting method, it accrues interest daily and recognizes that interest income as it is accrued, not when it is actually paid to the bank.

Temporary, Intermediate, and Permanent Records

Records of bank transactions may be classified as temporary or permanent. Many daily bank transactions are first entered on adding machine tapes, teller machine records, and transaction slips. These temporary records lose their value as transactions are completed in other areas of the bank. The information from teller machine records, for example, subsequently becomes part of the bookkeeping function. The bank usually retains microfilm copies or electronic imaged documents, transactions, and records.

Permanent records are those that must be kept longer, as required by law or bank policy. For example, copies of customers' bank statements and records of purchases and sales of securities for customers' accounts are stored for long periods in designated archives.

Journals and Ledgers

In accounting, a journal is a book of original entry. Each processing area in a bank usually has some form of journal in which daily transactions are posted as they occur. Eventually, entries are transferred from journals to the bank's ledgers, which are records of final entry. For example, daily journal entries of loans made by branch office loan departments eventually become part of the bank's ledger records. (Exhibit 10.2 summarizes the basic accounting records and reports.)

In the typical bank, a general accounting department maintains a general ledger, in which all financial information from every department and branch is consolidated to determine the daily financial condition of the bank. In addition to the general ledger, subsidiary ledgers, which are components of the general ledger, are normally maintained for specific types of accounts, such as demand deposit accounts, savings accounts, loans, and fixed assets.

In many cases these entries are prepared and posted electronically. Gone are the days when bank accountants bent over giant ledger books recording entries. Now we are more likely to see someone sitting at a personal computer keyboarding entries directly into the accounting system.

Today, journals and ledgers are readily identified by the level of security they have in the bank's computer system. Access by employees who enter the data is limited to certain parts of the accounting function and entries are recorded with an employee identifier to know who made the entry.

Financial Statements

Banks maintain two basic financial statements (reports) that convey all the essential information about a bank's current financial condition and the financial results it has achieved. The statement of condition, also called the balance sheet, is prepared as of a specific date; for example, it reports total assets, liabilities, and capital accounts of the bank as of December 31. The income statement, also called the profit-and-loss statement, covers the bank's operations over an extended period, such as the quarter or the year ended December 31, and

---

Exhibit 10.2 Accounting Records and Reports

Accounting Journal or Ledger	Bank Equivalent
Journal—book of original entry	Teller machine record of a $200 customer deposit
Subsidiary ledger—component of the general ledger for a specific account type	All banking transactions done today that affect demand deposit accounts
General ledger—all financial information from every department is consolidated	A consolidation of every transaction from every department of the entire bank
Financial statement—balance sheet and income statement	Financial statement—a consolidation of the general ledger put into a generally accepted accounting format

shows all revenues and expenses and the resulting profit or loss. Both the balance sheet and the income statement are updated every day.

Once a year, a bank will issue a complete picture of its operations and financial condition through the **annual report**. This report is management's summation of the bank's achievements over the course of the year. In this colorful, multi-page report, management summarizes significant achievements and future plans, and can report on its perspective of the bank's year. Often, the annual report will contain a detailed analysis of operations and the financial condition of the bank.

Statement of Condition

The **statement of condition**, or **balance sheet**, lists all of the company's assets and liabilities, and the stockholder equity (net worth). A statement of condition can be a snapshot of the assets, liabilities, and capital of a bank or a company on any given day, or it can be a monthly, quarterly, or annual average of the balance in those particular asset, liability, or capital accounts. Exhibit 10.3 is an example of a typical balance sheet, or statement of condition, of a financial institution.

The following major categories of assets are listed on a bank's statement of condition:

- cash on hand and due from banks (coin and currency held in the bank's vault, checks that are in the process of collection, and balances with correspondent banks and the Federal Reserve)
- investments (obligations of the federal government and its agencies, obligations of state and local units of government, and stock in the Federal Reserve, if the bank is a member)
- loans (all indebtedness to the bank, usually subdivided by category)

- fixed assets (real estate owned by the bank; furniture, fixtures, and equipment)
- other short-term assets (such as fed funds sold and securities purchased under the agreement to resell)

The following types of liabilities appear on the bank statement of condition:

- deposits (all money owed to customers, subdivided into demand, savings, time deposits, domestic, and global deposits)
- taxes payable (all federal, state, and local taxes that must be paid)
- dividends payable (if the directors have approved payment of a dividend to the stockholders but the actual disbursement has not yet been made)
- other short-term liabilities (such as fed funds purchased and securities sold under the agreement to repurchase)

Various other statements of condition assets and liabilities may be listed, depending on the size and scope of the bank's operations. Assets and liabilities are always listed in the order of liquidity so that the first item in each category is the most current and most easily converted into cash. Therefore, "cash and due from banks" is the first asset shown, while "deposits" is the first liability listed. Besides showing the balances in the asset and liability accounts, the statement of condition also provides information used to calculate certain performance measurements (see the Performance Measurements section).

An important point is the listing of loans on the balance sheet. Regulatory authorities and the Internal Revenue Service agree: Banks should recognize that, despite their best efforts, not all their outstanding loans will be repaid as scheduled. Therefore, each bank calculates a loan loss reserve, a reserve amount for possible loan losses on the basis of past

Exhibit 10.3 Consolidated Statement of Condition: Assets, Liabilities, and Stockholders' Equity

Assets

(In thousands of dollars)	December 31 20XX	December 31 20XX	Change
Cash and due from banks	$ 1,649,334	$ 1,332,586	$ 316,748
Overseas deposits	458,313	460,396	(2,083)
Investment securities:			
U.S. Treasury securities	881,081	982,654	(101,573)
Securities of other U.S. government agencies and corporations	199,318	243,420	(44,102)
Obligations of states and political subdivisions	738,813	396,948	341,865
Other securities	88,278	92,032	(3,754)
Total investment securities	1,907,490	1,715,054	192,436
Trading account securities	14,846	66,140	(51,294)
Funds sold	168,600	108,450	60,150
Loans (net of reserve for loan losses and unearned discount)	9,715,728	8,074,132	1,641,596
Direct lease financing	147,860	134,472	13,388
Premises and equipment, net	133,506	132,320	1,186
Customers' acceptance liability	372,835	248,271	124,564
Accrued interest receivable	133,840	123,719	10,121
Other real estate owned	34,332	13,668	20,664
Other assets	103,939	131,711	(27,772)
Total assets	$ 14,840,623	$ 12,540,919	$ 2,299,704

Liabilities and Stockholders' Equity

(In thousands of dollars)	December 31 20XX	December 31 20XX	Change
Demand deposits	$ 3,543,141	$ 2,937,065	$ 606,076
Savings deposits	3,585,808	3,485,886	99,922
Savings certificates	1,635,215	1,391,107	244,108
Certificates of deposit	1,827,420	1,601,707	225,713
Other time deposits	424,592	313,811	110,781
Deposits in overseas offices	1,468,003	722,950	745,053
Total deposits	12,484,179	10,452,526	2,031,653
Funds borrowed	897,189	924,501	(27,312)
Long-term debt	44,556	43,766	790
Acceptances outstanding	373,022	249,088	123,934
Accrued taxes and other expenses	142,756	122,064	20,692
Other liabilities	171,904	122,890	49,014
Total liabilities (excluding subordinated notes)	14,113,606	11,914,835	2,198,771
Subordinated notes:			
8.25% capital note to Wells Fargo & Company, due 20XX	25,000	25,000	——
4.5% capital notes due 20XX	50,000	50,000	——
Total subordinated notes	75,000	75,000	——
Stockholders' equity:			
Capital stock	94,461	94,461	——
Surplus	300,036	251,512	48,524
Surplus representing convertible capital note obligation assumed by parent corporation	10,065	14,589	(4,524)
Undivided profits	247,455	190,522	56,933
Total stockholders' equity	652,017	551,084	100,933
Total liabilities and stockholders' equity	$ 14,840,623	$ 12,540,919	$ 2,299,704

experience with losses, the quality of its current loan portfolio, and the economic and political climate. Each bank is permitted to reduce its total loan amount by this reserve. The loan loss reserve is not an advance admission by the bank that the full amount of the reserve will always be used for charge-offs; rather, the reserve is a "best guess" at the possibility of loan loss-protection against events that may take place in the future.

Unless a bank is insolvent, its total assets are greater than its total liabilities. The excess of assets over liabilities is the **net worth** of the bank and is shown in its capital accounts. Net worth is also called stockholder equity. A fundamental equation in accounting states that total assets must equal total liabilities plus net worth; that is, if all liabilities of the bank were to be paid through the use of assets, the institution's net worth would remain. The standard equation is:

Assets = Liabilities + Net Worth (Stockholders' Equity)

For example, if the total assets of a bank were $10,000 and total liabilities were $9,000, the net worth of the bank (stockholder's equity) would be $1,000 (assets of $10,000 minus liabilities of $9,000).

Did You Know?

Two banks are among *Business Week*'s S&P Top 50 U.S. corporations ranked on sales growth, profits, shareholder return, and other criteria:

MBNA (#35)

Wells Fargo (#39)

In 1997, there were seven banks in the top 50. This decline can be explained in part by the growth of the technology sector of the economy.

If you look carefully at a statement of condition in an annual report, you might see other types of assets and liabilities that are not included in the totals. These are *contingencies* for financial events that could occur in the future, so they are not considered part of the current financial picture.

Income Statement

The **income statement**, or **profit-and-loss statement**, lists all categories of income by source and all expense categories. Expenses are shown subtracted from income, reflecting either the profit or the loss experienced by the bank for a specified period. Exhibit 10.4 is an example of an income statement.

The following major sources of bank income are typically listed in order of size and importance:

- interest on loans
- interest and dividends on investments
- fees, commissions, and service charges

The major items of expense, also listed in order of size and importance, are as follows:

- interest paid on deposits
- salaries, wages, and benefits
- taxes (federal, state, and local)

The bank's income statement produces a net, or bottom line, figure representing revenues less expenses. This net figure is usually translated into earnings per share (see the Earnings Per Share section), from which stockholders know how much each share of outstanding stock earned in the designated period. If the bank's total expenses for the period exceed its income, the net figure is negative, indicating a loss. The bank can use the income statement to analyze its profits and determine its major sources of income and expense. It also can compare its categories of

Exhibit 10.4 **Consolidated Statement of Income (in Thousands of Dollars, Except Per Share Data)**

| | Year ended December 31 | |
	20XX	20XX
Interest income:		
Interest and fees on loans	$ 823,415	$ 693,463
Interest on funds sold	6,429	3,496
Interest and dividends on investment securities:		
U.S. Treasury securities	69,938	59,883
Securities of other U.S. government agencies and corporations	16,520	25,228
Obligations of states and political subdivisions	22,504	15,846
Other securities	7,067	7,268
Interest on overseas deposits	24,394	37,658
Interest on trading accounts securities	4,419	3,478
Direct lease financing income	33,371	32,560
Total interest income	1,008,057	878,880
Interest expense:		
Interest on deposits	463,733	414,832
Interest on federal funds borrowed and repurchase agreements	35,193	33,019
Interest on other borrowed money	17,751	12,882
Interest on long-term debt	21,232	19,079
Total interest expense	537,909	479,812
Net interest income	470,148	399,068
Provision for loan losses	41,028	46,379
Net interest income after provision for loan losses	429,120	352,689
Other operating income:		
Trust income	21,635	19,649
Service charges on deposit accounts	25,511	24,254
Trading account profits and commissions	(268)	1,690
Other income	43,797	23,324
Total other operating income	90,675	68,917
Other operating expense:		
Salaries	168,085	145,746
Employee benefits	41,028	32,126
Net occupancy expense	34,919	31,636
Equipment expense	20,648	19,234
Other expense	94,331	68,317
Total other operating expense	359,011	297,059
Income before income taxes and securities transactions	160,784	124,547
Less applicable income taxes	73,484	61,076
Income before securities transactions	87,300	63,471
Securities gains (losses), net of income tax effect of $(1,233) in 20XX and $48 in 20XX	(1,020)	40
Net income	$ 86,280	$ 63,511
Income per share (based on average number of common shares outstanding):		
Income before securities transactions	$4.03	$3.16
Securities transactions, net of income tax effect	(.05)	—
Net income	$3.98	$3.16

income and expense with those of peer banks. If its expenses are higher than its peers, the bank can adjust its operations to bring them in line with other institutions. There are many reference materials, such as data from the Federal Reserve Bank, that allow banks to make peer comparisons.

Performance Ratios

The income statement is a good source of information for determining whether the bank has had a profit or a loss. To determine the profitability and performance level of a financial institution, however, more information is examined, such as the use of assets, the amount of investment required to produce earnings, the organization's financial strength and stability, and the earnings-per-share. These figures show how effectively the bank uses its resources to earn a profit. Various ratios have been developed to show the performance, or profitability, of a bank. They are used by internal management, investment analysts, and state and federal regulatory authorities. The measures most widely used are

- return on assets
- return on equity
- capital ratio
- net interest spread
- earnings per share

Return on Assets

Return on assets is a good measurement of the profitability of a bank because it shows how well a bank is putting its assets to work to produce income. The **return on assets (ROA)** is calculated by dividing a bank's earnings (before securities gains or losses) by its average total assets during the period

(exhibit 10.3). For years many banks established a target ROA of 1 percent. Exhibit 10.5 shows that the median ROA for a group of 26 banks with assets between $20 billion and $70 billion increased from 1.27 for the year ended 1998 to 1.41 for the year ended 1999. Like any other financial ratio, the ratio is compared with that of other similarly sized banks. An ROA of 1.43 may be average for one group of banks of a certain size but would be extremely high for another group of banks with much larger assets. Usually, but not always, the larger the assets, the smaller the ROA.

Return on Equity

The second key measure of bank profitability is **return on equity (ROE).** The ROE, in effect, measures the rate of return a bank has achieved in relation to the funds invested in it. This ratio is calculated by dividing a bank's earnings (before securities transactions) by the average dollar amount of total equity during the period (exhibit 10.3). The term equity describes the ownership interest represented by stockholders' investment in the bank, plus retained earnings. Because a bank's total assets are always far greater than its equity, the ROE is always significantly higher than the ROA. This ratio is of particular interest to potential investors, because it indicates the bank's ability to put invested funds to work producing income. An ROE of 15 percent is considered good for many banks (exhibit 10.6). However, for the year ended 1999 the median ROE for 33 super-regional banks with assets between $20 billion and $70 billion was 16.73, reflecting the increased profitability and increased efficiency of banks for the past several years.

Exhibit 10.5 **Return on Assets (ROA)**

Commercial Banks with Assets of $20 Billion to $70 Billion

Name	City	State	1999 ROA	1998 ROA	1998 Ranking
Greenwood Trust Co	Greenwood	DE	4.33	*	
MBNA America Bank NA	Wilmington	DE	3.99	3.87	1
Bank One Michigan	Detroit	MI	2.08	***	
National City Bank	Cleveland	OH	1.89	1.45	13
Comerica Bank	Detroit	MI	1.85	1.64	8
PNC Bank NA	Pittsburgh	PA	1.54	**	
Crestar Bank	Richmond	VA	1.53	1.15	24
Bank One Arizona NA	Phoenix	AZ	1.51	1.87	2
Wachovia Bank NA	Winston-Salem	NC	1.50	1.28	16
Firstar Bank NA	Cincinnati	OH	1.49	***	
Branch Banking & Trust Co	Winston-Salem	NC	1.47	1.51	12
Norwest Bank Minnesota NA	Minneapolis	MN	1.46	1.65	6
Summit Bank	Hackensack	NJ	1.44	1.43	14
Huntington National Bank	Columbus	OH	1.42	1.06	28
Union Bank of California NA	San Francisco	CA	1.35	1.63	9
Manufacturers & Traders Tr Co	Buffalo	NY	1.33	1.25	19
Regions Bank	Birmingham	AL	1.32	1.21	21
State Street Bank & Trust Co	Boston	MA	1.27	1.08	27
Union Planters Bank NA	Memphis	TN	1.27	0.93	31
Bank One Texas NA	Dallas	TX	1.27	1.25	20
Fleet Bank NA	Jersey City	NJ	1.24	1.13	25
Mellon Bank NA	Pittsburgh	PA	1.22	1.79	4
Suntrust Bank Atlanta	Atlanta	GA	1.18	*	
Lasalle Bank NA	Chicago	IL	1.17	1.18	22
Mercantile Bank of Trenton NA	Trenton	MO	1.12	**	
Northern Trust Co	Chicago	IL	1.11	1.11	26
		Median	1.43	1.27	

* — Assests of less than $20 billion
** — Assests of more than $70 billion
*** — Asset size based on a 1999 merger
Source: FDIC Call Report, Fourth Quarter, 1999

Capital Ratio

Many bank failures in the 1980s and early 1990s made bank regulators, investors, and customers pay particular attention to the financial strength and stability of financial institutions. Large loan write-offs caused many of those bank failures. When the bank cannot absorb loan losses with current earnings, and its losses exceed its loan loss reserves, the loss must be taken out of the capital account. For many banks that failed, capital was completely or nearly completely depleted.

When a prospective bank submits its charter application, regulatory authorities question the dollar amount of capital that has been contributed by the incorporators. The bank's original capital consists of the number of shares purchased, multiplied by the price per share. When the bank begins to operate and to generate profits, retained earnings are added to the original capital. The bank may also sell addi-

Exhibit 10.6 Return on Equity (ROE)

Commercial Banks with Assets of $20 Billion to $70 Billion

Name	City	State	1999 ROE	1998 ROE	1998 Ranking
Greenwood Trust Co	Greenwood	DE	34.82	*	
MBNA America Bank NA	Wilmington	DE	31.68	34.24	1
Bank One Michigan	Detroit	MI	28.64	***	
National City Bank	Cleveland	OH	28.27	21.40	5
Norwest Bank Minnesota NA	Minneapolis	MN	24.65	23.41	4
State Street Bank & Trust Co	Boston	MA	21.90	18.15	17
Comerica Bank	Detroit	MI	20.60	20.65	6
Summit Bank	Hackensack	NJ	20.47	19.37	10
Crestar Bank	Richmond	VA	20.47	16.12	21
Bank One Texas NA	Dallas	TX	20.18	18.74	12
Bank One Arizona NA	Phoenix	AZ	19.67	27.72	2
Branch Banking & Trust Co	Winston-Salem	NC	19.43	18.95	11
Huntington National Bank	Columbus	OH	18.13	14.05	25
PNC Bank NA	Pittsburgh	PA	18.11	**	
Regions Bank	Birmingham	AL	18.01	15.16	22
Northern Trust Co	Chicago	IL	17.61	18.37	16
Firstar Bank NA	Cincinnati	OH	16.73	***	
Wachovia Bank NA	Winston-Salem	NC	15.95	14.65	23
Lasalle Bank NA	Chicago	IL	15.30	18.44	15
Southtrust Bank NA	Birmingham	AL	14.61	13.97	26
Mercantile Bk of Trenton NA	Trenton	MO	14.41	**	
Union Planters Bank NA	Memphis	TN	14.30	10.50	31
Fleet Bank NA	Jersey City	NJ	14.25	13.54	28
Union Bank of California NA	San Francisco	CA	14.08	17.96	18
Manufacturers & Traders Tr Co	Buffalo	NY	14.01	14.11	24
Chase Bank of Texas NA	Houston	TX	13.84	12.79	29
Mellon Bank NA	Pittsburgh	PA	12.23	18.52	14
Amsouth Bank	Birmingham	AL	11.64	*	
Harris Trust & Savings Bank	Chicago	IL	11.25	*	
Suntrust Bank Atlanta	Atlanta	GA	10.41	*	
Bank One NA	Columbus	OH	8.16	17.45	19
Chase Manhattan Bank USA NA	Wilmington	DE	7.80	12.77	30
Bankers Trust Co	New York City	NY	−16.91	**	
	Median		16.73	18.06	

* — Assests of less than $20 billion
** — Assets of more than $70 billion
*** — Asset size based on a 1999 merger
Source: FDIC Call Report, Fourth Quarter, 1999

tional shares of its stock, thereby increasing its capital base.

In bank examinations, federal and state authorities try to determine whether a bank's capital is adequate to support its operation. The third measure of bank profitability, then, is the capital ratio, determined by dividing the bank's total capital by its total assets.

Capital serves as a cushion for temporary losses. It also helps protect uninsured depositors, depositors whose balance exceeds the insurance coverage limit, and holders of liabil-

Exhibit 10.7 **Equity Capital Ratio**

Commercial Banks with Assets of $20 Billion to $70 Billion

Name	City	State	1999 Capital Ratio	1998 Capital Ratio	1998 Ranking
MBNA America Bank NA	Wilmington	DE	13.08	11.46	1
Bankers Trust Co	New York City	NY	12.10	**	
Suntrust Bank Atlanta	Atlanta	GA	10.82	*	
Chase Manhattan Bank USA NA	Wilmington	DE	10.01	10.23	2
Mellon Bank NA	Pittsburgh	PA	9.77	9.82	3
Manufacturers & Traders Tr Co	Buffalo	NY	9.54	9.16	7
Union Bank of California NA	San Francisco	CA	9.40	9.34	4
Wachovia Bank NA	Winston-Salem	NC	9.39	9.33	5
Fleet Bank NA	Jersey City	NJ	9.34	8.71	11
Greenwood Trust Co	Greenwood	DE	9.19	*	
Comerica Bank	Detroit	MI	9.16	8.57	12
Firstar Bank NA	Cincinnati	OH	9.16	***	
Union Planters Bank NA	Memphis	TN	8.29	8.86	9
Bank One Arizona NA	Phoenix	AZ	8.27	6.84	24
Lasalle Bank NA	Chicago	IL	8.21	6.15	31
PNC Bank NA	Pittsburgh	PA	8.13	**	
Mercantile Bk of Trenton NA	Trenton	MO	8.11	**	
Amsouth Bank	Birmingham	AL	8.04	*	
Bank One Michigan	Detroit	MI	7.64	***	
Huntington National Bank	Columbus	OH	7.56	7.86	14
Crestar Bank	Richmond	VA	7.40	7.01	27
Southtrust Bank NA	Birmingham	AL	7.36	7.60	16
Branch Banking & Trust Co	Winston-Salem	NC	7.19	8.18	13
Northern Trust Co	Chicago	IL	7.07	6.24	29
Regions Bank	Birmingham	AL	6.93	7.41	17
Summit Bank	Hackensack	NJ	6.89	7.25	19
Chase Bank of Texas NA	Houston	TX	6.82	7.40	18
Bank One NA	Columbus	OH	6.52	6.40	28
Bank One Texas NA	Dallas	TX	6.37	6.50	27
Harris Trust & Savings Bank	Chicago	IL	6.19	*	
National City Bank	Cleveland	OH	6.11	6.63	26
Norwest Bank Minnesota NA	Minneapolis	MN	5.42	5.82	32
		Median	8.12	7.60	

* — Assests of less than $20 billion
** — Assests of more than $70 billion
*** — Asset size based on a 1999 merger
Source: FDIC Call Report, Fourth Quarter, 1999

ities in the event the bank is liquidated. Nationwide, the capital ratios for banks generally range between 6 percent and 8 percent. (Exhibit 10.7 shows that the mean capital ratio for the 32 super-regional banks with assets between $20 billion and $70 billion was 8.12 for the year ended 1999.) This means that 92 percent to 94 percent of total assets are financed through various liabilities. For this reason, banking is often referred to as a highly leveraged industry; in other words, it is extremely dependent on debt (borrowed money in the form of deposits and other short-term liabilities) to function.

Net Interest Spread

Net interest spread is the difference between interest earned (from loans) and interest paid out (for deposits). Banks seek a net interest spread of 2.75 percent to 3 percent. This means that if a bank averaged 7 percent on the rate that it charged to borrow money, then it should expect to pay 4 to 4.25 percent on average for deposits (7% − 4% = 3%). The higher the net interest spread, the greater the spread between

Exhibit 10.8 **Net Interest Spread**

Commercial Banks Assets of $20 Billion to $70 Billion

Name	City	State	1999 NIS	1998 NIS	1998 Ranking
Greenwood Trust Co	Greenwood	DE	8.19	*	
Bank One Arizona NA	Phoenix	AZ	5.66	5.96	1
Union Bank of California NA	San Francisco	CA	5.01	4.90	7
MBNA America Bank NA	Wilmington	DE	4.98	5.09	3
Bank One Michigan	Detroit	MI	4.95	***	
Chase Manhattan Bank USA NA	Wilmington	DE	4.65	5.02	5
Union Planters Bank NA	Memphis	TN	4.33	4.22	13
Wachovia Bank NA	Winston-Salem	NC	4.32	4.16	16
Bank One NA	Columbus	OH	4.31	5.66	2
National City Bank	Cleveland	OH	4.25	4.38	9
Fleet Bank NA	Jersey City	NJ	4.24	4.18	14
Chase Bank of Texas NA	Houston	TX	4.20	4.38	8
Firstar Bank NA	Cincinnati	OH	4.19	***	
Regions Bank	Birmingham	AL	4.19	4.36	11
Comerica Bank	Detroit	MI	4.18	4.10	19
Huntington National Bank	Columbus	OH	4.18	4.09	20
Manufacturers & Traders Tr Co	Buffalo	NY	4.15	4.32	12
Bank One Texas NA	Dallas	TX	4.08	4.14	18
Crestar Bank	Richmond	VA	3.99	3.88	23
Amsouth Bank	Birmingham	AL	3.99	*	
Summit Bank	Hackensack	NJ	3.98	4.14	17
Southtrust Bank NA	Birmingham	AL	3.78	3.76	25
PNC Bank NA	Pittsburgh	PA	3.77	**	
Mellon Bank NA	Pittsburgh	PA	3.77	3.86	24
Branch Banking & Trust Co	Winston-Salem	NC	3.70	3.95	22
Mercantile Bk of Trenton NA	Trenton	MO	3.55	**	
Lasalle Bank NA	Chicago	IL	3.41	3.37	29
Norwest Bank Minnesota NA	Minneapolis	MN	3.21	3.43	27
Suntrust Bank Atlanta	Atlanta	GA	2.92	*	
Harris Trust & Savings Bank	Chicago	IL	2.45	*	
State Street Bank & Trust Co	Boston	MA	1.94	2.15	31
Bankers Trust Co	New York City	NY	1.69	**	
		Median	4.17	4.16	

* — Assests of less than $20 billion
** — Assets of more than $70 billion
*** — Asset size based on a 1999 merger
Source: FDIC Call Report, Fourth Quarter, 1999

rates for the bank. Theoretically, the profit should also be greater if the bank's other expenses remain constant.

In recent years, banks have been able to see net interest spreads exceeding 4 percent because of the strength of the economy. In 1999, the net interest spread for 32 banks with assets between $20 billion and $70 billion was 4.16 (See exhibit 10.8). These numbers reflect the strong economy of the late 1990s as well as bank management's need to provide a strong return to shareholders.

Earnings Per Share

Another measure of bank profitability is the earnings per share. **Earnings per share (EPS)** is calculated by dividing the bank's net income by the average number of shares of its stock outstanding during the period. Growth and EPS commonly are regarded as the key indicators of bank performance. In establishing income goals for the next year, some banks use EPS as a measurement. For example, a bank that earned $3.50 per share in the previous year may establish a goal of $4 per share for the current year. When compared with the market price of a share of stock, EPS also provides a means of determining how well the bank stock is regarded in the marketplace. This comparison of the earnings of the bank to the price of the stock is called the price-earnings ratio, or the price-earnings multiple.

A complete analysis of a bank's performance requires detailed attention to each of these four ratios for several years, rather than a focus on any one ratio for a single year. For example, a bank's board of directors and senior management may make a heavy commitment of resources in one particular year to enter a new service area or expand the bank's

branch system. A substantial addition to the bank's reserve for possible loan loss in a single year likewise is considered a one-time aberration. To identify trends, ROA, ROE, capital ratio, and EPS all are measured over time.

Impact of Financial Data

Financial data produced by a financial institution are important not only to the management and board of directors, but also to stockholders, potential stockholders, regulators, other financial institutions, employees, customers, and prospective customers.

Impact on Shareholders or Investors

Current shareholders are particularly interested in a bank's financial data, because data may have an immediate impact on the stock share value. If financial data indicate that earnings for the bank are up, and that the bank can meet its financial obligations and has a sound capital base, then the stock value should continue to rise. (Bank stock is still subject to market conditions, and fluctuates depending on external forces beyond the bank's control.) If the financial data indicate that the bank will earn less this year than it earned last year, the stock value typically declines. (On the other hand, if earnings are down because the bank had a one-time earnings loss resulting from unusual loan losses, and the bank can show that future earnings will rise, then the stock value may increase.)

Whatever the case, the bank's financial data must be accurate, because they have direct impact on the stock value and therefore affect stockholders. Potential shareholders such as the Jayson investment group in situation 1 are also concerned about the earnings and financial stability of the bank. The decision to invest is not made solely on the financial data produced by the bank, but it is influenced by those data.

Impact on Regulators

Bank regulators are also concerned with the data produced by banks. While they are interested in all the performance ratios, they are particularly interested in the capital ratio, which indicates the financial stability and strength of the organization. Because of numerous bank failures in the late 1980s, regulators have increased capital requirements for many financial institutions and monitor performance ratios on a continuing basis. The first hint of a problem in the ratios, especially the capital ratio, raises a flag to bank regulators.

Impact on Other Financial Institutions

Financial institutions judge their own performance relative to their peers, as well as against their own goals. They study the ratios of comparable banks as a way of judging their own performance in the marketplace. Financial institutions, especially those interested in acquiring other banks, are interested in the financial results of those other banks. Potential acquirers are looking for bargains; if a bank's performance ratios indicate inefficiency and marginal declines, that bank could be a prime candidate for acquisition. The potential acquirer may be able to reduce expenses, eliminate inefficiencies, and take advantage of economies of scale to turn a lackluster bank into a top performer.

Impact on Customers

A prudent customer will carefully shop for a banking relationship. In the past, consumers did not seem particularly concerned about the strength of financial institutions. However, since accounts are insured only up to $100,000 by federal deposit insurance, many people today are concerned about the financial strength of their bank or potential bank. Those customers with large sums of money not only shop interest rates, but also shop financial stability in organizations; they spread their deposit dollars among a number of financial institutions to reduce the risk of loss. The couple in situation 3 who are retiring to the Southwest can review the financial data on several institutions before selecting the one (or more) they feel is the safest for their retirement funds.

Impact on Employees

The financial data produced by a bank also have a direct and indirect impact on the bank's employees. Many employees take pride in the financial results of their organization and are interested in how their bank compares with competitors. Employee salaries, bonuses, benefits, and compensation can be directly tied to the organization's performance. Many banks have compensation plans for executive management that are based not only on the performance of their institution but also on its performance in relation to other financial institutions. Bank management and employees work to increase shareholder value; because of the impact that financial data have on shareholders, management and employees do everything in their power to ensure that the financial results are positive. After all, without customers there would be no deposit accounts, no loans, and no duties to perform.

Planning and Budgeting

Banks do not achieve financial results automatically. They plan carefully, set earnings objectives, and structure the balance sheet. Like all businesses, banks prepare budgets and monitor their performance daily, weekly, and monthly to locate the causes of variances in their budget. In addition to managing its overall financial performance and results, the bank also measures the performance of the individual activities that ultimately produce the financial results. It establishes performance standards for both quantity and quality, and measures itself against those standards and against the performance of peer banks.

Budgeting

The budget is the financial plan for attaining the goals set by management. Although budgeting varies from one financial institution to another, the basic concept is the same: Budgeting means establishing a financial plan for the coming year and perhaps another plan for the next three to five years.

Most financial institutions base their budgets on the amounts that were spent the previous year. For example, the bank may establish a goal or policy that non-interest expense will not exceed previous-year expenditures by more than 4 percent.

Each bank sets its own time frame for the budget. For example, for banks on a calendar-year accounting basis (the accounting year starts in January), the budget process typically starts in July or August and runs through October or November.

A financial institution's budget cannot include deficits; that is, expenses cannot exceed income. All expense hardware, software, facilities, supplies, communication, transportation, education, training, conferences, salaries, and other items must be included in the budget. The bank also budgets for income, including service charges, interest income, and other sources of non-interest income.

In preparing a budget, the financial institution needs to project interest expense and interest income. This process is difficult, because the bank not only projects and anticipates loan volumes and deposit volumes, but it also projects and anticipates interest rates and the impact that those interest rates will have on interest expense and interest income.

Budgeting is not an exact science, but management does its best to project expenses and income, formulate a budget, and strive to meet it. If the budget is prepared properly, the bank will go a long way toward meeting its plan.

Monthly Variance Reports

After the budget process has been completed and the budget (financial plan) is put in place, the bank strives to meet the targets. Most banks typically prepare monthly variance reports that indicate where expenditures have exceeded the budgeted amount or where income has failed to reach the income target. Budgets are usually prepared by cost center and profit center. A **cost center** is a unit in a bank, such as the proof department, that does not generate income: a profit center, such as a branch, does produce income. Even though a cost center does not generate income for the bank, it is vital to making the overall operation of the institution a success. Each profit and cost center manager is responsible for reviewing that center's variances from the budget and determining the causes of variances.

Unforeseen circumstances cause variances from the budget. For example, sometimes an expenditure is incurred later than anticipated; sometimes an expenditure becomes unnecessary and is eliminated from the budget, and sometimes center managers cannot plan for variations in volumes. For example, an unexpected increase in the volume of deposited items means an unexpected volume of processing (chapter 6) and a corresponding increase in processing fees. Center managers focus on offsetting unexpectedly high expenses by cutting back other areas of expense to stay within the overall budget. Of course, the bank also may look for other sources of income to offset unforeseen expenses.

Banks usually do not adjust the budget once it is in place. Instead, they can offset negative variances in one part of the budget with cost reductions in another part of the budget. Variances that cannot be offset that way—such as large loan charge-offs, for example—are identified as permanent variances from the budget. The bank documents these permanent variances and prepares for the negative impact they will have on profitability.

Many financial institutions base the center managers' compensation and bonus plans on meeting the budget. In those cases, center managers have not only a corporate interest in meeting the budget but a personal interest as well.

Performance Measurements

The financial plan, or budget, is in itself a performance measurement—the ultimate performance measurement in terms of measuring the success of a financial institution. These measurements are known as efficiency ratios. Banks can measure the number of employees-to-assets or employees-to-equity to compare themselves with peer group banks. In addition to the budget, however, many financial institutions also establish performance measurements for specific units and/or specific employees within the bank to measure productivity or quality or both. Both factors ultimately affect the bottom line and contribute to profitability.

Productivity

Productivity performance measurements evaluate the bank against itself and against other financial institutions in its market area and elsewhere. These measurements are used by cost center managers to determine how well they themselves, their cost center, and their employees are performing. Department managers also use these measurements to compare month-by-month or year-by-year productivity. From these comparisons, a manager may identify potential trends in productivity.

Did You Know?

The top five world banking companies in assets are:

Deutsche Bank AG	Frankfurt, Germany
Citigroup	New York, USA
BNP Paribas	Paris, France
Bank of Tokyo LTD	Tokyo, Japan
Bank of America Corp.	Charlotte, USA

(American Bankers Association)

For example, the proof department manager may measure the department's productivity and find that proof operators are encoding items at the rate of 1,300 per hour this month, versus 1,250 per hour last month, versus 1,150 per hour during the same month last year. This measurement tells the proof manager that productivity has increased since last year and has been affected by some of the programs the manager implemented.

However, the proof manager may find that the bank's average number of items per hour is lower than the industry norm or lower than the average of another financial institution; perhaps other proof departments in other banks using similar types of systems are encoding an average of 1,800 items per hour. The difference may be attributed to the methods by which the measurements were taken, to a different type of training program, to the types of documents being encoded, or to a problem in production. Whatever the cause, using performance measurements can alert the proof manager to a potential problem.

Quality

In addition to measuring productivity, the proof manager may also measure the quality of the work. For example, the manager might determine that the average proof operator in the department makes one error per 1,000 items encoded. By comparing this with previous error rates in the same department, the proof manager can identify trends. Proof managers can also measure the quality produced by their shop versus another institution; as a result, they may be able to increase the number of encoded items per hour and reduce the number of errors.

By increasing productivity—that is, increasing the number of items per hour produced by operators—the manager may then be able to substantially reduce the number of operators, the number of pieces of equipment, and the service maintenance cost as well. Improving quality reduces the number of rejects, thereby reducing the amount of manual intervention to correct errors. In addition, measuring quality performance benefits customer service, because customer deposits are encoded correctly the first time.

Performance Standards

Besides measuring performance and making comparisons, many financial institutions establish performance standards by function for both productivity and quality. For example, the proof manager, after determining the current level of performance, may set a performance standard of 1,600 items per hour per operator. Then the manager can implement programs for increasing productivity to meet that standard.

The same is true for quality standards. If the bank is currently making errors at the rate of one error per 1,000 items encoded, it may want to establish a new standard of one error per 1,400 items encoded. After a standard has been set, it can be used to measure performance of the department or of individuals.

Other examples of performance standards for improving quality include mailing statements within one business day of the statement date, or keeping customers waiting in line no longer than five minutes, or ensuring that no customer will have to hold longer than 30 seconds when calling the customer service department. Although such performance standards are not tied directly to the bank's financial plan, they do have an impact on it.

Summary

Bank accounting systems are designed to record, present, and interpret all the information that results from each day's transactions. The figures are essential to the bank's planning function, are required by federal and state regulatory authorities, and are expected by the bank stockholders and customers. If a bank cannot provide data on its profitability, it risks losing public confidence. The financial strength displayed by each institution is a benchmark used by customers to determine the best banks in which to place their funds.

Bank accounting systems generally use double-entry bookkeeping as a proof and control technique, and they always develop two basic reports: the balance sheet (statement of condition) and the income statement. All reports showing the bank's financial condition are submitted whenever required by authorities; quarterly balance sheets and income statements are made public, and detailed accounting information is used internally for a variety of important purposes.

Although the income statement reflects whether a bank has made a profit and actually shows the amount of profit that the bank has made, the income statement alone is not a complete measure of a bank's profitability. The bank also uses certain performance ratios: return on assets, return on equity, capital ratio, net interest spread, and earnings per share. These performance ratios reflect the bank's financial stability and ability to earn income from its assets. The financial data reported by the bank have significant impact on stockholders, regulators, other financial institutions, customers, and even employees. Consequently, the financial institution ensures the accuracy of financial data and does everything it can to ensure maximum profitability for the organization, consistent with sound principles of liquidity and safety.

The bank also establishes a financial planning process, including a budget for both expenses and income and a system for monitoring variances from the budgeted amounts. In addition, the bank manages those variances. Performance measurements are another element of financial planning. On the basis of performance measurements, the bank can evaluate its internal performance and the performance of specific departments and employees. It can then compare its own current and previous performance and measure itself against peer banks. Banks also establish performance standards and work toward achieving them. These standards exist to improve productivity and quality, both of which lead to increased profitability for the organization.

Review and Discussion Questions

1. Why is accurate financial data so important to federal and state regulators? To bank shareholders and investors? To customers?

2. Distinguish between cash and accrual accounting methods.

3. What is a bank's largest asset and largest liability? What are its largest income and expense items?

4. What are the four primary performance ratios?

5. Why is the accurate reporting of financial data important for customers?

6. Why is it important for a bank to establish a financial plan (a budget)?

Additional Resources

Analyzing Financial Statements. Washington, D.C.: American Bankers Association, 1998.

Financial Accounting: A Business Perspective. Chicago: Irwin Professional Publishing, 1998.

Web Resources

Federal Deposit Insurance Corporation (FDIC) www.fdic.gov

The reports of condition and income and thrift financial report www2.fdic.gov/Call_TFR_Rpts/

The Risk Management Association www.rmahq.org

U.S. Securities and Exchange Commission www.sec.gov

11

MARKETING AND THE CUSTOMER SERVICE FUNCTION

Learning Objectives

After completing this chapter, you will be able to do the following:

* define marketing and describe the elements of the marketing concept
* answer the questions "What do customers want from their bankers?", "How do customers buy?", and "What can be done to make customer contacts positive?"
* discuss the importance of relationship building and selling bank services
* discuss marketing research, its three profiles, and primary and secondary data sources
* list and describe the stages in the development process of a new product
* define the bolded terms that appear in the text

Introduction

Do you know that when you participate in the community, deal appropriately with an unhappy customer, or solicit customer opinions, you are helping to market your bank's products and services?

Situation 1

It's Saturday afternoon and you are sitting in the bleachers watching a Little League baseball game. Your bank's logo appears on the shirts and hats of one of the teams—evidence of your bank's team sponsorship. Your bank has encouraged its employees to show support for the team, which is what brings you here today. You will be handing out candy bars to both teams at the end of the game. One of the parents approaches you and asks if your bank also sponsors the concert series in the park during the summer. When you answer "yes," the parent wants to know why your bank is so involved in the community. How do you respond?

Situation 2

An obviously upset customer passes you at the customer service desk and gets in line to wait for a teller. You approach the customer and ask if there is anything you can do to help. The customer angrily explains that the bank bounced his mortgage check. In addition to having to pay a late fee to the mortgage company for not having his payment in on time, he has to pay what he considers an "exorbitant" fee to the bank for the returned check. He maintains he has never had an overdraft in the 15 years he has had his accounts with your bank and does not see how you could have let this happen to him. How can you diffuse his anger, solve his problem, and retain the banking relationship?

Situation 3

Janet Paul has been a customer of yours for several years. She fits the profile of the target market for a new checking account product your bank is considering offering. Her name came up on a list generated by your bank's computer as a prospect for a focus group to gauge customer reaction to the new product. You call her to invite her to participate. What can your bank gain from seeking her participation?

While the deposit, payment, and credit functions are still the foundation of banking, banks today find it necessary to focus on a variety of support areas to respond to the needs of their customers. The success or failure of an institution can often be measured by how efficiently quality products and services have been brought to the financial marketplace. The marketing function of the bank addresses how such a task is accomplished, and it requires the cooperation of all areas in the bank to ensure success. This chapter describes how a marketing philosophy that is properly integrated throughout the bank organization enhances the marketing function. The chapter also looks at bank customers to reveal their likes and dislikes, how they prefer to be serviced, how they make purchasing decisions, and how bankers can best relate to them. Finally the chapter addresses the development of new products.

Marketing in a Banking Environment

Marketing Defined

While marketing and research about markets have been functions of the business world for a long time, they are relatively new concepts for banking. Banks have traditionally had marketing departments that had little interaction with the rest of the bank. The situation is rapidly changing as more banks see marketing as a function that requires participation by the whole institution.

What is marketing? The most common definition of marketing is "human activity directed at satisfying needs and wants through exchange processes."[1]

Human activity means that people are involved in satisfying the need for products and services. Needs are things that individuals must have for basic comfort and survival. Once the basic needs are satisfied, people have wants that they believe will enhance their quality of life. In the broadest sense, people need food, shelter, and clothing. They may want steak and lobster tails, a million-dollar house, and designer clothing. In financial services, customers need a savings account or a mortgage loan. They want the best interest rates or payment terms.

In marketing, the thing exchanged is commonly called a **product**, which can be any object or service that satisfies a customer need or want—hence the definition of marketing as human activity directed at satisfying needs and wants through exchange processes. Banking is a service industry, rather than a consumer or producer goods industry; nevertheless, there is much disagreement and con-fusion in banking about the use of the words products and services. Some people feel that calling banking services "products" camouflages the fact that a service industry's marketing challenges are different from those of a product-related industry. On the other hand, some people feel that certain banking services, such as checking accounts, savings accounts, certificates of deposit, and loans, deserve to be called products. In this chapter, as throughout the text, both terms are used. This reflects their common uses as well as their subtle differences.

The Marketing Concept

The guiding principle of the most successful marketing firms is known as the **marketing concept** (exhibit 11.1). The marketing concept is based on the philosophy that the objectives of an organization are best reached by identifying the needs and wants of its customers, and meeting those needs and wants through an integrated, efficient, organization-wide effort supported by senior management. Recognizing that the marketer and the consumer are part of a broader society, another element may be added to this concept: marketing should be carried out in a socially responsible manner.

The marketing concept is a philosophy and a frame of mind that permeates the entire organization; it is also a basis for decision-making and a guide for effectively managing resources. Marketing, then, is not an activity that a business undertakes; rather, it is an organizational philosophy that influences and directs all the operations of a bank or other business. The four elements that support the marketing concept are customer orientation, profit, total company effort, and social

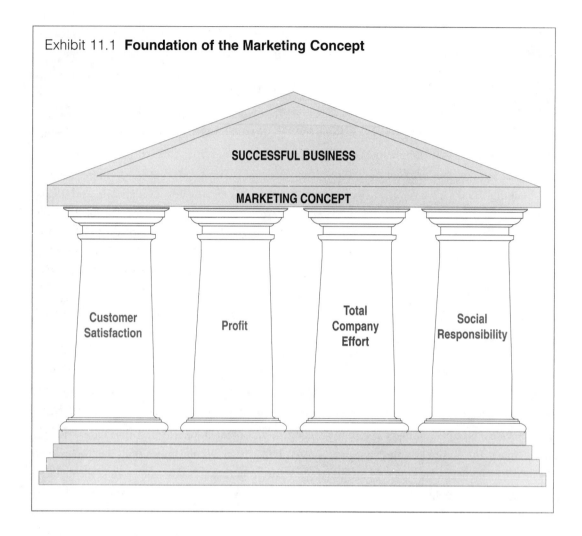

Exhibit 11.1 **Foundation of the Marketing Concept**

SUCCESSFUL BUSINESS

MARKETING CONCEPT

Customer Satisfaction

Profit

Total Company Effort

Social Responsibility

responsibility. When these four "pillars" are in place, they help ensure the success of a business.

The following sections cover each element of the marketing concept in detail and show how it applies to the business world.

Customer Orientation

The marketing concept recognizes that customer satisfaction is the "business" that all businesses are in. A truly marketing-oriented company believes that its financial objectives will be best served by identifying its target market and recognizing and responding to that market's needs and wants. Marketing expert J. B. McKitterick once said that, under the marketing concept, it is not important to be skillful in making the customer do what suits the interest or convenience of the firm, but to be skillful in inducing the firm to do what suits the interest of the customer.[2]

There are several good business reasons for including customer orientation in the marketing concept. Highly satisfied customers tend to be repeat purchasers, and it is much more expensive to generate a new customer than to provide additional service to an existing one. Satisfied customers are also more loyal, less likely to stray to competitors, and less price-sensitive than customers who are not highly satisfied. They are also more likely to direct referrals to your bank.

Profit

The marketing concept does not imply that customer satisfaction is the only objective of an organization. It recognizes that to reach profit objectives, there must be a balance between customer satisfaction and profitability. Indeed, the marketing concept believes that profit objectives can best be met by providing customer satisfaction.

The highly successful marketing organization finds ways to use its resources in the most efficient way possible consistent with customer wants and needs. A bank might improve customer satisfaction by offering a checking account with no fees, service charges, or minimum-balance requirements. However, a checking account is one of the most costly products offered by a bank, and it would be inadvisable to price the product this way. From a marketing perspective, the ideal approach would be to design checking products to meet the customers' needs and wants, and then to select the most acceptable service charges and minimum-balance combinations while earning a profit for the bank. Many banks now offer a range of checking accounts, from basic, low-cost, minimum services accounts to elaborate, interest-bearing accounts that require high minimum balances and provide numerous additional services, such as safe deposit boxes. The bank that builds more value into its checking accounts from the customer's perspective can attract more customers at a slightly higher price than can competitors offering fewer checking account benefits. Greater customer satisfaction improves earnings by increasing fee income and deposit balances.

Total Company Effort

The marketing concept must become the philosophy of the entire organization, not just the marketing department. In banks, as in other organizations, the importance of effectively integrating and coordinating the activities of employees is based on a simple truth: The people who work for the business are the business. A firm markets itself every time a customer interacts with an employee. If a teller is rude when greeting a customer, then as far as the customer is concerned, the bank is rude. The question is not whether the teller should engage in marketing, because marketing is inherent in the job. The question is whether the teller will market the bank's services effectively. Effective integration of the marketing concept throughout the bank's operations increases the likelihood that the teller's job, and all other jobs, will be performed in a manner consistent with the marketing concept.

With the marketing concept, every department of the bank sees itself as serving the bank's customers in some way. While only some employees deal directly with customers, employees who do not have this direct contact understand how the work they do affects the customer. For example, the proof operator knows that an encoding error will lead to an error on the statement, which will cause a problem for the customer. The customer will then call or visit the bank to get the problem resolved, creating additional work for customer service staff. In a marketing-oriented, customer-focused bank, all employees understand that "if you aren't serving the customer directly, you're serving someone who is."

Social Responsibility

Social responsibility is an important part of the marketing concept, especially for banks, which provide a quasi-public service. It is quite possible for a company to satisfy its customers yet be in conflict with the well-being of society as a whole. For example, a firm might market a product that satisfies a number of consumers but dangerously pollutes the environment or harms some type of wildlife. Increased sensitivity to social responsibility has resulted in some banks switching from styrofoam and paper cups to reusable glass, ceramic, or plastic coffee mugs, recognizing the environmental harm caused by non-biodegradable waste. Since banking is a paper-intensive industry, most banks have major programs in place to recycle used, shredded paper.

Banks are expected to play an active, socially responsible role in civic affairs. It is not unusual for a bank to mandate that its officers be involved with local service organizations. Through their community relations programs, banks often support the arts, scholastic achievement, and amateur sporting events. Frequently, a bank will take the initiative in addressing a specific cause, such as promoting neighborhood improvement or developing recreational opportunities for youth. In situation 1, you were approached by a community member who asked about your bank's involvement in the community. You would respond that your bank is not just a business, but a member of the community and therefore committed to adding to the community's quality of life.

Some aspects of social responsibility have been mandated by banking regulation. Since the passage of the Community Reinvestment Act, banks are subject to periodic examinations and are rated on the extent to which they meet the credit needs of all segments of the communities they serve.

Customer Relationship Management

Assessing and Responding to Customer Attitudes

The marketing concept requires a customer-oriented approach, yet how do we know what the customer wants? In 1999, the American Bankers Association Communications Council funded the third study of customer attitudes and banking knowledge, originally conducted by the Gallup Organization in 1994. This follow-up study was conducted by Mathew Greenwald & Associates in conjunction with the ABA Communications Council.[3] The original survey established a benchmark by which to measure customer satisfaction or dissatisfaction with banks and gave banks a deeper insight into the overall image of the industry. In addition to reevaluating attitudes in these areas, the new study looks at the perspectives of people from different generations. The results are being studied by bankers across the country to better define and market their products and services.

Several key findings of the study reveal customer attitudes and expectations, and suggest some new approaches to bank marketing. As exhibit 11.2 shows, 79 percent of bank customers feel very or somewhat favorably towards the banking industry. This is almost 10 percent higher than in the second survey, taken two years earlier.

The study had other good news for banks.

- Banks are seen as the most active industry in the community. Computer companies (55 percent), insurance companies (44 percent), and credit unions (46 percent) all scored lower than banks at 72 percent.
- 81 percent of the public surveyed agree that the U.S. banking system is financially healthy.
- 74 percent of the public surveyed use a bank most often for financial services, compared to 16 percent for credit unions and 10 percent for other institutions.

- 90 percent of bank customers are satisfied with the financial institutions they use most often. Almost half of these customers are very satisfied. These are very strong numbers.
- Compared to other financial services companies, banks are considered to be on the leading edge of technology by nearly two-thirds of their customers.
- 74 percent of bank customers feel banks do a good job of protecting confidentiality.

The news was not all good, however, and there is still work to be done.

- Roughly 40 percent of the respondents feel banks do a fair job of helping people meet financial goals, develop financial plans, and save for retirement.
- As shown in exhibit 11.3, the clear majority of the customers surveyed still access the bank through the traditional branch.
- While banks do very well with traditional bank products, at the time of the survey, relatively few customers purchased insurance, variable annuities, or individual stocks from banks.

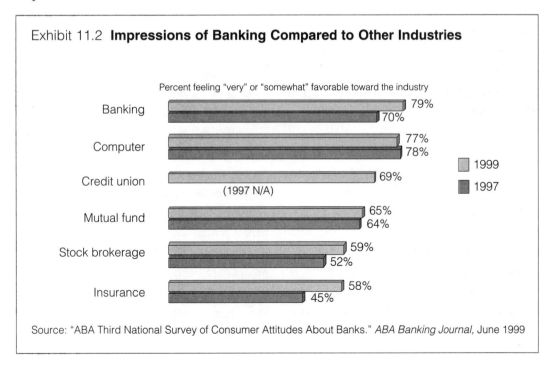

Exhibit 11.2 **Impressions of Banking Compared to Other Industries**

Percent feeling "very" or "somewhat" favorable toward the industry

Industry	1999	1997
Banking	79%	70%
Computer	77%	78%
Credit union	69%	(1997 N/A)
Mutual fund	65%	64%
Stock brokerage	59%	52%
Insurance	58%	45%

Source: "ABA Third National Survey of Consumer Attitudes About Banks." *ABA Banking Journal*, June 1999

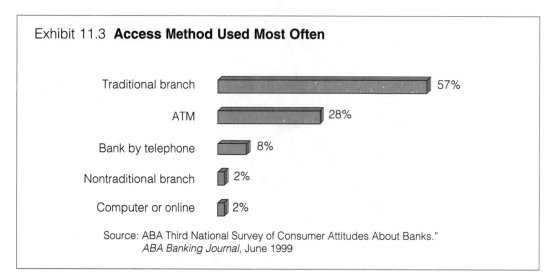

Exhibit 11.3 **Access Method Used Most Often**

Access Method	Percentage
Traditional branch	57%
ATM	28%
Bank by telephone	8%
Nontraditional branch	2%
Computer or online	2%

Source: ABA Third National Survey of Consumer Attitudes About Banks."
ABA Banking Journal, June 1999

- 62 percent of customers do not feel that banks are flexible in meeting their financial needs; however, these numbers have been declining from 64 percent in 1997 and 70 percent in 1994.

This study comes at a time when bankers are already addressing changes in customer attitudes, needs, and desires. Bankers are now seeking answers to the questions, "What do customers want from their bankers?" "How do customers buy?" and "What can be done to make customer contacts positive?" in order to improve the results from their marketing efforts.

What Do Customers Want From Their Bankers?

When asked what they want in a bank, customer responses mostly fall into the following categories:[4]

- responsive service
- competent staff
- a customer perspective
- courteous treatment
- reliable service
- products that meet consumers' needs
- a professional appearance

- easy access to staff and funds
- financial privacy

Responsive Service: Customers want their bankers to appear to be ready and willing to serve them. Responsive service makes it abundantly clear that you want and value their business. It means

- acknowledging customers as they approach
- being ready to help them
- taking responsibility for the problems they present
- functioning as a team with other bank employees—all having the same goal
- solving problems promptly and accurately
- going the extra mile to resolve special problems in a friendly and caring manner
- listening carefully to understand the customers' needs

Competent Staff: Customers expect bankers to be professional. They expect the bank employee they are dealing with to have the skills and knowledge needed to explain the bank's products and services and answer questions clearly. They expect to be directed to the products and services that will be most useful to them. Competent staff have the effect of reassuring customers that their money is in good hands.

A Customer Perspective: Communication with customers recognizes customers' needs. Both written and spoken communication should be in clear, concise language from the customer's—not the bank's—point of view. "Preauthorized automatic transfers are available with this account" may be operationally correct, but the following shows more of a customer perspective: "You can arrange to have funds automatically transferred from your checking account to your money market savings account, making regular saving easier for you."

Courteous Treatment: Customers expect bank staff to be friendly, thoughtful, and efficient, and to treat them with respect. They want to hear "thank you" when the transaction is concluded, and "excuse me" when the representative turns away from them. Customers expect consideration for their personal feelings and sensitivity toward their financial situations.

Reliable Service: Customers automatically expect a certain level of service from their banks. They expect their statements to arrive on time and to be correct; they expect renewal notices for their certificates of deposit; they expect electronic banking services to be available when they need them; and they expect problems to be resolved quickly. Bank advertising raises expectations in other areas, promising, for example, a quick response to a loan request. Reliable service means meeting and exceeding these customer expectations.

Products that Meet Consumers' Needs: Customers expect banks to have the standard banking products, and they expect each of those products to have specific benefits. For instance, they expect that

- a bank will offer a range of checking, savings, certificate of deposit, and credit services

- their savings accounts and certificates of deposit will earn a competitive rate of interest
- interest rates on loans will be competitive and payback terms will reflect customer needs
- investment services will allow customers to tailor a portfolio to meet their investment goals.
- electronic services such as the Internet, telephone banking, and direct deposit will make banking more convenient for them

A Professional Appearance: Customer attitudes are shaped in part by the appearance of the bank facility and its employees. Confidence is eroded by dirty or disorganized facilities and unprofessionally attired staff. Customers expect the office where they bank to look like a solid, safe place to put their money, and they expect the employees to dress professionally. A bank that fails to do this gives the impression that it does not respect its customers—and that it doesn't deserve their respect.

Easy Access to Staff and Funds: Customers expect the bank's services and people to be available when and where they are needed. The customer service area can be either inviting (open, well-lit platform) or discouraging (small, cluttered offices). The latter puts obstacles between the customer and you. Automation has helped banks give customers greater access to their money through automated teller machines and other electronic services that will be discussed in later chapters.

Financial Privacy: As the amount of personal information that is stored and transmitted electronically grows, so does consumer concern for the confidentiality of that information. Part of the Gramm-Leach-Bliley Act (chapter 2) addresses a financial institution's obligation to protect its customers' privacy. The act further prevents financial institutions from sharing account information with an unaffiliated third party (such as an employer or other creditor) without the customer's expressed permission. Banks have always placed a priority on protecting customer account information. The Gramm-Leach-Bliley Act provides additional assurance to customers that the industry will continue to protect their personal, private information.

How Does the Customer Buy?

Understanding how a customer "buys" is important to the marketing function. Purchasing—the buying process—usually happens in four phases (Exhibit 11.4):

• needs identification
• prepurchase activity or searching
• making the purchase decision
• postpurchase feelings or anxiety

Identifying a Need: The starting point for any purchase is an unsatisfied need. There are two types of needs. Recognized needs are needs of which the customer is aware. For example, a young woman who has just graduated from college realizes that she needs to establish credit. A couple leaving on a trip realize they need traveler's checks. A regular savings account customer realizes that she could be earning more interest by investing in a certificate of deposit. Unrecognized needs (needs of which the customer is unaware) are also very common. The college graduate may not know the credit options available to her. A customer who frequently bounces checks may not realize he needs overdraft protection. A customer may not be aware that a short-term loan might be more cost-effective than closing a certificate of deposit before maturity for short-term use.

Identifying customer needs is a prerequisite for successful marketing. If a bank product does not fill a need or is marketed to satisfy a need that customers do not feel, the product will not be successful.

Prepurchase Activity: Once a need is identified, the customer begins to search for the best way to satisfy the need. The level of effort expended in this search depends to a large extent on the cost, durability, and complexity of the product or service being sought. When purchasing a bank product, for example, the customer may look through the ads in the newspaper to compare the certificate of deposit rates offered by competing financial institutions. Your bank's own customers may then call your bank for more information or literature.

Customers search longer and more carefully when shopping for a mortgage loan or a home equity line of credit. Both these products are relatively complicated and require that the customer gain more knowledge about the various terms and conditions of the numerous products available on the market. Prepurchase activity might include talking to other people, reading consumer information pamphlets, making an appointment to talk with a bank loan officer, or requesting a loan application.

Making the Purchase Decision: When deciding whether to buy, the customer uses information gathered during the prepurchase phase to weigh the advantages and disadvantages of the product or service, compare the relative merits of alternatives, and select among various features. In the context of banking, this might mean choosing the term of a certificate of deposit or applying for a fixed-rate versus an adjustable-rate mortgage.

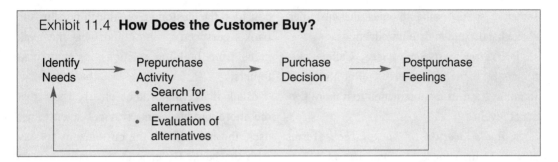

Exhibit 11.4 **How Does the Customer Buy?**

Identify Needs → Prepurchase Activity
• Search for alternatives
• Evaluation of alternatives
→ Purchase Decision → Postpurchase Feelings

The purchase decision is often the result of a difficult choice, and the choice becomes more difficult as the product or service becomes more complex.

Postpurchase Feelings: After the customer makes a purchase, a period of assessing the purchase decision inevitably ensues. The customer wants assurance that he or she made the right choice. Many customers experience anxiety, especially if the purchase decision was difficult or some attractive alternatives had to be rejected. Was the decision the right one? Were the most appropriate features selected? Will the customer be better off than before? Such questions occur to most customers as they reevaluate a product or service following its purchase.

Bankers, aware of this stage in the consumer buying process, take steps to ease whatever anxieties the customer might have as well as reassure him or her, and offer evidence that the customer has made a good decision.

In the banking world, reassuring new customers might entail sending them welcome letters or calling to thank them for their business and offering further assistance and guidance. Answering customers' questions after they have deposited their money or signed the loan papers is also a good way of reducing their postpurchase anxieties. What the banker needs to remember is that a customer generally needs continuing support after having made the purchase. In banking, the customer's postpurchase feelings are influenced by every transaction, every communication, and every experience with the bank.

What Can I Do to Make Customer Contacts Positive?

Making the customer feel important is a fundamental objective of a bank employee. A customer who perceives poor treatment feels that he or she does not matter or is unimportant to the bank. This may lead to discomfort in dealing with bank employees and ultimately to the customer taking his or her business elsewhere. In contrast, a satisfied customer feels important and believes that the bank values his or her business. The following seven simple rules of customer contact will help you make customers feel important with each interaction:

1. *Make eye contact*. Looking the customer in the eye as he or she approaches and then frequently making eye contact during the transaction acknowledges that you think this individual is important.

2. *Smile*. A smile communicates warmth. By smiling, you tell customers you are happy to be of service to them and are glad they do business with the bank.

3. *Acknowledge and greet the customer*. Acknowledging and greeting customers promptly when they approach the customer service area makes them feel welcome and comfortable stating their business. The customer service repre-

sentative should stand to greet the customer, shake hands, and initiate introductions.

4. *Use the customer's name.* Calling customers by name makes them feel at home and familiar. It raises the interaction to a more personal level.

5. *Avoid overuse of bank jargon.* Terms such as "truncation," "demand deposit," "foreign bank," and "amortizing" might be familiar to you, but may not be to your customer. Initials like PMI, APY, and even certificate of deposit may draw blank stares. Unless absolutely necessary for regulatory purposes, avoid using technical bank terms when a simpler explanation will suffice.

6. *Use expressions of courtesy.* "Please," "thank you," and "excuse me" are used liberally in all customer contact situations.

7. *Respond in a positive fashion.* Responding in a helpful, cheerful, interested manner to whatever the customer says lets the customer know you are ready and willing to help. Even when the customer is upset or angry, you should calmly show your willingness to listen.

In situation 2, the customer's anger can be diffused by using a combination of the above principles. If you make eye contact, smile, call him by name, and express genuine concern for his problem you will be successful in opening the lines of communication. Once this happens, it is easier to find an acceptable solution to the problem. You may, for example, reverse the fees incurred by the customer (if this truly is his first overdraft) and offer overdraft protection to keep it from happening again.

Building Relationships through Selling Bank Products and Services

Thus far, the chapter has looked at customer attitudes and customer contacts. It's time to consider the customer relationship from the bank's perspective—how and what the bank gains from building relationships with customers.

Bank marketing studies clearly show that the more products and services a customer uses, the more likely the customer is to stay with the bank. By encouraging customers to use multiple products and services, therefore, the bank builds a long-term, hopefully profitable customer relationship. While customers who use just one bank product or service can certainly be profitable, they are far less loyal. It is much easier to close one savings account than to close multi-faceted banking, investment, and insurance accounts.

Older bankers may still remember the days when there was little or no competition for bank services. Banks just had to open the doors in the morning and the customers would come streaming in. Banks were the only place in town to get basic financial services and they did not have to put much effort into "selling" their products. Now competition comes from every possible corner and selling the bank's products and services has become necessary for survival. Banks must understand the financial selling process, actively promote their products and services, offer electronic alternatives to traditional banking, and assist customers in making purchasing decisions in order to distinguish themselves from their bank and non-bank competitors.

Everyone in the bank is involved in selling bank products and services to customers, whether or not they are in the sales department! The best way all bank employees can build additional product and service relationships with customers is through a sales technique called **cross-selling**. Cross-selling is the practice of inducing users of one or more products or services to buy or use additional products or services. To cross-sell, bankers must constantly be aware of opportunities. For example:

- a teller who notices a customer with a large savings account balance may suggest a certificate of deposit.
- a loan officer who helps a customer finance a new car may suggest an insurance review with the bank's insurance subsidiary
- a calling center employee may suggest Internet banking or telephone banking to a customer who inquires about an account statement or current history

Cross-selling may involve nothing more than "planting a seed"—suggesting a service to customers and giving them time to think it over. Over time, the seed (idea) is nurtured by the banker who reminds the customers how the product or service will benefit them. As the idea "takes root," many of these customers will purchase the product with the following result:

- the bank expands the customer relationship
- the customer benefits from a needed product or service
- the customer, realizing the banker has his or her best interest at heart, will be more inclined to seek out this banker when additional financial needs arise

Marketing Research

Marketers use a variety of information in order to market a product or service effectively. Knowledge about the product itself is not enough; the banker also uses information on the target market for the product and how it compares with the competition. Getting ready to market a product or service involves a great deal of research. Some information is already in the bank's computer, waiting to be tapped. Other information is more difficult to find and may involve surveys, outside research, or

intensive web surfing. The Internet has proven to be an excellent resource for research material. Many banks subscribe to research firms through the Internet, which allows them to gather relevant information instantly.

A bank needs readily available, up-to-date information relating to its customers, its market, and its competitors in order to market effectively. Collecting basic market information facilitates developing these three basic profiles.

Customer Profile

Successful marketers know their customers. Banks need the information to answer questions such as "Who are our customers?", "How do our customers differ from those of competing banks?", and "How do our customers differ from other residents of the market area?" (For example, are the bank's customers younger or older than the overall market?) A customer profile normally includes information about age distribution, occupation, educational level, income, geographic location, and ethnic composition. Such information may be obtained from internal data such as bank customer files, surveys of customers, or information collected during account opening.

A customer profile should be created for commercial customers also. Such data might include the number of commercial customers by type of business, balance size, number and types of services used, length of banking relationship, geographic location, and profitability.

Market Profile

The financial health of a bank is tied to the economic well-being of the geographic area it serves. A market profile provides management with the information it needs to identify potential problems and opportunities in both the retail and commercial markets. Much of the information is widely available from a variety of sources, particularly through the Internet, but keeping the information current requires special monitoring of economic trends.

A market profile defines the boundaries of a bank's primary trade area (the geographic area from which 75 percent of the bank's business is derived) and the secondary trade area (the broader area from which the balance of its business comes). It also includes the number and value of housing units, population data, and demographic information in those geographical areas.

On the commercial banking side, the market profile normally includes the number, types, and locations of businesses in the trade area. Ideally, management also should have specific data about every firm or merchant in the area, including information about the nature of the business, its approximate sales volume, the number of employees, and its current banking affiliations. Such information forms the foundation of an effective officer-calling program.

Competitive Profile

In today's banking market, competitors abound and, therefore, bank marketing decisions take into account competitors' marketing strategies (that is, their product offerings, pricing, hours, and services) and their likely reactions to the bank's own marketing activities.

A bank's competitive profile answers such questions as "Who are our competitors?", "What are their services and how are they priced?", "What is each institution's market share?", "Who is the market leader (if there is one)?", and "How do our services, facilities, hours, and staff compare with theirs?"

Consider the following scenario: A bank in an older urban area hired a marketing research expert to analyze its possibilities for expansion. The researcher soon discovered that the bank did not have even the most basic market information with which to begin, so the researcher began compiling the information needed to create profiles of the bank's customers, markets, and competition.

In the course of developing the customer profile, the researcher discovered that the bank had customers who were substantially older than the customers of other banking institutions in the city, and a core of high-balance savings accounts, but a customer base that was aging and dying and was not being replaced.

Without corrective action to appeal to a younger market, the bank was destined to lose even more market share at its present locations and to have limited appeal in the new markets it wanted to enter.

Updating Market Data

Management requires a continual flow of up-to-date information on the customer, the market, and the competition. Customer bases continually change as residents and businesses move in and out of trade areas. Also, the local economy of the trade area is affected by the state and national economies, both of which are dynamic. Thus the basic market information is updated constantly.

Market Data Sources

Some market profile information can be derived from secondary data, which is information that has already been collected for another purpose either inside or outside the bank. For example, information from a profile of installment loan customers or a list of new homes built in a particular district could be used when marketing a new loan product. Primary data is information that is collected for a specific purpose. Customers could be surveyed, for example, to determine their preference for checking account choices.

A bank's internal information reveals information about customers' behavior in relating to the bank. Most banks store this type of information on databases called marketing customer information files (MCIFs). There are varying degrees of complexity in MCIFs, but they all help track vital information on customers, products and services, competitors, demographics, and more. With an MCIF, for example, banks can learn the proportion of customers having one, two, three, or more services with the bank. Banks can monitor the number of accounts and balances in checking, savings, and loan accounts opened and closed as well as where the traffic in the area is heaviest, to anticipate changing demands for services.

Secondary information about the local market can be obtained from external sources such as the Census Bureau, local chambers of commerce, and municipal offices. Information on competitors can be obtained from published reports put out by the regulatory agencies.

Data regarding competing banks' services and pricing can be obtained through their websites or by direct contact, posing as prospective customers. The Internet has a wealth of information that helps with the information-gathering.

Survey research can generate information in response to a specific need, especially regarding customer motivation and needs, opinions, knowledge, attitudes, and behavior.

New Product Development

Banks are on a continuous quest for new products to attract new customers and retain old ones. Developing a new product is a multiphase process. It begins with getting new product ideas, testing the concept, and conducting a business analysis. The product is then developed and test marketed before being introduced to the marketplace. Finally, the effectiveness of the product is evaluated relative to its objectives.

Getting New Product Ideas

A company that is eager for new product ideas can conduct a formal search of the market. In a bank, such ideas might come from ongoing research to help identify consumer banking needs that are not being met, or they might come from management or other employees. Some firms offer cash incentives to employees for generating new product ideas. More recently, new product ideas have been coming from advances in technology. Ideas for new products occasionally come from the banking regulators. The money market deposit account arose from this source. The purpose of idea generation is to find, in a structured, goal-oriented manner, new ways to serve the bank's customers in a meaningful way.

Screening New Products

Ideas for new products are screened against product objectives, product policy, and company resources. Not every new product idea can or should be pursued. A preliminary judgment is made as to whether an idea deserves further study. In an aggressive and imaginative bank, an unusual idea that first appears to be unworkable and not within present regulatory constraints will not be screened out until it has been evaluated in more detail. Each idea for a new product is evaluated to determine its impact on existing products.

The development of the NOW account, the predecessor to interest-bearing personal checking accounts, was spearheaded by a small, persistent bank in Maine. It found an ingenious way to evade a regulation banning the payment of interest on demand deposits by offering negotiable orders of withdrawal (which work like checks) on savings accounts.

Testing the Concept

This is a crucial phase in new product development. Concept testing is a function of consumer marketing research, but it does not simply entail asking a large number of consumers what they think of a new product idea. This type of questioning fails to elicit the underlying attitudes, beliefs, and concerns that consumers might have about a new product, and it does not provide insight into how they would actually behave if the product were available. There would be no frozen foods in our grocery stores today if the industry had been guided by preliminary consumer reaction to the concept.

Instead, it is better to first assemble small focus groups to explore reaction to a new product concept. This type of research is more effective at drawing out feelings and motivations that may affect the acceptance of the new product. It can also provide insight into how the product might be positioned or promoted. The customer in situation 3 can provide valuable help to the bank by giving honest reactions to a potential product.

Business Analysis

Business analysis is designed to show whether there is sufficient demand for the product, and if the product fits in with the bank's overall goals and objectives. Research and other methods are used to analyze projected use, market share, and so forth. This information is used to develop preliminary objectives, select the target market, and plan a marketing strategy. If management approves the recommendation, the product development coordinator will pull together the group necessary for developing the product. Exhibit 11.5 demonstrates the new product development process.

Developing the Product

During this stage, the bank determines if it is feasible to produce or provide the product or service at a cost and quantity that will make its final price attractive to customers. The product features that will be particularly important to consumers are identified at this point and clearly highlighted as the product is being designed. This is also the stage at which the promotion, distribution, and pricing strategies are considered and developed. The development stage involves production of prototypes or samples of the new product. In banking, the development phase for a new savings product would require modification of the savings computer system by the programming staff,

Exhibit 11.5 **New Product Development**

Getting New Product Ideas
What is the need in the marketplace?

↓

Screening New Products
What is the initial reaction against the bank's objectives,
other products, and company resources?
Are there regulatory constraints?

↓

Testing the Concept
What do the small focus groups say?

↓

Business Analysis
Is there sufficient demand for the product?
Does it fit with the bank's goals and objectives?

↓

Developing the Product
What will the features be?
How will the bank promote, distribute, and price the new product?

↓

Test Marketing the Product
What target markets will the bank test the product in?
How will the bank promote the product in those markets?

↓

Introducing the Product
How will the bank introduce the product?
What impact will this product have on the existing product line?

↓

Evaluating the Product
How does the progress of the new product meet the company's goals?
What adjustments are necessary?

---

the design of forms and documents to be used to set up the accounts, and the writing of procedures for the branch staff to follow in completing the forms and processing them.

Test Marketing the Product

Consumer goods manufacturers usually test market new products. It is not unusual for a company to try out a new product in one or two geographic markets, perhaps using a different promotional approach in each market to test their relative effectiveness.

Test marketing is increasing in banking, too. One benefit of test marketing is that the bank can assess customer response as well as familiarize employees with the planned new products.

Test marketing can be expensive and time consuming, however, and can offer competitors an opportunity to quickly copy the bank's new product or service. Therefore, it is beneficial to move quickly from the test marketing stage to a full-scale implementation or roll-out of the product.

Introducing the Product

This is the stage at which a company commits its resources to a full-scale introduction of the product to the market. Introducing a new banking product requires heavy involvement by the marketing department. A great deal of money is invested in advertising and sales promotions. Ideally, the training director has undertaken programs to ensure that each customer contact employee thoroughly understands the service and how to sell it (that is, knows its benefits as well as its features). Also it is critical to inform all staff members of the advertising campaign that has been launched so they can be prepared for customer inquiries. The launching of a new product often is tied to an employee incentive campaign to boost initial sales. At the same time, the bank might offer a premium to the customer for purchasing the new product.

At this stage, it is also important to assess the impact of the new product on existing product lines. Is a new savings product draining funds from existing accounts or drawing new deposits?

Evaluating the Product

The final stage in developing a new product involves monitoring the progress of the new product in relation to the company's goals. No product development plan is complete if it fails to include a system for monitoring the results of the plan. Effective monitoring enables the bank to make adjustments to the new product where needed, as well as to gain additional knowledge that will facilitate the introduction of the next new product. One of the purposes of the evaluation stage is to learn from experience.

Summary

Marketing is human activity directed at satisfying needs and wants through exchange processes. Many banks have adopted a marketing concept to promote their products more effectively. The elements of the marketing concept are customer orientation, profit, total company effort, and social responsibility.

Customers want responsive and reliable service, competent and courteous treatment, a customer perspective, and products that meet their needs. They also want their bankers to have a professional appearance and to be accessible. Bank customers go through the same stages to buy bank products and services as they do to purchase other consumer goods, beginning with a need. They search for alternatives in the prepurchase phase, make decisions in the purchase phase, and are anxious about their purchases in the postpurchase phase. Bankers have many ways to make customers comfortable with their purchases, and comfortable with the bank overall. Simple acts like making eye contact and smiling go a long way toward enhancing the customer relationship.

The more products and services a customer uses, the more likely he or she is to stay with the bank. Cross-selling is an effective way to enhance each customer relationship.

Before marketing a product, bankers conduct research on the customer and the market. There are many sources of internal and external data to use for this research. Bankers can also conduct focus groups and surveys to supplement existing data.

Banks are continually introducing new products to the marketplace in order to remain competitive. New products begin with ideas that are screened, tested, and analyzed before being developed. The new product is test marketed and then introduced to the marketplace. The product is then evaluated to determine if it has met its objectives.

Review and Discussion Questions

1. Explain the four elements in the definition of the marketing concept.

2. What are the four phases of the buying process?

3. How can cross-selling improve customer relations?

4. Describe each of the three profiles in marketing research.

5. List the eight steps in sequence of new product development.

Notes

1. Philip Kotler, *Marketing Management—Analysis, Planning, and Control.* Englewood Cliffs, N.J.: Prentice-Hall, 1984.

2. J.B. McKitterick, *The Frontiers of Marketing Thought.* Chicago: American Marketing Association, 1957. p. 8.

3. *ABA Customer Service Survey: ABA Banking Journal Supplement*, June 1999.

4. Bank Marketing Association, *Service Quality Management.* Parts adapted by permission of the publisher. Chicago: Bank Marketing Association, 1990. pp. 1–7.

Additional Resources

ABA Bank Marketing Magazine. Washington, D.C.: American Bankers Association

ABA/BMA Bank Marketing Departments: Analysis of Staffing and Structure, Washington, D.C.: American Bankers Association.

Bank Marketing Expenditures. Washington, D.C.: American Bankers Association, 2001.

Cross-Selling Deposit Products. Washington, D.C.: American Bankers Association, 1999.

Effective Referrals. Washington, D.C.: American Bankers Association, 1999.

Evolution of Bank Call Centers Vol. III: The Call Center Takes Center Stage. Washington, D.C.: American Bankers Association , 2000.

Evolution of Bank Call Centers Vol. IV: Benchmarks and Best Practices. Washington, D.C.: American Bankers Association, 2001.

Identifying and Leveraging Target Markets. Washington, D.C.: American Bankers Association, 1998.

Introduction to Relationship Selling. Washington, D.C.: American Bankers Association, 1999.

Marketing for Bankers. Washington, D.C.: American Bankers Association, 1998.

Web Resources

ABA Banking Journal www.banking.com/aba
ABA Financial Client Satisfaction Index
   www.clientsatisfaction.com/
American Bankers Association www.aba.com
Bank Marketing Association www.bmanet.org
CACI Marketing Systems
   www.demographics.caci.com

12

SPECIALIZED PRODUCTS AND SERVICES

**"If you'd like to press 1, press 3.
If you'd like to press 3, press 8.
If you'd like to press 8, press 5..."**

Learning Objectives

After completing this chapter, you will be able to do the following:

- define the four elements of a trust, explain the three legal requirements for bank trust services, and discuss the American Bankers Association principles that trust departments follow
- describe the basic trust services including settling estates, administering trusts, guardianships, and personal agency services, and corporate agency and employee benefit services
- explain how the Gramm-Leach-Bliley Act has affected the nature of brokerage services offered by banks and list the Office of the Comptroller of the Currency (OCC) guidelines for brokerage product sales
- describe safe deposit services and explain why banks have strict procedures for granting access to safe deposit boxes
- discuss three functions of an international department through a review of letters of credit, Eurodollars, global currency exchanges, and global credit operations
- differentiate among the different insurance product offerings
- define the bolded terms that appear in the text

Introduction

Being familiar with your bank's specialized products and services will help you serve customers with very specific needs. The following situations demonstrate this.

Situation 1

A retired businessman wants to revise his will. Ten years earlier he had named his daughter as executor. However, in the past decade, his assets have grown considerably and he has acquired works of art and overseas real estate. Although he still wants his daughter involved in settling his estate after he dies, he would also like the services of a professional. Is there someone in your bank to whom you could refer this customer?

Situation 2

San Francisco Machine Tools Corporation has negotiated with a firm in Germany to purchase a quantity of machine tools at a specific price. The U.S. firm wants to make sure the contract is fulfilled before it pays for the merchandise, but the German company wants to be sure it will be paid before it ships the merchandise. What can San Francisco Machine Tools do to address both concerns?

Situation 3

Fred Sightseer, a customer of your bank, is traveling in Europe. While in Poland, he sees a crystal vase that he wants to bring home to his wife. He's never seen anything like it and knows she will love it. Fred takes out his credit card to pay for the purchase. Before Fred left for his trip, he asked you whether his credit card could be used in Europe. What did you tell him? How does this work?

Full-service banking in the new millenium has a different meaning than it had just a few short years ago. In the past, the bank was considered to be offering full banking services if it offered checking accounts, savings accounts, certificates of deposit (CDs), and several types of loans. Now, in addition to these services, customers expect a full-service bank to offer a wide range of financial services, including financial and estate planning, brokerage, and various forms of insurance.

Many banks, especially smaller community banks, do not yet have the resources to offer the full range of new banking services. They are solving this problem in creative ways to ensure that their customers have access to all that is available. Some are seeking the help of outside vendors or other banks to provide these services. Known as "outsourcing," banks are hiring third parties to perform certain functions, instead of purchasing equipment and hiring personnel for those purposes. Banks are also experimenting with joint ventures, where two or more banks join forces to perform certain functions. A joint venture can reduce processing costs by sharing personnel, equipment, software, and transportation costs. The cost of new technology, such as image technology, can be spread across two or more banks. While outsourcing and joint ventures are not specifically addressed, keep these concepts in mind as you read this chapter and the next. It will help you understand how banks are keeping up with the explosion of new products and services.

Banks now are striving to meet a customer's total financial needs rather than focus on a customer's core deposits. This chapter examines the various specialized services offered by banks and explains why banks offer them not only to remain competitive, but to survive. Included are trust department services, brokerage and investment services, safe deposit services, global banking, and insurance.

Trust Department Services

A **trust** is a relationship in which one party holds property for another party, based on agreements and laws. There are four elements to a trust:

- the trust corpus, or the body of the trust
- the trustor or settlor
- the trustee
- the beneficiary

The trust corpus, or the body of the trust, is the property for which the trust is created. It can consist of any type of property such as cash, stocks, bonds, real estate, or any other item or thing of value. The trustor ("settlor" or "grantor" are terms also used for trustor) is the person creating the trust. For example, a grandparent who establishes a trust for the benefit of a grandchild is called the settlor or the trustor. The trustee is the person or entity, such as the bank, that takes control of the trust property and administers the trust. The trustee actually takes legal title to the property. The **beneficiary** is the person for whose benefit the trust was established. In the example above, the grandchild is the beneficiary of the trust.

In the early years of U.S. banking, trust services were considered specialized and were offered only by a trust company. Through the years, these trust companies assumed some or all of the commercial bank's functions, accepting demand and time deposits and extending credit. They obtained state banking charters and became known as bank and trust companies. It was not until the Federal Reserve Act of 1913 that national banks were allowed to offer trust services. Though those services still must be offered by a separate company, or through a separate trust division in most banks, they are as much a part of banking as deposits and loans.

Trust departments offer both individuals and corporations a full array of services that are highly specialized. For example, the trust department may be asked to manage a portfolio of stocks and bonds and may have full authority to make investment decisions on behalf of the beneficiary; this requires the services of a trained investment manager. Or the trust department may be asked to manage properties with significant amounts of timber. In this case, the trust department may employ a full-time forester. The point here is that the trust department employee, while an employee of the bank, may specialize in a field totally unrelated to the banking business.

Trust services are a natural complement to other banking services and facilitate development of a total financial relationship, while generating fees for the bank. If a bank fails to offer comprehensive trust services, customers might look elsewhere and move their entire banking business as well.

Principles of Trust Institutions

Three specific legal requirements apply to trust operations. The first provides that no bank may begin offering trust services without first obtaining approval from the proper authorities. A national bank that wishes to establish a trust department first applies for permission from the Comptroller of the Currency; the Federal Reserve and the Federal

Deposit Insurance Corporation (FDIC) also review the request. State-chartered banks obtain their trust powers from the banking departments of their respective states.

To meet the second legal requirement, a bank sets aside securities of unquestioned value, such as U.S. government obligations, as a form of collateral against the proper performance of trust duties. Through this requirement, all clients who are affected in any way by trust department operations enjoy an additional measure of safety over and above any federal insurance coverage that may apply. This same requirement applies to a bank's handling of public funds accounts, as discussed in chapter 4.

The third legal requirement on trust operations is found in state laws that set maximums on the fees banks can charge for certain services.

In addition to the legal requirements imposed on trust departments, the American Bankers Association has published a list of basic principles that banks follow:

- application of the prudent person principle
- segregation of trust assets
- separation of policymaking and auditing
- acquisition of specialized skills
- prevention of conflicts of interest

Prudent Person Principle

A court opinion issued in 1830 held that a trustee must act faithfully and with sound discretion as a prudent, intelligent person would act under similar circumstances. This **prudent person principle** requires that banks act with all the caution, skill, diligence, and sense of responsibility that a prudent person would display. A prudent person is expected to exercise more care in handling someone else's property than in handling his or her own. The risks a trustee might willingly take when dealing only with his or her own assets should not be taken when dealing with the property of others.

Segregation of Trust Assets

The assets of each individual trust are kept separate from those of all other trusts and from the bank's own assets. The trust departments of many banks are physically segregated from the rest of the institution with their own vaults, data processing equipment, and other facilities. In the past, an imaginary wall existed between the trust officers and their counterparts in other areas of the bank. Now they exchange information more freely and join in meetings with accounts that they share. Often this exchange provides the customer with additional services such as asset management, private banking, and financial planning, which creates a broader base with which to satisfy all of the customer's needs.

Separate Policymaking and Auditing

A special committee of the bank's board of directors sets policies concerning investments and the size and type of trust relationships the bank will accept. Also, there is a separate audit of the trust department, distinct from any audits conducted in other areas of the bank.

Acquisition of Specialized Skills

A bank is expected to use all of its expertise, plus all the skills it can reasonably acquire, in conducting trust operations. Banks seek to improve their skills to render even better service to their clients. Each institution regularly reviews all its trust operations and the qualifications of its employees in an effort to identify possible areas of improvement.

Prevention of Conflicts of Interest

The final ABA principle, specifically designed to prevent any conflicts of interest, is aimed at the practice of self-dealing. It states that a bank (1) should have no personal interest whatsoever in any investments bought or sold for trust funds and (2) should not purchase from itself any property from any of its trusts. All dealings between the bank's directors, officers, and staff members on the one hand, and its trust funds on the other, are prohibited.

Personal Fiduciary Services

Depending on the needs of its market and the volume of business it is able to produce, a bank may offer any or all of the following trust services to individuals:
- settling estates
- administering trusts
- administering guardianships
- administering personal agency services

Settling Estates

When a person dies, with or without a will, someone must take control of that person's affairs. The person who has died, the decedent, may have outstanding debts or taxes to be paid, and ultimately the assets of the decedent, which are referred to as the **estate**, must be distributed to the decedent's heirs. Many individuals leave a **will** to take care of their affairs after their death, describing the property they own and its location, and designating the beneficiaries to whom the property will be left and the person or entity that will settle the estate. The person designated in the will to settle the estate is referred to as the executor (executrix is the seldom-used female form). The executor can be a close relative, one of the heirs of the estate, the bank, or some combination of these. The retired businessman in situation 1 will probably name his daughter and his bank trust department as co-executors in his will.

A decedent who leaves a valid will according to state law typically names the executor and directs how the estate is to be distributed. The will may also be used to designate guardians of the decedent's minor children. Depending on the amount of property left by the decedent and whether all the property was held jointly, an estate may or may not need to be established. If an estate must be established, wills must be admitted to probate in most cases. Probate is a special court that examines and approves a will, confirms that the executor is qualified, and confirms the process by which assets will be transferred to the heirs and the beneficiaries.

If the decedent dies without leaving a valid will or has left no instructions for distributing the estate, the estate is distributed in accordance with the laws of the state. The court also appoints guardians for minor children of a decedent who was the sole surviving parent. If the decedent dies without a will, if the will is invalid, or if the executor cannot or will not serve, the court appoints an administrator.

The duties of executors and administrators are basically the same; they follow these steps in sequence:

- Take inventory to determine the exact value of the estate. Every asset of the decedent is itemized and a dollar value is shown for each.
- Take control of some or all of the assets, as necessary.
- File necessary federal and state tax returns and pay all necessary taxes on the basis of the value of the estate.
- Settle all debts and claims against the estate.
- Distribute the remaining assets, either according to the terms of the will or as directed by state laws.

When a bank acts as administrator or executor, it is legally liable for maintaining detailed records and accounting to the court and beneficiaries for all its actions.

Administering Trusts

The most common types of trust funds administered by banks are testamentary trusts, living trusts, and charitable and institutional trusts.

Testamentary trusts are created under the terms of a decedent's will. As trustee under a testamentary trust, a bank is responsible for managing the assets turned over to it by the executor or administrator and for paying the income to the beneficiaries, as specified in the will. Living trusts do not involve a decedent. They are created voluntarily by an individual who executes a trust agreement and transfers certain property to that trust. Often, the individual no longer wishes to manage his or her affairs because of sickness or excessive traveling. The trustee then manages those assets for the trust.

The trust agreement contains all the provisions for the formation of the trust, the payment of interest, and the payment of proceeds or distribution of the trust property to the beneficiaries.

Charitable and institutional trusts are established when a university, hospital, or charitable organization turns over cash, securities, or property to the bank. The bank's duties then involve active management of the investments that have been and will continue to be made.

Administering Guardianships

Another closely related service offered by bank trust departments is the administration of guardianships. **Guardianship** (sometimes called conservatorship) is established by court order for the benefit of a minor or incapacitated person. A minor is defined by state laws as one who is not of legal age; an incapacitated person is one who has been declared incompetent because of illness or senility. By law, the trust department periodically provides an accounting to the court to prove that all the proceeds were used for the person's benefit.

Administering Personal Agency Services

In addition to trust services, trust departments in banks also offer **agency services**. There is a significant legal difference between the role of agent and that of trustee. While trustees assume legal title to the property that is turned over to them, agents do not. Agents are given specific authority by an individual who retains legal title to the asset.

The most common agency services for individuals are safekeeping, custody, investment advisor, and investment manager.

- In safekeeping, the bank accepts, holds, and returns upon request the stocks, bonds, or other assets that the individual delivered to it.
- Custody services include safekeeping of assets plus collection of income for the individual. A custodian may buy and sell securities for the individual only when specifically instructed to do so. Banks can provide custody services for individuals, as well as for correspondent banks, and agencies of government.
- When acting as an investment advisor, the bank performs all the general duties of a custodian plus other responsibilities granted to it by the individual. For example, in handling securities for the individual, the bank may review the individual's investments from time to time and suggest retention, sale, exchange, conversion, or purchase of new securities. In addition, as investment advisors, banks often handle real estate in addition to securities. In these cases they collect rental income, pay the taxes on the property, provide for its upkeep and maintenance, and disburse any net income directed by the owner.
- An investment manager performs all of the above duties. In addition, the customer expects the investment manager to make financial decisions based on previously established parameters.

Corporate Fiduciary Services

Corporate Agency Services

For corporations and agencies of government, banks provide agent, registrar, and paying agent services.

- As a transfer agent on behalf of a corporation, the bank is responsible for changing the title of ownership on the corporation's shares of stock. This is necessary when shares change hands. The old shares must be canceled and new shares issued in the name of the new stockholder.
- Each corporation establishes the maximum number of shares of stock that may be issued. As registrar, the bank maintains records of the number of shares canceled and reissued so that an overissue cannot take place.
- As a paying agent (also called dividend disbursing agent) the bank is responsible for making all payments of interest or dividends to the holders of the shares of stock or the bonds issued by a corporation or unit of government. A paying agent is also responsible for redeeming all debt issues as they mature.

Employee Benefit Services

One of the fastest-growing and most competitive areas of trust services involves trust funds maintained for the employees of corporations and banks. **Employee trusts** may result from union negotiations, fringe benefit packages, or an increased emphasis on the social responsibility of the employer to provide for the well-being of employees.

A business may establish a **pension trust** or **profit-sharing trust** and make regular contributions into a trust fund. The duties of a bank in handling pension and profit-sharing trusts, whether for its own employees or for the personnel of another corporation, involve receiving regular corporate contributions, investing those contributions, maintaining detailed records to show the accrued value for each employee, making all disbursements, and providing detailed data on every transaction. An employer's payments into a profit-sharing fund fluctuate according to each year's net profits.

Another employee benefit service is the 401(k) plan. These 401(k)s are salary deferral plans to which employees contribute a percentage of their wages; companies may also contribute on their employees' behalf. The plans are managed by the trust department for its own employees or for other banks and companies. Fund managers handle corporate as well as employee contributions. They do all tax reporting and year-end accounting and reporting, arrange payouts, and complete disbursements. Bank trust department personnel will often work with the company to make investment decisions.

Investment and Brokerage Services

The Gramm-Leach Bliley Act was described in chapter 2. It authorizes bank subsidiaries or financial holding companies to own brokerage firms, allowing banks to provide their customers with this financial service. For many years, banks watched as savings deposits were withdrawn from banks and reinvested in mutual funds, stocks, and other brokerage products. This disintermediation of billions of dollars from the banking system occurred because banks could not offer competitive interest rates. With the passage of the Gramm-Leach-Bliley Act, banks now can offer products—not FDIC insured—that compete directly with brokerages and investment firms. Banks are now faced with the challenge of organizing themselves to expand into the brokerage service arena. This section focuses on this challenge.

Brokerage Service Organization

Banks are organized in a number of ways to offer brokerage services. Some banks sell mutual funds and other brokerage products through a third party; the licensed full-service brokerage sets up shop on the bank's premises, and the bank is paid a fee. Although banks earn less in fees this way than from performing the service themselves, third-party brokerage has certain advantages: The bank has no responsibilities relative to the service, while making it available to its customers.

Some banks have formed joint ventures with broker-dealers to sell securities. Under these arrangements, employees work for both the bank and the broker-dealer; however, the licensed broker-dealer must supervise the brokerage functions performed by the bank employee.

Banks also sell brokerage products through their own discount brokerages. The brokerage units are formed either as subsidiaries of the bank or as affiliates of the financial holding company. These units sell a full range of investment products and services but do not offer investment advice. Discount brokerage services are typically less expensive than full-service brokerages.

Banks that want to sell securities and offer investment advisory service form full-service brokerages. These brokers are typically formed as subsidiaries of the bank or the financial holding company. They can perform the same services as a brokerage house, including underwriting and holding equity securities.

Once a bank decides how to organize its brokerage function, it must determine how it wants to make the services available to its customer base. Some have completely separate brokerage operations that are physically separate from the bank. In these banks, employees are not involved at all in the operations of the brokerage company. Other banks take the opposite position and use their existing retail delivery system to sell the brokerage securities. The branch system is already in place and could give banks an advantage over other competitors.

Bank Regulator Concerns

The explosion of bank brokerage services requires both the Federal Reserve and the Office of the Comptroller of the Currency (OCC) to issue guidelines for banks to follow when selling brokerage products. The OCC guidelines advise banks to:

- adopt a statement describing the features of the sales program and the roles of bank employees and third-party entities.
- market non-deposit products in a manner that does not mislead or confuse customers about the products or the risks. To the extent possible, banks should separate the retail deposit-taking and retail non-deposit sales functions.
- prohibit bank employees, particularly tellers, from offering investment advice. The OCC strongly discourages employees who accept retail deposits from selling retail non-deposit investment products.
- refrain from offering uninsured retail investment products with a product name identical to the bank's name.
- conspicuously disclose that investment products
  - are not FDIC insured.
  - are not obligations of the bank.
  - are not guaranteed by the bank.
  - involve investment risk.

- obtain a signed statement from customers that they have received the disclosures.
- determine the appropriateness of the product recommended to the customer.
- properly train bank employees to sell investment products.
- avoid compensation programs that give salespeople the incentive to sell non-deposit investment products rather than a more suitable option.
- comply with all applicable state and federal restrictions on transactions involving the bank's fiduciary accounts.
- maintain a compliance program to ensure compliance with the guidelines and any other applicable requirements.

The Financial Plan

The key to the success of any customer's investment program is the financial plan. A well-crafted financial plan will help a customer achieve his or her investment goals, whether it is a comfortable retirement, college for the children, purchasing a house, or estate planning. It can help to minimize taxes while providing funds for unexpected emergencies.

Financial plans can mix short-term and long-term goals. They can enhance existing plans or begin an entirely new one. Inherent in all financial plans is the customer's willingness to tolerate risk. Typically, an investment strategy is broken into three parts. The balance and types of investments within each category reflect the customer's tolerance for, or aversion to, risk. These categories are:

- Safe, secure, liquid products
- Products that generate income
- Investments that grow or appreciate in value

Safe assets are traditional bank products like checking, savings, and certificate of deposit (CD) accounts. They are used to meet everyday life expenses and often provide a small investment return. Many of these products are FDIC insured (providing safety) and are very liquid.

Income assets provide customers with greater income-earning potential. These assets are not meant to provide growth in the value of the investment. Rather, they provide a regular income stream for the investor. These investments are not normally FDIC insured and the income generated can be taxable or tax deferred.

Finally, growth assets are purchased for their potential to increase in value. Stock and other equities are the most common examples of these. Again, even though banks may now offer these products, they are not FDIC insured.

Product Offerings

Many brokers have access to a long list of products and services to meet the needs of the customer's financial plan. Of the many options, three major product categories will be highlighted in this section—stocks, bonds, and mutual funds.

Stocks

Stock is the evidence of actual ownership in a company. It is traded from one investor to another, through stock exchanges. There are many forms of stock, including common (the most widely available) and preferred. The owner of stock is referred to as a shareholder or stockholder. Stocks of different companies fulfill many investment goals—from the most conservative to the most aggressive. They can

provide growth and/or income. Regardless of the company, stock is a higher risk investment than an insured bank product like a certificate of deposit. The principal value of an investment in stock is not guaranteed. When the stock is sold, it might be worth more or less than its original purchase price. Historically, however, the value of stocks has outpaced the rate of inflation, making them a popular long-term investment choice.

Bonds

Bonds are loans that investors make to governments and corporations. By purchasing bonds, investors are loaning money to these entities, in exchange for a set rate of interest. Interest is usually paid on a regular basis and the principal amount of the bond is repaid on a predetermined maturity date. Bonds can be issued by corporations, the United States Treasury, or municipal authorities. Some bonds are tax-free, meaning income generated by these bonds would be exempt from federal, state, and/or local income taxes. The risk associated with investing in bonds is based on the quality of the issuer the bond. U.S. government bonds are considered very low risk (if not risk-free) because they are backed by the full faith and credit of the United States. The government can raise the money to repay these bonds by additional borrowing or by increasing taxes.

Mutual Funds

Mutual funds are a collection of stocks, bonds, and other investments owned by a group of investors and managed by a professional investment company. Mutual funds are an extremely popular investment vehicle because they give investors access to professional management and more types of stock than most would be able to purchase on their own. The risk in the funds is spread over all of the stocks, bonds, and other investments in a portfolio. The dividends and interest earned by the investments are divided among those investors who hold shares in the fund. Since all of the investors' money is pooled, the professional investment company has considerably more buying power than it would if it were investing for each individual. Exhibit 12.1 shows how mutual funds work.

Safe Deposit Services

The safe deposit facilities at banks today offer the same basic service that goldsmiths provided many years ago in accepting valuables from clients for safekeeping. Then, as now, the key word is *protection*. By their very nature, banks have secure vaults for the protection of currency, securities, and collateral. It is logical that they would extend the use of those facilities to customers for a fee. However, safe deposit services are not offered solely because they are a traditional part of banking. They are also considered a business tool—to attract customers or prevent existing depositors from seeking banking services elsewhere.

With proper identification and documentation, a bank may establish a safe deposit relationship with:

- an individual
- an individual together with a deputy (agent) whom he or she appoints and whose rights are comparable to those of an attorney-in-fact (chapter 4)
- two individuals jointly
- a sole proprietor

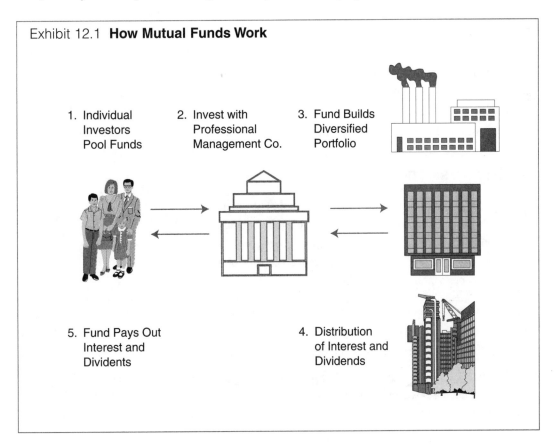

Exhibit 12.1 **How Mutual Funds Work**

1. Individual Investors Pool Funds
2. Invest with Professional Management Co.
3. Fund Builds Diversified Portfolio
5. Fund Pays Out Interest and Dividends
4. Distribution of Interest and Dividends

- a partnership
- a corporation (In the case of a corporation, the bank must obtain a separate corporate resolution authorizing the safe deposit relationship.)
- a fiduciary

Whenever a safe deposit box is rented, the bank must obtain appropriate signature cards. Typically, these cards include the terms of the contract between the customer and the bank. The bank then assumes responsibility for the adequate protection of the customer's property.

The customer renting a safe deposit box has every right to expect that the identical property placed in the box will be protected and can be retrieved during normal banking hours. Frequently, this property is unique and cannot be replaced. Family heirlooms, valuable documents, stamp collections, and jewelry, for example, must remain in the same condition as when the customer placed them in the box; no substitution or change is acceptable. In contrast, a depositor who gives the bank $100 in currency cannot expect to receive the identical bills back when a withdrawal is made.

Each bank that offers safe deposit services must be aware of the liability it faces and pro-vide protection for the safe deposit customer. If a customer claims that certain valuables have been removed without his or her authorization or knowledge, the burden of proof is usually on the bank to prove that it did everything possible to provide protection. Any evidence of a bank's negligence in its daily safe deposit operations, or any proof of defects in the vault's construction or maintenance, may convince a judge or jury that the customer is entitled to damages.

Exhibit 12.2 lists common safeguards that should be part of every safe deposit program.

Right of Access

The safe deposit signature cards and contract clearly stipulate who is allowed to have access to a box. Possession of a key *does not* establish right of access. The best precaution a bank can take to avoid any future claims is to require each individual desiring access to sign an access card that can be compared with signature cards already on file. The bank may require additional identification, such as a PIN for access. It is in the bank's best interest to establish strict procedures for safe deposit per-

---

Exhibit 12.2 **Safe Deposit Safeguards**

- Keys to unrented boxes are under dual control at all times.
- No member of the bank's staff accepts custody of a customer's key.
- Safe deposit boxes are opened in private rooms only.
- Bank personnel have no knowledge of the contents of a box.
- Customers cannot leave their boxes unattended.
- When a customer terminates the safe deposit relationship and returns the keys to the bank, the box is opened under dual control to verify that it is empty.
- All safe deposit boxes require a bank key and a customer's key to open. The bank's key is never referred to as a master key, because this might give the impression that the bank has one key that opens every box.
- In the event of a customer's death or declared incompetency, state and local laws regulate disposition of the box's contents.

sonnel. This protects against unauthorized access to the safe deposit box. Employees must implement these procedures with extreme care at all times. This protects the customers as well as the bank.

Questions often arise concerning the insurance that covers safe deposit boxes. The contents of a safe deposit box, which are not known to the bank, are not specifically insured, nor does federal deposit insurance apply. Normally, the general liability policy of the bank will offer insurance protection against losses.

Global Banking

Global banking has become a critical factor in the profitability of many major U.S. banks. Even in institutions where the volume of international business does not require the facilities of an independent department, the demand for foreign trade services grows each year. While major U.S. banks will have a fully staffed global banking department, smaller banks may rely on a larger bank to act as a correspondent to provide these specialized services.

In today's world, countries are increasingly dependent on one another, and money knows no geographic boundaries. Electronic transfers of funds move billions of dollars every day among Hong Kong, London, Tokyo, Paris, Frankfurt, and the major cities in the United States. The primary international services offered by banks fall into three major categories:

- payments
- deposits
- credits

Before any U.S. stock exchange opens in the morning, the activity, trends, and foreign exchange quotations are already available from the exchanges in London and Tokyo. Any

economic change in foreign markets directly affects the United States. For large U.S. banks, the entire world is their marketplace.

In expanding their international operations, U.S. banks are simply following the lead of their corporate customers, which saw the huge potential for sales and profits in foreign countries and quickly began to market their products globally. Today the output of these corporations flows steadily from every part of the United States to other parts of the world. In many cases, large money center banks have duplicated this pattern of overseas growth.

Global Payments Services: Letters of Credit

Of all the global services now offered by banks, the best known and most frequently used is the commercial letter of credit. A buyer of goods often requires assurance that the merchandise being bought will conform exactly to specifications, while a seller of goods often requires assurance of payment after the goods have been shipped. As described in situation 2, where a San Francisco merchant wants to purchase goods from a German company, without some independent guarantee that the right merchandise will be sent and that payment will be made, importers and exporters would be hesitant to trade. Letters of credit satisfy the requirements of both parties and minimize the risks of international trade. A **letter of credit (L/C)** is an instrument issued by a bank, substituting the credit standing of the bank for the credit standing of the importer (buyer) of goods. It guarantees that the bank will pay the exporter (seller) if all the terms of the contract are met. At the same time, it protects the buyer by assuring that no payment will be made unless and until the contract has been fulfilled. With a reputable bank in the middle, both parties are willing to trade.

Most letters of credit are irrevocable, although a revocable letter of credit can be written. An **irrevocable letter of credit** stipulates that no changes can be made without the full consent of both the buyer and the seller. The application for an irrevocable L/C clearly states that the credit cannot be revoked. Letters of credit may also be issued on either a sight basis, which calls for immediate payment once the terms are met, or a time basis, which specifies a later date by which the payment must be made.

A letter of credit provides some protections for the issuing bank against either party not honoring its commitment. Usually the letter of credit stipulates that the bank

- maintains a security interest (chapter 8) in all property covered by the contract
- is not responsible for physically counting or otherwise examining the actual goods being ordered
- bears no responsibility for the genuineness of any document submitted to it

The San Francisco company (the importer) in situation 2 applied for a letter of credit. The importer's bank in San Francisco will review the application. By approving the application,

the bank is accepting the importer's guarantee to reimburse it after the bank pays the seller. The California bank thus becomes the **issuing bank** under the letter of credit. It notifies the German bank specified in the letter of credit that the L/C is being opened. The German bank, known as the **advising bank,** often a correspondent of the issuing bank, then contacts the exporter.

The exporter is now the beneficiary of the letter of credit and will be paid, provided all the terms and conditions of the original contract are met. The required documents, for which the seller has made arrangements, provide the evidence that the contract has been fulfilled.

If all conditions are met, funds will flow from the issuing bank in California to the paying bank in Germany, and the bank in California will then recover the funds from the buyer's account.

In addition to their value as instruments that finance foreign trade, letters of credit serve many other global and domestic purposes. For example, a **standby letter of credit**, also known as a performance letter of credit, may be used to assure payment of construction contracts or long-term sales contracts, or to cover other debts of someone who needs to use a bank's credit standing to reinforce his or her own.

Standby letters of credit have been used in large numbers by construction contractors in favor of municipalities in the United States as a means of making sure site improvements are made for large housing developments. Through these letters of credit, the issuing banks guarantee to the municipal authorities that curbs, streets, and major site improvements will be made if the contractor defaults. Exhibit 12.3 shows a standby letter of credit.

In some cases, an L/C issued by one bank requires a further guarantee of payment through a larger, more prestigious bank. The second bank that agrees to undertake the responsibility to make payment in addition to the obligation of the issuing bank thus confirms the guarantees, and the L/C is called a confirmed letter of credit.

Global Deposit Services: Eurodollars

The large-scale expansion of overseas branch networks by U.S. banks, plus the creation of

---

Exhibit 12.3 **Standby Letter of Credit**

GOODWIN NATIONAL BANK
3848 Third Avenue
Goodwin, MI 48136
(313) 250-6626

IRREVOCABLE LETTER OF CREDIT NO. 68520

DATE 3/20/01

Beneficiary Name: Advance Design Concepts, Inc.
Address: 865 Independence Drive
                     Toronto, Canada M5K 2H6

Gentlemen:

We hereby open our Irrevocable Letter of Credit No. 68520 in your favor, available by your drafts drawn on Goodwin National Bank, Goodwin, MI, at sight for any sums not exceeding in total $100,000, for the account of Brewster Killington Associates, Powell, MN.

The drafts must be accompanied by your signed statement certifying that Brewster Killington Associates has not performed or paid (give reason for drafting a Letter of Credit), and that demand for payment has been made and the performance has not been forthcoming from Brewster Killington Associates.

All drafts drawn under this credit must be marked "Drawn under Goodwin National Bank, Letter of Credit No. 68250, dated 3/20/01." Any amendments to the terms of this credit must be in writing over the authorized signature of this Bank.

Except as otherwise expressly stated, this Credit is subject to the "Uniform Customs and Practices for Documentary Credits."

We hereby agree with you that each draft drawn under and in compliance with the terms of this credit will be duly honored if presented on or before 12/31/03.

Very truly yours,

Joyce M. Creighton
Senior Vice President

"offshore" facilities in locations such as the Bahamas and the Cayman Islands, provided global corporations with depositories into which they could place the funds derived from their local operations.

The term **Eurodollar** was first introduced into the language of banking in the 1960s. Eurodollars are simply U.S. dollars that have been deposited outside of the United States. They differ from domestically deposited dollars only in terms of their technical locations and can easily be brought back to the United States by the banks' head offices.

If a corporation deposits $1 million with a bank in the United States, the value of that deposit to the bank is immediately reduced by the reserve required by the Fed. On the other hand, when Eurodollars are recorded on the offshore bank's books they are not subject to reserve requirements. Therefore, if deposited overseas in the form of Eurodollars, the entire $1 million theoretically represents loanable or investable funds for the bank. This provides additional funds to invest when compared with domestic deposits.

No interest rate restrictions apply to Eurodollars; a bank may pay any interest rate it sees fit to attract them. The hundreds of billions of Eurodollars that now exist constitute a major source of funds for large banks. At the same time, they have proved extremely attractive to domestic corporations because of the interest yield. The net result is that the largest U.S. banks now generally report more than half of their total deposits as "foreign." The bulk of these foreign deposits can be found in interest-bearing relationships, such as large-denomination time deposits.

The Eurodollar should not be confused with the European Currency Unit (ECU). The ECU is now referred to as the "euro" after its intro-

duction on January 1, 1999. The euro is the official currency of a group of countries (the European Union) that includes Austria, Belgium, Finland, France, Germany, Ireland, Italy, Luxemburg, the Netherlands, Portugal, and Spain.

Global Currency Exchanges

Another component of global banking is the exchange of currency and checks into and out of currencies from different countries. World commerce knows no boundaries and companies must be able to easily exchange money from one currency to another. This is accomplished through the world's banking system, in which the U.S. banking system is a key player. International departments of large banks monitor the exchange rates of the world's currency so they know how to exchange dollars for francs, pounds, or drachmas. These exchanges can be calculated immediately, allowing all the parties involved to move money around the world in seconds, without any party taking undue risk or exposure.

Consider Fred Sightseer in situation 3. His charge goes to the merchant's account in Poland and gets deposited in Polish currency. The bank electronically transmits Mr. Sightseer's card information to a central clearing house, which transfers it back to the U.S., converts the charge to U.S. dollars, and posts the charge to the customer's credit card account.

Global Credit Operations

U.S. banking also has an international presence as a provider of credit to individuals, businesses, and governments. However, global lending is perhaps the primary concern of the largest U.S. banks today. Here, the credit is extended chiefly to foreign governments, their agencies, and authorities.

The nature of global lending has changed drastically in the past decade or so. Formerly, international banking was primarily the business of commercial banks. But as governmental barriers around the world have fallen, investment banks, corporations, and individual investors have assumed a greater role. The rise in the participation in global banking of investors other than commercial banks can be seen most clearly in the thousands of investors and owners of shares in international mutual funds.

Insurance

Under the Gramm-Leach-Bliley Act, banks now have the ability to offer insurance products. Financial holding companies (FHC) and financial subsidiaries may sell insurance products like insurance agents, or they may act as brokers by offering product lines from several different insurance companies.

Financial subsidiaries, however, cannot underwrite insurance and annuities. The law does say that if subsidiaries of banks are already engaged in underwriting insurance and annuities they can continue to do so (banks were allowed to get involved in smaller towns, which gave them additional income streams), but new bank subsidiaries cannot start to offer underwriting services for insurance and annuities.

However, FHCs can underwrite all types of insurance, including title insurance and annuities. This means a bank can now compete with the local insurance agent, through its FHC, by offering the same types of insurance products,

Did You Know?

Increasingly, banks are selling more than credit life insurance. Dental insurance is sold by 5.3 percent of the large banks ($1 billion+ in assets), 16.7 percent of medium banks ($250 million–$1B), and 11 percent of smaller banks (<$250 million). You can also get homeowners insurance and disability insurance from many banks.

ABA Securities Association

or it can underwrite insurance just as the large insurance companies (like State Farm and Allstate) do.

Product Offerings

Many banks are currently investigating whether or not to offer insurance and, if so, what products to offer. They have many options, including the following:

- credit life insurance, which pays off the insured loan if the borrower dies while the loan is still open.
- property insurance, which covers homes, cars, boats, jewelry, and anything else that consumers can own.
- casualty insurance, which provides protection against serious or fatal injury. An example of this is your health coverage at work.
- life insurance, which provides for survivors upon the death of the insured.
- title insurance, which protects homeowners from financial loss due to ownership problems. This differs from property insurance in that it protects the *title* of the property, rather than the property itself. For example, if, after you purchased property in good faith, someone came forward with a valid claim on the

property due to an incorrect survey report, the title insurance would reimburse the investment you had in the property.

- annuities, which are investment vehicles that have a fixed, regular payment made for a specific period of time, or for the life of the person insured under the plan. Individuals invest in annuities most often for retirement planning since, after they are fully paid according to contract terms, annuities provide regular income.

Summary

In addition to the basic banking products such as checking and savings accounts and loans, banks offer an array of specialized services to meet the needs of specific market segments. Some of the major specialized services offered by banks are trust services, global banking services, and brokerage and insurance services.

Banks offer trust and agency services to individuals and corporations. The major services that banks typically offer include settling estates; administering trusts and guardianships; and safekeeping, custody, transfer agent, registrar, and paying agent services.

In offering these trust services, the bank hires employees with specialized capabilities to manage the assets of the trust customers. A bank's trust department also executes its duties as a fiduciary without any conflicts of interest. The primary duty of the bank is to its customers; therefore, the bank segregates the trust assets to ensure that there are no conflicts of interest.

For many years, savings deposits were withdrawn from banks and reinvested in mutual funds, stocks, and other brokerage products. This disintermediation of billions of dollars from the banking system occurred because banks could not offer competitive interest rates. With the passage of the Gramm-Leach-Bliley Act, banks can now offer products that compete directly with brokerages and investment firms. Banks are now faced with the challenge of organizing themselves to expand into the brokerage service arena.

Bank safe deposit services benefit both the customer and the bank. Extreme care must be taken to control access to safe deposit boxes, ensuring that only the authorized owner has access to the box.

More than ever before, banking involves a worldwide market. Banking activities today include far more than the basics of attracting and retaining deposits, processing payments, and extending credit. To remain competitive, banks offer services to their customers that transact international business. Letters of credit are a basic international service offered by banks. This product helps protect the interests of both the buyer and the seller of goods in the international marketplace.

Again as a result of the Gramm-Leach-Bliley Act, banks can now offer insurance products to their customers through financial holding companies. This makes banks competitive with insurance agents and companies.

Review and Discussion Questions

1. What legal requirements must be met in order for banks to offer trust services?

2. What are the major reasons why banks offer brokerage products?

3. Why is it necessary to prepare a financial plan before investing?

4. Why do banks have strict procedures for granting access to safe deposit boxes? What do these procedures include?

5. How does a letter of credit issued by a bank protect the interests of both the buyer and the seller of goods?

Additional Resources

Bank Insurance Survey Report. Washington, D.C.: American Bankers Association, 2000.

Global Banking. Washington, D.C.: American Bankers Association, 1999.

Investment Basics and Beyond. Washington, D.C.: American Bankers Association, 1998.

Referring Insurance and Annuities Customers. Washington, D.C.: American Bankers Association, 1999.

Trust Basics. Washington, D.C.: American Bankers Association, 1998.

Trust Operations. Washington, D.C.: American Bankers Association, 1998.

Web Resources

ABA Insurance Association
www.aba.com/ABAIA/default.htm
ABA Securities Association
www.aba.com/ABASA/default.htm
American Bankers Association
www.aba.com
Securities and Exchange Commission
www.sec.gov

13

ELECTRONIC FINANCIAL SERVICES

I'm gonna ace this test!
I snuck in my dad's "Smart Card"...

Learning Objectives

After completing this chapter, you will be able to do the following:

- describe how electronic funds transfer systems facilitate purchases through point-of-sale (POS) transactions and transfer funds quickly and safely through automated clearing houses (ACH)
- explain how banks meet the needs of corporate clients by offering electronically delivered cash management services
- discuss the home banking options available to consumers through the telephone and the Internet
- distinguish among the functions of three types of bank cards, including debit, credit, and smart cards
- discuss some of the systems developed to provide security and prevent loss in the electronic realm
- discuss the impact of new legislation authorizing the use of electronic signatures
- define the bolded terms that appear in the text

Introduction

Electronic financial services have changed the nature of banking more quickly and more completely than any other innovation in the history of banking. As the following situations show, consumers take for granted many conveniences that were just dreams a decade ago.

Situation 1

Joan and John Newcomer have recently moved to a new town. They decide to join the local health club and are given the option of having their monthly fee automatically deducted from their checking account. Later that day, they call their insurance company to change their address and transfer their accounts to a local agent. Again, the agent asks if they would like their payments deducted monthly from their account. The Newcomer's already use automatic deduction for their mortgage payment and know how convenient that is. They readily agree to use this service for both their health club membership and insurance premiums. How does this work?

Situation 2

On her way home from work, Liz withdraws $100 in cash from the ATM outside her bank. She then goes in to the bank and deposits her $700 paycheck at the teller window. Finally, she stops at the kiosk in the bank lobby and authorizes a $406 payment on her car loan. Later that evening, Liz sits down at her computer and accesses her bank account through the Internet. She checks her balance and prints out a statement of the activity on her account. All of the transactions she made just a short time before appear on the screen. What other banking services are available to Liz over the Internet?

Situation 3

An employee of a large computer chip manufacturer has stolen several blank paychecks and has forged an authorized signature on one of these checks, payable to a fictitious person for whom he has false identification. He presents the check to you at the teller window and, because of an agreement with this company to cash checks for employees, you cash the check. Emboldened by the seeming ease of the fraud, the employee does the same thing the next week. This time, however, there is a stop payment order on the check and the employee is detained by the bank security officer. What bank service alerted the company to this fraud?

This chapter discusses the areas where electronic financial services—including funds transfer, home banking, and bank cards—have had the greatest impact. Security concerns and loss prevention are also addressed.

Electronic Funds Transfer Systems

The fast and reliable flow of funds through the banking system has long been dependent on electronic systems. Originally these systems were developed for bank-to-bank use only. Fedwire is a good example of a system that used early computers and dedicated phone lines to facilitate the electronic debiting and crediting of bank accounts. However, the demand of merchants and corporations for access to banking technology brought about many of the changes in electronic funds transfer systems today. Consumers and merchants now also benefit from this through the use of point-of-sale transactions for the purchase of goods and services. Automated clearing houses provide instant access to funds by electronically crediting and debiting transactions. Corporations also benefit from cash management services that rely on electronic systems.

Point-of-Sale Transfers

Most card-based transactions are done through a **point-of-sale (POS) terminal**. This is a terminal at the seller's place of business where customers can use credit, debit, and smart cards to pay for purchases and services. POS systems are completely electronic. Customer entries initiate a debit to the customer's account and a credit to the seller's account. Use of debit cards results in an instant posting (debit) to the customer's transaction account at a financial institution; use of a credit card posts the transaction to the customer's pre-approved line of credit; and use of a smart card immediately reduces the amount of money stored on the card's microchip. Exhibit 13.1 shows how debit cards are used in POS transactions.

In many cases, customers are asked to provide a **personal identification number (PIN)** to complete a point-of-sale transaction. This protects the customer from unauthorized use of the card. PIN numbers are one of the primary means of safeguarding against bank card fraud. Customers should be advised to select unique numbers for their PINs, avoiding birthdays and other numbers that might be "guessed" by others.

Point-of-sale transactions eliminate the need for cash, benefiting all parties involved.

Although merchants usually pay a small fee for each POS transaction, the fee is offset by the savings related to reduced cash handling and storage. Customers appreciate the convenience of not having to carry large amounts of cash to conduct business, or not having to write checks and being asked to produce many forms of identification. Banks benefit from POS because the transactions are handled through processing centers. The information, received electronically, is simply entered on the bank's books for both the customer and the merchant. Banks also save money on cash handling costs twice—once when the customer gets the cash and again when the merchant brings the cash back to the bank for deposit.

Automated Clearing House

The Automated Clearing House (ACH) network is a nationwide electronic payment system used by financial institutions, corporations, and consumers. It helps customers get their money faster. By using ACH, a corporate customer or government entity can make payments to consumers or other organizations without issuing a check, and can obtain payment from a customer electronically.

Corporations and government entities use the ACH network for various reasons. First, an ACH transaction costs less than a paper-based transaction that uses checks. Second, using the ACH system eliminates the labor and materi-

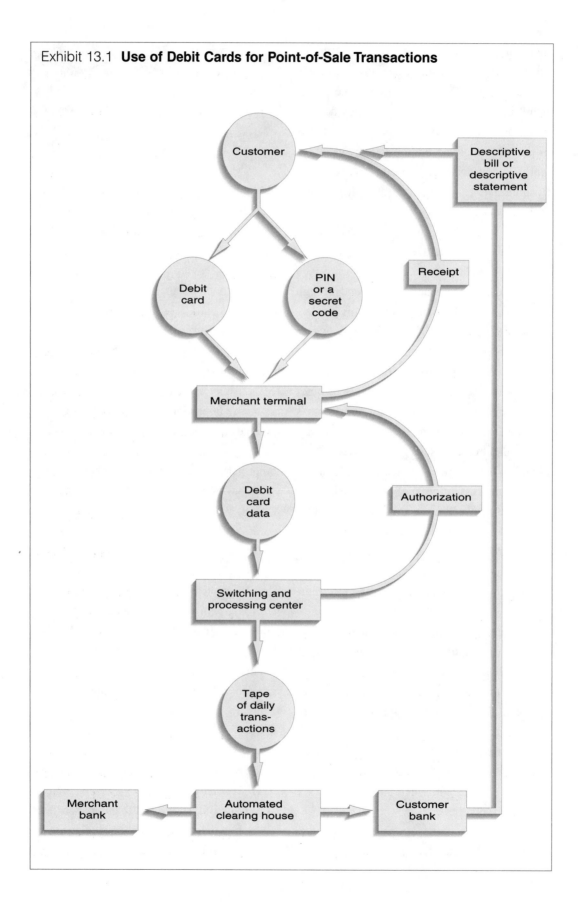

Exhibit 13.1 **Use of Debit Cards for Point-of-Sale Transactions**

Customer

Debit card

PIN or a secret code

Receipt

Descriptive bill or descriptive statement

Merchant terminal

Debit card data

Authorization

Switching and processing center

Tape of daily trans-actions

Merchant bank

Automated clearing house

Customer bank

als needed to print paper documents. Finally, corporations like ACH transactions because their proceeds are made available to them earlier than they are when checks are used.

For the same reason, recipients like ACH (direct deposit) payments. For example, an employee who is paid by the employer via ACH is assured of receiving his or her pay on the payroll date and of having the funds available in his or her account on the same day. On the other hand, an employee who is paid by check by the employer may not receive his or her pay on the payroll date, and the employee's bank may not make the funds available immediately if the check is drawn on an out-of-state bank.

In addition to making payments and receiving payments from other companies, corporations also use ACH to transfer funds from their accounts at one bank to their accounts at another bank. Corporate customers may initiate ACH transactions through a number of methods, depending on the capability of their bank. The corporation could deliver a magnetic tape to the bank containing the ACH transactions, or it could transmit the ACH transactions directly to the bank's computer via the Internet or other electronic means.

Many banks, including relatively small ones, offer customers ACH services via personal computer. The customer prepares the ACH transactions through personal computer software like Quicken or Microsoft Money, and transmits the transactions to the bank electronically.

Another form of ACH item is a pre-authorized payment. These payments are automatically debited from a bank account on a regular, pre-approved basis. The customer authorizes a merchant to charge his or her account for a predetermined amount on a specific day. The Newcomers in situation 1 will use pre-authorized payment for their health club membership and insurance premiums—two very common uses.

Some corporate customers use the services of third-party processors. These companies, which typically process payrolls, prepare the ACH entries for the corporation and deliver them to the corporation's financial institution or directly to the financial institution's ACH processor. Using third-party services allows the corporation to use the ACH without originating the transactions.

Cash Management Services

In the early 1950s, commercial banks recognized the unique needs of their corporate customers and began to offer **cash management** services. Corporations with significant billings and payments wanted to put their money to work instead of leaving balances in non-interest-bearing demand deposit accounts. Cash management services help corporations get their money faster, keep it longer, and put it to work while it is in the bank. Although the needs of large corporate customers, governmental agencies, and other financial institutions differ from those of individuals and small businesses, large and small governments and corporations can all benefit from cash management services. These services include

- collecting income and payments more quickly and efficiently (getting money faster)
- managing and reconciling outgoing payments more efficiently (keeping it longer)
- obtaining timely and complete information on the status of their bank accounts (putting it to work better while it is in the bank)

Electronic systems are the basis of cash management services that make business easier and more profitable for many companies. All of the following cash management services—lockbox, cash concentration, controlled disbursement, and zero balance accounts—rely on electronic transactions to give corporate customers greater access to and use of their funds.

Lockbox Service

Lockbox services help companies get access to their money faster. Uncollected funds have no real value to the depositor or the bank that has given immediate provisional credit for deposited checks. Before the advent of lockbox services, a customer would mail a payment directly to a company. These payments, whether to a business, a unit of government, a correspondent bank, or a university, were subject to mail delays, processing and deposit delays, and collection delays. The cash management service that addresses this problem is called lockbox.

Lockbox services speed up the collection process by having payments sent directly to a post office box managed by the bank, rather than to the company. The customer mails his or her electric bill payment, for example, to this post office box rather than to the electric company. The bank retrieves this payment directly from the lockbox, deposits it immediately, and sends the company a record of the customers who have made payments. Since the check does not have to pass first through the electric company, delays in deposit and collection are eliminated. The lockbox service improves availability of funds. The fee charged by the bank is offset by increased funds availability, and the net cost to the company is lower than if the company did the processing itself.

Exhibit 13.2 compares a payment made directly to a corporate customer with a payment made to a corporate customer through a lockbox. In the bottom example, the funds are wired and therefore can be received electronically that day. In the top example, the funds may take a week to be received by the corporation, and it may be several more days before the funds are collected and available.

Cash Concentration

Cash concentration is a service banks offer to corporations that have accounts at numerous banks and want to concentrate or pool the balances in one account (called the concentration account). The corporation initiates ACH debits, electronic checks drawn on their accounts at other banks. These ACH debits are deposited with the concentration bank and sent to the paying banks, where the debits are charged to the proper accounts. Exhibit 13.3 shows the flow of the debits (charges). In this example, the corporation originates three ACH debits in the amount of $400,000 each, drawn on banks B, C, and D. The debits are deposited with bank A on the settlement date, which is the date charges will be made to the accounts at banks B, C, and D. Bank A gives the corporate customer credit for the $1.2 million and makes the funds available to it. Through the use of the ACH and cash concentration, the corporate customer is able to concentrate the $1.2 million previously located in several banks into the one account maintained with bank A. This $1.2 million in Bank A can then be invested at a higher rate of return than the corporation could get on three smaller balances of $400,000 each.

Controlled Disbursement Accounts

A **controlled disbursement account** is drawn on an affiliate of the bank or a branch of the

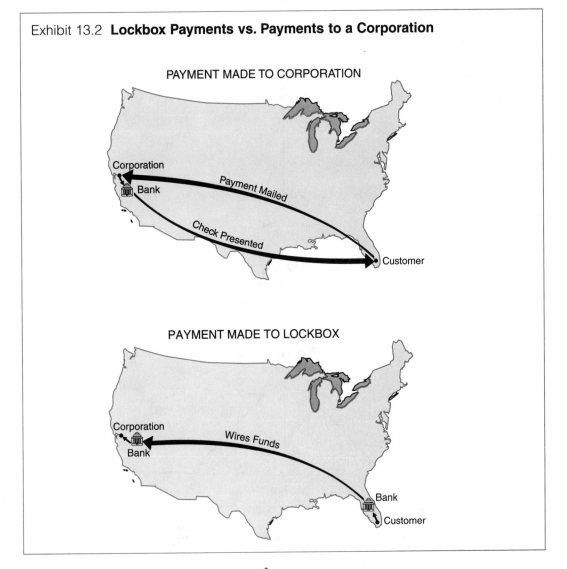

Exhibit 13.2 **Lockbox Payments vs. Payments to a Corporation**

PAYMENT MADE TO CORPORATION

Corporation
Bank
Payment Mailed
Check Presented
Customer

PAYMENT MADE TO LOCKBOX

Corporation
Bank
Wires Funds
Bank
Customer

primary bank, and processed at another check processing facility. As the checks are presented for payment, the paying bank accumulates totals throughout the processing day and advises the corporate customer of the total amount of checks that will be paid on the account that processing night.

The Federal Reserve offers a similar product, called **payer bank services**, that allows the bank to report to the corporate customer the total amount of checks that will be posted against the account on that processing night. The payer bank provides the Federal Reserve with the routing transit number and the account number of the controlled disbursement account. The Federal Reserve accumulates the totals during its processing and transmits the total of the checks to be presented on that account. The bank then notifies the corporate customer of the total amount of checks that will be posted to the account that processing night.

In either case, the corporate cash manager can fund the account by transferring money from investment accounts, or direct the bank to fund the account from the company's line of credit.

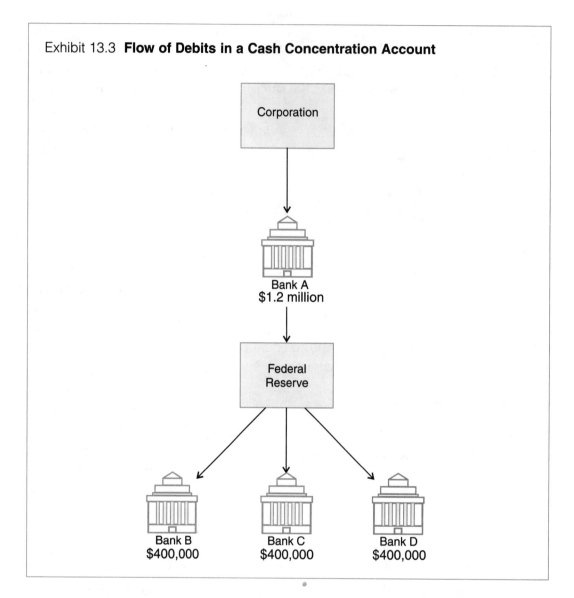

Exhibit 13.3 **Flow of Debits in a Cash Concentration Account**

Corporation

Bank A
$1.2 million

Federal
Reserve

Bank B
$400,000

Bank C
$400,000

Bank D
$400,000

Zero Balance Accounts

The **zero balance account** is a bank account owned by a customer in which the balance is always maintained at zero. The customer writes checks on the account, and as the checks are presented to the bank for payment, the bank automatically transfers funds from another account, the investment account, to maintain the account balance at zero. For example, if $150,000 worth of checks are presented for payment against the zero bal- ance account, the bank deducts the checks from the account and automatically transfers $150,000 from the investment account. The investment account earns interest until the checks are presented for payment. Or the cus- tomer may fund the zero balance account from a line of credit established with the bank, and then pay down the line of credit with excess funds.

In some cases the bank and the customer may agree to another number rather than zero. This threshold number permits the customer to increase the deposit earnings or decrease line of credit interest payments. At the same time, the bank is able to offset some of its costs by having a higher threshold than zero.

Direct Deposit and Fedwire

Direct deposit and Fedwire were covered earlier in the text. Direct deposit (chapter 4) provides customers with the convenience of having their employer or the government deposit payroll, Social Security, or other payments directly into the customer's account. Not only does this electronic transaction give the customer access to the funds sooner than if payment had been made by check, it provides greater security over paper checks, which can be lost or stolen.

Fedwire (chapter 3) is an electronic money transfer service provided by the Federal Reserve. Customers, usually large corporations and other financial institutions, instruct the Fed to transfer funds from the customer's account to the account of a beneficiary. Using Fedwire reduces float in the system and provides a fast, secure means of transferring large sums of money.

Home Banking

With the large increase in access and use of personal computers, **home banking**, the service that allows a customer to perform banking transactions at home is now a necessity for most banks. In the early 1980s, bankers thought customers would flock to home banking if given the opportunity, but for many reasons, they did not. Technology was not as reliable or as user-friendly and convenient as it is today.

Home banking has finally taken off. Customers are more comfortable with technology and demand the convenience home banking brings. Now customers can have access to their accounts and other information 24 hours a day without ever leaving home. Banks are investing a great deal of money to develop effective home banking systems—often with software companies as partners.

Telephone Banking

With an account number and a touch tone phone, customers can get answers to routine questions about balances, loan rates, checks paid, deposit rates, credit card payments, and so forth through telephone banking. Telephone banking systems have built-in security measures to prevent unauthorized access. The newer systems go beyond the automated voice response by providing a link to a "human" operator who can answer more complex questions, take loan applications, and open accounts. Using an automated system in a call center provides a great convenience to customers while reducing the number of calls that need to be handled by bank employees, allowing bank employees to concentrate more on detailed, specialized customer service.

Internet Banking

More and more customers are using their home or office PCs to access personal and business account information, including balances, transaction history, and tax information. Consumers are paying bills, purchasing stocks and bonds, and even applying for loans. While some banks offer their own online banking systems, many are partnering with major providers of **personal financial management (PFM)** software, such as Intuit, Microsoft, and MECA. Using these software programs, customers can upload and download between the bank and the PFM to keep all their records synchronized. This information is transmitted to the bank via the customer's Internet service provider.

Experts are predicting that Internet banking will see explosive growth within the next few years. Exhibit 13.4 shows how many banks, by asset category, had transactional websites as of March 1999. Exhibit 13.5 shows how this service has grown since 1995.

Deposit Services

Through Internet banking, consumers can check their balances, review their account deposit history, reconcile activity on their accounts, and transfer funds among accounts.

Balance Inquiries: Customers have the ability to see up-to-the-minute account balance information online. Liz in situation 2 did not pause to write down her transactions in her check register. She knew that when she got home she could get her balance and evidence of the day's transactions on the Internet.

Deposit Histories: Like Liz in situation 2, customers can view interim statements revealing current account activity or they can access previous statements to review past transactions. Some banks offer an electronic statement that is e-mailed to the customer each month, in place of the traditional paper statement. Others allow customers to view electronic images of their paid checks, front and back, while sitting at their computers.

Account Reconcilement: When tied to a PFM or the company's accounting system,

Exhibit 13.4 **Banks and Thrifts with Transactional Websites by Asset Category***

Asset Category	Number of Institutions	Percent of Institutions
Over $100 Billion	5	71%
$10 Billion to $100 Billion	32	39%
$1 Billion to $10 Billion	58	13%
$500 Million to $1 Billion	40	10%
$150 Million to $500 Million	158	8%
Less than $150 Million	197	3%

*As of March 31, 1999
Source: FDIC

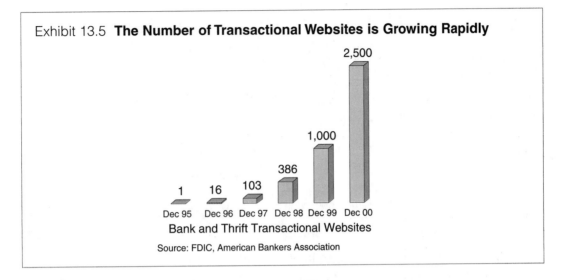

Exhibit 13.5 **The Number of Transactional Websites is Growing Rapidly**

Bank and Thrift Transactional Websites

Source: FDIC, American Bankers Association

customers can download a file from the bank that contains all the activity on their account, including checks paid, deposits made, and transfers posted. Customers then compare this information to their own records. Items that cannot be matched must be manually approved before they can be posted for reconcilement. When the matching process is done, the PFM or accounting system completes the reconcilement, posts a summary of the debits and credits, and informs the customer if the account is in balance. While individual consumers may download this information monthly, a business may reconcile its records more frequently because of the greater volume of activity. The thief in situation 3 was very likely caught by an account reconciliation system where the bank's list of checks paid did not match the company's list of checks written.

Account Transfers: Customers can access their accounts on the bank's system and make transfers among these accounts through either their PFM or accounting systems. Customers can even schedule recurring transfers, instructing the bank's computer system to make these transactions automatically. Generally, the bank will provide the customer with a confirmation number once a transfer is completed.

Payments

Payment services are often a two-part process—receiving bills electronically and paying these bills electronically.

Electronic Bill Presentment: Large companies, such as utility or credit card companies, offer a service to their customers whereby they notify the customers by e-mail when a payment is due. The notification may include a printable electronic statement or, less often, the statement might be sent separately by mail. Electronic bill presentment saves the company postage and handling costs. Some companies combine this service with pre-authorized payment. Customers can pre-authorize payment to be charged from their account at each billing cycle. On the specified date, the company issues an ACH item, which electronically debits the customer's account. The debit and a detailed description appear on the customer's monthly statement. Exhibit 13.6 shows the anticipated growth in electronic bill presentment services.

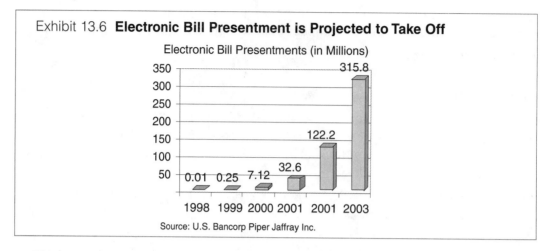

Exhibit 13.6 **Electronic Bill Presentment is Projected to Take Off**

Electronic Bill Presentments (in Millions)

Source: U.S. Bancorp Piper Jaffray Inc.

Electronic Bill Payment: This service allows customers to pay all of their bills electronically, eliminating the need to write and mail checks. Electronic bill payment is often part of the customer's PFM software and is done by accessing the Internet, the bank, or a bill paying company. Typically, customers complete an "electronic check" with the payee, amount, and date the amount is to be paid. This information is transmitted electronically to the bill payer, who follows the customer's instructions and makes the electronic payment through an ACH directly to the payee. In cases where the payee cannot accept electronic payments, such as for more personal or local checks, the bank or bill-paying company will write a check and deliver it through the mail. Just as with bill presentment, customers have the option of pre-authorizing payment for recurring transactions. To maintain security, access to the sites requires the use of a password. Information passed from the customer to the bank and from the bank to the customer is encrypted (explained below).

Lending

Internet-based loan services are fast becoming as available to consumers as deposit and payment services.

Online Applications: Customers apply for loans online from the comfort of their homes or offices. Banks vary in their sophistication in dealing with the applications once they are received. Some print out paper copies and submit the application to their regular, manual processing procedures. Others use sophisticated software that processes everything electronically, including ordering and processing the credit report, evaluating the application using credit scoring, and notifying the applicant (see chapter 8). Everything in this process is electronic, with the possible exception of the loan closing. Consumers have been slow to accept electronic loan applications, preferring in many cases to meet face-to-face with a loan officer.

Financial Calculators: Many banks now post financial calculators on their websites as a service to their customers. Customers use these calculators to figure out monthly payments for certain amounts, terms, and interest rates. Using this tool, they can determine if it is worth while to refinance a mortgage or to finance a car for two or four years. Customers also can print amortization schedules that show how their payments are being credited, and what happens to the loan if they make larger principal payments. These calculators give customers greater control over their financial affairs by letting them see different payment scenarios.

Links and Partnerships

The Internet has provided tremendous opportunities for businesses that provide similar services to link together. The PFM software mentioned earlier provides Internet links to the banks, insurance companies, and mortgage companies that do business with them. Some Internet sites act as information clearing-houses. A customer shopping for a mortgage, for example, can go to a clearing-house site and find many different mortgage providers, mortgage calculators, home insurers, inspection services, and other related information. By clicking on the company name, customers are automatically linked to more information, generally on the company's website. Customers also can have businesses on the site bid for their service by describing the type of loan they are looking for and waiting for the mortgage companies to e-mail rates and terms. Then customers can choose the most advantageous mortgage. Companies pay a membership fee to be listed on each site.

Bank websites can act also as information providers. A typical bank website might include links to the following:
- locations of branches and hours
- product information
- company history
- employment opportunities
- links to non-profit sites that the bank sponsors
- a company directory for e-mail contact
- electronic banking
- financial calculators

- stock tickers
- check order companies

Web-only Banks

Recent years have seen the emergence of **web-only banks**. These banks are only available to customers through the Internet. They do not have traditional "bricks and mortar" branches. Web-only banks offer deposit, payment, and loan services, but often do not offer the full range of auxiliary services that traditional banks provide. Since they do not have the overhead of traditional banks, web-only banks can offer higher deposit interest rates on insured deposits, and lower borrowing rates. At the time this text was written, most web-only banks were about a year old and none was older than five years. It is still too early to predict the impact these banks will have on the financial services marketplace.

Bank Cards

As mentioned in the beginning of this chapter, bank cards offer customers convenient use of their money without the need for cash. Bank cards fall into three main categories—debit cards, smart cards, and credit cards.

Debit Cards

Debit cards are plastic bank cards that allow customers to purchase goods and services by giving them direct access to balances in checking or savings accounts. Typically, a customer swipes a debit card through a POS card reader, enters a PIN if required, and completes a transaction to purchase things like groceries or gas. Refer to exhibit 13.1 to see how a debit card transaction flows through the banking system.

Smart Cards

These cards are sometimes referred to as "stored value cards." Storing the customer's account information, identification information, and a dollar value that has been electronically transferred to the card from the customer's account are some of its banking applications. The card is most useful for small purchases. The amount of the purchase is subtracted from the value in the microchip. When the balance gets low, customers can add money again electronically from their accounts. Carrying a smart card is like carrying cash without the risk of having the cash lost or stolen. While widely used in Europe, bank-issued smart cards are just starting to appear in the United States. The technology has been available for many years in Europe and will be found more and more in the United States.

Credit Cards

Credit cards were discussed at length in chapter 8 as a form of consumer loan, a line of credit. They are mentioned again here as one of the electronic options customers have to add convenience to their daily lives. Credit cards are used also to pay for goods or services at POS terminals or through the Internet and to obtain cash through ATMs.

Loss Prevention: Electronic Financial Services

Consumers are naturally concerned about maintaining the security of their financial information and transactions in the electronic realm. They want to know how banks are protecting the data they are transmitting and the financial records that reside on the bank's website. Consumers will only fully accept this new medium if they can be convinced that their information is completely protected.

Internet Security Concerns

As more and more people transact business on the world wide web, security concerns become much greater. Customers often place security among their top three concerns in web-based commerce. The banking industry has worked with software engineers and designers to devise software programs that can ensure the safe movement of data through the phone lines and other Internet connections. Some of the results of this collaboration include the following:

Encryption Code

Encryption code systems protect information being exchanged between two systems. The source location sends out data that is "scrambled" and can only be read by the receiving location. The receiving location "unscrambles" the data and rearranges it in logical form. Netscape Navigator and Microsoft Internet Explorer both offer encryption code in their software as a way of protecting data integrity.

Firewall Security

Firewall security is usually software or hardware that provides a "wall" between two systems. It may allow customers to read information provided on a system but will not allow them to change it. For example, a customer can access his or her account history from a personal computer over the Internet. Firewall security prevents the customer from being able to change the records—like changing a deposit amount from $100 to $1,000.

Anti-virus Technology

Viruses are mini computer programs that often attach themselves to e-mail. Once a virus attachment is opened, it executes a program that can render a computer useless. More sophisticated viruses will replicate themselves and infect other computers in a network—possibly disabling an entire company.

Companies such as Norton and McAfee offer anti-virus software that protects computer systems against viruses. In addition to detecting viruses in computer files, these software programs scan incoming e-mail messages for any of the virus programs recognized by the software. The software automatically quarantines the infected files until the computer operator or system administrator eliminates the virus or e-mail.

To keep up with the latest viruses, many banks update their virus protection software regularly. Some even provide daily updates of virus fixes to prevent any possible contamination of their systems.

Bank Card Loss Prevention

Bank card fraud involves the use of a stolen card or number to fraudulently purchase goods or services. The potential for loss is great with bank card fraud, since the criminal can make a significant number of purchases, often before the victim even knows the card is missing. For example, consider the shopper who, while loaded down with packages, is the victim of a pick-pocket in a crowded mall. The thief now has the victim's bank card and identification, and can attempt to use the card at the mall, or to make phone, mail-order, or electronic purchases. Several hours later, the victim realizes the card is missing and reports the theft to the

bank. By then, however, the thief may have purchased or ordered several thousand dollars worth of merchandise.

Bank card information can be obtained in a number of ways, including:

- taking a card from a stolen wallet or handbag (as in the above example)
- stealing a card or statement from a mailbox or from within the postal delivery service
- copying of information by sales associates or servers, from a card presented for a legitimate transaction
- buying account information sold by dishonest card issuer employees
- stealing statements from files or trash cans
- retrieving carelessly discarded sales receipts

System Safeguards

As discussed in chapter 4, Regulation E of the Electronic Funds Transfer Act addresses bank card usage and responsibility. Under Regulation E, consumer liability due to bank card fraud is limited to $50. Card issuers absorb the bulk of the losses resulting from fraudulent transactions. While customers' direct losses are restricted, high losses to the industry eventually translate into higher interest rates and service charges. Card issuers have therefore made limiting this loss a priority. The following safeguards are some of the ways card issuers are addressing this problem.

- To thwart mailbox theft, most cards sent through the mail are not activated until the customer calls a toll-free number to do so. This confirms that the card holder received the card and it is not in the hands of a thief. In addition, the issuer will often send a follow-up notice stating that the card has been sent and needs to be activated. If the card has not been received, the customer can alert the issuer.

- Many cards require a personal identification number (PIN) to use the card. This makes the card useless to anyone who does not know the PIN.

- Cards have expiration dates that must be used in conjunction with the account number to have a transaction approved.

- Card holders are asked to sign the backs of their cards so their signatures can be compared to the signature at the point of purchase. Merchants can verify that the signatures match.

- Card issuers now use sophisticated software to monitor account activity. Any unusual increase in activity on an account, such as an uncharacteristically high volume of spending, increased use of mail order, or use in atypical parts of the country, will place a warning on the account. The card issuer might freeze or flag the account until the transactions can be verified with the legitimate holder.

Electronic Signatures

In June 2000, President Bill Clinton signed legislation that allows the use of electronic signatures on contracts. This bill gives the same legal recognition to digital signatures for providing consent to online transactions as is held by written signatures for non-electronic transactions.

An electronic signature is much more than a digitized copy of a signature. Digitized signatures are nothing more than a picture scanned into a computer file. Electronic signatures are actually mathematical algorithms or procedures that attach to a document and insure that no change has been made to the original document. They also ensure that the source of the document is, in fact, the "signer" of the contract. If the signature is not real or if the document has been altered, the algorithms will not match and the electronic document will not be valid. This is comparable to changes on a paper contract that render it invalid.

Current technology uses software that allows customers to place an electronic signature on an electronic document, transmit the documents to a business or individual, and have the document carry the same legal standing as a signed paper contract. Another part of the legislation permits electronic copies of documents to have the same legal standing as paper documents.

Summary

Electronic financial services have made the financial system faster, more accurate, safer, and more profitable for banks, consumers, and businesses. Point-of-sale transfers allow the purchase of goods and services without the use of cash. Automated clearing houses facilitate the transfer of funds in the banking system so that customers can make payments and get their money faster.

Businesses benefit from the many electronically-based cash management services that banks offer, including lockbox, cash concentration, controlled disbursement accounts, and zero balance accounts.

Home banking is finally catching on, as technology becomes more reliable and user-friendly. Customers can use the telephone and the Internet to meet most of their banking needs, including making payments, transferring funds among accounts, and applying for loans. Many bank sites provide links to related services and provide tools for customers to calculate payment options. Web-only banks are emerging in the market place.

Bank cards offer customers the convenient use of their money without the need for cash. Debit cards give direct access to balances in checking or savings accounts. Credit cards access a line of credit. Smart cards store information, including a sum of money, on a microchip embedded in the card. Use of the card reduces the value, which can be replenished electronically.

To address security concerns, the banking industry uses encryption codes and firewall security systems. Soon, consumers will be able to use secured electronic signatures to sign contracts and transact other business online.

Review and Discussion Questions

1. Why do banks and merchants encourage point-of-sale transactions?

2. Why did banks begin to offer corporate cash management services to corporate customers?

3. Describe the advantages of electronic bill presentment to utility or credit card companies.

4. How do debit cards, credit cards, and smart cards differ?

5. What is firewall security and how does it work?

Additional Resources

ABA Bankers News. Washington, D.C.: American Bankers Association.

ABA Banking Journal. New York: Simmons-Boardman Publishing Corp.

Alternative Delivery Systems: Trends and Issues. Washington, D.C.: American Bankers Association, 1998.

Web Resources

American Bankers Association www.aba.com

Federal Bureau of Investigation www.fbi.gov

Federal Deposit Insurance Corporation www.fdic.gov

NACHA - Electronic Payments Association www.nacha.org

APPENDIX
SUMMARY OF FEDERAL RESERVE REGULATIONS

A 12 CFR 201

Extensions of Credit by Federal Reserve Banks

Governs borrowing by depository institutions at the Federal Reserve discount window

B 12 CFR 202

Equal Credit Opportunity

Prohibits lenders from discriminating against credit applicants, establishes guidelines for gathering and evaluating credit information, and requires written notification when credit is denied

C 12 CFR 203

Home Mortgage Disclosure

Requires certain mortgage lenders to disclose data regarding their lending patterns

D 12 CFR 204

Reserve Requirements of Depository Institutions

Sets uniform requirements for all depository institutions to maintain reserve balances either with their Federal Reserve Bank or as cash in their vaults

E 12 CFR 205

Electronic Fund Transfers

Establishes the rights, liabilities, and responsibilities of parties in electronic funds transfers and protects consumers when they use such systems

F 12 CFR 206

Limitations on Interbank Liabilities

Prescribes standards to limit the risks posed by obligations of insured depository institutions to other depository institutions

G 12 CFR 207

Disclosure and Reporting of CRA-Related Agreements

Regulation implementing provisions of the Gramm-Leach-Bliley Act that require reporting and public disclosure of written agreements between insured depository institutions or their affiliates and nongovernmental entities or persons made in connection with fulfillment of Community Reinvestment Act requirements

H 12 CFR 208

Membership of State Banking Institutions in the Federal Reserve System

Defines the requirements for membership of state-chartered banks in the Federal Reserve System; sets limitations on certain investments and requirements for certain types of loans; describes rules pertaining to securities-related activities; establishes the minimum ratios of capital to assets that banks must maintain and procedures for prompt corrective action when banks are not adequately capitalized; prescribes real estate lending and appraisal standards; sets out requirements concerning bank security procedures, suspicious-activity reports, and compliance with the Bank Secrecy Act; and establishes rules governing banks' ownership or control of financial subsidiaries

I 12 CFR 209

Issue and Cancellation of Federal Reserve Bank Capital Stock

Sets forth stock-subscription requirements for all banks joining the Federal Reserve System

J 12 CFR 210

Collection of Checks and Other Items by Federal Reserve Banks and Funds Transfers through Fedwire

Establishes procedures, duties, and responsibilities among (1) Federal Reserve Banks, (2) the senders and payors of checks and other items, and (3) the senders and recipients of wire transfers of funds

K 12 CFR 211

International Banking Operations

Governs the international banking operations of U.S. banking organizations and the operations of foreign banks in the United States

L 12 CFR 212

Management Official Interlocks

Restricts the management relationships that an official in one depository institution may have with other depository institutions

M 12 CFR 213

Consumer Leasing

Implements the consumer leasing provisions of the Truth in Lending Act by requiring meaningful disclosure of leasing terms

N 12 CFR 214

Relations with Foreign Banks and Bankers

Governs relationships and transactions between Federal Reserve Banks and foreign banks, bankers, or governments

O 12 CFR 215

Loans to Executive Officers, Directors, and Principal Shareholders of Member Banks

Restricts credit that a member bank may extend to its executive officers, directors, and principal shareholders and their related interests

P 12 CFR 216

Privacy of Consumer Financial Information

Implements the provisions of the Gramm-Leach-Bliley Act that prohibit a financial institution from disclosing nonpublic personal information to third parties that are not affiliated with the financial institution

Q 12 CFR 217

Prohibition against Payment of Interest on Demand Deposits

Prohibits member banks from paying interest on demand deposits (for example, checking accounts)

S 12 CFR 219

Reimbursement to Financial Institutions for Providing Financial Records; Recordkeeping Requirements for Certain Financial Records

Establishes rates and conditions for reimbursement to financial institutions for providing customer records to a government authority and prescribes recordkeeping and reporting requirements for insured depository institutions making domestic wire transfers and for insured depository institutions and nonbank financial institutions making international wire transfers

T 12 CFR 220

Credit by Brokers and Dealers

Governs extension of credit by securities brokers and dealers, including all members of national securities exchanges; see also Regulations U and X

U 12 CFR 221

Credit by Banks or Persons other than Brokers or Dealers for the Purpose of Purchasing or Carrying Margin Stocks

Governs extension of credit by banks or persons other than brokers or dealers to finance the purchase or the carrying of margin securities; see also Regulations T and X

V 12 CFR 222 (Proposed)

Fair Credit Reporting

Proposed regulation to implement the notice and opt-out provisions of the Fair Credit Reporting Act applicable to financial institutions that give their affiliates certain information about consumers

X 12 CFR 224

Borrowers of Securities Credit

Extends to borrowers who are subject to U.S. laws the provisions of Regulations T and U for obtaining credit within or outside the United States for the purpose of purchasing securities

Y 12 CFR 225

Bank Holding Companies and Change in Bank Control

Governs the bank and nonbank expansion of bank holding companies, the divestiture of impermissible nonbank interests, the acquisition of a bank by individuals, and the establishment and activities of financial holding companies

Z 12 CFR 226

Truth in Lending

Prescribes uniform methods for computing the cost of credit, for disclosing credit terms, and for resolving errors on certain types of credit accounts

AA 12 CFR 227

Unfair or Deceptive Acts or Practices

Establishes consumer complaint procedures and defines unfair or deceptive practices in extending credit to consumers

BB 12 CFR 228

Community Reinvestment

Implements the Community Reinvestment Act and encourages banks to help meet the credit needs of their communities

CC 12 CFR 229

Availability of Funds and Collection of Checks

Governs the availability of funds deposited in checking accounts and the collection and return of checks

DD 12 CFR 230

Truth in Savings

Requires depository institutions to provide disclosures to enable consumers to make meaningful comparisons of deposit accounts

EE 12 CFR 231

Netting Eligibility for Financial Institutions

Defines financial institutions to be covered by statutory provisions regarding netting contracts—that is, contracts in which the parties agree to pay or receive the net, rather than the gross, payment due

From Federal Reserve website: www.federalreserve.gov/Regulations/

ANSWERS TO REVIEW AND DISCUSSION QUESTIONS

Chapter 1

1. If all bankers are supposed to be "selling" the products and services of the bank, why is sales a major career avenue for bankers?

    Even though all bankers are salespeople for the bank, banks must focus on the sale of their products and services in order to be competitive. In larger institutions, the sales teams specialize according to product. Retail banking, business banking, insurance sales, investment products, and trust services are all examples of sales avenues open to today's bankers.

2. What are non-traditional bank services and why do banks want to provide these?

    Non-traditional bank services include insurance and brokerage. Because of legislation passed in 1999, banks, insurance companies, and brokerage firms can now enter each other's businesses. Banks want to offer these non-traditional products in order to compete on an equal basis with these other providers and to provide a full range of services to their customers.

3. How do banks contribute to their communities?

    In addition to providing credit to help individuals and businesses in the community, banks contribute their time and efforts to enriching communities. Bank employees have a history of service to charitable organizations and banks sponsor many community-minded events.

4. What is the difference between a typical commercial bank and a financial holding company structure?

A typical commercial bank has a corporate structure. It is owned by the stockholders and overseen by a board of directors. A financial holding company is a corporation that owns the bank's (or banks') stock. It may own more than one bank and banking-related organizations like mortgage companies and brokerage services.

5. Why are banks willing to give up some of their independence and use outside vendors or other banks for services?

It is no longer cost-effective or easy for banks to keep up with the technology and other services they need to do business. They seek outside companies to provide many services, ensuring access to the latest technology without having the costs of employees and support. While banks may be giving up some of the independence and ability to customize that they enjoyed in the past, these new alliances are providing significant cost savings and a high level of service.

Chapter 2

1. Describe the banking period prior to the passage of the National Bank Act.

The political climate prevented government involvement and control in the banking industry. Virtually anyone could operate a bank, regardless of whether there was enough capital or expertise. Consequently, the early U.S. banking system evolved with a lack of discipline and supervision. Just prior to the National Bank Act, the country suffered through the period of wildcat banking when bank failures were routine and public distrust ran high.

2. What is meant by the term "dual banking system?" Does the dual banking system exist today?

The term dual banking system refers to the fact that both national banks and state-chartered banks developed over the course of U.S. history. These two structures still exist today, and although there are differences with respect to examinations, some regulatory common ground was achieved with the passage of the Monetary Control Act of 1980.

3. How did the Federal Reserve Act solve the problems of pyramided reserves and check collection?

The Federal Reserve Act established a central bank with branches in 12 geographic districts. This allowed reserves to be maintained at Federal Reserve branch banks all across the country, thus solving the problem of pyramiding reserves at money center banks. The act further avoided pyramiding by giving the Federal Reserve the authority to change reserve requirements and to extend overnight credit to its members for reserves.

The Federal Reserve Act also used the 12 geographic districts to accommodate the check collection process in a more expedient manner. Any Federal Reserve branch could receive checks from constituents within its district, regardless of whether those checks were drawn on a bank nearby or on a bank thousands of miles away.

4. What impact did the Great Depression have on the banking system?

Economic growth before the Great Depression was fueled by the 1920s stock market boom, which was financed by banks. When the stock market crashed and the Great Depression arrived, bank loan losses soared, and capital was depleted. Over 8,300 banks failed, and customers lost about $7 billion in deposits.

5. What does disintermediation mean?

The role of a financial intermediary is to bring borrowers and savers together. Disintermediation occurs when depositors withdraw account balances from banks and other financial intermediaries in order to obtain higher rates elsewhere, thus eroding the supply of loanable funds to potential borrowers.

6. How does the Gramm-Leach-Bliley Act protect a consumer's right to financial privacy?

Privacy provisions in the Gramm-Leach-Bliley Act give customers the right to instruct their bank not to provide information on their behalf to non-affiliated third parties, prevent the financial institution from providing account information to unaffiliated third party marketers or telemarketers, require financial institutions to establish a privacy policy and to make this policy available to customers annually, and require the financial institution to be sure that it protects the security and confidentiality of its customers' information.

Chapter 3

1. List the four basic duties of the Federal Reserve?

The Federal Reserve's duties fall into the following four general areas:
- Conducting the nation's monetary policy by influencing the money and credit conditions in the economy in pursuit of full employment and stable prices
- Supervising and regulating banking institutions to ensure the safety and soundness of the nation's banking and financial system and to protect the credit rights of consumers

- Maintaining the stability of the financial system and containing systematic risk that may arise in financial markets
- Providing certain financial services to the U.S. government, to the public, to financial institutions, and to foreign official institutions, including playing a major role in operating the nation's payment system.

2. How is the Federal Reserve structured?

The Federal Reserve is broken into 12 districts, each with a Federal Reserve bank, most with branches. Each Reserve bank is governed by a nine-member board of directors. A Board of Governors, appointed by the president and confirmed by the senate, supervises the entire Federal Reserve system.

3. What services are offered to banks by the Federal Reserve?

The Federal Reserve offers the following services:
- coin and currency
- check clearing and collection
- wire transfer
- automated clearing house (ACH)
- settlement
- securities safekeeping

4. How is the Fed used to implement regulatory legislation?

When Congress passes regulatory legislation, it directs the Fed to issue requirements to implement the provisions of the act or law. The Fed then has the authority to ensure compliance with these regulations.

5. Describe how banks create money.

Banks create demand deposits when they make loans; the loans come into the banking system as demand deposits (deposits that increase the money supply).

6. Briefly describe the tools of monetary control, and explain how the Fed uses them.

The tools of monetary control are reserve requirements, the discount rate, and open market operations. The Federal Reserve uses these tools to manage the growth of the money supply and achieve national economic objectives.
- The Fed requires banks to set aside a portion of their deposits in a non-interest-bearing reserve account at the Federal Reserve as a means of safeguarding customer deposits. It

uses changes in the reserve requirement to decrease or increase the amount of money a bank has available to lend.

- The Fed influences loan demand and the easing or tightening of credit through the discount rate. The discount rate is the rate charged by the Fed on loans it makes to financial institutions.
- By far the most powerful tool available to the Fed in its role as the agent of monetary policy is the open market operations of the Federal Open Market Committee (FOMC). The FOMC is responsible for system-wide administration of monetary policy. One of the basic functions of the FOMC is to determine the amount of government obligations (bills, notes, and bonds) to be sold and redeemed each week.

Chapter 4

1. Why is the deposit function so important to depositors?

   The deposit function provides customers a safe place to keep their coin and currency as well as a means to collect amounts received through checks and other items. The deposit function also provides convenient access to a wide array of payment mechanisms, and provides the foundation upon which the payments and credit functions operate.

2. Why is it important to properly identify a person opening an account?

   Identification is important to comply with legal reporting requirements for tax information and to detect money laundering. It is also critical to avoid the liability and losses of fraudulent activity that might be perpetrated by dishonest and unscrupulous people.

3. When opening accounts, why is it important for banks to establish the authority of the customer to use the account? What three steps does the bank take to accomplish this when opening an account?

   When an account is opened, the bank enters into a contractual relationship that gives the customer the ability to extend credit to himself or herself, provides the customer with the vehicle to convert checks and other instruments into cash, and creates a number of other situations that could result in a loss to the bank. Three steps the bank takes to open an account include:
   - establishing the identity of the person opening the account
   - determining that the person has the legal capacity to open the account
   - ensuring that the person is authorized to open the account

4. Distinguish between a cash item and a non-cash item.

   Cash items are processed in bulk and can be accepted for immediate and provisional credit, which is reflected by the timely update of an account's ledger balance. Non-cash items require special handling, are not processed in bulk, and are only recognized for credit after collection and payment is completed. Examples of cash items include checks, coin, and currency, while a good example of a non-cash item would be a draft with documents attached.

5. List several ways customers can make deposits.

   Customers can make deposits in several ways, including:
   • in person at the teller's window
   • at the drive-in teller's windows
   • via night depository
   • at ATMs
   • using electronic (direct) deposit
   • via telephone or wire transfer
   • via mail deposits

6. What is the purpose of Regulation DD, and how has its enactment benefited bank customers?

   The purpose of Reg DD is to assist customers in comparing deposit accounts offered by various financial institutions. It has provided disclosure guidelines to help customers compare one bank's products with another bank's products.

Chapter 5

1. Define the term "negotiable instrument."

   As defined by Section 3-104 of the UCC, a negotiable instrument is "an unconditional promise or order to pay a fixed sum of money, with or without interest or other charges described in the promise or order." Furthermore, it must be payable on demand or at a specific time, and it must be payable "to bearer" or "to order."

2. List the parties to a check.

   The parties to checks and drafts are the drawer, the drawee, and the payee. With a check, the drawee is the bank that holds the checking account. Once a drawee accepts a check or draft, then the drawee becomes an acceptor.

3. Distinguish among a cashier's or treasurer's check, a teller's or official's check, and a certified check.

A cashier's or treasurer's check is a check issued by a bank and drawn on that bank; thus, the bank is both the drawer and the drawee. A teller's or official's check is similar to a cashier's check but is issued by a bank and then drawn on another bank or payer. Even though a teller's check is drawn on another bank, the drawer bank is obligated to fund the payment of the check. A certified check is a check that has been accepted by the bank on which it is drawn. The certification process transforms an instrument to a guaranteed obligation of the drawee bank.

4. Distinguish between a check payable to bearer and a check payable to an identifiable person.

An instrument payable to an identifiable person would be issued to an actual person or a legal entity, such as a corporation. If the instrument is not payable to an identifiable person, the instrument is considered payable to bearer, and the payee would likely be "cash" or "bearer."

5. Explain the difference between a "blank endorsement" and a "special endorsement" and discuss when each is used.

A blank endorsement consists simply of the signature of the payee or other holder of the instrument. A blank endorsement can be used for any purpose and allows flexibility and ease of transfer.

In a special endorsement, not only does the previous holder sign the instrument, but the holder also names the party to whom rights to the instrument are being transferred. For example, the endorser would add the line "Pay to the order of," which implies that the endorser intends the transferee to negotiate the instrument further.

6. Discuss how holder in due course affects the banking system.

A holder in due course provides depositary banks and others involved in the check clearing process protection from loss due to dishonored items. Without this protection, the involved parties would not be willing to take the risk, and the banking system could not operate.

Chapter 6

1. Describe the difference between paying a check and cashing a check.

A teller pays a check when giving cash to a person who presents a check that is drawn on that teller's own bank. A teller cashes a check when giving cash to a person who presents a check drawn on another bank.

2. What tests must a check pass to be properly payable?

The check is examined to ensure that it does not have any forged or unauthorized signatures, alterations, stop payment order, or other reason why the depositor would object to the bank's paying the check.

3. What functions are typically performed in the item preparation, encoding, and proof functions and what are their purposes?

Item preparation includes removing such impediments as staples, paper clips, and rubber bands. Also, single-item deposits are often separated, and all work is bundled and prepared in the proper order for distribution to proof operators for balancing and encoding.

The encoding function involves placing key data into MICR information on all bank documents (checks, deposits, loan coupons, etc.). All documents are usually encoded with the dollar amount, but may also need the account number and routing or transit identification to be inscribed. The encoded MICR data allow these documents to be processed on high-speed capture equipment for efficient transaction posting and disposition of check clearings.

The proof function involves balancing each individual transaction, ensuring accuracy at the point of origin so that transactions will be posted to the right accounts for the right amounts. This is where it is determined if debits = credits. Customer and bank errors can both be corrected through this process.

4. Describe the item capture and sorting process, including the information that is typically captured.

Item capture involves taking the following information from the check:
- Dollar amount
- Debit or credit identification
- Account number
- Check or serial number
- Application type (for example, loans or deposits)
- Float assignment and the number of items deposited
- Film picture or image of the item

The purpose of sorting is twofold: first, to sort items for cash letter preparation in the forward check collection process, and second, for internal purposes, such as sorting items for statement rendering or for the disposition of other MICR documents by certain departments of the bank.

5. What is electronic check presentment?

ECP involves transmitting MICR information via electronic wire instead of relying solely on a paper-based system. This electronic information precedes the delivery of paper items and checks, allowing for earlier posting of transactions by the payer bank.

Chapter 7

1. Describe the process of posting.

The applicable MICR data are read to capture transaction type (debit or credit), account number, amount, and check number. These paper-based transactions and electronic transactions are then merged before posting is initialized. Once posting is started, every transaction is subject to informational criteria such as sufficient funds, holds, and stop payments. When these criteria are satisfied, the transactions are either added to the account balance (if they are deposits or credits) or subtracted from it (if they are checks or debits).

2. Distinguish between in-filing and bulk filing.

In-filing refers to the process of manually performing the daily filing of checks into an individual account file denoted by a signature card. Bulk filing involves the daily accumulation of check bundles by statement cycles to be put in storage trays until detailed sorting in account number order is done at statement cutoff.

3. Under the revised provisions of Article 4 of the UCC, what is the customer's duty to examine the bank statement after it is made available to him or her by the bank?

The customer must examine the statement within 30 days and report any forgeries or alterations within that time.

4. Distinguish between outgoing returns and incoming returns.

Outgoing return items are checks, drafts, and other instruments returned by the paying bank. Incoming return items are checks, drafts, and other instruments that are received by the depository bank to be charged back to the depositor's accounts.

5. List several points tellers should keep in mind when dealing with a bank robber.

Tellers should remain calm, not act like heroes, trigger alarms when safe to do so, not talk to anyone after the robbery, get a good physical description, and attempt to remove from sight notes given by the robber.

6. Define identity theft and explain why it is such a serious problem for the victim.

Identity theft is the process of stealing a victim's social security number and other identifying information, and using it to purchase merchandise and services under the victim's name. Often, victims must spend countless hours contacting banks, creditors, and credit bureaus to report the fraud and correct their records. It is not uncommon for this type of fraud to resurface again after the first occurrence.

Chapter 8

1. List five reasons why the lending function is so important to the bank.

    1. Of the three cornerstones of banking—the deposit, payment, and lending functions—the lending function represents one of the most important sources of income.
    2. To qualify as a bank, a bank is legally required to make commercial loans.
    3. Lending is the most traditional element in the relationship between banks and their customers.
    4. The Community Reinvestment Act requires banks to meet the legitimate credit needs of the communities in which they operate.
    5. The quality of a bank's loans is often key to the institution's survival in today's economy.

2. Identify three Federal Reserve requirements for bank loans.

    1. Regulation B: prohibits discrimination in the process of extending credit.
    2. Regulation Z: requires lending banks to fully disclose all loan costs to the borrower in a uniform manner, expressed as an annual percentage rate (APR).
    3. Regulation BB: implements the Community Reinvestment Act which requires banks to meet the credit needs of the community

3. What roles do bank directors play in the overall lending function?

Bank directors represent the highest authority on policy-making for the lending function. Through membership on a loan committee, directors must do the following:
    • review the loan portfolio for meeting local credit needs and complying with the CRA

- authorize the assignment of credit authority
- determine the types of loans to be made
- conduct periodic reviews and audits
- tighten the standards when warranted and authorize all credits above a stipulated amount

4. Should loans be granted on the basis of collateral alone? Why or why not?

A loan request should not be approved solely on the basis of the value of collateral. If all of the other principles of credit are satisfied, then collateral can be used to strengthen the position of a loan.

5. Distinguish between construction loans and mortgage loans.

Construction loans are short-term extensions of credit that provide funds for completing a real estate project. Mortgage loans are permanent, long-term extensions of credit with a completed real estate project or improvement as collateral.

Chapter 9

1. Why has liability management become so important in banking?

Managing the liability side of banking has become increasingly important because interest-free deposits no longer can be expected to flow into the bank on a regular basis. Banks must work hard to attract new depositors, pay an affordable price for those deposits, and retain the deposits once they have been established.

2. What would be the consequences if a bank chose to overemphasize liquidity while neglecting other factors in funds management? What would be the consequences of overemphasizing safety at the expense of liquidity and income?

If a bank emphasized only liquidity, keeping large supplies of currency in its vaults as a protection for increasing customer demands for funds, the percentage of deposits available for lending would shrink, thus impairing the credit function and reducing income. The excess cash would also violate safety measures by being vulnerable to theft and fraud.

If a bank tries to achieve ultimate safety, it will never assume any risk in putting deposits to profitable use, and the potential to maximize loans will not be reached, resulting in lost income opportunities and failure to serve the credit needs of the community.

3. Distinguish between the discount rate and the prime rate.

   The discount rate applies to short-term credit extended by the Fed. In addition, the Fed has established a higher rate for its loans to depository institutions for periods of more than 30 days. The higher, flexible rate is used when a depository institution is under liquidity pressure and is unable to obtain funds on reasonable terms from other sources. The prime rate is a benchmark, base, or reference that a bank establishes from time to time in calculating an appropriate rate for a loan customer.

4. How can bank investments contribute to liquidity?

   Bank investments are considered as secondary reserves that can be converted into cash on very short notice.

5. Distinguish between credit risk and market risk.

   Credit risk pertains to whether the bank believes a borrower can repay a loan as scheduled. Market risk refers to the fact that market conditions and overall desirability determine the value of an investment, leaving the seller with little or no control over the outcome.

6. List the four types of holdings that typically make up a bank's investment portfolio.

   The four types of holdings are:
   - U.S. Treasury obligations
   - U.S. agency obligations
   - municipals
   - miscellaneous investments

Chapter 10

1. Why is accurate financial data so important to federal and state regulators? To bank shareholders and investors? To customers?

   Federal and state bank examiners always verify the accuracy of the bank's financial reports to determine the institution's true financial condition. Inaccurate financial data often result in a deeper probe by the examiners. Shareholders and investors require accurate financial data as a predictor of growth potential. Customers focus interest on the financial stability of the institution that is handling their money.

2. Distinguish between cash and accrual accounting methods.

Cash accounting records income and expense as cash is received and paid out, while accrual accounting records income at the time it is earned (regardless of when it is received) and records expenses at the time they are incurred (regardless of when they are paid).

3. What is a bank's largest asset? Its largest liability? Its largest income and expense items?

A bank's largest asset is loans, which generate the majority of revenues.
A bank's largest liability is deposits, which provide raw material for making loans.
A bank's largest income item is the interest income from loans, while the largest expense item is the interest paid on deposits. Its largest operating expense items are salaries and employee benefits.

4. What are the four primary performance ratios?

The four primary performance ratios are:
- return on assets
- return on equity
- capital ratio
- earnings per share

5. Why is the accurate reporting of financial data important for customers?

Accurate financial data helps customers choose the bank they want based on its stability and longevity. Customers not only shop interest rates, but also shop financial stability in organizations; they may spread their deposit dollars among a number of financial institutions to reduce the risk of loss.

6. Why is it important for a bank to establish a financial plan (a budget)?

A financial plan or budget allows a bank to plan expenditures carefully and to set earning objectives. A budget is the vehicle planners use to forecast future conditions.

Chapter 11

1. Explain the four elements in the definition of the marketing concept.

Customer orientation recognizes that customer satisfaction is the most important element in any business and that only a satisfied customer will purchase the product. The marketing concept also stresses reaching the bank's profit objectives. The marketing concept is a total company effort. It will not work if it is just the philosophy of the marketing department and not the whole bank. Finally, the marketing concept involves social responsibility in recognition of the bank's role in the community.

2. What are the four phases of the buying process?

Identification of a need, prepurchase activity, the purchase decision, postpurchase anxiety.

3. How can cross-selling improve customer relations?

Research has shown that the more products and services a customer uses at one bank, the more likely that customer is to be loyal to that bank. Cross-selling bank products to existing customers increases their commitment to the bank.

4. Describe each of the three profiles in marketing research.

The customer profile reveals who the customer is and how the bank's customer differs from those of competitors. The market profile looks at economic and other trends in the marketplace and provides management with the information it needs to identify potential problems and opportunities in both the retail and commercial markets. The competitive profile identifies the competitors and their products and services, estimates market share, and compares products and services.

5. List the eight steps in sequence of new product development.

The eight steps of new product development are:
1. getting new product ideas
2. screening new product ideas
3. testing the concept
4. business analysis
5. developing the product
6. test marketing the product
7. introducing the product
8. evaluating the product

Chapter 12

1. What legal requirements must be met in order for banks to offer trust services?

   The following legal requirements must be met:
   - No bank may begin offering trust services without first obtaining approval from the proper authorities.
   - The bank must set aside securities of unquestioned value as collateral against the proper performance of trust duties.
   - State laws must be followed regarding maximum fees banks can charge for certain services.

2. What are the major reasons why banks offer brokerage products?

   Banks recognize the appeal of mutual funds and other investment vehicles; they offer these services for the benefit of their existing customer base. These services help retain customers during periods of low interest rates and are capable of generating fee income along with increasing customer market share and penetration.

3. Why is it necessary to prepare a financial plan before investing?

   The financial plan is the key to the success of any customer's investment program. By having the investor outline his or her investment objectives, the financial planner can pick the appropriate vehicles to meet these objectives.

4. Why do banks have strict procedures for granting access to safe deposit boxes? What do these procedures include?

   It is in the bank's best interest to establish strict procedures for safe deposit personnel. This protects against unauthorized access to the safe deposit box. Employees must be trained to implement these procedures with extreme care at all times. This protects the customers as well as the bank.

5. How does a letter of credit issued by a bank protect the interests of both the buyer and the seller of goods?

   A letter of credit guarantees that the exporter (seller) will be paid if all the terms of the contract are met, and that payment on behalf of the importer (buyer) will not be made unless and until the contract has been fulfilled.

Chapter 13

1. Why do banks and merchants encourage point-of-sale transactions?

   Point-of-sale transactions eliminate the need for cash, benefiting all parties involved. Although merchants usually pay a small fee for each POS transaction, the fee is offset by the savings related to the costs of cash handling and storage. Banks benefit from POS because the transactions are handled faster and more efficiently through processing centers. Banks also save money on cash handling costs twice—once when the customer gets the cash and again when the merchant brings the cash back to the bank for deposit.

2. Why did banks begin to offer corporate cash management services to corporate customers?

   Banks recognized that corporations need to put idle funds to work in lieu of not receiving interest earnings on demand deposit balances. With this mindset, cash management services were designed to
   • collect income and payments more quickly and efficiently
   • manage and reconcile outgoing payments more efficiently
   • obtain timely and complete information on the status of their bank accounts

3. Describe the advantages of electronic bill presentment to utility or credit card companies.

   Electronic bill presentment saves postage and handling costs associated with sending invoices. Some companies combine this service with pre-authorized payment, which has the added advantage of reducing reliance on check payments. Customers can pre-authorize payment to be charged from their accounts at each billing cycle.

4. How do debit cards, credit cards, and smart cards differ?

   Debit cards give direct access to balances in checking or savings accounts. Credit cards access a pre-authorized line of credit. Smart cards store information, including a sum of money, on a microchip embedded in the card. Use of the card reduces the value, which can be replenished.

5. What is firewall security and how does it work?

   Firewall security is usually software or hardware that provides a "wall" between two systems. It may allow customers to read information provided on a system but will not allow them to change it. For example, a customer can access his or her account history from a home computer over the Internet. Firewall security prevents the customer from being able to change the records.

GLOSSARY

ABA Institution Identifier—A unique identifying number assigned by the American Bankers Association (ABA) under the national numerical system to facilitate the sorting and processing of checks. It has two parts, separated by a hyphen. The first part identifies the city, state, or territory in which the bank is located; the second part identifies the bank itself. The ABA Institution Identifier appears in the upper right-hand corner of checks as the numerator (upper portion) of a fraction.

ABA transit number—See **ABA Institution Identifier.**

acceptance—See **banker's acceptance.**

ATM access card—The plastic used by a cardholder to activate an automated teller machine for deposits, cash withdrawals, account transfers, balance inquiries, or other related functions.

account—A relationship involving a credit established under a particular name, usually by deposit or loan.

account analysis—The process of determining the profit or loss to a bank in handling an account for a given period. An account analysis report shows the activity involved, the cost of that activity (determined by multiplying unit costs by transaction volume), and the estimated earnings on average investable balances maintained during the period after all expenses have been listed.

accounting—The process of organizing, recording, and reporting all transactions that represent the financial condition and performance of a business, organization, or individual.

account reconcilement—A bookkeeping service offered to bank customers who use a large volume of checks. The service is designed to assist them in balancing their accounts. It may include numerically sorting checks, itemizing outstanding checks, and actually balancing the account.

accounts payable—Amounts that are due to vendors or suppliers.

accounts receivable—Short-term assets, representing amounts due from a vendor or supplier of goods or services that were sold on credit terms.

accrual accounting—The accounting method of recording all income when it is earned and all expenses when they are incurred.

acquisition—When one bank acquires another.

adjustable rate—See **variable rate loan**.

administrator—A party appointed by a court to settle an estate when (1) the decedent has left no valid will, (2) no executor is named in the will, or (3) the named executor cannot or will not serve. The legend "c.t.a." with the word "administrator" means that the terms of the will dictate the settling of the estate.

advising bank—A bank that has received notification from another financial institution of the opening of a letter of credit. The advising bank then contacts the beneficiary, reaffirming the terms and conditions of the letter of credit.

agency—The relationship between a party who acts on behalf of another, and the principal on whose behalf the agent acts. In agency relationships, the principal retains legal title to property or other assets.

agency services—Services provided by the agent on behalf of the individual who owns the asset.

agent—A party who acts on behalf of another by the latter's authority. The agent does not have legal title to the property of the principal.

allowance for loan losses—A balance sheet account designed to recognize the fact that all loans will not be repaid in full. The allowance is increased periodically by funds deducted from the organization's income. See **loan loss reserve.**

altered check—A check on which a material change, such as the dollar amount, has been made. Banks are expected to detect alterations and are responsible for paying checks only as originally drawn.

American Bankers Association (ABA)—Based in Washington, D.C., the American Bankers Association represents banks of all sizes on issues of national importance for financial institutions and their customers. The ABA, which was founded in 1875, brings together all categories of banking institutions, including community, regional, and money center banks and holding companies, as well as savings associations, trust companies, and savings banks.

American Institute of Banking (AIB)—Founded in 1900, the American Institute of Banking is a continuing education curriculum for the financial services industry. AIB programs are instructor-guided, include measurements of learning, and are designed to increase job skills and enhance knowledge. Completion of prescribed programs can lead to industry-recognized AIB diplomas and certificates, or assist in professional licensing requirements.

amortization—The gradual reduction of a loan or other obligation by periodic payments of principal and interest.

annual percentage rate (APR)—The true cost of credit on a yearly basis. Expressed as a percentage, the APR results from an equation that considers the amount financed, the finance charge, and the term of the loan. The APR is usually expressed in terms of the effective annual simple interest rate.

annual percentage yield (APY)—A percentage rate reflecting the total amount of interest paid on a deposit account, based on the interest rate and the frequency of compounding for a 365-day period.

annual report—Management's summation of the bank's achievements over the course of the year; often the report contains a detailed analysis of the financial condition of the bank.

asset—Anything owned that has commercial or exchange value. Assets may consist of specific property or of claims against others, versus obligations due to others (liabilities).

asset-liability management—The management of a bank's assets and liabilities to produce maximum long-term gains for the institution's shareholders. The program includes planning to meet liquidity needs, planning maturities to avoid excessive interest rate risk, and controlling interest rates offered and paid to ensure an adequate spread between the cost of funds and the return on funds.

asset recovery department—The department responsible for taking action on late loan payments and for restructuring loan terms.

attorney-in-fact—A party authorized by a bank's depositor to issue instructions to that bank regarding the account. The form by which the depositor grants this authority is called a power of attorney. The rights of an attorney-in-fact last until the depositor dies or revokes them.

audit—A formal or official examination and verification of accounts.

auditor—In banking, an individual, usually appointed by the bank's directors and reporting to them, who is responsible for examining any and all phases of the bank's operations.

automated clearing house (ACH)—A computerized facility that electronically processes interbank credits and debits among member financial institutions, avoiding the use of paper documents.

automated teller machines (ATMs)—Electronic facilities, located inside or apart from a financial services institution's premises, for handling many customer transactions automatically.

automatic transfer service (ATS)—A service by which a bank moves funds from one type of account to another for its customer on a preauthorized basis.

availability—The unrestricted access of a depositor to an account balance.

availability schedule—A list indicating the number of days, subject to the terms of Regulation CC, that must elapse before deposited checks can be considered converted into usable funds.

available balance—The portion of a customer's account balance on which the bank has placed no restrictions, making it available for immediate withdrawal.

average daily float—The portion of a customer's account balance that consists of deposited checks in the process of collection. Most banks average the float over a month.

backup withholding—The procedure by which a payer of interest must withhold a portion of that interest under certain conditions.

balance—The amount of funds in a customer's account. This term may refer to the book (ledger) balance, which simply shows the balance after debits and credits have been posted; the collected balance, which is the book balance less float; or the available balance.

balance reporting—A service offered by a bank to corporate customers wherein the bank reports balance and other transaction information to the company on a daily basis.

balance sheet—A detailed listing of assets, liabilities, and capital accounts (net worth), showing the financial condition of a bank or company as of a given date. A balance sheet illustrates the basic accounting equation: assets = liabilities + net worth. In banking, the balance sheet is usually referred to as the statement of condition.

balloon payment—The last payment on a loan when that payment is substantially larger than earlier payments.

bank card fraud—Use of a stolen bank card or account number to fraudulently purchase goods and services.

bank check—See **cashier's check.**

bank draft—A check drawn by a bank on its account with another bank.

bank examination—A detailed scrutiny of a bank's assets, liabilities, capital accounts, income, and expenses by authorized representatives of a federal or state agency. The purposes are to determine the bank's true financial condition, ensure that all applicable laws and regulations are being followed, and ensure that the bank is operating in a safe and sound manner.

bank holding company (BHC)—See **financial holding company.**

Bank Insurance Fund (BIF)—A fund created in 1989 under the Financial Institutions Reform, Recovery, and Enforcement Act that receives the deposit insurance premiums that banks pay to the FDIC.

bank marketing—Banker activity directed at satisfying the financial services needs and wants of bank customers through the exchange of products and services.

banknote—See **note.**

Bank Secrecy Act—Federal legislation that requires banks to report cash transactions that exceed $10,000 in any single day and requires that the bank maintain certain records (copies of checks paid, deposits, and so forth). The act is intended to inhibit laundering of funds obtained through illegal activities.

bank statement—See **statement.**

banker's acceptance—A time draft drawn on a bank and accepted by that bank. Also referred to as an acceptance.

basic money supply—The component of the money supply that includes coin and currency, demand deposits, and traveler's checks; also known as M1.

basis point—The movement of interest rates or yields, expressed in hundredths of 1 percent.

batch—A group of deposits, checks, records, or documents that have been assembled for processing and proving.

batch header—Accompanying the cash letter, it acts as an offset entry (credit) to the listed checks.

bearer—Any party who has physical possession of a check, security, or other negotiable financial instrument with no name entered on it as payee. Any bearer can present such an instrument for payment. A check made payable to cash is a bearer instrument.

beneficiary—The party who is to receive the proceeds of a trust, insurance policy, letter of credit, or other transaction.

bequest—A gift of personal property provided for in a will.

blank endorsement—The signature of the payee creating a bearer instrument that can be negotiated without any other endorsement.

board of directors—See **directors.**

Board of Governors—The seven-member group, appointed by the president of the United States and confirmed by the Senate for 14-year terms, that directs the overall operations of the Federal Reserve System.

bond—A long-term debt instrument. The issuer (a corporation, unit of government, or other legal entity) promises to repay the stated principal on a specified date at a specific rate of interest.

bookkeeping department—See Demand Deposit Department.

branch bank—A bank that maintains a head office and one or more branch locations. The ability to open branches within a state is subject to the laws of that state.

breach of conduct—A conflict of interest in which personal gain or self-interest take precedence over the employee's job duties.

brokerage firm—A firm that sells stocks, bonds, and mutual funds; not FDIC insured.

bulk cash—Rolled or bagged coin and/or banded currency.

bulk filing—A method of filing checks in bundles that are sorted by statement cycle.

business loans—Loans to businesses, repaid through sales of a company's goods or services.

bylaws—Formal rules and regulations adopted by the board of directors, describing the purpose and nature of the business, duties of the various officers, and other business matters.

call report—A sworn statement of a bank's financial condition as of a certain date, submitted in response to a demand from a supervisory agency or authority.

capital—An accounting term describing the excess of assets over liabilities. Capital accounts include the stockholders' investment in the bank, retained earnings, and borrowings in the form of notes or debentures.

capital ratio—A measure of profitability, determined by dividing the stockholders' equity by total assets.

capital stock—All the outstanding shares of a corporation's stock, including preferred and common shares. The total amount of a corporation's common and preferred stock is authorized by its charter or certificate of incorporation.

cash accounting—The accounting system that posts debits and credits only when money is actually received or paid.

cash advance—A loan obtained by a cardholder by presenting the card at a bank office or inserting it in an automated teller machine. The cardholder obtains cash through this process. The loan is an advance under the line of credit granted to the cardholder.

cash concentration—A service banks offer to corporations that have accounts at numerous banks and want to concentrate or pool the balances in one bank.

cash-in ticket—A ticket used by a teller as a substitute document for cash received in a deposit.

cash item—Any item that flows through the collection process without need of special handling, for which a bank is willing to give immediate but provisional credit to a customer's account.

cash letter—An interbank transmittal form, resembling a deposit slip, used to accompany cash items sent from one bank to another.

cash management—A family of bank services designed to speed up collection of receivables, control payments, reconcile accounts, provide information, and efficiently manage funds.

cash-out ticket—A ticket used by a teller to balance a deposit when cash is given to the customer or when checks are cashed.

cashier's check—A check drawn by a bank on itself. Since the drawer and drawee are one and the same, acceptance is considered automatic and such instruments have been legally held to be promises to pay.

cashing—Delivering money in exchange for a check drawn on another financial institution.

central information file—A data base of individuals' accounts with a bank.

certificate of deposit (CD)—A formal receipt issued by a bank for an amount of money, left with the bank for a specified amount of time (seven days or more). CDs usually bear interest, in which case they are payable at maturity or after a specified minimum notice of intent to withdraw. CDs may also be non-interest-bearing.

certified check—A depositor's check that has been stamped with the word "certified," with a signature and date. By certifying a check, the drawee guarantees that sufficient funds have been set aside from the depositor's account to pay the item. A certified check is a promise to pay and therefore is an obligation of the drawee.

charge-back fraud—A check fraud scheme in which funds are withdrawn against a deposit of worthless checks.

charge-off—A loan, obligation, or cardholder account that the bank no longer expects to collect and writes off as a bad debt.

chartered—Authorized by the federal government (in the case of national banks) or a state government (all other banks) to conduct a banking business under stated terms and conditions.

check—A demand draft drawn on a bank or other financial institution ordering the bank to pay the amount to the person presenting the check.

check clearing service—Service offered to financial institutions by Federal Reserve Banks and commercial banks to clear or present checks to the paying bank.

check routing symbol—The denominator (lower portion) of a fraction, appearing in the upper right-hand corner of checks drawn on Federal Reserve member banks. The ABA Institution Identifier is the upper portion of this fraction. The check routing symbol identifies the Federal Reserve district in which the drawee is located, the Fed facility through which the check can be collected, and the availability assigned to the check under the Fed schedule.

check safekeeping—See **check truncation.**

check truncation—Any one of several systems designed to reduce the physical workload of processing paper checks. In one approach the information on a check is converted into electronic impulses.

clearing—The process or method by which checks and/or other point-of-sale transactions are moved, physically or electronically, from the point of origin to a bank or other financial institution that maintains the customer's account.

clearing agent—The Fed or correspondent bank offering check collection services.

clearing alternatives—The various methods of presenting checks to the drawee bank.

clearing house association—A voluntary association of banks that establishes a meeting place for the exchanging and settling of checks drawn on one another.

Clearing House Interbank Payments System (CHIPS)—An automated clearing house operated by the New York Clearing House Association, used for interbank funds transfers for international customers. CHIPS handles large-dollar payment activity for thousands of accounts around the world and facilitates the settlement of international transactions.

club account—An account offered by a bank to encourage customers to make periodic small deposits for such future expenditures as Christmas or Hanukkah, vacations, or other purposes, usually within a year. These accounts are informal and may be interest-bearing.

code of ethics—A formal set of guidelines that represent a corporation's policies of corporate governance and individual conduct.

coin—Metallic money, in contrast to paper money (currency).

collateral—Specific property pledged by a borrower to secure a loan. If the borrower defaults, the lender has the right to sell the collateral to liquidate the loan.

collected balance—Cash in an account, plus deposited checks that have been presented to a drawee for payment and for which payment has actually been received. The collected balance is the customer's book balance minus any float.

collection item—Any item received by a bank for which the bank does not or cannot give immediate, provisional credit to an account. Collection items receive deferred credit, often require special handling, usually are subject to special fees, and do not create float. Credit for a collection is not posted to the customer's account until final settlement takes place. Also called **non-cash item.**

collection services—Services offered to financial institutions by Federal Reserve banks and commercial banks to collect funds for the paying bank.

co-maker—An individual who signs a note to guarantee a loan made to another party and is jointly liable with that party for repayment.

combined statement—A bank statement that combines information from a number of accounts. Depending on the software capabilities of the bank, the statement may contain checking, savings, time deposits, bank card usage, and loan information on one statement.

commercial bank—By law, an institution that accepts demand deposits and makes commercial loans. In practice, a financial institution that has the capacity to be a full-service provider of deposit, payment, and credit services to all types of customers and can offer other financial services, such as international and trust services.

commercial loan—Credit extended by a bank to a business.

commercial paper—Short-term, unsecured promissory notes issued by major corporations of unquestioned credit standing as a means of borrowing.

common stock—Securities evidencing ownership of a corporation and generally giving the shareholder voting rights. The rights of holders of common stock are inferior to those of holders of the corporation's bonds, preferred stock, and other debts.

Community Reinvestment Act (CRA)—A law passed in 1977 that requires banks and other financial institutions to meet the credit needs of their communities, including the low- and moderate-income sections of those communities. The act also requires banks to submit reports concerning their investments in the areas where they do business. A bank's compliance with the CRA is evaluated whenever the bank files a request for an expansion of business, such as an application for a new branch.

compensating balance—The non-interest-bearing balance that a customer must keep on deposit to ensure a credit line, gain unlimited checking privileges, and offset the bank's expenses in providing various services.

Competitive Equality Banking Act—Legislation passed by Congress in 1987 and containing provisions regarding availability to bank customers of deposited checks, the operations of non-bank banks (a non-bank bank is a financial institution owned by a nonbanking company that avoids being defined as a bank holding company for regulatory purposes), and the authority of banks to offer certain services. Title IV of this act is called the Expedited Funds Availability Act.

compliance program—The policies and procedures that a bank establishes and follows to ensure that it is obeying all applicable federal and state laws and regulations.

Comptroller of the Currency—An official of the U.S. government, appointed by the president and confirmed by the Senate, who is responsible for chartering, examining, supervising, and, if necessary, liquidating all national banks.

concentration account—A deposit account into which funds from other bank accounts are transferred.

confirmed letter of credit—A letter of credit, issued by one bank, on which a second bank undertakes the responsibility to honor drafts drawn in compliance with the terms of the credit.

conflict of interest—Related to ethics, when two interests are at cross-purposes with each other.

conservatorship—See **guardianship.**

construction loan—A short-term loan, often unsecured, to a builder or developer to finance the costs of construction. The lender generally requires repayment from the proceeds of the borrower's permanent mortgage loan. The lender may make periodic payments to the borrower as the construction work progresses.

consumer banking—The activities of providing financial services to individuals.

consumer lending—All types of credit extended to consumers, either individually or jointly, primarily for the purpose of buying goods and services for their personal use. Also referred to as installment credit, personal loans, or personal finance.

consumer loan—The general term for loans extended to individuals and small businesses.

contract—An agreement, enforceable at law, between or among two or more persons, consisting of one or more mutual promises.

controlled disbursement account—A demand deposit account on which the corporate customer writes checks and the paying bank advises the customer of the dollar amount of the checks that will be posted to the customer's account that night.

corporate bonds—Long-term debt obligations issued to investors by corporations to finance expansion.

corporate resolution—A document filed with a bank by a corporation. It defines the authority given to the corporation's officers and specifies who may sign checks, borrow on behalf of the corporation, and otherwise issue instructions to the bank and conduct the corporation's business. The powers listed in the resolution are granted by the corporation's directors.

corporate structure—An organizational structure with stockholders, directors, and officers.

corporation—A business organization treated as a legal entity and owned by a group of stockholders (shareholders). The stockholders elect the directors, who serve as the active, governing body to manage the affairs of the corporation.

correspondent bank—A bank that maintains an account relationship and/or engages in an exchange of services with another bank.

cost accounting system—An accounting system that relates all direct and indirect costs and expenses to specific functions performed.

cost center—A unit in a bank, such as the proof department, that does not generate income.

counterfeit checks—Checks scanned into a computer retaining the authorized signature, but changing the payee's name, amount, serial number, and date.

counterfeiting—The act of creating counterfeit money, that is, bogus coins and currency, made to appear genuine. Counterfeiting is a felony, making the perpetrators subject to long prison terms and heavy fines. The U.S. Secret Service, a bureau of the Treasury Department, is responsible for tracking counterfeiters.

credit—(1) An advance of cash, merchandise, or other commodity in exchange for a promise or other agreement to pay at a future date, with interest if so agreed. (2) An accounting entry to the right-hand (credit) side of an account, decreasing the balance of an asset or expense account or increasing the balance of a liability, income, or equity account.

credit analysis—See **loan analysis.**

credit card—A plastic card (or its equivalent) to be used from time to time by the cardholder to obtain money, goods, or services, possibly under a line of credit established by the card issuer. The cardholder is billed periodically for any outstanding balance. See **debit card.**

credit department—The unit in a bank in which all credit files on borrowers are maintained and analyzed. The department's work may also include answering inquiries from outside sources. A bank's credit files contain the history of each account relationship and include all correspondence, memoranda, financial statements, and other material that must be retained.

credit investigation—The stage in the lending process in which a formal investigation of the applicant's financial and economic condition is made.

credit risk—The bank's estimate of the probability that the borrower can and will repay a loan with interest as scheduled.

credit scoring—A technique that uses a mathematical formula to determine the likelihood that a borrower will repay a loan, given adverse circumstances.

credit union—A voluntary cooperative association of individuals having some common bond (for example, place of employment), organized to accept deposits, extend loans, and provide other financial services.

creditor—Any party to whom money is owed by another.

cross-selling—The practice of inducing users of one or more services to buy or use additional services.

currency—Paper money, as opposed to coin.

current assets—Cash and other items readily convertible into cash within one year, such as accounts receivable and inventory.

current liabilities—Short-term debts expected to be paid within one year, such as accounts payable.

custody—A banking service that provides safekeeping for a customer's property under written agreement and also calls for the bank to buy, sell, receive, and deliver securities and collect and pay out income only when ordered to do so by the principal.

daylight overdraft—(1) A shortage in a bank's reserve account at the Federal Reserve during business hours. (2) Any temporary overdraft in an account, resulting from payments made during business hours before incoming funds are actually received. Daylight overdrafts are cleared by the close of business on the same day.

debit—(1) An accounting entry that increases the balance of an asset or expense account or decreases the balance of a liability, income, or equity account. (2) A charge against a customer's balance or bank card account.

debit card—A plastic card enabling the card-holder to purchase goods or services, the cost of which is immediately debited to his or her bank account. Debit cards activate point-of-sale terminals in supermarkets, stores, and gas stations. Together with credit cards, they are commonly referred to as bank cards.

decedent—A term used in connection with wills, estates, and inheritances to describe a person who has died.

declaration of loss—A statement signed by the purchaser or the payee that the official check has been lost or stolen and that the check has not been negotiated.

deed—A written instrument, executed and delivered according to law, used to transfer title to property.

default—(1) The failure of a borrower to make a payment of principal or interest when due. (2) The condition that exists when a borrower cannot or does not pay bondholders or note holders the interest or principal due.

deferred availability—A delay in the time frame within which deposited checks can be withdrawn and the funds used by the depositor. Under the terms of the Expedited Funds Availability Act, limits have been placed on the delays that banks can impose in making deposited checks available.

delivery—The transfer of possession of an item from one party to another.

demand deposit—Funds that may be withdrawn from a bank without advance notice. Checking accounts are the most common form of demand deposits.

demand deposit accounting—The processing, tracking, and posting of transactions affecting a bank's demand deposits and the accounting for those deposits.

Demand Deposit Department—The bank unit that maintains and updates all records of depositors' accounts.

demand draft—A written order to pay at sight, upon presentation. A check is a demand draft drawn on a bank or other financial institution offering demand deposits.

demand loan—A loan with no fixed maturity, payable whenever the bank calls for it or at the borrower's option. A demand note is used with this type of loan.

deposit—Any placement of cash, checks, or other drafts with a bank for credit to an account. All deposits are liabilities for a bank, since they must be repaid in some form at some future date.

deposit function—The banking process by which funds are accepted for credit to an account. In the case of checks, the function includes conversion of the items into available, usable funds.

deposit operations department—The bank unit that maintains and updates all records of depositors' accounts. See **demand deposit accounting.**

deposit slip—A listing of the items given to a bank for credit to an account. A copy of the deposit slip may be given to the customer as a receipt.

Depository Institutions Deregulation and Monetary Control Act—See **Monetary Control Act.**

deputy—An individual authorized to act for another in performing certain transactions, specifically in the case of access to a safe deposit box.

direct deposit—The process by which a payer delivers data by electronic means directly to the payee's financial institution for credit to his or her account. The most common example is the federal government program for direct deposit of Social Security payments. Direct deposit systems substitute bookkeeping entries, received electronically, for paper checks.

directors—The individuals, elected by stockholders, who comprise the board of directors and serve as the active, governing body of a corporation.

direct presentment—The method of check collection, also called direct sending, in which deposited checks are presented directly to their drawee banks for settlement.

direct sending—See **direct presentment.**

discount—Interest withheld when a note, draft, or bill is purchased, or collected in advance when a loan is made.

discount rate—The rate of interest charged by the Federal Reserve on loans it makes to financial institutions.

discount window—The lending facility of a district Federal Reserve bank, through which financial institutions borrow from the Fed on a short-term basis. The Fed closely monitors discount window activity to control borrowing by banks and other financial institutions.

dishonor—The refusal of a drawee or drawer (maker) to pay a check, draft, note, or other instrument presented.

disintermediation—The flow of funds from one type of account into another, from one financial institution to another, or from bank accounts into investments for the purpose of obtaining higher yields.

diversification—A method of decreasing the total risk of investments by investing funds in assets of different kinds.

dividend—A periodic payment, usually made on a quarterly basis, by a corporation to its stockholders as a return on their investment. All dividend payouts must be approved by the corporation's board of directors.

dividend disbursing agent—A bank service performed for a corporation in issuing periodic dividend payments to the corporation's stockholders as instructed by the corporation's directors. See **paying agent.**

documentary draft—A written order to pay, accompanied by securities or other papers to be delivered against payment or acceptance.

dormant account—A customer relationship that has shown no activity for a period of time.

double-entry bookkeeping—An accounting system based on the premise that for every debit there must be an equal, corresponding credit; therefore, all transactions are posted twice.

draft—A signed, written order by which one party (the drawer) instructs another (the drawee) to make payment to a third (the payee). In international banking, also called bill of exchange.

drawee—The party to whom the drawer issues instructions to make payment. In the case of checks, the drawee is a bank or other financial institution.

drawer—The party who gives the order to pay a draft.

drive-in window (drive-up window, drive-through window)—A convenience offered to the public, with a teller's window facing the outside of a bank building so that customers can transact their business without leaving their cars.

dual banking system—All commercial banks in the United States must be chartered, either by the state in which they are domiciled (state banks) or by the federal government through the office of the Comptroller of the Currency (national banks). The side-by-side existence of these two types of banks creates a dual system.

dual control—A bank security procedure requiring that two members of the staff be involved in a transaction.

e-business/e-commerce—Business conducted electronically over the Internet.

earnings per share (EPS)—The most common method of determining a company's profitability. It is obtained by dividing the net income by the number of outstanding shares of common stock.

electronic check presentment (ECP)—The transmission of the MICR line of checks by a presenting bank to the paying bank.

electronic funds transfer service (EFTS)—The use of automated technology to move funds without paper checks.

employee trusts—Pension and profit-sharing trust funds established by employers for the benefit of employees. The trustee, usually a bank, makes payments to the employees during employment, upon retirement, or at death, as designated under the terms of the trust.

encoding—The process of inscribing or imprinting MICR data on checks, deposit slips, debit and credit tickets, or other bank documents.

encryption code—Digital code that protects information being exchanged between two electronic systems.

endorsement—A signature (other than the signature of the maker, drawer, or acceptor) that is made on an instrument for the purpose of negotiating the instrument, restricting payment of the instrument, or incurring endorser's liability on the instrument.

endorser—Any person who makes an endorsement.

Equal Credit Opportunity Act—Federal legislation, passed in 1974, that requires all lenders and creditors to make credit equally available, without any type of discrimination.

equity—(1) The stockholders' investment interest in a corporation, equaling the excess of assets over liabilities and including common and preferred stock, retained earnings, and surplus and reserves. (2) In real estate, the interest or value an owner has in property, minus the amount of any existing liens.

escheat—The legal principle by which a state government is entitled to receive funds that have remained in dormant accounts for a period of time and whose owners have not been located.

escrow—The holding of funds, documents, securities, or other property by an impartial third party for the other two participants in a business transaction. When the transaction is completed, the escrow agent releases the entrusted property.

escrow agent—The third party in an escrow transaction, who acts as agent for the other two parties, carries out their instructions, and assumes the responsibilities of paperwork and funds disbursement.

estate—The sum total, as determined by a complete inventory, of all the assets of a decedent.

Eurodollars—Deposits that are denominated in dollars but are held in branches or banks outside the United States, especially in Europe.

executor—A party named in a decedent's valid will to settle an estate and qualified by a court to act in this capacity. A female executor is sometimes called an executrix.

Expedited Funds Availability Act (EFAA)—A portion (Title IV) of the Competitive Equality Banking Act of 1987 that requires financial institutions to make deposited funds available for withdrawal within certain time limits. The act was implemented by the Federal Reserve's Regulation CC.

Federal Deposit Insurance Act—The 1935 legislation (Banking Act of 1935) that amended the Glass-Steagall Act and authorized the FDIC to set standards for operations at FDIC-member banks, examine those banks to ensure compliance with the standards, take action to reduce the potential of troubled banks failing, and pay depositors if an insured bank fails.

Federal Deposit Insurance Corporation (FDIC)—The agency of the federal government, established in 1933 to provide insurance protection, up to statutory limits, for depositors at FDIC member institutions. All national banks and all Fed member banks must belong to FDIC; other commercial banks and savings banks may also join if they wish. Under the provisions of the Financial Institutions

Reform, Recovery, and Enforcement Act of 1989 (FIRREA), the responsibilities of FDIC were greatly expanded.

Fed funds—Member banks' excess reserves at the Federal Reserve, loaned on a daily basis to other banks. Fed funds are also used to settle fund transfers, with no float, among member banks.

Fed funds rate—The rate charged by an institution that sells Fed funds to another institution.

Federal Open Market Committee (FOMC)—The Federal Reserve committee that has complete charge of open-market operations, that is, the purchases and redemptions of all U.S. government obligations as part of monetary policy.

Federal Reserve Act—The 1913 legislation that established the Federal Reserve System.

Federal Reserve banks—The 12 district institutions that deal with member banks and maintain branches and check-processing centers as necessary. Each district bank is owned by the member banks in its district.

Federal Reserve (Fed) float—The difference between the dollar amount of cash items in the process of collection by the Fed and the availability credit given to sending banks by the Fed. The Fed actually receives payment from drawee banks only after presentation; however, in the meantime it often grants availability credit to the sending banks.

Federal Reserve notes—The paper money, constituting the largest part of the nation's money supply, issued by the 12 Federal Reserve banks and officially designated as legal tender by the federal government. Each such note is an interest-free promise to pay on demand.

Fedwire—The Federal Reserve's funds transfer service used by banks to complete customer wire transfer requests.

Federal Reserve System—The central monetary authority for the United States, created by the Federal Reserve Act of 1913 and consisting of the 12 district banks and their branches, plus the member banks that are the stockholders and legal owners. The Federal Reserve Board of Governors in Washington, D.C., exercises overall control over the nationwide operations of the system.

fiduciary—An individual, bank, or other party to whom specific property is turned over under the terms of a contractual agreement and who acts for the benefit of another party on a basis of trust and confidence.

financial holding company (FHC)—A corporation that owns, controls, or otherwise has the power over the voting stock in one or more banks. All bank holding companies come under the jurisdiction of the Federal Reserve.

Financial Institutions Reform, Recovery, and Enforcement Act of 1989 (FIRREA)—Legislation passed in 1989 as a result of the crisis among the savings and loan associations. FIRREA abolished the former Federal Home Loan Bank Board and Federal Savings and Loan Insurance Corporation and established the Office of Thrift Supervision and the Resolution Trust Corporation. The act also imposed new capital requirements on S&Ls, increased the FDIC insurance premium, and restricted interest rates on deposits and investment opportunities for S&Ls.

financial subsidiary—Created by the Gramm-Leach-Bliley Act, the entity that can engage in the sale of financial products without geographic limits.

firewall security—Software that puts a "wall" between two electronic systems, preventing one user from changing information provided by the other user.

fiscal policy—The planning of the federal government's revenue-producing and spending activities, directly affecting the federal budget and taxation.

float—The dollar amount of deposited cash items that have been given immediate, provisional credit but are in the process of collection from drawee banks. Also called uncollected funds.

floor-plan financing—Bank financing to dealers for the purpose of maintaining inventory.

forged check—A demand draft, drawn on a bank, that has been fraudulently altered or on which the drawer's signature is not genuine.

forgery—The legal term for counterfeiting a check or other document with the intent to defraud.

401(k) plan—A type of qualified retirement plan, under which an employee can make tax-exempt contributions to a fund and have those contributions matched in part by the employer's contributions.

fraud—Intentional misrepresentation of a material fact by one party so that another party, acting on it, will part with property or surrender a right.

full-service bank—A financial institution that not only accepts demand deposits and makes commercial loans but also offers services to meet all the financial needs of its customers.

funds management—(1) The continual rearrangement of a bank's balance sheet to maximize profits, to maintain adequate rate spreads and liquidity, and to make safe investments. (2) The management and control of all items on a balance sheet, including assets, liabilities, and capital, to optimize a bank's earnings without taking excessive risk or liquidity exposure. Also called balance sheet management.

Garn-St Germain Act—The name given to the Depository Institutions Act of 1982, authorizing the opening of new types of interest-bearing accounts and giving federal regulators additional powers to assist troubled banks and financial institutions.

general ledger—The consolidated, summary books of account in a bank, showing all changes in the bank's financial condition and bringing together all branch and departmental totals. Data from the bank's general ledger department are used for all call reports and to prepare the bank's statement of condition (balance sheet).

general obligation bond—A municipal obligation, backed by the full faith and credit of the issuer and therefore by the municipality's taxing power.

genuine signature—The actual, valid signature of a drawer without forgery.

Glass-Steagall Act—The 1933 Banking Act, which established the Federal Deposit Insurance Corporation, separated commercial banking from investment banking, and prohibited payment of interest on demand deposits.

Gramm-Leach-Bliley Act—This act permits financial holding companies to engage in a broad new range of activities financial in nature, while a financial subsidiary may engage in most of the new activities. It has provisions on financial privacy, ATM disclosures, and Federal Reserve oversight of financial holding companies.

growth assets—assets such as stocks, purchased for their potential to increase in value.

guardianship—The trust relationship, established by a court appointment, in which a trustee holds in safekeeping and manages certain property for the benefit of a minor or incompetent person. Also called a conservatorship.

hold—A restriction on the payment of all or any part of the balance in an account.

holder—The person in possession of an instrument if the instrument is payable to bearer or, in the case of an instrument payable to an identified person, if the identified person is in possession.

holder in due course—As defined in the Uniform Commercial Code, a party who accepts an instrument in good faith and for value, without notice that it has been dishonored, that it is overdue, or that there is any claim against it.

holding company—A legal entity that owns stock in other corporations and usually exercises control over them.

home banking—A group of bank services designed to enable customers to obtain current information about their accounts and initiate certain transactions through a telephone or computer terminal link to the bank.

home equity loan—A type of real estate credit in which the homeowner borrows against the value of his or her residence through a second mortgage. The lending bank frequently establishes a home equity line of credit against which the borrower can draw at any time.

house check—See **on-us check**.

identity theft—Fraud involving stealing a victim's identification and using it to open fraudulent accounts.

image statement—A bank statement that contains an image of the paid checks.

image technology—The process of converting a paper document to an image of the document and storing the image on a computer.

immediate credit—Credit for deposits immediately reflected in the book or ledger balance of an account.

in-clearing capture—The process whereby the Fed presents a cash letter to the paying bank and the paying bank prepares the items for capture, performs the capture run, and settles for the checks.

income—The third objective of funds management, the objective of the bank to generate income from investments.

income assets—Assets purchased for their income-generating potential.

income statement—A record of the income and expenses of a bank or business covering a period of time. Also called a profit-and-loss statement.

incoming return items—Checks, drafts, and other instruments that are received by the depositary bank to be charged back to depositors' accounts. See **return items.**

indirect loan—A loan involving three parties, including the borrower who obtains financing, a merchant (or dealer), and a financial institution.

individual account—An account opened for and owned by an individual.

individual retirement accounts (IRAs)—Tax-deferred accounts into which a customer, subject to the restrictions in the Tax Reform Act of 1986, can make deposits and earn interest for retirement purposes. Withdrawals from IRAs are not permitted, without penalty, until the depositor reaches age 59½.

in-filing—The process of filing checks in individual files by checking account number.

inflation—A continuing increase in the general level of prices in an economy, which results from increases in total spending relative to the supply of goods on the market. Inflation is also associated with increases in wages and production costs, and a decrease in purchasing power.

installment loan—A loan made to an individual or business, repaid in fixed, periodic payments.

institutional trusts—A trust fund established by a large investing body, such as a university or a corporate pension and profit-sharing plan.

insufficient funds—A banking term indicating that the drawer's balance does not contain sufficient funds to cover a check or checks. Commonly abbreviated as "NSF."

insurance draft—A draft issued by an insurance company to pay a claim.

insured bank—A bank that is a member of FDIC.

interest—Money paid for the use of money.

Internet banking—Use of home or office PCs to access personal account information like balances, transaction history, and tax information, in addition to paying bills and purchasing stocks and bonds.

Internet banks—Banks that exist solely on the Internet, usually without "bricks and mortar" branches.

investment—The exchange of money, either for a promise to pay at a later date (as with bonds) or for an ownership share in a business (as with stocks).

investment advisor—An agency service in which the bank performs all the duties of the custodian plus any duties requested by the owner.

investment bank—A financial institution that raises funds directly from investors and savers by acting as underwriters and distributors of securities.

investment portfolio—The sum total of the various securities owned by an individual, bank, business, institution, or unit of government.

irrevocable letter of credit—A commercial letter of credit that cannot be amended or canceled except by full mutual agreement between the parties.

issuing bank—A bank that issues a letter of credit, based on a customer's application.

joint account—A bank relationship in the names of two or more parties. Joint accounts may carry rights of survivorship or may be established on a tenants-in-common basis, without such rights.

joint tenancy—The holding of property by two or more parties on an equal basis, conveying rights of survivorship.

joint venture—An arrangement in which two or more banks join forces to perform certain functions with the intent of reducing costs and improving efficiency.

journal—An accounting record of original entry in which transactions are listed and described in chronological order.

Keogh account—A retirement account for self-employed individuals and their employees, to which yearly tax-deductible contributions can be made if the plan meets Internal Revenue Service requirements.

Key Book—A complete listing of the ABA Institution Identifiers assigned to all banks in the United States, so that any bank can be identified and located by its numerical designation.

kiting—Attempting to draw against uncollected or nonexistent funds for fraudulent purposes. A depositor issues a check, overdrawing an account at one bank, and deposits into that account a check drawn on insufficient or uncollected funds at another bank.

laundering—The practice of moving funds through numerous accounts and/or banks, one after another, in an attempt to conceal the source of the money. See **money laundering.**

ledger—An accounting record of final entry, into which transactions are posted after journal posting has taken place.

ledger balance—See **balance.**

legal lending limit—The maximum amount of money a bank can lend on an unsecured basis to a single borrower or a combination of financially related borrowers. The legal lending limit is established by law and is expressed as a percentage of the bank's capital and surplus.

legal reserves—The portion of a bank's demand and time deposits that must be kept in the form of cash or acceptable equivalents for the protection of depositors. Fed member banks maintain these reserves with the Fed in their district; other banks either use the Fed directly or use a correspondent bank that is a Fed member.

lending policy—A written statement of the guidelines and standards that a lender follows in making credit decisions. Lending policies in banks are established by the bank's directors.

less cash deposit—A deposit from which a certain amount is given back to the customer in cash. See **split deposit.**

letter of credit (L/C)—An instrument issued by a bank, substituting the credit of that bank for the credit of a buyer of goods. It authorizes the seller to draw drafts on the bank and guarantees payment of those drafts if all the stated conditions and terms have been met. Also called commercial letter of credit.

liability—Anything owed by a bank, individual, or business. A bank's largest liability is the sum total of its deposits.

liability management—The management and control of liabilities to optimize a bank's earnings without excessive risk or liquidity exposure.

LIBOR—London Interbank Offered Rate, an international money market interest rate that is the average rate offered by banks for the interbank placement of Eurodollars. It functions like the prime rate.

lien—A legal claim or attachment filed on record against property as security for the payment of an obligation.

line of credit—An expression of the maximum amount of credit a bank is willing to lend to a borrower. Confirmed lines of credit are made known to the customer; guidance lines of credit are for the bank's internal use only.

liquidity—(1) The ability of a bank, business, or individual to meet current debts. (2) The quality that makes an asset quickly and easily convertible into cash.

liquidity needs—The total amount a bank calculates as being necessary to cover estimated withdrawals and payments of funds and to meet the anticipated and legitimate credit demands of customers.

living trust—A trust fund that becomes effective during the lifetime of the trustor (settlor).

loan—A business contract in which a borrower agrees to pay interest for the use of a lender's funds.

loan analysis—A formal evaluation of the financial and economic condition of a potential borrower, appraising the borrower's ability to repay debt.

loan application—The first step in the lending process; the document that gathers preliminary information from the borrower.

loan closing—The point where all loan documents are complete, appropriate forms signed, funds disbursed, and documentation filed.

loan documentation stage—The stage in the lending process in which all forms necessary to secure the lender's interest and comply with state and federal requirements are obtained and completed.

loan interview—The step in the lending process in which the loan officer attempts to understand the borrower's needs and gathers initial, supporting documentation.

loan loss reserve—A balance sheet account established by a bank or other creditor, based on expectations of future loan losses. The loan loss reserve is built up through deductions from net income. As loan losses occur, they are charged to the reserve.

loan participation—The sharing of a loan to a single borrower by more than one lender.

loan review—The systematic review of the loan portfolio by directors and officers.

local check—As defined by Regulation CC and the Expedited Funds Availability Act, a deposited check that is drawn on another bank in the same Fed check processing region.

local clearing item—A check drawn on another local bank.

lockbox—A banking service in which a bank assumes the responsibility for receiving, examining, processing, and crediting incoming checks for a customer to reduce mail, deposit, and collection time.

magnetic ink character recognition (MICR)—The encoding of checks and documents with characters in magnetic ink so that they can be electronically read and processed.

maker—The party who issues a note and thereby makes himself or herself liable for a legal obligation.

margin—The excess of the value of collateral over the amount loaned against it.

margin requirement—Under Regulation U of the Federal Reserve Act, the minimum amount of money a customer must provide to buy stocks and bonds on credit.

market risk—The risk that the market value of a security will decrease because of interest rates and other market conditions.

market segmentation—Marketing strategy based on a bank organizing and concentrating its sales efforts on the similarities that exist within customer groups or market segments.

marketing concept—An organizational philosophy that establishes objectives of the company as customer orientation, profit, total company effort, and social responsibility.

marketing customer information file (MCIF)—A database built for marketing purposes by extracting selected data from the central information file.

master file—The updated record of the closing balance in each account at a bank. It is produced by merging the previous day's master tape with the current day's transaction tape (entry run).

matched funding—Funding a loan or other assets by issuing a liability with the same (matched) maturity or duration.

maturity—The date on which a note, draft, bond, or acceptance becomes due and payable.

member bank—A bank that belongs to the Federal Reserve System.

memo-post—An indication on a deposit account that an item will be posted to the account during the next posting period.

merger—The combination of two or more formerly independent firms under a single ownership.

MICR—See **magnetic ink character recognition.**

microfilm—The photographic process that reduces checks and other documents for record-keeping and storage purposes.

midnight deadline—A term defined in the Uniform Commercial Code as midnight of the banking day following the banking day of receipt of the item.

Monetary Control Act—The 1980 legislation that provided for the gradual phaseout of interest-rate ceilings, made all financial institutions subject to reserve requirements, and gave expanded powers to thrift institutions.

The full name is Depository Institutions Deregulation and Monetary Control Act.

monetary policy—The general term for the actions taken by the Federal Reserve to control the flow of money and credit.

money—Legal tender; coin and currency declared by a government to be the accepted medium of exchange.

money center—A city with an active money market and financial community, such as New York, Chicago, or San Francisco.

money laundering—The practice of moving large amounts of illegally obtained cash through many bank accounts to hide the source of the money.

money market deposit account—An account authorized in 1982 that is federally insured, provides easy access to the deposited funds, and pays an interest rate that is competitive with money market mutual funds.

money market instruments—Private and government obligations with a maturity of one year or less. These include U.S. Treasury bills, banker's acceptances, and commercial paper.

money market mutual fund—A mutual fund that pools investors' contributions and invests them in various money market funds.

money supply—The total amount of funds available for spending in the nation at any point in time. M1, the most commonly quoted measure of the money supply, is the sum total of currency, demand deposits, and other deposits subject to check withdrawal.

mortgage loan—Real estate credit, usually extended on a long-term basis with the mortgaged property as security.

municipals—Bonds issued by any state or local government or by a state or local government's agencies and authorities.

mutual savings bank—A savings institution that has no stockholders and is owned by the depositors, who elect the board of trustees to manage it. See **savings bank.**

national bank—A commercial bank that operates under a federal charter and is supervised and examined by the Office of the Comptroller of the Currency. The word national must appear in some form in the bank's corporate title. All national banks must belong to the Federal Reserve System and to the Federal Deposit Insurance Corporation.

national banknote—A national currency issued by national banks under the authority of the National Bank Act.

national numerical system—See **ABA Institution Identifier.**

negotiable instrument—An unconditional written order or promise to pay a certain sum of money. The document must be easily transferable from one party to another. Every negotiable instrument must meet all the requirements of Article 3 of the Uniform Commercial Code.

negotiable order of withdrawal (NOW) account—A type of account that permits the depositor to earn interest while at the same time having check-writing privileges.

negotiation—The transfer of possession of an instrument to a person who becomes a holder of the instrument.

net interest spread—The difference between interest income and interest expense.

net worth—The excess of assets over liabilities; the shareholders' equity in a bank or business.

night depository—A convenience facility provided for merchants who wish to deposit their receipts after business hours. A small vault, located inside a bank but accessible outside the premises, is used.

non-cash item—(1) See **collection item.** (2) An item that cannot be processed in bulk and requires special handling.

non-local check—As defined by Regulation CC and the Expedited Funds Availability Act, a deposited check that is drawn on another bank located in a different Fed check processing region.

non-member bank—A state-chartered bank that is not a member of the Federal Reserve System.

non-performing asset—See **non-performing loan.**

non-performing loan—A loan made by a bank to a customer on which no interest is being paid or accrued. Loans in this category are non-earning assets and usually are related to or precede foreclosure or charge-off.

note—A written promise to pay a specific amount either on demand or at a future date.

NOW account—See **negotiable order of withdrawal (NOW) account.**

Office of Thrift Supervision (OTS)—An agency of the Treasury Department, created by the Financial Institutions Reform, Recovery, and Enforcement Act of 1989 to regulate federally chartered savings and loan associations.

officer—Any executive of a bank or business to whom authority has been delegated, usually by the board of directors or senior management.

official check—See **cashier's check.**

offset—The bank's legal right to seize any funds that a debtor or guarantor may have on deposit and to apply those funds to a loan in default.

on-us check—A check deposited or negotiated for cash at the bank on which it is drawn. Also called house check.

open market operations—Sales and purchases of government obligations by the Federal Open Market Committee to influence the size of the money supply and to control the flow of money and credit. The Fed uses open market operations as its major tool for implementing monetary policy.

optical character recognition (OCR)—The electronic reading of numeric or alphabetical characters from printed documents. Also called optical scanning.

order—A written direction to pay money to someone.

organizational chart—Represents the organization at a particular moment in time and shows the skeleton of the organizational structure.

outgoing return items—Checks, drafts, and other instruments returned by the paying bank. See **return items.**

outsourcing—A term used to describe the process of a bank hiring a third party to perform the processing of certain functions for the bank.

outstanding check—An issued check that has not yet been presented for payment to, or paid by, a drawee.

overdraft—A negative (minus) balance in an account, resulting from the paying (posting) of checks for an amount greater than the depositor's balance.

overdraft banking—A service offered to demand deposit customers whereby checks drawn on insufficient funds are not returned to the presenter but are paid from funds under a line of credit.

participation—See **loan participation.**

partnership—A business venture operated by two or more individuals in non-corporate form. The rights, duties, and responsibilities of the partners are usually covered in a partnership agreement.

pay—To debit a check against a customer's account.

payee—The beneficiary of an instrument; the person to whom the note is payable.

payer bank services—Various check-related services offered to paying financial institutions by Federal Reserve banks.

paying—Giving cash for an on-us check.

paying agent—The service by which a bank disburses (a) dividends on a corporation's stock or (b) interest and principal on bonds and notes. Also called fiscal agent. See **dividend disbursing agent.**

paying teller—A bank representative responsible for the paying and cashing of checks presented.

pension—A fixed sum payable regularly to an individual or his or her family, usually by an employer after the individual's retirement from service.

pension trust—A trust fund established by an employer (usually a corporation) to provide benefits for incapacitated or retired employees, with or without their contributions.

Personal Financial Management (PFM) software—Software that facilitates electronic transactions between the bank and its customers.

personal identification number (PIN)—A series of numbers or letters used by a cardholder or randomly assigned by the card issuer to provide personal security in accessing a financial service terminal and prevent use of a bank card by unauthorized parties.

pigeon drop scheme—A scheme to defraud customers of cash in which two thieves convince a victim to advance money for a share in a large amount of found money.

platform—A term commonly used to describe the portion of a bank's lobby area where officers, new account representatives, and customer service personnel are located.

point of sale (POS)—The location in a merchant establishment where a sale is consummated by payment for goods or services received.

point-of-sale (POS) system—An electronic system by which the purchaser of goods or services can use a plastic card in a terminal at the seller's place of business, thereby initiating a debit to the cardholder's account at a financial institution and a credit to the seller's account.

postdated check—Bearing a future date. A postdated item is not valid until that date is reached.

posting—The process of adding deposits to an account balance and subtracting checks and other withdrawals.

power of attorney—The legal document by which one party is authorized to act on another's behalf. See **attorney-in-fact.**

preauthorized payments—A convenience service offered by banks to customers, enabling them to request that funds be transferred to a creditor's account on a regular, fixed basis.

presenting bank—A bank that forwards a deposited or cashed item to another for payment.

presentment—Demand for payment of a negotiable instrument made by the person entitled to payment.

price-earnings multiple—See price-earnings ratio.

price-earnings ratio—The comparison of the earnings of the bank to the price of the stock.

primary reserves—Bank reserves that provide immediate liquidity but do not generate income.

prime pass—The initial pass or run of items in the check capture process.

prime rate—A benchmark or guideline interest rate that a bank establishes from time to time and uses in calculating an appropriate rate for a particular loan contract. The prime rate is usually offered to the bank's most creditworthy customers, reflecting their deposit balances and financial strength.

principal—(1) The sum of money stated in an account, a contract, or a financial instrument; for example, the amount of a loan or debt exclusive of interest. (2) The primary borrower on a loan or other obligation. (3) A person who appoints another party to act for him or her as agent. (4) The property of an estate. (5) The individual with primary ownership or management control of a business.

probate—The judicial determination concerning the validity of a will and all questions pertaining to it. The first step in the settling of an estate. Also the name of the special court that handles probate matters.

product—In marketing, any good, service, place, idea, or other entity that is offered to a market for sale to satisfy a need or want.

profit-and-loss statement—See **income statement.**

profit margin—The difference between the selling price of a product or service and the costs involved. The profit margin is usually expressed as a percentage of the selling price.

profits—The excess of revenues over the costs incurred in earning them.

profit-sharing trust—A trust fund into which an employer contributes a portion of annual profit for the benefit of the employees.

promissory note—A written promise committing the maker to pay a certain sum of money to the payee, with or without interest, on demand or on a fixed or determinable future date.

proof—Any process that tests the accuracy of an operation or function. Also called balancing.

proof department—The unit in a bank that sorts and distributes checks and other work

and arrives at a control figure for all transactions.

proof machine—Equipment that simultaneously sorts items, records the dollar total of all items, provides totals for each sorted group, and balances the total to the original input amount.

proprietary fund—A mutual fund managed by a bank for its own customers.

proprietorship—See **sole proprietorship.**

provision for loan losses—A reserve, built up through one or more charges to current earnings, established to provide an allowance for possible future loan losses. The loan loss provision is based on actual experience, anticipated economic conditions, and management's expectation of potential credit problems.

provisional credit—Credit that was previously given but may be reversed if the item deposited is returned unpaid by the paying bank.

prudent person principle—A guideline stating that a trustee handling investments is required to act as a person of prudence, intelligence, and discretion would act in dealing with assets.

public funds account—An account established for any government, agency of government, or political subdivision.

pyramided reserves—The pattern of bank reserve funds that existed before the Federal Reserve System was established. In the pyramided reserves system, large amounts of bank reserves concentrated with banks in New York and, to a lesser extent, in other financial centers.

qualified endorsement—An endorsement on a check or other instrument, containing the words without recourse or similar language intended to limit the endorser's liability if the instrument is dishonored.

raised check—An item on which the dollar amount has been fraudulently increased.

reader/sorter—Electronic equipment with the ability to read, sort, and process MICR-encoded checks and documents.

receivables—The accounts that are owed to a business.

receiving bank—Any bank that accepts an item or receives paperless entries from an automated clearing house (ACH).

reconcilement—A process of comparing and balancing one accounting record against another to provide a proof.

redlining—The illegal and systematic exclusion of certain neighborhoods—usually high-risk, low-income areas—from eligibility for mortgages or other loans by actually or implicitly drawing a red line around the eliminated area on a map.

refinancing—(1) To retire existing loans or notes by changing their terms or by making new borrowing arrangements. (2) To retire existing securities by selling new issues.

regional bank—An institution located outside the nation's major money centers and serving a geographic area.

registrar—A bank or trust company appointed by a corporation to ensure that the number of shares of outstanding stock does not exceed the authorized limit. A registrar is agent for both the corporation and the stockholders, since it protects the interests of both.

repurchase agreements (repos)—Contracts between a seller and a buyer, in which a sale of securities takes place with a simultaneous agreement to buy back the same securities at a specified price on a stated date. Repos represent the most common form of overnight investment for corporate funds and usually involve federal government obligations.

reserve accounts—Accounts that are used by financial institutions to meet legal requirements. Reserves are kept either directly with the Federal Reserve or with a correspondent bank that is a Fed member.

reserve requirement—Portions of a bank's funds set aside to meet legal requirements and/or for known or potential expenses or losses.

resolution—See **corporate resolution.**

Resolution Trust Corporation (RTC)—An agency of the federal government created by the Financial Institutions Reform, Recovery, and Enforcement Act of 1989 (FIRREA) to oversee the liquidation of the assets of insolvent savings and loan associations.

restrictive endorsement—An endorsement that limits the future actions of the next holder. The most common example uses the words "For deposit only."

retail banking—Bank services offered to consumers and small businesses. The full-service commercial bank provides both retail and wholesale services. See **consumer banking** and **wholesale banking.**

retail lockbox—See **lockbox.**

return items—Checks, drafts, or notes that have been dishonored by the drawee or maker and are returned to the presenter. See **incoming return items** and **outgoing return items.**

return item services—Services provided to financial institutions by Federal Reserve banks to return dishonored checks to the presenter.

return on assets (ROA)—A financial measurement that indicates how efficiently a bank's assets are being used. It is usually determined by dividing net profits by average total assets.

return on equity (ROE)—A financial measurement that indicates how efficiently the bank's equity capital has been put to profitable use. It is usually calculated by dividing net profits by net worth.

returning bank—A bank that takes returned checks from a paying bank and returns them to the bank of first deposit in an expeditious manner.

revenue bonds—Obligations, usually municipal, issued to finance a specific project, with interest and principal to be paid out of the income arising from that project. These bonds are not backed by the full faith and credit of the issuer.

revolving credit—A line of credit that permits the borrower to withdraw funds or charge purchases up to a specified dollar limit. The outstanding balance may fluctuate at various times from zero up to the maximum amount. Also referred to as open-end credit.

right of survivorship—The right of one surviving tenant to take full possession of specific assets upon the death of the other tenant, subject to tax laws.

risk—The degree of possibility that a loss will be sustained in a loan, investment, or other transaction.

routing symbol—See **check routing symbol.**

safe assets—Assets like savings and checking accounts, purchased for safety and liquidity.

safekeeping—The banking service by which the bank issues a receipt for, maintains records of, and provides vault facilities for a customer's property. See **truncation.**

safety—The ideal perception by customers that a bank is in a position to honor all anticipated withdrawals of funds and that the bank, acting prudently, has taken all appropriate measures to protect the property entrusted to it and is not taking unwarranted risks.

savings account—An interest-bearing relationship used by a customer to accumulate funds. Savings accounts have no fixed maturity date.

savings and loan association (S&L)—A federally or state-chartered thrift institution, formerly known as a building society, that accepts various types of deposits and uses them primarily for home mortgage loans. By making deposits, the members of a cooperative S&L are actually buying stock in it. The lending powers of S&Ls were significantly expanded under the Monetary Control Act of 1980.

Savings Association Insurance Fund (SAIF)—Mandated by the Financial Institutions Reform, Recovery, and Enforcement Act of 1989, this fund under the control of the FDIC receives deposit insurance assessments from savings associations.

savings bank—A thrift institution specializing in savings accounts but also offering other types of deposit relationships, including checking accounts. Many savings banks are now federally chartered and are using the increased powers granted to them by the Monetary Control Act to make commercial loans and offer additional services. See **mutual savings bank.**

savings bond—A non-negotiable security issued by the U.S. Treasury Department and not subject to market fluctuations.

savings certificate—See **certificate of deposit.**

secondary market—A market for the resale of securities, such as the dealer market or a stock exchange, where ownership is transferred from one owner to another. The first sale of any security is in the primary market; all subsequent sales are in the secondary market.

secondary reserves—Funds invested in high-quality, short-term assets that can be quickly converted to cash without major loss.

secured loan—A borrower's obligation that includes the pledging of some form of collateral to protect the lender in case of default.

Securities Exchange Act—A congressional act that established the Securities and Exchange Commission (SEC). It imposed ongoing disclosure requirements for entities whose securities are publicly traded (for example, proxy statements, annual reports). It also gave the Federal Reserve the authority to set margin requirements.

security interest—An agreement securing a loan with collateral.

security officer—A bank representative who has been given responsibility for various phases of internal controls, such as loss prevention.

self-check digit—A suffix numeral used by bank computers, using a programmed formula to test the validity of a bank number or account number.

sending bank—A bank that forwards a deposited or cashed item to another for payment. Also called presenting bank.

service charge—A fee levied by a bank for services rendered.

settlement—Payment.

settlor—A person who creates a trust (such as a living trust) to become operative during his or her lifetime. Also called trustor, donor, or grantor.

share draft—A check-like instrument used by customers of credit unions as a payment medium and drawn against the issuer's deposit balance.

sight draft—A written order to pay upon presentation or delivery.

sight letter of credit—An instrument, issued by a bank, by which the bank's credit is substituted for that of the applicant and against which funds are paid immediately upon presentation of the documents evidencing a shipment of merchandise.

signature—A sign or mark made by the drawer or maker of a negotiable instrument. A signature may include a thumbprint and may be typed, printed, or stamped.

smart card—Cards that are embedded with a microchip that allows information to be stored on the card. Also called stored value cards.

sole proprietorship—A business venture owned and operated by one person.

special endorsement—An endorsement that names the party to whom an instrument is being transferred.

special power of attorney—A legal document that limits the authority of the attorney-in-fact to a specific duty or function; see **attorney-in-fact.**

split deposit—A transaction in which a bank customer wishes to have part of a check credited to an account and the remainder paid out in cash.

spread—(1) The difference between the return on assets and the cost of liabilities; the profit margin. (2) The difference between the buying rate and selling rate of a currency or marketable security, such as a stock or bond.

stale-dated check—An instrument bearing a date six months or more in the past, prior to its presentation. The Uniform Commercial Code states that banks are not required to honor such checks.

standby letter of credit—A letter of credit to be drawn on in the case of non-performance by the issuing bank's customer.

state bank—A commercial bank chartered by the state in which it is headquartered.

statement—The record prepared by a bank for a customer, listing all debits and credits for the period and the closing balance in the account. See **combined statement.**

statement of condition—See **balance sheet.**

statement savings—A savings account in which a periodic statement, usually computer-generated, replaces the traditional passbook.

stock—The generic term for the common and preferred shares issued by a corporation, evidencing ownership.

stockholders—The owners of the common and/or preferred stock in a corporation. Also called shareholders.

stop payment—A depositor's instructions to a drawee, directing the drawee not to pay a specific item.

subsidiary ledger—A component of the bank's general ledger, identifying individual areas and activities such as loans, types of accounts, and so forth.

super NOW account—A relationship that is interest-bearing and subject to check withdrawal. It is similar to a money market deposit account, but it (1) is not available to corporations, (2) subjects the funds to reserve requirements, and (3) has no limit on monthly transaction volume.

surplus—That portion of a bank's capital accounts derived from retained earnings over a period of time and from funds paid for shares of stock in excess of par value.

sweep account—A relationship in which all the funds in an account, over and above a specified figure, are automatically transferred into an investment pool or interest-bearing account.

tax-exempt bond—A qualifying municipal obligation on which the interest income is not subject to federal income tax. Depending on local statutes, the same bond may also carry exemption of interest from state and local taxation.

teller's check—An official bank check issued by a bank and drawn on another bank or payer.

tenants in common—The holding of property by two or more persons in such a manner that each has an undivided interest that, upon the death of one, passes to the heirs or devisee(s) and not to the survivor(s).

term loan—A bank loan with a maturity of less than one year.

testamentary trust—A trust fund created under the terms of a will.

time deposit—A relationship carrying a specified maturity date, usually bearing interest and restricting the depositor's ability to make withdrawals before the maturity date.

time draft—A written order directing payment at a fixed or determinable future date.

time letter of credit—A letter of credit containing a specific maturity date for payment.

TIN Certification—The process of confirming that a customer's tax identification number (TIN) is correct, that he or she is not subject to backup withholding, or that the customer is exempt from withholding. IRS form W-9 is required.

title document—An instrument that provides evidence of legal ownership of certain property.

trade name—A fictitious name used for business purposes, often indicating the nature of the business. The laws of many states require that trade names be legally registered.

transaction account—Under the terms of the Monetary Control Act of 1980, an account with a financial institution that allows for transfers of funds to third parties.

transfer agent—A bank or trust company that acts as agent for a corporation and effects changes of ownership of stock or bonds from one party to another.

transit item—A non-local item; a check whose drawee is not located in the area defined as local.

traveler's check—A negotiable instrument sold by a bank or other issuer in various denominations for the convenience of individuals who do not wish to carry cash. These checks are readily convertible into cash upon proper identification, usually by a signature in the presence of the cashing party.

treasurer's check—A check issued by a state bank and drawn on that bank. Banks often use treasurer's checks to pay their own obligations or to pay out loan proceeds.

Treasury bill—A marketable U.S. Treasury obligation with a life of one year or less, sold to the public at weekly auctions on a discount basis and in minimum denominations of $10,000. Also called T-bills.

Treasury bond—Obligation of the U.S. Treasury with a maturity of more than 5 years but less than 30 years.

Treasury note—Obligation of the U.S. Treasury with maturities greater than one year but less than five years.

truncation—A generic term for the various banking systems designed to reduce the need to send or physically handle checks for customers' accounts. See **safekeeping.**

trust—An agreement or contract established by agreement or declaration, in a will, or by order of a court, under which one party (the trustee) holds legal title to property belonging to another, with a specific benefit in mind.

trust company—A financial institution chartered specifically to offer trust services. It may also be authorized, under its charter, to provide general banking services.

trustee—The party holding legal title to property under the terms of a trust.

trustor—See **settlor.**

truth in lending laws—Federal and/or state legislation requiring that all lenders provide borrowers with full information as to the terms and conditions of loans.

uncollected funds—See **float.**

unconditional—A requirement in the definition of a negotiable instrument that the instrument not contain any conditions to payment.

underwrite—To assume a risk for a fee, especially in the case of investments. The underwriter of a securities issue assumes responsibility for its sale and remits the sale proceeds to the issuer.

undivided profits—An account in a bank's general ledger that is part of capital. It represents funds that have not been paid out as dividends or transferred to the surplus account.

Uniform Commercial Code (UCC)—The body of laws, adopted in whole or in part by most states, pertaining to financial transactions such as bank deposits and collections, letters of credit, and title documents.

unit bank—An institution that maintains no branch offices.

unit banking—The banking system operating in those states that prohibit branch banking.

unsecured loan—Bank credit extended without collateral.

updating—Modifying a master file with current information.

usury—Excessive, illegal, or punitive interest charges.

variable-rate loan—A loan that allows the lender to make periodic adjustments in the interest rate according to fluctuating market conditions. Also referred to as an adjustable-rate loan.

vault cash—(1) That portion of a bank's cash on hand that is left in its vault as an immediate reserve. (2) Cash on hand.

viruses—Mini computer programs that can disable a computer.

web-only banks—See **Internet banks**.

wholesale banking—The providing of bank services to corporations, units of government, institutions, and other non-retail entities.

wildcat bank—A pre-1862 bank that issued its own currency, established remote locations, and designated them as the only points at which that bank's notes could be redeemed for specie. Eliminated by the National Bank Act.

will—A formal, written, witnessed instrument by which a person gives instructions for the disposition of his or her estate.

wire transfer—See **Fedwire**.

working capital—The excess of a business's current assets over its current liabilities; the liquid funds available to a business for its current needs.

wrongful dishonor—Dishonor of a properly payable check by the paying bank.

yield—(1) In investments, the rate of return expressed as a percentage of the amount invested. (2) In loans, the total amount earned by a lender, expressed on an annual percentage basis.

zero balance accounts—A group of bank accounts maintained for the same customer and controlled by a master concentration account. All debits to the subsidiary accounts, in which no balances are kept, are offset through transfers of funds from the main account.

zero proof—A banking procedure in which all postings are successively subtracted from a control figure to arrive at a zero balance, thus indicating that all entries have been correctly posted.

INDEX

disclosures, 31

transactions, 76

automated transfer services (ATS), 56

automatic deduction, 248

automatic deposit, 54

availability, 173

availability schedule, 113

available balance, 69–70

available funds, 73

B

Baby Boomers, aging, 230

balance, 190

inquiries, 256

see also proof

balance sheet, 189, 190

bank cards, 259–260, 263

fraud, 261

information, 261

loss prevention, 261–262

safeguards, 261–262

bank directors, 186

banker's acceptances, 180

bank examiner scheme, 139

bank funds, management, 167–172

bank holding companies, 177

banking, 1–12

evolution of, 13–33

law, 42–43

Banking Act of 1935, 24

banking holidays, 22–23

Bank Insurance Fund (BIF), 29, 30

bank investments, 174–177

restrictions, 177

types, 177–180

typical portfolio, 177, 178

banknotes, 15–16

1857, 15

national, 17, 18–19

see also Federal Reserve notes

bank-provided endorsement, 91

banks

community, 7–8

organization, 8–9

ownership, 172

perception of, 213–214

regulatory authorities, 44

robbery, 122, 133–134, 135, 142

top five in assets, 202

Bank Secrecy Act, 136

bearer, 88

beneficiary, 229

bill of exchange, accepted, 180

blank endorsement, 89, 90

Board of Governors, Federal Reserve System, 38, 39

responsibilities, 40

rule-making authority, 42

bonds, 176, 236

book balance, 68–69

borrowers, 6, 22

borrowing, encouraging and discouraging, 48–49

bottom line, 192

brokerage firms, 25, 26

brokerage services, 234–237

organization, 234–235

broker-dealers, 234

budgeting, 201

budgets, 185

bulk filing, 126, 127–128, 129, 142

business analysis, 222

business organization, banks as, 8–9

business owners, 60–64

buying process, 216, 217

C

capacity, 67

capital ratio, 195–198

capital, 196–197

original, 195–196

requirements, national banks, 23

letters of credit, 239–240, 241

leveraged industry, 197–198

liabilities, 56, 80, 167, 190, 197
    deposit loss, 130
    management, 167–168, 181
    parties to negotiable instruments, 83–85, 118

LIBOR rate, 174

life insurance, 243

Lincoln, Abraham, 17

links, 259

liquidity, 168–170, 181, 190

loans, 8, 43, 45–46, 166, 167, 168, 172, 190
    customers, 6
    farmers and ranchers, 7
    losses, 195
    management, 167
    negotiation, 175
    portfolios, deteriorating, 27–28
    risk, 176

loan loss reserve, 190, 192

local banks, 15

local check, 73

local clearing item, 109

local items, 114–115

local needs, 38

lockbox services, 252, 253

London Interbank Offer Rate (LIBOR rate), 174

losses, 27

loss prevention, 121–143, 260

M

M1, 45

magnetic ink character recognition (MICR), 107, 109, 118
    line, 112, 132
    line, in-clearing capture, 123
    placement of data on checks, 108

mailbox theft, 262

management, internal, 186

margin requirements, lack of, 23

marked money, 133

market
    profile, 220
    risk, 176, 179

market crash, 22–23
    factors contributing to, 23

market data
    updating, 220–221
    sources, 221

marketing, 7, 9, 207–225, 235
    defined, 209, 224
    concept, 209–212

marketing customer information files (MCIFs), 221

marketing research, 219–221, 224

marketplace, expanding, 25–26

matched funding, 168

maturity, 168
    date, 56
    spacing, 177

mergers, 10, 12

MICR. *See* magnetic ink character recognition

minors, 60, 67

Monetary Control Act of 1980, 28, 40, 47

monetary policy, 36, 45
    administration, 49
    tools, 46–50

money center, 19

money creation, 8, 46, 51
    banks' role, 45–46

money laundering, 65, 136

money market deposit accounts (MMDA), 27

money market mutual funds, 25

money supply, 45, 49, 173
    growth rate, 45
    increasing and decreasing, 47

monthly variance reports, 201–202

mortgage rates, 36

mortgages, 2, 8

municipal bonds, 178–180, 181